CONSTITUTIONAL PRACTICE

The Foundations of British Government

Constitutional Practice

The Foundations of British Government

THIRD EDITION

Rodney Brazier

OXFORD
UNIVERSITY PRESS

*This book has been printed digitally and produced in a standard specification
in order to ensure its continuing availability*

OXFORD
UNIVERSITY PRESS

Great Clarendon Street, Oxford OX2 6DP

Oxford University Press is a department of the University of Oxford.
It furthers the University's objective of excellence in research, scholarship,
and education by publishing worldwide in

Oxford New York

Auckland   Cape Town Dar es Salaam Hong Kong Karachi
Kuala Lumpur Madrid Melbourne Mexico City Nairobi
New Delhi Shanghai Taipei Toronto
With offices in
Argentina Austria Brazil Chile Czech Republic France Greece
Guatemala Hungary Italy Japan South Korea Poland Portugal
Singapore Switzerland Thailand Turkey Ukraine Vietnam

Oxford is a registered trade mark of Oxford University Press
in the UK and in certain other countries

Published in the United States
by Oxford University Press Inc., New York

© Rodney Brazier 1988, 1994, 1999

The moral rights of the author have been asserted

Database right Oxford University Press (maker)

Reprinted 2007

ISBN 978-0-19-829811-3

For Margot and Vicky

PREFACE TO THE THIRD EDITION

This new edition appears during a time of unprecedented change in British constitutional law and practice. The Labour government that swept to power on May Day 1997 did so with an electoral mandate to introduce wide-ranging constitutional reforms, and those that are relevant to my themes are analysed in these pages. I will not write an exhaustive list of those reforms here, but some may be noted by way of example. The devolution of executive and legislative power to Scotland, Wales, and Northern Ireland is reflected in an expanded and retitled Chapter 1, and the constitutional consequences for the United Kingdom of the establishment of the Scottish Parliament are discussed in Chapter 9. While Chapter 3 on hung Parliaments has only been revised lightly, its content will assume greater importance if the voting system for the House of Commons is altered following the national referendum to which Ministers are committed. The coming to office of the first Labour government for eighteen years has caused much rewriting of Chapter 4 on the transfer of power, an event which has also explained further the relationship between the Labour Party's constitution and a Prime Minister's constitutional authority. The new Ministerial Code—itself in part a consequence of some Conservative Ministers' political and personal difficulties—is noted in several places. Detailed changes in practice in both Houses of Parliament are described. The publication from time to time of former Ministers' memoirs and diaries continues to provide a rich source of information about governmental practices. By using them as well as all the other sources available to me I hope that this new edition will provide an authoritative and up to date source of British constitutional practice.

Many people helped me in writing this book or in preparing this new edition. Several serving and retired Ministers and civil servants are acknowledged in footnotes: they gave me their time even over small details, and I am most grateful to them. The Information Offices of both Houses have been models of efficient public service, as always. Mr G. F. Lock, then the Assistant Librarian of the House of Commons Library, kindly read the original Chapter 10 in draft—although any errors which remain there, or elsewhere, are my sole responsibility.

I have tried to describe and explain British constitutional practice as it obtains in October 1998.

R.B.
University of Manchester

CONTENTS

Table of Statutes   xiii

1. THE CONSTITUTION OF THE UNITED
   KINGDOM   1
   Devining the constitution   1
   The territorial context of the constitution   5
   Reforming the constitution   9

2. CHOOSING A PRIME MINISTER   11
   General election   12
   Resignation through illness or old age   14
   Voluntary retirement   18
   Emergency coalition   20
   Loss of the party Leadership   23
   Conclusions   28

3. GOVERNMENT FORMATION FROM A HUNG
   PARLIAMENT   30
   The political negotiations   32
   The Queen   37
   A caretaker government   44
   The second dissolution   45
   Conclusions   50

4. THE TRANSFER OF POWER   52
   The Prime Minister takes office   55
   Matters legal, conventional, and political   56
   The Cabinet chooses itself   63
   The Sovereign's influence   67
   Ministers take office   70

5. THE PRIME MINISTER   73
   The electorate's choice   75

Power over Ministers   76
The highest profile; patronage; dissolution   90
The direction of departments   96
A Prime Minister's weaknesses   98
Conclusions   103

6. THE CABINET   105
   Cabinet business   105
   Cabinet committees and ministerial meetings   113
   Confidentiality of proceedings and papers   124
   Conclusions   131

7. MINISTERS AND DEPARTMENTS   132
   Ministerial titles   132
   Departments   138
   The use of non-departmental Ministers   141
   Ministers' conduct   143
   Ministers' pay and conditions   158

8. THE OPPOSITION   160
   The Leader of the Opposition   160
   Constitutional duties of the Opposition   167
   The shadow government   171
   Shadow into substance   176

9. CONSTITUTIONAL MONARCHY   183
   The Queen's usual powers   184
   The Queen's reserve powers   189
   The Queen and the Scottish Parliament   197
   Continuity and succession   202

10. THE HOUSE OF COMMONS   205
    Elections, Members, and parties   205
    The Commons and the government   212
    Members' influence on the government   220

11. THE HOUSE OF LORDS   235
    Acquiring and losing membership   235
    Organization in the House   244
    The work of the Lords   246

Lords and government in conflict 255

Assessment—and reform? 261

12. THE CONSTITUTIONAL POSITION OF THE JUDGES 265

Appointment, pay, and promotion 266

Judges and Parliament 276

Extra-judicial activities 282

Tenure, discipline, and removal 287

Reform 296

Appendices

A. Senior Ministers since 1945 302

B. The Party Leadership Election Rules 304

C. The formal resignation and appointment of Ministers:
A memorandum by the Clerk of the Privy Council 310

Index 317

TABLE OF STATUTES

Abortion Act 1967   286
Accession Declaration Act 1910   204
Act of Settlement 1701   204, 288
  s. 3   243
Act of Union with Ireland 1801   235
Act of Union with Scotland 1707   235
Administration of Justice Act 1968
  s. 1(1)(*a*)   237, 270
Administration of Justice Act 1973
  s. 9(1)(*a*)   274
  s. 9(5)   275
Administration of Justice Act 1985
  Part II   228
Aircraft and Shipbuilding Industries Act 1977   258
Appellate Jurisdiction Act 1876   270
  s. 5(1)   60, 273
  s. 6   270, 288
  s. 25   237, 270
Appellate Jurisdiction Act 1887
  s. 5   237
Armed Forces Act 1996   206
Bill of Rights 1689   204
British Nationality Act 1981
  s. 50(1)   207, 243
Consolidated Fund Act 1816
  s. 2   312
Copyright, Designs and Patents Act 1988   130
Courts Act 1971   293, 298
  s. 17(4)   289
  s. 21(3)   267
  s. 21(5)   289
  s. 21(6)   289
  s. 21(7)   274
  s. 24   264, 274, 283

Courts and Legal Services Act 1990
   s. 71   237, 266, 267, 268, 269, 270
   s. 75   283
   Schedule 10   237, 266, 267, 268, 269, 270
   Schedule 11   283
Crime (Sentences) Act 1997   282
Criminal Justice Act 1988
   s. 35   260
   s. 36   260
Defence (Transfer of Functions) Act 1964
   s. 2   133
Dock Work Regulation Act 1976   259
Education (No. 2) Act 1986
   s. 47   259
European Communities (Finance) Act 1995   220
Family Law Reform Act 1969
   s. 1(4)   206
   Schedule 2   206
Forfeiture Act 1870
   s. 2   243
Government of Ireland Act 1914   257
Government of Wales Act 1998   7, 263
Health Service Commissioners Act 1993   213
House of Commons (Clergy Disqualification) Act 1801   208
House of Commons Disqualification Act 1975
   s. 1(1)   282
   s. 2(1)   57
   s. 2(2)   57
   s. 4   208
   s. 9(1)   135,136
   Schedule 1   208, 282
   Schedule 2   135
House of Commons (Redistribution of Seats) Acts 1944 to 1979   195
Human Rights Act 1998   9, 10
   ss. 4, 5   9
   ss. 6–9   10
Industrial Relations Act 1971   121
Insolvency Act 1986
   s. 427   209, 243
Interpretation Act 1978
   s. 5   133
   Schedule 1   133

Judicial Committee Act 1833
  s. 1   60
Judicial Pensions and Retirement Act 1993   285
  s. 26   237, 289
  Schedule 5   237, 289
Justices of the Peace Act 1997
  s. 5   288
  s. 6(1)   266
  s. 7   288
  s. 11(2), (3), (4)   268, 289
  s. 13   267
  s. 14(2), (3), (4)   268
  s. 16(1), (3), (4)   268, 289
  s. 18   268
  s. 19   267
  s. 26   266
Land Registration Act 1988   238
Law of Property (Miscellaneous Provisions) Act 1994   248
Life Peerages Act 1958
  s. 1   236
  s. 1(3)   236
Local Government Act 1974
  Part III   213
Local Government Act 1985
  s. 1   195
Local Government (Interim Provisions) Act 1984
  s. 1   195
  s. 2   260
Meeting of Parliament Act 1694   206
Mental Health Act 1983
  s. 141   209
  Part II   243
Ministerial and other Pensions and Salaries Act 1991
  s. 1   159
  s. 3   158
  s. 4   159
  s. 5   159
Ministerial and other Salaries Act 1975   55, 57, 60
  s. 1(1)   55, 57, 72, 134, 158
  s. 1(2)   60
  s. 1(4)   57
  s. 2(1)   42, 210
  s. 2(2)   210

s. 3(1)(*b*)   135
s. 4   158
Schedule 1   55, 57, 72, 134
Ministerial and other Salaries Act 1997   158
Ministers of the Crown Act 1937   55
s. 5   161
Ministers of the Crown Act 1964   57
s. 1   141
s. 2(1)(*a*)   141
Ministers of the Crown Act 1974   57
Ministers of the Crown Act 1975   62, 140
s. 1(1)   62, 140
s. 1(2)   140
s. 2(1)   62, 134, 161
s. 2(2)   161
s. 3   134
s. 4
s. 5   63, 141
s. 8(1)   132
Ministers of the Crown (Transfer of Functions)
  Act 1946   62, 140
National Audit Act 1983   229
s. 1(1)   93
National Loans Act 1968
s. 1(5)   257
Naval Discipline Act 1957   206
Northern Ireland Act 1998   8
Northern Ireland (Elections) Act 1998   8
Northern Ireland (Entry to Negotiations, Etc.) Act 1996   8
s. 4   8
Official Secrets Act 1911   110
s. 2   110, 122, 125–6
Official Secrets Act 1989   110, 126
ss. 1–6   126
s. 2   126
s. 3   126
s. 4   126
s. 7(1)   126
s. 9   126
s. 12(1)   126
Parliament Act 1911   190, 191, 256
s. 1   192
s. 1(1)   257

s. 1(2)	257
s. 2(1)	195, 256, 257
s. 3	257
s. 5	256
s. 7	194, 205
Parliament Act 1949	190, 191, 256, 257
s. 1	257
Parliament and Local Elections Acts 1917 and 1918	190
Parliament and Registration Act 1916	190
Parliamentary Commissioner Act 1967	213
s. 1(2)	93
Parliamentary Constituencies Act 1986	195
s. 3	41
Schedule 2, para. 1(4)	41
Parliamentary and other Pensions Act 1972	209
Parliamentary and other Pensions Act 1987	209
Parliamentary and other Pensions and Salaries Act 1976	209
s. 5	
Parliamentary Pensions etc. Act 1984	209
Paymaster General Act 1835	
s. 4	312
Peerage Act 1963	11, 242
s. 1(1)	242
s. 1(2)	22, 242
s. 1(3)	242
s. 2(1)	22, 242
s. 2(2)	242
s. 3(1)	242
s. 3(2)	243
s. 4	235
s. 5	236
s. 6	236
Schedule 1	242
Police and Criminal Evidence Act 1984	
s. 83	93
Schedule 4	93
Prevention of Terrorism (Temporary Provisions) Act 1989	110
Private International Law (Miscellaneous Provisions) Act 1995	248
Prolongation of Parliament Acts 1940 to 1944	190
Promissory Oaths Act 1868	71, 310
s. 3	71, 310
s. 5	71, 310

Schedule 71, 310, 312, 313
Prosecution of Offences Act 1985 109, 260
  s. 1(1)(*a*) 109
  s. 2(1) 109
  s. 2(3) 109
  s. 3(1) 109
Public Order Acts 1936 and 1986 110
Re-election of Ministers Act 1919 208
Reform Act 1867 4
Regency Act 1937
  s. 1(1) 203
  s. 2(1) 203
  s. 3(1), (2) 203
  s. 4(2) 203
  s. 6(1) 202, 203
  s. 6(2A) 203
  s. 6(3) 203
  s. 8(2) 202
Regency Act 1943
  s. 1 203
Regency Act 1953
  s. 1(1) 203
  s. 3 203
Regional Development Agencies Act 1998 8
Representation of the People Act 1884 4
Representation of the People Act 1918 4
Representation of the People Act 1928 4, 147
Representation of the People Act 1969 4
Representation of the People Act 1981
  s. 1 209
  s. 2 209
Roman Catholic Relief Act 1829
  s. 9 208
Scotland Act 1998 6, 134, 197, 263
  s. 2 200
  s. 2(6) 199
  s. 3 200
  s. 3(1)(*b*) 198
  s. 3(2) 198
  s. 19 197
  s. 28(2) 200
  s. 28(3) 200
  s. 28(7) 200

ss. 29–33 200
s. 45(1) 199
s. 45(2) 199, 201
s. 45(3) 198, 201
s. 45(7) 199
s. 46(1) 198
s. 46(2) 198
s. 46(3) 198
s. 47(1) 198
s. 47(2) 198
s. 47(3) 199
s. 49(4) 199
s. 53 200
s. 84(4) 199
s. 84(5) 199
s. 95 294
ss. 98–103 200
Schedule 6 200
Sexual Offences Act 1967 276
Sexual Offences (Amendment) Act 1976 228
Sheriff Courts (Scotland) Act 1971
   s. 12 294
Solicitors Act 1974
   s. 38 283
Succession to the Crown Act 1707 204
Supreme Court Act 1981
   s. 1(1) 269
   s. 1(2) 60, 273
   s. 2(1) 269
   s. 2(2) 60
   s. 2(2)(a) 273
   s. 2(4) 269
   s. 2(5) 269
   s. 4 269
   s. 4(1) 60
   s. 4(1)(a) 273
   s. 4(1)(e) 269
   s. 4(4) 269
   s. 4(5) 269
   s. 5 269
   s. 5(1) 60
   ss. 10–13 269
   s. 11(2) 288

s. 11(3) 288
s. 11(8) 291
s. 11(9) 291
s. 12(1) 274
s. 12(3) 274
s. 12(5) 275
s. 146 267, 274, 283
Supreme Court of Judicature Act 1873 270
Trade Union and Labour Relations (Amendment) Act 1976 258
Tribunals of Inquiry (Evidence) Act 1921 154
War Crimes Act 1991 257
War Damage Act 1965 280
Welsh Church Act 1914 257

1

THE CONSTITUTION OF THE UNITED KINGDOM

Devining the constitution

This book seeks to describe and analyse the current working of British central government. It is written from the perspective of a constitutional lawyer who believes that the opinions of Ministers, civil servants, politicians, historians, and other academic writers are as helpful in divining the meaning of the British constitution as the views of those who may be learned in the law. The emphasis is placed on the organization and powers of the government, although two chapters are devoted to Parliament entirely in its own right (rather than as just an adjunct through which governments achieve and retain their authority), and a final chapter considers the constitutional position of the judiciary. As the book is concerned with constitutional and political issues affecting central government, not with detailed administration, the organization of the civil service is omitted. It is important to understand both how governments come to office and the nature of their powers, not least because the tradition of highly centralized administration in London is still very strong and has helped to endow any government with considerable authority over the nation's affairs. (It remains to be seen how that state of affairs will be affected by the present government's programme of constitutional reform.)[1] The task undertaken is, therefore, to identify the hands in which that power lies and to set forth the institutions and procedures through which it is exercised.

Wherever possible the approach is prescriptive. The aim is to explain in any particular situation what may and should appropriately be done. Where prescription is not possible, perhaps because there is a clear divergence of opinion between the political parties as to what the constitution ordains, the reasons behind those differences are explained and then ways forward are suggested which are in keeping with my perception of the spirit of the

[1] On which see the final section of this chapter.

constitution. If such differences fall to be tested it will obviously be for those with the ability to practise the tenets of the constitution to decide which course to take, and what is suggested in these pages may be of some assistance. An example is provided by the clutch of problems which could arise on the election of a hung Parliament. Before each of the general elections in the 1980s and that of 1992 the return of a House of Commons in which no party would have an absolute majority of seats was awaited with bated breath almost as much by certain commentators as by the smaller political parties. All were disappointed, and so two key questions did not need to be answered. One was whether the Conservative and Labour Parties were right to believe that the largest party in such a House is entitled to form a minority government, or whether the Liberals, then the SDP, and then the Liberal Democrats were nearer the mark in insisting that a coalition, or some parliamentary pact short of coalition, should be tried first. The other question was whether (as Labour thought) a Prime Minister at the head of a minority government is automatically entitled to a dissolution on request at any time of his choosing, or whether (as the smaller parties believed) a dissolution might only be granted if no other government could be formed from the existing House. Now no one can know whether the Conservative and Labour Parties will remain as the only parties of government, the ins and the outs, particularly because reform of the voting system is on the cards.[2] The failure, however, of any other party or grouping to translate the multi-party politics which exist in the country (as demonstrated by the millions of non-Conservative and non-Labour votes cast in recent general elections) into a multi-party House of Commons seems to show that, without electoral reform, two-party parliamentary politics are as entrenched as at any time since the 1930s. But in case a hung Parliament is returned, answers to hung Parliament questions are offered here.[3] Speculation must not, however, be open-ended about other things that are most unlikely to happen in this country. The political parties in the main believe in basic fair play (although not to the extent of even trying to reach a consensus on the reform of the unfair electoral system); they accept the fundamental principles of western liberal democracy; they usually follow a rough and ready collection of Queensberry rules. Accordingly, the unthinkable need not be thought, or at least not for too long.[4]

---

[2] A referendum on that issue has been promised in the light of the Report of the Independent Commission on the Voting System: see the final section of this chapter.

[3] See Chapter 3.

[4] Some such questions (such as what would happen if a government defeated on a vote of confidence refused either to recommend a general election or to resign) are considered in Chapter 9.

Overriding concern for the practical working of government is one reason for the unusual title of this book. Another is that the whole system of British central government is based on practice, not law. (There is, of course, an increasing amount of statute law which must be and is taken into account.) The choice of title underlines the fundamental and these days uncontroversial point that an understanding of central government requires a detailed consideration of 'rules' which are not rules of law properly so called. Large tracts of the constitution are subject only to these 'rules', such as, for example, the powers of the Sovereign, the existence of and relationships between the Prime Minister and the Cabinet, the relationships between the government and Parliament, between the two Houses (and the internal working of each), and the appointment and disciplining of the judiciary. Whether to label these 'rules' as conventions, principles, doctrines, practices, understandings, maxims, or precepts; whether the courts recognize or declare them; which of them (if any) are binding (and if so why), and what consequence (if any) flows from the breach of any or all of them, are questions which are amply explored elsewhere.[5] John Mackintosh thought that the difference between law and convention was unimportant, because in the development of the constitution both rested on the necessities of political life: laws could be repealed or conventions changed if that were found to be desirable.[6] But that difference is very important for those who are most intimately concerned in Westminster and Whitehall with the daily working of central government. For them, the possible solutions to any given problem require answers to severely practical questions. Does a particular solution require legislation, or could it be achieved by administrative or procedural means? If legislation would not be needed, then would that particular solution be in accordance with precedent and practice? If it would not be in such accordance, could its adoption be justified to Parliament and to the general public? Arcane examination of the nature of constitutional conventions is of very little use to these practitioners, and to that end it is eschewed here; but it is hoped that it is quite clear in this book whether any proposition is or is not one of law, so that the means of bringing about any alteration to it would be equally apparent.

Even by the time of the last edition of his still valuable work on Cabinet government, published in 1959, Sir Ivor Jennings remained convinced that

---

[5] For a review and consideration of the literature see Rodney Brazier, 'The Non-Legal Constitution: Thoughts on Convention, Practice and Principle' (1992) 43 *Northern Ireland Legal Quarterly* 262.

[6] John Mackintosh, *The British Cabinet* (3rd edn., 1977), p. 12.

it was necessary to keep in its pages Victorian constitutional precedents back as far as 1841, the year in which Sir Robert Peel became Prime Minister for the second time.[7] In the main he also kept to a minimum any consideration of recent events. For the last edition of his book on the Cabinet before his untimely death, John Mackintosh felt justified in ignoring events before the Reform Act 1867, the statute which he felt established a broadly representative House of Commons and consequently representative government as we now know it.[8] On the other hand he was, unlike Jennings, completely ready to take advantage of the very latest noteworthy happenings which threw light on the Cabinet system, whether revealed through autobiographies, biographies, published diaries and letters, or leaks. Now the twenty-first century is imminent, it would seem odd to postulate the constitutional practice appropriate to that century by reference to what happened in the nineteenth and also by failing to give whatever proper consideration is possible to recent constitutional and political developments. An awful lot of water has flowed under Westminster Bridge since Queen Victoria died, and only information from the twentieth century, and ideally from after 1945, is deployed here. Even after the passage of the Representation of the People Act 1884, only a mere 60 per cent or so of the adult male population (or about 28 per cent of the whole adult population) had the vote.[9] All adult men, and women over 30, had to wait until the Representation of the People Act 1918 for the franchise; not until the Representation of the People Act 1928 were women equated with men in being entitled to vote at 21.[10] So the principle of fully representative democracy was only enshrined in law some 70 years ago, and it is *that* democracy upon which modern British government is based.

Other important things, too, have occurred in recent decades and they must be fully taken into consideration if a realistic picture of the contemporary constitution is to be drawn. Since 1945 the power of the Prime Minister in relation to the Cabinet has continued to grow, so that an incumbent may do more by virtue of personal authority, rather than as a result of collective ministerial decision, than was previously the case.[11] Again, it was not until 1965 that the Conservative Party fell into line with the Labour and Liberal Parties by adopting a formal and democratic

---

[7] Sir Ivor Jennings, *Cabinet Government* (3rd edn., 1959), pp. 8–13.

[8] Mackintosh, n. 6 above, pp. 18–20.

[9] See Colin Turpin, *British Government and the Constitution: Text, Cases and Materials* (2nd edn., 1990), p. 19.

[10] The voting age was lowered to 18 by the Representation of the People Act 1969.

[11] This is described in Chapters 5 and 6.

procedure through which to elect its Leader, so that the need for the Queen to exercise her personal judgement in the choice of a new Prime Minister has been further reduced, although not completely removed.[12] That, and other developments, show a desirable trend towards politicians taking primary responsibility for the resolution of political crises. Moreover, the formalization of the Shadow Cabinet system (in the Conservatives' case as late as 1964), and the reorganization of government departments (beginning in the same year) have greatly affected the composition and membership of any Cabinet.[13] What amounts to an adverse vote in the House of Commons requiring either a dissolution or the government's resignation has also altered in the last 30 years.[14] Ministerial responsibility, too, has been affected by a number of political developments, including the introduction of the departmental select committees in 1979[15] and the increased use of committees in the House of Lords since 1974,[16] which have both altered how each House elicits information from Ministers and civil servants. For all these, and other reasons, it is essential where it can be done to turn to the more recent pages of constitutional history for guidance as to the meaning of the British constitution as we approach the year 2000, rather than to the older, and in some cases inappropriate, volumes.

The territorial context of the constitution

This book is concerned with British central government. The powers that are being devolved to the nations and regions of the United Kingdom will reduce the authority of Westminster and Whitehall, and it is therefore useful to outline those powers as a correction to what would otherwise be an inaccurate picture.

The United Kingdom of Great Britain and Northern Ireland is a unitary sovereign state.[17] That basic constitutional position will not change when the Scottish Parliament, the Welsh Assembly, and the Northern Ireland Assembly begin their work. All three bodies will depend for their authority on the powers devolved to them through their constituent Acts, passed by the Parliament of the United Kingdom. None of those bodies will be

---

[12] See Chapter 2.
[13] See the respective explanations given in Chapters 4 and 7.
[14] See Chapter 10.   [15] See Chapter 10.   [16] See Chapter 11.
[17] The exercise of its sovereignty, of course, is conditioned by several factors, not least the legal obligations resulting from membership of the European Union.

able to enlarge the powers devolved without the consent and legislative approval of the Westminster Parliament. Nor will the new system be federal in character: that would have required, for example, special protection for the new bodies against encroachment on their rights by the Westminster Parliament, and there will be no such legal protection. Moreover, all three of the main British political parties remain committed to the continuing integrity of the United Kingdom.[18] Subject to that, Scotland, Wales and Northern Ireland will enjoy greater autonomy within the United Kingdom as the third millennium approaches.

Under the Scotland Act 1998[19] the powers to be retained to the Westminster Parliament are set out, and the Scottish Parliament will have legislative powers in all other matters (subject to detailed exceptions). The main areas which will be reserved to the United Kingdom Parliament are the constitution (including the Crown,[20] and the Parliament of the United Kingdom itself); foreign affairs and relations with the European Union; the civil service; defence; the fiscal, economic and monetary system; employment and social security legislation; and other specified matters which it is thought should remain subject to national control or operation. Apart from those reserved matters, the Scottish Parliament will be able to pass Bills which, when they receive royal assent, will be known as Scottish Acts, and which will constitute primary legislation in Scotland. Vast areas of life in Scotland, therefore, will be subject to laws made by Scots in Edinburgh, and Westminster's writ will no longer run. Disputes about the legal power of the Parliament to enact a particular Bill will be resolved by a reference to the Judicial Committee of the Privy Council. The Scottish Parliament will receive a block grant each year from Westminster,[21] to spend according to its wishes, and it will also have the power to vary the basic rate of income tax upwards or downwards by 3p. The Scottish Parliament will be elected by the additional member system of proportional representation: one member will be elected from each of the present 73 parliamentary

---

[18] The Scottish National Party, by contrast, regards the 1998 arrangements as a staging-post towards independence, and Sinn Fein sees them as a step towards a unified Republic of Ireland. The Liberal Democrats aspire to a federal United Kingdom, which would maintain the cohesion of the country as a whole.

[19] On which see *Scotland's Parliament*, Cm. 3658 (1997). The people of Scotland approved the government's general plans for a new Parliament by a substantial majority at a referendum in 1997.

[20] For the constitutional relationships between the Queen and the Scottish Parliament, see Chapter 9.

[21] The Secretary of State for Scotland will have primary responsibility for obtaining an appropriate annual amount for this grant: the office of Secretary of State for Scotland will continue, but his role will be reduced.

constituencies, and a further 56 members will be allocated on the basis of votes cast for the various political parties at each Scottish general election. It will be a fixed-term Parliament, being dissolved every four years (although it could be dissolved earlier if the Parliament so voted by a two-thirds majority or if it could not agree on whom to nominate as First Minister), for there will be a First Minister and a Scottish Executive of Ministers and junior Ministers, drawn from the Parliament.[22] The Parliament itself will nominate one of its number to be First Minister; its Presiding Officer will recommend his name to the Queen for formal appointment. The first elections to the Scottish Parliament are expected in 1999 with the Parliament functioning by the end of that year or early in 2000.

The Welsh Assembly will be a more modest body. Under the Government of Wales Act 1998[23] the Assembly will consist of 60 members, elected by the additional member system every four years. It will take over most of the functions of the Secretary of State for Wales (whose office will, however, remain for the time being). The Welsh Assembly (unlike its Scottish counterpart) will have no power to enact primary legislation, which will continue to be passed for Wales at Westminster. One consequence of that is that (unlike in Edinburgh) the question of what is or is not a reserved matter will not arise. But the Assembly will have the authority to enact secondary legislation which is currently within the remit of the Secretary of State for Wales, and it will be able to express its views on policy in the principality and exert some control over quangos there. In effect the Assembly will exercise, or have influence over the exercise of, the powers hitherto enjoyed by the Welsh Office. The Assembly will have control of the annual sum which has, up to now, been made available to the Welsh Office to disburse—and which amounted to £7 billion in 1997. The Assembly will work (as in Scotland) through a Cabinet-style system, headed by a First Secretary and an Executive Committee of Secretaries. The First Secretary will be nominated by the Assembly. The first elections to the Assembly will be held in 1999.

For obvious reasons the road to the devolution of power back to Northern Ireland has been a long and bloody one.[24] That made the all-party agreement which was concluded on Good Friday 1998 the more

[22] See R. Brazier, 'The Scottish Government' [1998] *Public Law* 212.

[23] On which see *A Voice for Wales*, Cm. 3718 (1997). The people of Wales voted in favour of a Welsh Assembly—just—in a referendum held in 1997. The vote was 50.3 per cent in favour and 49.7 per cent against, on a 50.3 per cent turnout.

[24] For an account see S. A. de Smith and R. Brazier, *Constitutional and Administrative Law* (8th edn., 1998), pp. 50–7; Brigid Hadfield, *The Constitution of Northern Ireland* (1989).

remarkable.[25] Under it, Northern Ireland was once more to have a devolved legislature, with full legislative and executive authority over matters which are currently within the remit of the Northern Ireland Office. A Northern Ireland Assembly would be able to pass Bills (requiring royal assent) on such matters.

Accordingly agriculture, economic development, education, the environment, and health would be the principal areas for which the people of Northern Ireland would resume responsibility, while matters such as security and external relations would remain the responsibility of the British government. As well as a legislature there would be an Executive Committee drawn from it, consisting of a First Minister, a Deputy First Minister and ten other Ministers, the membership being allocated according to the numbers of seats secured in the legislature. To take account of the unique divisions in Northern Ireland, decisions in the legislature and in the Executive Committee would be arrived at, for certain matters, by specified majorities.

The people of Northern Ireland gave the Good Friday agreement their overwhelming backing at a referendum[26] held on 22 May 1998. On a turnout of 81 per cent, 71 per cent voted for the agreement. The Northern Ireland (Elections) Act 1998 was swiftly passed in order that a Northern Ireland Assembly could be elected and take part in the preparations to give effect to the Good Friday agreement. That Assembly, consisting of 108 members elected by single transferable vote (STV), with six members from each of the 18 parliamentary constituencies, was elected in June 1998. The Northern Ireland Act 1998 was passed subsequently to provide the detailed legislative framework for Northern Ireland's new constitutional arrangements, based on the Good Friday agreement.

Progress is also being made towards the devolution of power from Westminster to the regions of England. The Labour government plans, first, to introduce regional development agencies throughout England, and the Regional Development Agencies Act 1998 has been passed for the purpose. Then, in time, if the view develops in any English region that it wants greater democratic control of its affairs the government will provide the opportunity for a referendum in that area; if the result is a vote in favour of a regional elected assembly, legislation would be enacted at Westminster to provide it. The people of London are ahead of the rest of England, for they

[25] The text was published as 'The Agreement' in Cm. 3883 (1998). The agreement had been negotiated by representatives elected to a forum under the terms of the Northern Ireland (Entry to Negotiations, Etc.) Act 1996.

[26] It was held under the Northern Ireland (Entry to Negotiations, Etc.) Act 1996, s. 4.

were able to vote at a referendum in 1998 on whether they wished to have a Mayor of London and a London Assembly, together constituting a new Greater London Authority. Londoners did vote in favour (albeit on a very low turnout). The new Mayor and London Assembly will be elected for the first time in 1999, and will be a significant political force in the nation's capital. Other English cities may decide that they, too, would like to have an executive mayor.

Reforming the constitution

The Labour government which swept to power on May Day 1997 did so committed to make many and vital reforms to the British constitution.[27] In this endeavour it was supported fully by the Liberal Democrats.[28] Legislation to give effect to the first tranche of its constitutional reform programme is well advanced. As has just been seen, devolution legislation has been enacted, as has the Human Rights Act 1998 to give remedies in domestic law for breaches of the European Convention on Human Rights, and a Freedom of Information Bill is to be introduced into Parliament.[29] Reform of the House of Lords, and possible reform of the voting system for the House of Commons, are also being taken forward.[30]

One of the effects of these measures will be to tilt the balance of constitutional power in the United Kingdom away from London and towards other institutions and indeed towards citizens themselves. The practical effect of the Human Rights Act 1998, for example, will be to restrict the sovereignty of the British Parliament—not openly, as a matter of law (for that would be too much to expect MPs to bear), but rather more subtly as a matter of practice. Thus if a court is satisfied that a provision in legislation is incompatible with any right secured under the European Convention, it may make a declaration to that effect.[31] The legislation will not be struck down in the way that, for instance, the United States Supreme Court can strike down unconstitutional legislation; but the ball will be tossed into

---

[27] For the story see R. Brazier, *Constitutional Reform* (2nd edn., 1998), ch. 3.

[28] Indeed, in an unprecedented move the new Prime Minister formed a Joint Consultative Cabinet Committee with equal numbers of Ministers and Liberal Democrat parliamentarians. The two parties had agreed a Joint Report on Constitutional Reform before the 1997 general election.

[29] On which see *Your Right to Know*, Cm. 3818 (1997).

[30] See respectively Chapters 10 and 11.

[31] Human Rights Act 1998, ss. 4, 5.

Parliament's court to enact amending legislation to remove the incompatibility. Parliament's technical legal sovereignty is retained: but in practice it is difficult to envisage a case in which the government and Parliament would do other than move to enact correcting legislation. Moreover, when a Minister introduces any Bill into Parliament he must now state either that its provisions are compatible with the Convention rights, or that, although the Bill is incompatible, he wishes Parliament to proceed with it. That new duty[32] should ensure that Ministers will scrupulously avoid introducing legislation that would deny citizens their Convention rights (or, in extreme cases, Ministers will have to declare openly that they wish Parliament to legislate inconsistently with those rights). That will limit Parliament's notional power to legislate on any matter as it might like.[33]

By the end of this Parliament the British constitution will embrace, as well as our traditional institutions, a Scottish Parliament and Welsh and Northern Ireland Assemblies, and a London Mayor and Assembly. The courts will be able to give redress for breaches of the European Convention on Human Rights, and in practice Parliament will have to amend legislation that is incompatible with that Convention. There will be a Freedom of Information Act which will give citizens much greater access to official information. It may be—depending on the result of a national referendum—that future elections to the Parliament of the United Kingdom will take place under a new voting system, which may produce far more hung Parliaments than we are accustomed to. Hereditary peers may no longer sit in the House of Lords; some progress will have been made towards transforming that House into a more democratic chamber. In short, the constitution of the United Kingdom will look very different by the early years of the new millennium.

---

[32] Ministers have been bound in practice to check that draft legislation is compatible with the European Convention on Human Rights, but they were under no duty to make the declarations now required under the Human Rights Act.

[33] If a public authority acts in a way which is incompatible with the Convention rights a citizen affected by that action may seek judicial remedies: Human Rights Act 1998, ss. 6–9.

2

CHOOSING A PRIME MINISTER

The appointment by the Sovereign of a Prime Minister is an act done by virtue of the royal prerogative. In theory the Queen could commission anyone she pleased to form a government. But in practice such a notion is entirely removed from reality, because of course today the royal discretion is subject to several limiting factors, the most important of which is that in making an appointment she should commission that person who seems able to command a majority in the House of Commons. The other restraints are that the person chosen must be a Member of Parliament (or be about to occupy his seat as an MP after a general election), must not be a peer (unless he can disclaim his peerage under the Peerage Act 1963 and seek a seat in the House of Commons), and must usually be the elected Leader of his party. It is possible to go further than noting these limitations and to argue that, although the formal *appointment* of a Prime Minister is a prerogative act, the actual *choice* no longer normally lies with the Queen at all: in that sense the selection of a new Prime Minister does not depend upon any prerogative power. For, the argument runs, in most cases (say after a general election) the identity of the politician who is to remain or is to become the Prime Minister is obvious. Further, each of the political parties now has machinery for electing its Leader,[1] so that there should be no repetition of controversial events like those of 1957 and (particularly) of 1963, when the Queen had to become involved in the actual evolution of a new Prime Minister as distinct from his formal appointment to office.[2]

---

[1] For the current rules see Appendix B. The Leader of the Conservative Party used to be elected by MPs taking the Conservative whip, in a system which allowed for more than one ballot so that candidates could be eliminated to ensure that the victor received an overall majority of the votes cast on the final ballot. Since 1998, however, each member of the Conservative Party has been able to vote for the Leader in a postal ballot. Labour's electoral college system is examined below. The Liberal Democrats conduct a postal ballot of their members throughout the country.

[2] In 1957, when Sir Anthony Eden resigned, the Queen consulted Sir Winston Churchill (presumably as a former Conservative Prime Minister) and the Marquess of Salisbury (Lord President of the Council and Leader of the House of Lords in Eden's government). Both

Today, it might be said, the party election machinery would make the choice, in consequence of which the Queen would probably be insulated from the contenders and from having to prefer (or seem to prefer) one man or woman rather than any other. This restrictive view of the prerogative is generally correct, but the royal prerogative of choice, as distinct from that of appointment, of a new Prime Minister is not dead, but dormant. There could still be far from fanciful instances in which the Queen would have to act without the protection of any prior party election of a Leader. Suggestions will be made in this chapter, however, which might keep to a minimum the involvement of the Queen and her prerogative and which would make the maximum use of parliamentary democracy.

General election

There have been 26 changes this century of Prime Minister or of government or of both. Of those changes, 10 involved a person becoming Prime Minister by being able to form a government after a general election, ousting a sitting government;[3] 11 concerned succession to the office through the resignation of a member of the same party but not entailing the collective resignation of the government;[4] two involved a change of party

---

recommended Macmillan rather than the only other candidate, R. A. Butler. Lords Salisbury and Kilmuir had polled individual members of Eden's Cabinet. The Queen did not ask Eden for advice about the succession, but at his resignation audience he indicated his debt to Butler: Vernon Bogdanor, *The Monarchy and the Constitution* (1995), p. 94. For published accounts, see, for example, Harold Macmillan, *Riding the Storm* (1971), pp. 180–5; Lord Butler, *The Art of the Possible* (1971), pp. 195–7; and Lord Kilmuir, *Memoirs: Political Adventure* (1961), p. 285. In the ferocious 1963 battle, there were at various times a number of candidates to succeed Macmillan. He tried to ensure that (in his words) 'the customary processes of consultation' about the Leadership were carried out as widely as possible within the Conservative Party, but the controversy over the methods and the result remains. Lord Home 'emerged'. For published versions, see, for example, Alistair Horne, *Macmillan 1957–1986* (1989), ch. 18; Randolph Churchill, *The Fight for the Tory Leadership* (1964), especially chs. 6–10; Lord Home, *The Way the Wind Blows* (1976), pp. 180–5; Harold Macmillan, *At the End of the Day* (1973), ch. 15; Lord Butler, above, pp. 241–50; and Iain Macleod, 'The Tory Leadership', *The Spectator*, 17 January 1964. See also Geoffrey Marshall, *Constitutional Conventions* (1984), pp. 29–32.

[3] MacDonald (1924); Baldwin (1924); MacDonald (1929); Attlee (1945); Churchill (1951); Mr Wilson (1964); Mr Heath (1970); Mr Wilson (March 1974); Mrs Thatcher (1979); and Mr Blair (1997).

[4] Balfour (1902, succeeding his uncle Salisbury); Asquith (1908, in succession to the dying Campbell-Bannerman); Lloyd George (1916, taking over the war coalition from Asquith); Baldwin (1922, succeeding the dying Bonar Law); Baldwin (1935, replacing MacDonald as head of the 'National Government'); Chamberlain (1937, on Baldwin's retirement); Eden (1955, on Churchill's oft-delayed but encouraged retirement); Macmillan (1957,

government without a general election;[5] and on three occasions the resignation of the Prime Minister was a constitutional device to enable him to form a new government—on two occasions to form a coalition,[6] on the other to break up a coalition and to create a one-party government.[7]

It is trite to observe that there are only three possible results of a general election. The sitting government and Prime Minister may be sustained in office with an absolute majority in the House of Commons (as in 1906, 1918, 1922, 1931, 1935, 1950, 1955, 1959, 1966, October 1974, 1983, 1987, and 1992). Or the government party might lose the election, one other party being returned with an overall majority (as in 1924, 1945, 1951, 1964, 1970, 1979, and 1997). Last, the electoral system might produce a hung Parliament, that is, one in which no single party has an absolute majority in the House of Commons. This is rare: it happened at the two general elections in 1910, in 1923, in 1929, and then not again until February 1974.[8]

The constitutional consequence of the first result is that the Prime Minister continues in office, refreshed if the number of his party's seats has increased, relieved that, even if his majority has been reduced, he is at least left with a majority.[9] He does not need to see the Queen, for the use of the prerogative in relation to the Prime Ministership is not required. The practical effect of the second result is, of course, dramatic. The day after polling, when the result is clear,[10] the defeated Prime Minister will seek and obtain

succeeding Eden on his illness); Sir Alec Douglas-Home (1963, succeeding Macmillan on *his* illness); Mr Callaghan (1976, having been elected Leader of the Parliamentary Labour Party on Mr Wilson's retirement); and Mr Major (1990, on his election to the Conservative Leadership, Mrs Thatcher having withdrawn from the contest).

[5] When Campbell-Bannerman formed a Liberal government in 1905 after the resignation of Balfour, and when the Conservatives broke up Lloyd George's coalition in 1922 to install Bonar Law.

[6] The 1915 coalition under Asquith in succession to his Liberal administration, and the 'National Government' in 1931, headed by MacDonald who had been Prime Minister of a minority government immediately before that.

[7] The 1945 caretaker Conservative government formed by Churchill after Labour had refused to continue the wartime coalition until the defeat of Japan, as Churchill would have preferred. See Sir Winston Churchill, *The Second World War*, vol. vi, *Triumph and Tragedy* (Penguin, 1985), ch. 35, especially pp. 508–19. A list of senior Ministers since 1945 is given in Appendix A.

[8] The details and the consequences are considered in the next chapter.

[9] As, for example, when Attlee's 1945 government, which had been returned with a majority of 146, found itself with a majority of only eight after the 1950 general election; or the late Conservative government, whose 1987 majority of over 100 was reduced to 21 in the 1992 contest.

[10] In 1979, Mr Callaghan resigned *before* the election returns had given the Conservative Party an absolute majority, but it was obvious from the trend of voting and computer forecasts that this was coming. In the event, the Conservatives secured a 43-seat absolute majority.

an audience of the Queen to offer his resignation and that of his government, and (perhaps) to give advice about his successor. A defeated Prime Minister need not offer advice about a successor when the Leader of the Opposition has been returned with a homogeneous majority Commons party behind him.[11] The Prime Minister will appreciate that he could not form a government from the new House and have its confidence; the victorious Leader obviously could, and no doubt the Queen will know the election results as quickly and in the same manner as anyone else—by watching the television or listening to the radio. But the constitutional niceties may be maintained: even when the course of action is clear, as in 1997, when Mr Major had to make way for Mr Blair, it may be preferable for the Queen to be advised whom to send for in order to preserve the comfortable notion that at the change of an administration, an event which must be inextricably linked with party politics, the Queen still acts only on ministerial advice. (An oddity can, however, be noted here. Unless the outgoing Prime Minister is scrupulous about the order in which he presents his remarks and resignation to the Queen at his farewell audience, the Queen might in fact not be acting on ministerial advice at all if the resignation precedes any recommendation. She would then merely be hearing advice from a former Prime Minister. But in the excitement of a government being turned out by the electorate, such minutiae are easily overlooked.) In neither of these results does the prerogative of choice of a new Prime Minister have any role. The third possible consequence of a general election, however—the return of no single party to the Commons with an absolute majority of seats—may lead to a change of Prime Minister and could involve that prerogative. The formation of a government from a hung Parliament involves so many questions that the whole of the next chapter is devoted to it.

Resignation through illness or old age

Since 1900 seven Prime Ministers have resigned their office while the government has remained otherwise intact, their departure being forced by ill health or old age or both. The men concerned were Salisbury (1902), Campbell-Bannerman (1908), Bonar Law (1923),[12] MacDonald

---

[11] A former Prime Minister has written that the outgoing Prime Minister need not give advice in such circumstances: Harold Wilson, *The Governance of Britain* (1976), p. 24.

[12] Campbell-Bannerman resigned as Prime Minister on 6 April and died on 22 April 1908; Bonar Law resigned on 20 May 1923 and died the following October.

(1935),[13] Churchill (1955),[14] Eden (1957)[15] and Macmillan (1963).[16] The pressure of high office in modern Britain leading to, or exacerbating, an illness, or an impossible political situation for which an illness could provide the opportunity for an honourable exit, both mean that the constitutional process will continue to have to provide from time to time a new Prime Minister from an existing government, the intention being that the government, having the confidence of the House of Commons, should continue in office. How would that process work today?

The easiest answer would depend upon a happy combination of circumstances. If there were no urgency about the transfer of office, with no emergency actual or imminent, there would be no need for an unseemly rush—and more importantly no need to involve the prerogative of choice. The ordinary party election machinery would be used to elect a new Leader of the party forming the existing government; the outgoing Prime Minister would wait for that election result, (perhaps) recommend his successor, and then resign. The new Leader would then be appointed. This certainly could be the procedure if the reason for the resignation were old age, as with Churchill, for an additional few weeks in office could scarcely make much difference. On the other hand, what might be termed the 'alarmist' view deserves to be examined. Party elections can be relatively slow affairs. The transfer of office from Mr Wilson to Mr Callaghan in 1976, for example—a case of voluntary retirement which will be considered below—took three ballots and three weeks to complete. The election of Mrs Thatcher in 1975—the Conservatives being in opposition at the time—took two ballots and nearly two weeks; but the transfer from Mr Major to Mr Hague in 1997 took three ballots and six

---

[13] MacDonald had been the titular head of the 'National Government' since its formation. His health declined through those years, and although he remained in that government as Lord President of the Council under Baldwin after his final resignation as Prime Minister in 1935, he resigned with Baldwin in 1937 and died later in that year.

[14] Churchill was extremely reluctant to leave office because he believed that he could promote peaceful coexistence between the Soviet Union and the West. He was finally convinced that he should go in April 1955 at the age of 80. For an account of the struggle to ease him from office, see Harold Macmillan, *The Tides of Fortune* (1969), pp. 533, 537, 539–41, and 544–5.

[15] Eden bore the British responsibility for the Suez invasion in 1956, but it was a recurrence of a debilitating illness which forced his resignation in January 1957. For his own account, see Sir Anthony Eden, *Full Circle* (1960), pp. 581–4; and see Robert Rhodes James, *Anthony Eden* (1986), ch. 14.

[16] He had to resign quite suddenly in order to undergo surgery which would need prolonged recuperation, an event which he termed in his autobiography a 'stroke of fate': Harold Macmillan, *At the End of the Day* (1973), ch. 15. Macmillan thought he had cancer: in later life he often remarked that he need not have resigned: see Horne, n. 2 above, p. 542.

weeks.[17] The 'alarmist' might argue that such a period would be intolerable if the country faced any grave emergency; and moreover that, even when comparative calm reigns, there is an ever-present need for someone to hold the office of Prime Minister, blessed with the authority which that office brings. So, for example, on this view a latter-day stricken Eden could not and should not be expected to stay in office despite his illness until a successor were elected; or if some economic emergency gripped the nation and the Prime Minister's health collapsed, a replacement with the political and moral authority to govern would be needed much faster than any party's election system could supply one. At first sight this argument seems to render the use of the party election inappropriate and the employment of the royal prerogative of choice as in, say, 1963, the more attractive. But objections can be seen on a moment's reflection. If a Labour government were in office at the relevant time, it would be difficult to see how that Party would accept anyone other than an elected successor to be Prime Minister, particularly after the Party's statement in 1957 that it would not expect anyone to accept office as Prime Minister unless he had first been elected Leader of the Parliamentary Labour Party.[18] This attitude is perhaps reinforced both by the manner of the exit of Mr Wilson in 1976 (involving a voluntary and leisurely retirement from office), and by the Party's election rules introduced in 1981, which are underpinned by the desire for greater party participatory democracy. If a Conservative government were in power, the prospect of another 'emergence' would remind the Party of the divisions on Eden's resignation and the open warfare which surrounded Macmillan's resignation. And given the Party's use in 1990 of its election machinery to oust Mrs Thatcher and to elect a successor, the Conservatives would now insist on a Party election to choose a new Leader.

A solution is suggested which combines the requirements of always having someone, with next to no power vacuum, at the helm, together with

[17] The election of Mr Heath as Leader of the Conservative Party in July 1965, on the other hand, took only six days, thus showing that, depending on the circumstances, a party election can be concluded fairly speedily. Sir Alec Douglas-Home had announced his intention to resign the Leadership on 22 July at a meeting of the 1922 Committee; nominations were called for by 26 July, and although Mr Heath did not have the arithmetical lead for outright victory over his rivals Mr Maudling and Mr Powell when the result was announced on 27 July, they immediately withdrew, and Mr Heath's name alone was placed in nomination for the second ballot the following day and he was declared to be the winner. See George Hutchinson, *Edward Heath* (1970), pp. 138–44 and Appendix III to that book for the details and the then current election rules.

[18] See Geoffrey Marshall and Graeme Moodie, *Some Problems of the Constitution* (5th edn., 1971), pp. 47–8; see also the Labour Party Constitution, cl. VII and the Parliamentary Labour Party's Standing Orders, s. I. 1 (explained in Chapter 8).

what today may be taken as being the common preference in the political parties for the Leader (and hence Prime Minister) to be elected. Save for the case where a Prime Minister is to resign as the result of advanced years, and therefore where speed is not essential and an ordinary party election could take place, the following course of action is proposed to find a new Prime Minister for a continuing government. First, the outgoing Prime Minister would inform the Queen and his parliamentary party of his illness and desire to resign.[19] Secondly, the Queen would ask the Prime Minister's deputy (if there were one), or the number two in the order of precedence in the Cabinet list[20] (if there were no formal deputy), to take charge of the government, while retaining his portfolio, but *without* appointing him Prime Minister.[21] He would look after the government on as much of a care and maintenance basis as circumstances permitted, deciding only urgent matters and then only with Cabinet consent if this were possible.[22] Thirdly, the government party would proceed to an election as expeditiously as might be and, when a successful candidate was elected, the Prime Minister (if able, or the deputy or number two if not) would recommend him as successor, resign, and the new Leader would kiss hands on appointment as Prime Minister.[23] In such a way the democratic ideal would be preserved; at no time would the government be rudderless, and the Queen would remain isolated from party politics.

[19] For the suggested procedure if the Prime Minister were to die suddenly, see n. 23 below.

[20] The Cabinet 'pecking order' can be seen in the list of Ministers published periodically in *Hansard*. That order is taken to be the Prime Minister's. Labour's 1981 rules provided (until 1993) that the elected Deputy Leader would become Leader, if a vacancy occurred while the Party was in government, until a new Leader was elected at a Party conference. Now (see S.O. 5(3)), a Labour Cabinet may appoint a Cabinet Minister as acting Leader until a Leadership election could be held.

[21] This could be seen to be analogous to two historical episodes. Eden asked Butler, the Lord Privy Seal, in 1956–67 'to preside at Cabinet meetings' during the Prime Minister's illness (see Sir Anthony Eden, n. 15 above, p. 569), and Macmillan asked Butler (then First Secretary of State) in 1963 'to take charge of the Government' during the former's illness (see Lord Butler, n. 2 above, p. 241). In both cases Butler retained his portfolio.

[22] Powers which are personal to the office of the Prime Minister could not be exercised until a new Leader was elected and Prime Minister was appointed. Although some of these powers are quite important, it is difficult to see why, if they should fall to be used in the interim, they could not wait. For a useful compilation of some of these powers, see E. C. S. Wade and A. W. Bradley, *Constitutional and Administrative Law* (12th edn., 1997), pp. 288–91.

[23] If the Prime Minister were to die suddenly, I suggest that the procedure set out in the text should still be followed, omitting references to the outgoing Prime Minister. No Prime Minister has died in office this century, although there have been some near misses: see n. 12 above. Had Mr Wilson died during his premiership Labour MPs would have been summoned to a meeting within 48 hours and an exhaustive ballot would have been held there and then. The new Leader would then have been appointed Prime Minister by the Queen, who had

It might be objected that for a politician to act as a 'caretaker' might in itself enhance his chances in the subsequent Leadership election, simply by his being seen to fulfil the duties of the office of Prime Minister.[24] But it is equally possible that he could spoil any chances he might have had by making some political slip. And even if the 'caretaker' solution is still disliked, would not a strong argument in its favour be that the automatic selection of the 'caretaker' by virtue of his position preordained either by the stricken Prime Minister or (in the case of a Labour government) by his position as Deputy Leader of the Labour Party[25] would ensure that that selection would keep the Queen above the party infighting, and overall would ensure that the royal prerogative of choice of a new Prime Minister in this context would have no part to play?

As a matter of strict law, party elections can neither preclude nor preempt the prerogative of choice.[26] If a Prime Minister indicated that he wished to resign because he was ill, the Queen would indeed be acting in accordance with constitutional law if she were then and there to accept his resignation and appoint a successor after taking whatever soundings seemed appropriate. But that law has upon it a rich gloss of practice, realism, and political sophistication which, I suggest, would preclude a repeat of events such as those which occurred in 1963. This gloss was added when all the parties came to accept the desirability of Leadership elections—that is, after 1965.

Voluntary retirement

A Prime Minister might find himself in the still unusual but fortunate position of being able to decide for himself when to retire, with no pressure to do so from his party, still healthy, not too advanced in years, and with no

---

apparently approved the plan. See Tony Benn, *Out of the Wilderness: Diaries 1963–1967* (1987), p. 263. Macmillan told Selwyn Lloyd in 1958 that he had informed the Queen that, in the event of Macmillan's death, she should seek Lord Home's advice, and that his choice of his own successor would have been Derick Heathcoat-Amory: see D. R. Thorpe, *Selwyn Lloyd* (1989), p. 309.

[24] Thus, Butler might twice have thought that acting as head of the government, in 1956–67 and in 1963, might ultimately help his accession to the Conservative Leadership. In neither case, however, did it. Both episodes took place, of course, before the Conservative Party had Leadership election rules: the 1963 event encouraged the adoption of such machinery.

[25] See n. 20 above.

[26] This statement will be considered more fully below when the Labour Party's 1981 Leadership rules are considered.

wish to hold ministerial office again. In this century only two men have been in such a situation: Baldwin in 1937 and Mr Wilson in 1976.

Voluntary retirement provides the means for the simplest choice of a new Prime Minister save only for the outright victory of an opposition party at a general election. Provided that the outgoing politician considers that he is fully capable of carrying out the functions of his office until his successor is chosen,[27] all that he needs to do is to inform his Cabinet, party, and the public of his intention,[28] await the outcome of the ballot, go to the Queen to advise her of the circumstances and to resign.[29] Thus the democratic process is seen to be carried out, crowned by the dignity of the Queen's appointment of a person to be Prime Minister who, through that process, is patently the choice of his party.

One potential danger to this dignity may be inherent in the election itself, which could provide yet another example of the modern weakness of the convention of collective Cabinet responsibility.[30] The candidates in the Leadership election might feel obliged to show their party colleagues why they should be preferred,[31] and this could lead to the espousal of policies alternative to those of the government and of the outgoing Prime Minister. In the 1976 changeover, for instance, Mr Benn produced a statement which was little short of an alternative manifesto.[32] This development should not, however, cause concern. It would be extremely odd if the various candidates did not have different policies, or different interpretations of policies, from which their party was to make a choice. If the party electorate is to make an informed choice, those differences should be made

---

[27] If he thinks that he is not so capable, then the procedure outlined above on the use of a caretaker could apply.

[28] Mr Wilson informed the Queen and the Speaker in 1975 of his intention of retiring, and he made his plans clear to the Cabinet and public on 16 March 1976. For Mr Callaghan's account of his succession as Prime Minister see James Callaghan, *Time and Chance* (1987), pp. 390–4.

[29] In *The Governance of Britain* (1976), p. 22, Harold Wilson states that the Prime Minister resigns *and then* informs the Queen of the result of the ballot. Strictly, as was pointed out earlier, the Queen would not be acting on ministerial advice once the Prime Minister had actually resigned.

[30] On ministerial responsibility, see Chapter 7.

[31] Mr Wilson's successor in 1976, however, did not: he remained aloof, allowing his managers to gather the votes.

[32] But as Mr Benn said during the election to choose a successor to Mr Wilson as Leader of the Parliamentary Labour Party and thus as Prime Minister, 'If a man stands to be Prime Minister or Leader of a great party, the people are entitled to know the platform on which he stands'. In his campaign in 1981 for the Deputy Leadership of the Labour Party, which was in opposition at the time, Mr Benn was criticized for advocating some policies (such as on Northern Ireland) which were not in accordance with those of the Shadow Cabinet of which he was a member.

20 CONSTITUTIONAL PRACTICE

public. Our constitutional system is now mature enough to recognize this so as to eschew any idea of a need for anything like an 'agreement to differ' for the duration of the campaign.[33] It has to be accepted that, if a sitting government is to elect a new Leader, collective responsibility must at least be viewed very liberally throughout the election of the new Leader and Prime Minister.[34]

Emergency coalition

From the easiest way of identifying a new Prime Minister it is now necessary to examine a more difficult case: the need to form a coalition government from an existing House of Commons as a result of an emergency of such a grave character that only a government composed of representatives of more than one party would have the political authority to take the measures necessary to meet it.[35] If it is agreed by the leading politicians of the main parties that the circumstances requiring an emergency coalition exist, and that a coalition could be formed which would have the confidence of the Commons, then the major question must be: who is to lead it? Three possibilities present themselves.

The sitting Prime Minister might be thought to be the most appropriate choice.[36] The events of August 1931 are so well known that only the salient features will be noted here.[37] Realizing that the minority Labour government which he had formed in 1929 could not—indeed, would not—take effective measures against the economic and financial storm which was battering Britain, MacDonald decided to resign. Urged on by George V, however,[38] he agreed to take office again as Prime Minister of a 'National

[33] This is not to say that in Parliament at least the Cabinet's policy must be advocated and defended.

[34] Another objection might be that, whatever other criticisms might be made of the prerogative of choice in (say) 1957 and 1963, it did at least produce a Prime Minister quickly, thus to a degree avoiding uncertainty which (it is always claimed) is bad for economic and industrial affairs. Against this perfectly legitimate point of view must be balanced the advantage of a democratic election producing a Leader who is unarguably the choice of his party.

[35] This is not the same as the consequences of a newly elected Commons in which no party has an overall majority, which are discussed in the next chapter.

[36] As was MacDonald in 1931 (at least by George V and MacDonald himself), but as Chamberlain was not in 1940 (mainly because Labour refused to serve under him).

[37] For accounts of this episode, see Reginald Bassett, *1931: Political Crisis* (1958); David Marquand, *Ramsay MacDonald* (1977), pp. 604–70; and Sir Harold Nicolson, *King George V* (1952), chs. 26–7.

[38] 'The King impressed on the Prime Minister that he was the only man to lead the country through the crisis and hoped that he would reconsider the situation. His Majesty told him

Government', including the Conservative Party and the Samuelite Liberals, both of which groups readily fell in with the plan. MacDonald failed to convince all but an embarrassingly small number of his Labour colleagues to join him in the 'National Government', which was returned with an enormous Commons majority at the general election of 1931—in which the Labour Party was smashed.[39] To take another set of circumstances, there might (again) be an obvious choice of man or woman to head the new coalition who was not the Prime Minister. Thus, in the First World War, dissatisfaction with Asquith's leadership led to the emergence of Lloyd George as Prime Minister in 1916, and, in the Second, Churchill was chosen by general consent, even though he was not the first choice of (among others) George VI[40] to take over from Chamberlain. Baldwin succeeded MacDonald in 1935 in continuance of the 'National Government', and Chamberlain similarly followed Baldwin in 1937.[41] In only the Asquith–Lloyd George transfer was there real controversy over the transfer of power. But, thirdly, there could be the case of a coalition being essential, the sitting Prime Minister being unacceptable, and *no* clear successor being present. Indeed, the position could be more complicated if none of the party Leaders was acceptable, which could happen if, for example, not even the gravity of the emergency could override personal antagonisms. How in this situation—and indeed in the other two types of coalition crisis just outlined—could the royal prerogative be exercised in a manner which would protect the user from allegations of political partisanship? Is there any solution of a general character to the problems which could arise with a present-day creation of a coalition which might reconcile the desire of the political parties for a role in the choice of the new Prime Minister with what could be an unavoidable personal selection of a new Prime Minister made by the Queen? A tentative suggestion is offered here, in an attempt

---

that the Conservatives and Liberals would support him in restoring the confidence of foreigners in the financial stability of the country': Sir Clive Wigram, Private Secretary to George V, quoted in Sir Harold Nicolson's *King George V*, p. 464. No one today considers that the King acted with anything other than total propriety throughout this crisis.

[39] The results were: Conservatives 471 seats, National Labour 13, Samuelite Liberals 33, Simonite Liberals 35, Lloyd George Liberals 4, Labour 46, Independent Labour Party 6.

[40] As George VI recorded in his diary on 10 May 1940, Chamberlain and the King 'had an informal talk over his successor. I, of course, suggested Halifax, but he told me H. was not enthusiastic . . . I was disappointed . . . as I thought H. was the obvious man' (quoted by Sir John Wheeler-Bennett, *King George VI: His Life and Reign* (1958), pp. 443–4. The King was then easily persuaded to send for Churchill.

[41] The 'National Government' was really a Conservative government, with 471 Conservative MPs dominating it with the support of a small band of Liberals and an even smaller group of National Labour men.

to keep the prerogative of choice out of the political fray. As will be seen, it could not work in all circumstances.

Clearly, if a broad consensus is desired rather than a royal selection based on limited soundings, some form of election will be necessary. Equally plainly, however, an individual party election carried out under the current party rules could be of little help: it would be confined to one party when the whole point of the exercise would be to identify a Member of Parliament who would have cross-party support in a coalition. In this unique (and infrequent) contingency, should not the House of Commons itself take up the task of choosing the new Prime Minister? The existing government would, if feasible, continue in office until he or she was appointed. Candidates would allow themselves to be nominated for the office, and as soon as possible a secret ballot would be held of all MPs under (say) the superintendence of the Speaker.[42] The first-past-the-post system would have to be used because presumably the emergency would not allow the time for any form of exhaustive election.[43] If Parliament stood adjourned— as it did in August 1931—the Speaker and the Lord Chancellor could recall it, acting on the existing Prime Minister's request.[44] The man or woman receiving the most votes would be recommended by the Prime Minister to the Queen to form a coalition government. The Queen would then receive the outgoing Prime Minister's resignation and exercise the prerogative to appoint the new one. Thus, even at a time of serious constitutional crisis, the ideal of election might work in harmony with the royal prerogative.

Of course, this scheme is tentative, and objections to it can easily be foreseen. Urgency of the hypothetical crisis might require a choice within hours, not days, in which case the former manner of use of the prerogative, advised as best as may be, would have to be relied upon. Moreover, if one party had a substantial Commons majority, its candidate might be assured of election, regardless of the views of the other parties. This would not, however, necessarily follow. MacDonald was accepted by the Conservative Party and the Samuelite Liberals in 1931 to head the 'National Government', even though Labour was in a minority in the Commons and

---

[42] It is safe to assume that the successful candidate today would be an MP. He could be a peer only if he had made it clear that he intended to disclaim his peerage and seek a seat in the Commons, assuming that he came within the provisions of the Peerage Act 1963—broadly, that he had succeeded to the peerage within the previous 12 months (s. 1(2)) or that he had been an MP when he succeeded, and had disclaimed it or would disclaim it within one month (s. 2(1)).

[43] The election would be organized 'through the usual channels'—the Leader of the House and his shadow, the Whips, and representatives from the minor parties.

[44] House of Commons Standing Order 13; sessional orders of the House of Lords.

MacDonald's new creation, the National Labour Party, was minuscule. Again, how could the suggested scheme operate at all if Parliament were not just adjourned but dissolved when the need for a coalition arose? It could not: the prerogative of choice would have to be activated. And after the Labour Party's adoption of a widely based electoral college to elect its Leader,[45] an election confined to MPs alone might be too narrowly based for its taste and thus be unacceptable to it.[46]

Loss of the party Leadership

No Prime Minister has enjoyed his tenure of office without criticism from his own parliamentary party from time to time; some have faced revolts within their own party on particular issues;[47] a few have, in effect, been forced from office by their own party.[48] The introduction in 1965 of formal rules governing the election of the Conservative Leader, so that all the main parties have Leadership election machinery, has affected the security of Prime Ministers. The Conservative Party coup in 1990 demonstrates that a Prime Minister has merely a leasehold on power, and that the lease may be terminated by his party. Mr John Major has also shown that a Conservative Leader can seek a formal renewal of that lease. Both events will be described now.

By 1990 Mrs Thatcher—who had led the Conservatives to three consecutive general election victories—had come to be seen by the Party as an electoral liability.[49] The poll tax was widely and deeply unpopular; her belligerent style towards what was then still the European Community had become very troubling for the Cabinet. She refused to countenance changes to either aspect of her policy. Sir Geoffrey Howe, the Deputy Prime Minister, suddenly resigned from the Cabinet over her attitude

---

[45] To be discussed shortly.

[46] But would it be preferable to a choice made from Buckingham Palace?

[47] It is impossible to think of a government, certainly since the Second World War, which has not faced such revolts, resulting in changes in policy or open defeat in the Commons.

[48] The most recent and dramatic example was the eviction of Mrs Thatcher in 1990. Other instances may be seen in Churchill's reluctant retirement in 1955, and the rejection of Chamberlain in May 1940 when his majority of about 200 fell to 81 in the debate on the Norwegian campaign as a result of Conservative abstentions and votes against him.

[49] Mrs Thatcher had been challenged for the Leadership by a back-bench Conservative MP, Sir Anthony Meyer, in 1989. It was the first-ever Leadership challenge to a Conservative Prime Minister under the Party's 1965 rules. Although Mrs Thatcher beat him easily, 60 MPs declined to vote for her.

towards Europe, and his personal resignation statement[50] had a profound effect in undermining Conservative support for the Prime Minister. Mr Michael Heseltine, then a back-bench MP, announced that he would challenge Mrs Thatcher for the Conservative Leadership. Although she subsequently beat him in the first ballot with the votes of 204 Conservative MPs to Mr Heseltine's 152, that did not give her the required 15 per cent majority for victory.[51] She immediately announced her decision to fight on into the second round of balloting, but she then consulted senior Party figures (including the Chairman of the Conservative Party Organization, the Chairman of the 1922 Committee, and Lord Whitelaw), and saw individually nearly all the members of the Cabinet. The preponderance of advice to her was that she risked defeat in the second ballot. Mrs Thatcher then withdrew from the contest. Two Cabinet colleagues, Mr John Major and Mr Douglas Hurd, joined Mr Heseltine in that ballot: the result was victory for Mr Major.[52] Mrs Thatcher resigned as Prime Minister, and Mr Major kissed hands as her successor.[53] Twelve days had elapsed since Mr Heseltine's announcement. Perhaps the primary significance of these events for the future may be that what Conservative MPs have done once they could do again.

By 1995 Mr Major as Prime Minister had endured several years' criticism of his leadership from within the Conservative Party, and particularly from Conservative MPs. He therefore decided in June of that year to trigger a leadership contest by resigning as Leader of the Conservative Party (but not as Prime Minister). Perhaps he expected to be returned unopposed: but Mr John Redwood resigned as Secretary of State for Wales in order to fight the election. Both men, in effect, issued manifestos. Mr Major won on the first ballot, although 89 Conservative MPs voted for Mr Redwood and a further 22 abstained or spoiled their ballot papers.[54]

After the election in 1997 of Mr William Hague as party successor to Mr Major the Conservative Party set about revising the rules for the election of its Leader, both to widen the franchise and to simplify procedures. The principles underlying the new rules (which are given in Appendix B) are

---

[50] See 180 H.C. Deb. 461 (13 November 1990).

[51] The then current rules appeared as Appendix B in the second edition of this book.

[52] Mr Major was two votes short of an overall majority: he scored 185 votes, to Mr Heseltine's 131, and Mr Hurd's 56. The runners-up immediately withdrew, and the Chairman of the 1922 Committee declared Mr Major to be the winner.

[53] For full accounts, see R. Brazier, 'The Downfall of Margaret Thatcher' (1991) 54 *Modern Law Review* 471; Alan Watkins, *A Conservative Coup* (1991), and *The Road to No. 10* (1998), pp. 211–34; Margaret Thatcher, *The Downing Street Years* (1993), ch. 28.

[54] See R. Brazier, 'The Resignation of John Major' [1995] *Public Law* 513.

that, in future, the Leader of the Conservative Party will be elected by all Party members through a postal ballot; that a winning candidate will need merely to obtain 50 per cent or more of the votes cast; and that, although Conservative MPs will no longer alone elect the Leader, the 1922 Committee will have the exclusive right to nominate candidates, and its Chairman will be in charge of each contest.

How secure is a Labour Prime Minister? Although at the time it was seen as no more than the correction of an anomaly, only at the Labour Party's annual conference in 1979 was the formal position of the Leader of the Parliamentary Labour Party brought into line with the *de facto* position by his being accorded the title of 'Leader of the Labour Party'.[55] The changes in the method of electing the Leader, introduced at the special conference at Wembley in January 1981, and the 1980 requirements about reselection of candidates have, however, possibly laid a constitutional minefield.

Broadly, the rules require that an electoral college choose the Leader.[56] A weighted voting system is used, giving 66 per cent of the votes to the Party outside Parliament—33 per cent to trade unions and other affiliated organizations, 33 per cent to the constituency Labour parties—leaving the previously autonomous Parliamentary Labour Party (PLP) with only 33 per cent. The system was first used in 1981 to elect the Deputy Leader.[57] In 1983, on the retirement of Mr Foot, Mr Kinnock was elected Leader by the electoral college and Mr Hattersley was elected Deputy Leader.[58] On Mr Kinnock's retirement after the 1992 general election, Mr John Smith was elected Leader by the electoral college, with Mrs Margaret Beckett as Deputy Leader.[59] It was last used, following Mr Smith's death in 1994, to elect Mr Tony Blair as Leader and Mr John Prescott as Deputy Leader.[60]

---

[55] Constitution, cl. VII. 1.

[56] Labour Party Conference Rule 5. See also Dawn Oliver, 'The Constitutional Implications of the Reforms of the Labour Party' [1981] *Public Law* 151.

[57] The incumbent, Mr Healey, narrowly retained the post on the second ballot with 50.426 per cent, beating Mr Benn (49.574 per cent). The revised 1981 constitution provides for the Deputy Leader in opposition to become Leader automatically if 'the Party Leader, for whatever reason, becomes permanently unavailable' (S.O. 5(4)), until a new Leader is elected at a Party conference. The status of the Deputy Leader has thereby been enhanced.

[58] He obtained over 71 per cent of the electoral college votes to his nearest rival's 19 per cent. Mr Hattersley was elected Deputy Leader in a separate ballot, securing over 67 per cent of the votes.

[59] Mr Smith obtained 91.016 per cent of the votes to Mr Bryan Gould's 8.984 per cent. Mrs Beckett secured 57.303 per cent to her nearest rival's 28.129 per cent.

[60] Mr Blair received 57 per cent of the votes for Leader to Mr Prescott's 24.1 per cent and Mrs Margaret Beckett's 18.9 per cent. Mr Prescott won the Deputy Leadership by 56.5 per cent to Mrs Beckett's 43.5 per cent.

There must be an annual election, even if Labour is in power, if one is required by the annual Labour Party conference. This system could present three separate constitutional problems. The first is centred on the attitude of the PLP. Now, the Leader of that parliamentary party with an overall majority is entitled to be asked to form a government. Under the old system, the Leader of the PLP would be seen to enjoy the confidence of that body because it had elected him through an exhaustive ballot.[61] The obvious danger under the 1981 arrangements is that, given the overwhelming percentage of votes from outside the Commons, a new Leader might have little support in the PLP. Leaving aside for present purposes the polarizing of the different parts of the Party which would take place,[62] the constitutional issue may be highlighted by examining a hypothetical House of Commons. Suppose that a Labour Prime Minister, A, with an overall majority gives notice of his intention to retire as soon as a new Leader is elected (following the Wilson precedent of 1976). The electoral college elects B,[63] mainly through trade union and constituency votes. But it is obvious, through public statements, media polls, and so on, not only that B would have fared badly under the old PLP electoral system, but that another MP, C, would have won convincingly under it, because in this example the PLP is to the right (or to the left) of the Party outside the House of Commons. B enjoys the full-hearted support of only a small percentage of the PLP. Assuming, as it seems safe to do, that the opposition parties would not support B as Prime Minister in the Commons, his parliamentary majority just does not exist. What 'right' would B have to become Prime Minister? One plausible result might, of course, be that the PLP would make the best of it, tolerating B as their Leader because he was the choice of the Party. The consequences of rejecting him could be (a) a fatal split in the Labour Party as a whole; (b) an utterly confused state of party politics in the Commons; and—most serious of all in the immediate term for Labour—(c) the danger that the Queen might refuse to appoint B Prime Minister because of his obvious lack of a Commons majority.

---

[61] He could, of course, have lost that confidence, but it is noteworthy that since 1945 there have been only three contests for the Leadership otherwise than on the retirement (Attlee in 1955 and Wilson in 1976) or death (Gaitskell 1963 and Smith 1994) of the Leader. And a Labour Prime Minister, under the old system, could not be challenged: see the now superseded Standing Orders for the Election of the Officers and Parliamentary Committee of the PLP in Opposition, S.O. 9.

[62] One direct result was the emergence of the Social Democratic Party in April 1981, 12 sitting Labour MPs initially joining it, and several others defecting to it later.

[63] Candidates must be a 'Commons Member of the Parliamentary Labour Party': Labour Party Conference Rule 5.2(c).

Constitutional development could be thrown back to before 1965, with the Queen exercising the prerogative of choice based on the best advice available to her. No one in the Labour Party would want that; the Party outside Parliament would be outraged;[64] the Sovereign would be seen, however unavoidably, to be taking sides. And there would be no solution in appointing a Labour Prime Minister conditionally on a request for a dissolution, because were Labour to be returned to power the Leadership question would still be there.[65] A compromise (which by definition would not satisfy everyone) can be suggested. It would avoid, on the one hand, the use of the prerogative of choice in appointing C as Prime Minister (not as Leader of the Party but as the Leader of the majority of the PLP) and, on the other, an automatic use of prerogative of appointment to install B (as Leader of the Party), knowing that he had no Commons majority. The PLP could conduct a poll of its members to test which man had the greater support.[66] Presumably, in the hypothesis presented, C would win[67] and he would become Prime Minister. Even as this is written, howls of anger from Labour ranks can be imagined, but every political party must remember that it cannot effect changes in British constitutional law or practice merely by changes in its internal rules if the consequence of those changes clashes with clear constitutional practice.[68]

A second difficulty could arise from the Labour Party rule (again dating from 1981) that a Leader in office as Prime Minister can be challenged for

[64] See n. 18 above, about the Party's insistence that no one should become a Labour Prime Minister without first having been elected Leader of the Party.

[65] For the Queen to appoint the Leader of the Opposition as Prime Minister conditional on such a request would be a gambler's throw indeed, for what if Labour were to win the general election? This can be distinguished from the Whitlam affair in Australia in 1975 only because the Opposition Leader *did* win the election. Again, what would have been the consequences if the dismissed Labour Prime Minister had won? See further P. G. Polyviou, *Annual Survey of Commonwealth Law* (1976), p. 16; Sir John Kerr, *Matters for Judgment* (1978); Gough Whitlam, *The Truth of the Matter* (1979); and Gareth Evans (ed.), *Labor and the Constitution 1972–1975* (1977).

[66] There is now no provision at all in the Labour Party's constitution for this. To the contrary, in November 1981 the Parliamentary Labour Party accepted new standing orders which included the provision that the PLP should accept as its Leader and Deputy Leader the people voted into those positions by the electoral college. Yet what the PLP does it can undo.

[67] Admittedly *he* might not have a Commons majority either, because those who were loyal to B would not support C. In that case, the Queen would have to take an active role in consulting party Leaders. But to invite the Leader of the Opposition to form an administration on condition that he recommend a dissolution would be unwise: see n. 65 above.

[68] The adoption by Labour of the election of its Leader by the PLP, and by the Conservatives of such a system based on Conservative MPs in 1965, constituted changes in internal rules but did not offend against constitutional practice—unless the old-fashioned view is adhered to that the royal prerogative should remain absolutely free in this matter, a view which I emphatically reject, as do other modern writers.

the Leadership at a Party conference if an election is requested by a majority of the conference on a card vote.[69] The Conservative Party spectacularly changed its Leader and Prime Minister in 1990: why should the Labour Party not follow suit one day? Both parties have a requirement that there be an annual Leadership election if one is duly requested. The Conservative Party has no record of loyalty to failed Leaders or Prime Ministers. So is it safe to be sanguine about Labour's procedures, given the mood which deepened in the early 1980s and which strives for even greater accountability in the Labour Party, of which this rule is an example? I suggest that an attempt may well be made at some future Labour Party conference to dislodge a Labour Prime Minister, even though this may seem highly unlikely at present given Mr Blair's success so far. If any such attempt were successful, the Leader would have to resign as Prime Minister. Whether his successor took over smoothly would depend on the issues discussed above in relation to the Leadership changing hands in a hypothetical House of Commons.

The last major problem potentially caused by changes in Labour rules in 1980 is that every Labour MP must undergo a reselection process.[70] This must happen once in each Parliament.[71] It is very unlikely that a Labour Prime Minister would be deprived of his seat in this way, but it deserves to be noted that, however unwittingly, a piece of machinery has been created which could be used locally to deprive a Labour Prime Minister of his seat. *If* this were ever done, then unless some other constituency took him on board in time for the general election, or perhaps unless he stood and won in his constituency as some kind of independent Labour candidate with at least PLP support, then, on the declaration of the result in his constituency, he would lose any right to remain Prime Minister. Labour might be in the extraordinary position of winning a general election with its Leader outside Parliament.

Conclusions

From this survey, three broad conclusions may be drawn.

(1) The idea that the role of the Queen has been reduced in the selection of a new Prime Minister to that of cypher is in most instances correct. The

---

[69] Labour Party Conference Rule 5.4(b). See also n. 61 above.

[70] Labour Party Conference Rule 4.A.11.

[71] Ibid. The National Executive Committee of the Labour Party has advised constituency parties that a short list of one (i.e. the sitting MP) should not be acceptable to the general management committee of the constituency if there is another candidate or candidates.

political parties have quite legitimately taken over some of the choices which the Sovereign has previously had to make, sometimes in controversial circumstances.

(2) It is, however, wrong to assume that the prerogative of choice of a new Prime Minister is as limited today as might have been supposed. Although some ways have been suggested in this chapter in which procedures might be adapted to ensure an element of democratic choice so that so far as possible the prerogative of choice could be kept in the background, a number of instances have been outlined where its use would be difficult to avoid. These are where:

(a)   a coalition is needed, either as a matter of extreme urgency (so that there is no time for any party election), or when Parliament is dissolved;

(b)   the Labour Party's electoral college chooses a Leader when Labour is in power who is rejected by the Parliamentary Labour Party;

(c)   a Labour Prime Minister is ousted from the Leadership by the electoral college, and

(d)   a Labour Prime Minister is denied his parliamentary seat through the mandatory reselection procedure and no other seat can be found for him in time for the next general election.

(3) Thus, although there has undoubtedly been a shift of constitutional responsibility from the Sovereign to the political parties, enhancing the dignity of the head of state while, where possible, making the choice of a head of government more democratic, there remain sufficient possible circumstances in which the Queen would have to exercise her prerogative of choice unaided by the parties. It is much too soon to consign that part of the royal prerogative to the lumber room wherein lie discarded bits of constitutional law and practice.

It is to the tricky question of how a Prime Minister is chosen on the return of a hung Parliament that attention is turned in the next chapter.

3

GOVERNMENT FORMATION FROM A HUNG PARLIAMENT

The election of a hung Parliament[1] presents a broad range of possible procedures and resulting government structures: there are precedents this century which provide a dazzling array of choice.[2] So a Prime Minister, having failed to secure a majority at the general election, might resign immediately,[3] or stay in office to negotiate a coalition,[4] or wait to meet Parliament to have his fate decided on the motion on the loyal address in reply to the Queen's Speech.[5] The Sovereign might take some part in the resolution of the crisis,[6] or none.[7] There could be a protracted succession,[8] or a resolution almost as speedy as if the electorate had returned a majority government.[9] The administration which emerged could vary in its composition from a minority government enjoying no support from other parties,[10] to a minority government with negotiated aid from others so as to ensure some degree of stability,[11] to a majority coalition of two[12] or three parties,[13] or

---

[1] Two useful books are Vernon Bogdanor, *Multi-party Politics and the Constitution* (1983) and David Butler, *Governing Without a Majority: Dilemmas for Hung Parliaments in Britain* (2nd edn., 1986). See also Rodney Brazier, *Constitutional Texts* (1990), ch. 1, and (for suggested changes to the relevant practices) *Constitutional Reform* (2nd edn., 1998), pp. 133–8.

[2] The main precedents will be evaluated later.   [3] As did Baldwin in 1929.

[4] As did Mr Heath in February 1974.   [5] Baldwin took this course in 1923.

[6] As did George V, indirectly through his Private Secretary, in 1923–24.

[7] The Queen did not have to intervene following the election of the February 1974 hung Parliament.

[8] The longest this century lasted from the 6 December 1923 general election to the appointment of MacDonald at the head of the first and minority Labour government on 22 January 1924, a period of six weeks.

[9] As in February–March 1974, a period of only four days.

[10] Such as the minority Labour governments of MacDonald (January to November 1924) and Wilson (March to October 1974).

[11] Like the Lib.-Lab. pact which sustained the minority Callaghan government in office from March 1977 to July 1978. The pact did not follow a general election, nor did the governments indicated in nn. 12–14 below.

[12] As with the Conservative–Liberal Unionist government from 1900–5 (although overwhelmingly Conservative).

[13] The 'National Government' of 1931 to 1940.

even a national coalition of all the main parties.[14] And behind all that would be another uncertainty: if the successor government were to be defeated on an early vote of confidence, would the Queen be obliged to permit a further turn of the constitutional roulette wheel by granting a second dissolution of Parliament?

It seems from all this that there are no 'rules' about government formation from a hung Parliament. Such uncertainty in an area of major importance in the constitution may cry out for regulation, but the only 'rule' in such circumstances is open-ended and unhelpful, namely that in choosing a Prime Minister the Queen should commission that person who appears best able to command the support of a stable majority in the House of Commons, or, failing such a person, that politician who seems able to form a government with a reasonable prospect of maintaining an administration in office.[15] This does not take us very far. How, for example, could the Queen identify that person who *might* command a majority in the House of Commons of minority parties, and how would she resolve the possible and conflicting claim of the Leader of the largest minority party to form a minority government?

Moreover, the precedents—especially those in which a minority administration was formed—have to be approached with caution, as they were (as will be explained later) political accommodations arrived at as the result both of the political realities of the day and of the personal relationships between the party Leaders. Such relationships have varied and will vary greatly from time to time, making inter-party co-operation more, or less, likely.[16] Accordingly, those precedents should not be considered as being rule-constitutive.

The likelihood today of achieving agreement in advance of an inconclusive general election about relevant rules is remote, given the attitudes of the Leaders of the parties. The Leaders of the Conservative and Labour Parties have insisted at recent general elections that, as their respective parties would win an outright majority, discussions about a hung Parliament would be pointless—although during the 1980s and the early 1990s

---

[14]   The wartime coalition of Lloyd George of 1916 (which lasted until 1922) was formed from a hung Parliament, but not that of Churchill (1940 to 1945).

[15]   See the formulations given in, for example, S. A. de Smith and R. Brazier, *Constitutional and Administrative Law* (8th edn., 1998), pp. 168–71; E. C. S. Wade and A. W. Bradley, *Constitutional and Administrative Law* (12th edn., 1997), pp. 262–5; O. Hood Phillips, *Constitutional and Administrative Law* (7th edn., 1987 by O. Hood Phillips and P. Jackson), pp. 318–22.

[16]   Baldwin's animosity towards Lloyd George contributed to his part in the break-up of the latter's government in 1922. It would have been difficult to envisage a peacetime coalition between Mrs Thatcher and any Labour Leader.

successive Labour Leaders asserted that if Labour were to emerge as the largest minority party after an election the Labour Leader would be entitled to form a minority administration after the resignation of the Conservative government. The Liberal Democrats (and their predecessors), however, have actively campaigned for a coalition government to be formed from any hung Parliament and have rejected the formation of a minority administration out of hand.[17] Given the absence of all-party agreement on appropriate government formation procedures, the setting up of an inter-party conference or a Royal Commission to work towards agreed rules might not be worth while.[18] Equally, it would be astonishing if the Queen were to publish what her attitude would be in such a crisis, partly because it would be wholly outside any previous practice, but mainly because a precondition of such publication would be ministerial advice to make it, which in the light of the stance of the main party Leaders would not be likely to be forthcoming.[19] Yet the return of hung Parliaments could become routine if the present voting system were to be changed to one based on a more proportional method.

These matters expose the Queen to pressure to decide political questions, with the inherent risk of criticism however she might answer them. In the absence of rules about forming an administration from a hung Parliament the present purpose is to suggest a number of procedures which would help to preserve the perceived political neutrality of the head of state, ensure that as far as possible politicians would take responsibility for the resolution of political issues, and facilitate the effective continuance of government during any period of crisis. The first stage to be considered concerns the political negotiations which might take place after an inconclusive election but before the Queen became involved to any significant extent.

The political negotiations

After a general election in which the electorate records a decisive verdict the political debate may slacken. After the election of a hung Parliament,

---

[17] For an analysis, see R. Brazier, 'An Alliance Veto of a Minority Government?' [1985] *Public Law* 545.

[18] Those two devices are suggested by David Butler, n. 1 above, p. 105. The case for a more wide-ranging constitutional body is argued in Brazier, *Constitutional Reform* (1991), ch. 2.

[19] Butler, n. 1 above, pp. 132–3 suggests that the Queen could publish 'during a time of political peace' what her response would be to a request for a dissolution by a minority Prime Minister, but he does not address my point about the need for ministerial advice being obtained for such publication.

however, that debate will intensify: the political parties could well disagree on the type of government which should be installed; some party activists might be ready to denounce the heresy of co-operation or (worse) coalition with the adversaries of the late campaign; evidence of bias against one party or for another on the Queen's part might be sought—all to be relayed to the nation by the media. In such a situation it is suggested that the guiding light ought to be that the political crisis should if possible be resolved by politicians—in a phrase, that there should be political decisions, politically arrived at. If followed, such a guiding light would help to refute any allegation that a non-elected head of state had imposed a particular solution on the elected House instead of allowing that House, through the party Leaders, to arrive at a conclusion. It would also enhance the Queen's impartiality as between the political parties and between individuals,[20] which would be crucially important if a political compromise were to prove impossible, when only the Queen could end the succession crisis.

Support for such a guiding light can be obtained from the aftermaths of three hung Parliaments that have been elected this century,[21] in 1923,[22] 1929,[23] and February 1974.[24] In May 1923 Baldwin succeeded the dying Bonar Law as Prime Minister and, although the government which he took over had a majority of 37 seats and had only been elected in the previous November, he obtained a dissolution to seek a mandate for protection against the import of foreign manufactures. The Conservatives secured only 258 seats in the December 1923 general election, with the free-trade parties obtaining 191 seats (for Labour) and 159 seats (for the combined Asquith and Lloyd George Liberals, reunited against protection). Several outcomes were theoretically possible: a minority Conservative government, as being the largest minority; a Liberal–Labour free-trade

[20] The Queen's inevitable interventions in the fight for the succession to Macmillan in 1963, and to a lesser extent in choosing a successor to Eden in 1957, raised accusations that she had been forced to choose between contenders within the Conservative Party. For the published accounts see, Chapter 2, n. 2.

[21] The two general elections of January and December 1910 resulted in hung Parliaments, but as Asquith's government remained in power throughout they are not helpful in this analysis and are disregarded here.

[22] For detailed accounts of the six-week succession crisis in 1923–24, see David Marquand, *Ramsay MacDonald* (1977), pp. 296–305; Kenneth Rose, *King George V* (1983), pp. 324–7; Sir Harold Nicolson, *King George V* (1952), chs. 22 and 23; Vernon Bogdanor, n. 1 above, pp. 91–107. George V caused soundings to be made by his Private Secretary after the 1923 election about what his attitude should be if a request for a further dissolution were made, but he did not intervene directly in the government formation after that election.

[23] See David Marquand, n. 22 above, pp. 483–91.

[24] See Harold Wilson, *The Governance of Britain* (1976), pp. 25–6 and *Final Term: The Labour Government 1974–1976* (1979), pp. 9–11.

coalition; a Liberal–Conservative coalition (or at least co-operation between them in the House) so as to keep out Labour (which had never held office before), or a minority Labour government. Baldwin decided to stay in office and to meet the new Parliament.[25] The Labour Party would not countenance coalition.[26] Baldwin would not join a coalition—after all, he had played an important role in destroying Lloyd George's coalition government in 1922 and, in his words, he had 'killed one coalition and would never join another'.[27] The Liberals would offer no support to the Conservative Party which had fought the election to end free trade; and, as Asquith put it, if there were to be a Labour government for the first time it would be in a minority and 'it could hardly be tried in safer circumstances'.[28] A minority Labour government was inevitable, and Labour and the Liberals combined to defeat Baldwin's government by 72 votes on the King's Speech. Baldwin resigned, and George V—in his first personal intervention in the crisis—appointed MacDonald Prime Minister in January 1924.[29] The outcome had been dictated by the politics of the day and by the attitudes of the party Leaders, not by the King.[30] The second hung Parliament was returned in 1929. Labour became the largest minority party, with 288 seats, with Baldwin's second government obtaining 260 seats and the Liberals 59 seats.[31] Several of the factors which had militated against coalition only five years earlier were still present, and Baldwin

[25] His first inclination, having lost what his critics claimed was an unnecessary general election, was to resign forthwith as Prime Minister and Leader of the Conservative Party, but he subsequently changed his mind, perhaps at the King's urging. 'The Prime Minister came to see me and I asked him not to resign but to meet Parliament and see what happens': George V's diary for 10 December 1923 (quoted in Kenneth Rose, n. 22 above, p. 324). Vernon Bogdanor thinks that Baldwin had already decided to stay before that audience, so that the King's role in the episode has been exaggerated: n. 1 above, p. 97.

[26] The National Executive Committee resolved on 12 December 1923 that the 'Parliamentary Party should at once accept full responsibility for the Government of the country without compromising itself with any form of coalition': The Times, 14 December 1923.

[27] Quoted in Sir Harold Nicolson, n. 22 above, p. 495. He could not foresee 1931.

[28] Quoted in R. W. Lyman, The First Labour Government (1957), p. 86.

[29] MacDonald, as Leader of the second-largest party after the 1923 general election, was Leader of the Opposition. Sir Ivor Jennings has written in his Cabinet Government (3rd edn. 1959), p. 32 that 'The rule is that on the defeat and resignation of the Government the Queen should send first for the Leader of the Opposition'. This rule, however, fails to take account in a hung Parliament of a possible majority coalition which might or might not include the Leader of the Opposition.

[30] George V's Private Secretary, Lord Stamfordham, had acted as an important channel of information from the party Leaders to the King.

[31] The Conservatives had a larger share of the popular vote than Labour, 38.2 per cent to 37.1 per cent, a phenomenon repeated at the February 1974 election of a hung Parliament (Conservative 37.9 to Labour 37.1).

resigned immediately.[32] The King accordingly sent for the Leader of the Opposition from the previous Parliament, MacDonald, who formed his second minority administration: beyond formally appointing MacDonald, George V was required to perform no function. Strong support for the suggested guiding light of political decisions, politically arrived at, is provided by the most recent instance of a hung Parliament, that of February 1974. A Conservative majority of 16 at the dissolution disappeared at the polls, Labour becoming the largest minority with 301 seats, the Conservatives second with 296, the Liberals with 14 and the United Ulster Unionists with 11.[33] Mr Heath had an audience of the Queen on the day after the election to inform her of the political situation, and saw the Leader of the Liberal Party, Mr Thorpe, over the weekend to offer Liberal places in a coalition Cabinet and a Speaker's Conference on electoral reform.[34] The Liberals in the event rejected the offer, and on Monday 4 March Mr Heath resigned. As the Labour Shadow Cabinet had already made it publicly known that it was prepared to form a minority administration with no help from the other parties,[35] the Queen appointed Mr Wilson Prime Minister. Once again the new government had emerged from a hung Parliament with no recourse to the Sovereign.

In 1923, 1929, and 1974 the party Leaders resolved the crises. In each case the result happened to be a minority government. In the circumstances, there was no alternative. But the situation has since changed in two respects. First, the Liberal Democrats (and their predecessors) have been adamant that a coalition and only a coalition be formed from a hung Parliament. A pre-condition for Liberal Democrat support of such a coalition would be an agreement on policy. The Liberal Democrats' view has been that the political situation could only be addressed adequately by a coalition

[32] He told the King's Private Secretary that 'He was beaten and he accepts it and thinks this sporting attitude will count in his favour next time. If he hangs on they will say, "Here is a man clinging to office, he won't take his defeat, he is trying to prevent the Labour Party from enjoying their victory" ': Keith Middlemas and John Barnes, *Baldwin* (1969), p. 527. By 1929 there was a readier recognition that universal suffrage meant that seats won in Parliament represented the will of the electorate more closely than had been the case before that suffrage.

[33] The Scottish and Welsh Nationalists achieved a total of nine seats, there were two Independents, a Social Democratic and Labour member from Northern Ireland, and the Speaker. The Ulster Unionists no longer took the Conservative whip.

[34] The Ulster Unionists might have been available—at a price—to join Mr Heath's proposed coalition, and had they done so he would have had a nine-seat majority: see Phillip Whitehead, *The Writing on the Wall* (1985), p. 113; Cecil King, *Diary 1970–1974* (1975), p. 348. The Unionists were offered the Conservative whip, but they declined it: Lord Whitelaw, *The Whitelaw Memoirs* (1989), p. 135.

[35] Their statement was reported in *The Times*, 2 March 1974.

government, not by an 'unstable' minority administration.[36] If in such a Parliament the Liberal Democrats could find support from MPs in other parties so as to constitute a majority in the House, then the consensus for minority government which was forced on the parties in 1923, 1929, and 1974 would no longer exist, and if the traditional parties of government clung to their anti-coalition positions[37] a conflict would be produced which the Queen would have to end. The second change is that, if some of the political parties were to embrace the idea of a coalition, a pre-condition might be a change in the party leadership on the part of a potential coalition partner. One analogy, not involving the aftermath of a general election, comes from 1940, when neither the Labour Party nor the Liberals would join a coalition under Chamberlain, who eventually resigned to make way for Churchill.[38] In the 1983 and 1987 general election campaigns the Alliance parties indicated that a change in the Leadership of the Conservative Party might have to take place before they would join a Conservative–Alliance coalition.[39] If a party which was challenged in that way stood by its Leader, a minority administration might have to result. Alternatively, if it agreed to change its Leader, there would be a significant delay in forming the successor coalition until the change in Leader had been made. That delay would be exacerbated by the formal Leadership election procedures which all the parties have. All involve formal nominations and secret ballots. The

[36] The Liberal Democrat threat to vote down a minority government is not very convincing, because the other main opposition party (or a large section of it) would have to vote with them to achieve that result and that party would have to be prepared (as the Conservatives in 1974 were not) to face the financial cost of a quick second election and the possible antagonism of the electorate. In 1998 the Liberal Democrat conference agreed to co-operate with the Labour government if invited to, whether in a formal coalition or otherwise. But such co-operation would have to be approved first by the Liberal Democrat Executive and by the parliamentary party, as well as (in certain circumstances) the party conference itself and the party membership. This followed the unprecedented formation by Mr Blair of a Joint Consultative Cabinet Committee, including Liberal Democrat parliamentarians. Its main task was to take forward constitutional reform, about which there was much common ground between the two parties.

[37] Conservative antipathy can be traced back to Baldwin's hatred of Lloyd George. The Conservatives have only taken part in coalitions this century in wartime and at a time of financial emergency—the 'National Government' of 1931. Mr Heath suggested a 'Government of National Unity' in the October 1974 manifesto *Putting Britain First* but the idea died with his loss of the Conservative Leadership in 1975. Labour's antagonism was perhaps historically class-based and was bitterly reinforced by MacDonald's break-up of the Labour Party in 1931.

[38] Churchill was Prime Minister for five months before reluctantly accepting the Leadership of the Conservative Party: see Martin Gilbert, *Finest Hour: Winston Churchill 1939–1941* (1983), pp. 347–8, 829, 835–7.

[39] As the Leader of the Liberal Party put it: 'we cannot get rid of Thatcherism without getting rid of her. So she would have to step down to make way for a new Tory leader more in the "one nation" mould of Winston Churchill or Harold Macmillan': speech at Westminster to the Liberal Youth Day rally, 15 May 1985.

Heath–Thatcher transfer in 1975 took seven days; the Wilson–Callaghan changeover in 1976 took three weeks;[40] the Thatcher–Major transition in 1990 took almost two weeks, and the Major–Hague transfer took six weeks.[41] Thus an embryo coalition might have a gestation period of some weeks before it could be born.[42]

I have argued that after an inconclusive general election the guiding light should be: political decisions, politically arrived at. If the party Leaders were to agree within a few days that a majority coalition could not be formed and that a minority government should take office (as in 1974) the succession question would be decided. The Queen, acting on the views of the party Leaders as published[43] and presumably as communicated to her by the Prime Minister, would perform without controversy her dignified function of receiving the outgoing Prime Minister's resignation and appointing his minority successor.[44] (The only constitutional problem which could subsequently occur would be if the minority Prime Minister were to seek within a short time a further dissolution: this is discussed later.) Alternatively, a majority coalition might turn out to be on the cards, with or without a change in the Leadership of one party, but the largest minority party might insist that it had a right to take office on its own.[45] In such a case of irreconcilable disagreement the suggested guiding light would be extinguished and the Queen would have to become involved. It is her role in that delicate situation which will now be examined.

The Queen

The King or Queen for the time being is not a mere piece of mechanism but a human being carefully trained under circumstances which afford exceptional chances of learning the business of politics.[46]

---

[40] See Patrick Cosgrave, *Margaret Thatcher* (1978), ch. 2; Harold Wilson, *Final Term*, n. 24 above, pp. 236–9.

[41] See Chapter 2.

[42] The party election rules are in given in Appendix B. Labour's electoral college system could prove the longest by far. The resultant delay would enhance the need for a caretaker government, a point which is developed later.

[43] As they were in 1923 and 1974: see nn. 26 and 35 above. Before the 1997 general election the Liberal Democrats stated publicly that their policy of 'equidistance' between the other two parties had been abandoned in favour of co-operation with the Labour Party in a hung Parliament.

[44] It might be, of course, that the Prime Minister was going to succeed himself.

[45] It is unlikely that the parties representing a majority of seats would both fail to agree on a coalition *and* seek to vote down a minority government at the earliest opportunity.

[46] Sir William Anson, *The Law and Custom of the Constitution* (4th edn., 1935), ii. 61.

The Queen is clearly in a unique position to observe the business of politics. She has been head of state for nearly 50 years, during which time she has presided over 12 general elections and has seen 10 different Prime Ministers.[47] She is well informed, receiving all Cabinet papers and minutes and Foreign and Commonwealth Office telegrams. Her former Prime Ministers have paid tribute to her assiduity, her knowledge of national and international problems, and her accumulated political knowledge and experience, all of which became apparent to them through their weekly audiences.[48] It is therefore possible greatly to exaggerate the extent to which the Queen would need to seek advice as to what steps she should take following the election of a hung Parliament.

Her closest adviser would in the first instance be her Private Secretary, currently Sir Robin Janvrin. The office of Private Secretary[49] was created by Queen Victoria in 1861 and the holder has become a major source of professional advice, through knowledge of the leading politicians and by absorbing published and other opinions of constitutional writers. He is appointed personally by the Sovereign: there is no scope for political interference in the appointment.[50] There is a precedent for the Private Secretary, following an inconclusive election, acting both as a conduit for the party Leaders' views and as an active gatherer of them. From the general election of December 1923 until the Conservative landslide of 1924, George V's Private Secretary Lord Stamfordham conducted informal and confidential talks which helped to install MacDonald's first government and to inform the King of the attitude of the Leaders to any parliamentary defeat of it and of the issues involved in any consequent request for a dissolution. Nevertheless, it would be doubtful, I suggest, whether today a Private Secretary should be asked to perform a similar function, partly because of the risk that he might be perceived as being an establishment

---

[47]   She could say with even greater force than her grandfather, who reigned for 25 years, that 'My Ministers come and go and are relieved of their duties, but I am here always': George V to Lady Desborough, quoted in Kenneth Rose, n. 22 above, p. 106.

[48]   See Harold Macmillan, *Riding the Storm* (1971), p. 344 and *Pointing the Way* (1972), p. 30; Lord Home, *The Way the Wind Blows* (1976), p. 201; articles by Lord Home, Lord Wilson of Rievaulx, and James Callaghan, *The Sunday Times Magazine*, 13 April 1986 (on the occasion of the Queen's 60th birthday); Margaret Thatcher, *The Downing Street Years* (1993), pp. 17–18. During the BBC television programme *Elizabeth R* in 1992, the Queen commented 'Occasionally [I can] put one's point of view, and perhaps [the Prime Minister] hadn't seen it from that angle'.

[49]   On the office, see Sir John Wheeler-Bennett, *King George VI: His Life and Reign* (1958), Appendix B; Vernon Bogdanor, *The Monarchy and the Constitution* (1995), ch. 8; H.C. 29 (1971–2), pp. 30–41.

[50]   There may be, however, informal discussions with Ministers about senior appointments in the Royal Household: see 567 H.L. Deb. 134–5 (written answers 19 December 1995).

figure rather than as a purely neutral conveyer of information to the Sovereign, and mainly because an intermediary who saw the Leaders privately would be an inadequate substitute for the Queen receiving their opinions personally and according to a fair procedure.[51] Another potential adviser whom the commentators either overlook or rule out as being an inappropriate source of information is the outgoing Prime Minister. A Prime Minister who had failed to obtain a majority at a general election would be following precedents if he were to resign immediately,[52] or if he were to stay to see if he could form a coalition,[53] or if he were to wait and meet Parliament.[54] He is in theory entitled to remain in office until defeated on a vote of confidence.[55] Since MacDonald's resignation in 1924, however, none has waited to meet Parliament.

Three assertions have been made about an outgoing Prime Minister's constitutional position: first, that he is under no duty to give advice about his successor, but is under a duty to offer it if asked; secondly, that it would none the less be *improper* for the Queen to elicit his opinion, and thirdly that resigning Prime Ministers have not in modern times in fact sought to volunteer a view on the succession.

The first proposition must be right, especially if at his final audience he resigns and then speaks about his successor, for clearly his opinion could not be classified as ministerial advice but as the view of a former (albeit the most recent) Prime Minister.[56] As Harold Wilson has written: 'Contrary to widespread belief, there is no duty on the prime minister, still less any inherent right, to recommend the man to be sent for'.[57]

The second assertion, that it would be improper for the Queen to seek the outgoing Prime Minister's views, must be challenged. David Butler has written that:

there could be even greater problems if [the Queen] were obliged, in default of anyone else, to act on the advice of a lame-duck Prime Minister. It would be widely

---

[51] That suggested procedure will be outlined shortly. I do not consider the idea of an *informateur*, that is, a respected honest broker who might act on the Queen's behalf, to be worth consideration. Such an idea has received considerable criticism (see, for example, Butler, n. 1 above, pp. 88–91; Bogdanor, *Multi-Party Politics and the Constitution* (1983), pp. 129–33; and for implicit rejection, Marshall, *Constitutional Conventions* (1984), pp. 43–4), and no support.

[52] Baldwin (1929).   [53] Heath (1974).   [54] Baldwin (1923–24).

[55] On what is a vote of confidence, see P. Norton, 'Government Defeats in the House of Commons: Myths and Reality' [1978] *Public Law* 360 and Chapter 10.

[56] This point was explained earlier.

[57] *The Governance of Britain* (1976), p. 22. Similarly, he has put it in *Final Term*, n. 24 above, p. 239 that 'Contrary to the views of some text-book writers, a retiring Prime Minister does not advise the Queen who should be sent for, still less is there any truth in one proclaimed view . . . that if the Queen asks for advice she must accept it'.

seen as outrageous if, in an essentially adversarial situation, the umpire had to act on the advice of one of the protagonists.[58]

Vernon Bogdanor comments that 'It would be absurd, for example, [for the Queen] to ask a Prime Minister just defeated in the Commons or at the polls for advice as to his successor'.[59] But if a hung Parliament were elected, what could be more natural and less objectionable than the Queen asking the outgoing Prime Minister for the benefit of his experience over the next step? This would not be on the basis of seeking ministerial advice, as he would be resigning, but rather on the basis that that person had served the Queen as Prime Minister, perhaps for some years,[60] and that his opinion would be one piece of information which the Queen might wish to have. What weight she attached to it would be another matter. Just because a Prime Minister had lost a general election should not turn him into a pariah to be ushered from the Queen's presence as quickly as possible before he could add an inappropriate gloss on the bare act of resignation. The third proposition, that advice by a resigning Prime Minister has seldom been given in modern times,[61] must be qualified. The office of Prime Minister has changed hands 25 times since 1900. A perusal of the published materials shows that in five cases when the main opposition party won a majority at a general election it is not recorded whether advice was given,[62] perhaps because such advice was redundant, so that those cases can be ignored. Of the remaining 19 situations, advice was definitely given in nine transfers— half that total.[63] There is no record either way in seven other transfers;[64] advice was certainly not given in the remaining four.[65] Even if the seven unknown cases shifted to the 'no advice' column, advice has actually been

---

[58] See n. 49 above, p. 80.

[59] 'No Overall Majority: Forming a Government in a Multi-party Parliament' (Constitutional Reform Centre, 1986), p. 4.

[60] And perhaps having formed a close relationship: see, for example, the Queen's letter to Harold Macmillan after his retirement, quoted in his *At the End of the Day* (1973), pp. 518–19.

[61] See Butler, n. 1 above, p. 91.

[62] 1924 (MacDonald to Baldwin), 1951 (Attlee to Churchill), 1964 (Douglas-Home to Wilson), 1970 (Wilson to Heath), and 1979 (Callaghan to Thatcher).

[63] 1916 (Asquith to Lloyd George), 1931 (MacDonald succeeding himself), 1935 (MacDonald to Baldwin), 1937 (Baldwin to Chamberlain), 1940 (Chamberlain to Churchill), 1945 (Churchill to Attlee), 1955 (Churchill to Eden), 1963 (Macmillan to Home), and 1976 (Wilson to Callaghan).

[64] 1902 (Salisbury to Balfour), 1905 (Balfour to Campbell-Bannerman), 1922 (Lloyd George to Bonar Law), 1929 (Baldwin to MacDonald), 1974 (Heath to Wilson), 1990 (Thatcher to Major), and 1997 (Major to Blair).

[65] 1908 (Campbell-Bannerman to Asquith), 1923 (Bonar Law to Baldwin), 1924 (Baldwin to MacDonald), 1957 (Eden to Macmillan).

tendered almost as often as not this century in situations in which the succession was not automatic after a general election. I stress that this does not
show any 'right' to advise, merely that, as a matter of published record,
advice has been given more often than is sometimes recognized.[66]

Thus if the result of the party Leaders' negotiations were to be anything
other than a speedy agreement on a minority government, the Queen
would have to intervene using her own knowledge and skill, with her
Private Secretary at her elbow, and, if she wished, receiving the views of
the outgoing Prime Minister. Her intervention would be to receive the
differing opinions of the party Leaders and to commission a new Prime
Minister.

Suppose that a general election were to give Labour 290 seats, the Conservatives 260, the Liberal Democrats 80 seats,[67] and others 20.[68] As the
largest minority, Labour might claim the right to form a minority administration, whereas the Conservatives and the Liberal Democrats might be
ready to form a majority coalition government. The precedents of 1923,
1929, and 1974[69] all point to Labour's solution, and so in that sense it would
be prudent for the Queen to commission a Labour Prime Minister. But I
have already argued that those precedents are not prescriptive. Accordingly, the Queen might consider it to be her duty to commission a Conservative–Liberal Democrat coalition as having the better prospect of
reasonable stability, especially if those parties threatened to vote down a
minority Labour government at the earliest opportunity. How should the
Queen decide between those competing aims in a fair manner which
would leave the political decisions to politicians?

It is suggested that the Queen should hear the views in audience of each
party Leader in turn in order of their seat strengths in the new House.[70] So
in the hypothetical example she would receive in turn first the Leader of

[66] The Queen could consult former Prime Ministers and senior Privy Counsellors (as in
1957). George V's device of an all-party conference at Buckingham Palace, to which he
resorted four times, would not be apposite in choosing a new government from a hung Parliament. If such a conference were necessary, it could just as expeditiously take place away
from Buckingham Palace and thus take away the media spotlight. The Queen could, moreover, inform herself just as well through an alternative procedure now to be discussed.

[67] That would constitute a doubling of their current representation.

[68] Northern Ireland returns 18 MPs: Parliamentary Constituencies Act 1986, s. 3 and
Schedule 2, para. 1(4). The overwhelming majority will be Unionists. The Scottish and
Welsh Nationalists might account for the remaining handful.

[69] These were analysed above.

[70] It would be a nice question who would go first if the two leading parties tied (as they did
in December 1910). Personal convenience should, perhaps, dictate the order, and that would
sensibly be made public.

the Labour Party, then the Leader of the Conservative Party, then the Leader of the Liberal Democrats, then the Leaders of the parties from Northern Ireland, and so on.[71] The outgoing Prime Minister would be one of these. Such audiences would bear the advantages that the Queen would be following the electorate's choice as reflected in the seats given by it to the parties; no Leader could feel piqued at not being consulted, or at being consulted after some other Leader for no apparent reason, and the Queen would be informing herself personally of the Leaders' views, so that no one could allege that his views might have been distorted by an intermediary. The views of all the party Leaders, regardless of how few MPs they led, should be so obtained, for *not* to consult them all, especially in a close result, could be damaging: just a handful of votes in a Commons division could be crucial to the continuance of a government.

Let it be supposed after the hypothetical election result posed earlier that in the audiences the Labour Leader were to urge the Queen to appoint him Prime Minister of a minority government, and that subsequently the Conservative Leader[72] were to wish to see if an anti-Labour coalition could be formed with the Liberal Democrats, or perhaps were to tell the Queen that some Conservative MPs wanted to ally with that party and that time would be needed to test party opinion. In his later audience the Leader of the Liberal Democrats would make plain his enthusiasm for a coalition solution.[73] Armed with that information the Queen would be unwise immediately to commission anyone as Prime Minister—not the Labour Leader (because there could well be a Commons majority against him), not the Conservative or the Liberal Democrat Leader (because she would have an insufficient guarantee of a viable coalition to persuade her to take the novel step of appointing anything other than a minority administration from a hung Parliament). I suggest that it would be more prudent if, through the outgoing Prime Minister,[74] the Queen were to tell the Leaders that if she were to receive evidence (again through the outgoing Prime Minister) of a

---

[71] Any dispute about the number of seats held by any party could be resolved by whoever had been Speaker in the old Parliament (or a deputy if he were not re-elected): at this stage, before the new Parliament had met, there would be no elected Speaker. The Speaker can already be called upon to decide who is Leader of the Opposition by reference to numbers of seats (Ministerial and other Salaries Act 1975, s. 2(1)), and he might now be called upon to rule on the rights of opposition parties to Opposition Days, again based on seat strengths (Standing Order No. 13(2), (3)).

[72] One of these two Leaders may be assumed to be outgoing Prime Minister.

[73] There is no point in speculating here what might be the attitudes of the other parties.

[74] It will be argued shortly that he should remain in office throughout the succession crisis as caretaker Prime Minister.

copper-bottomed agreement on a majority coalition, its leadership, proposed disposition of ministerial offices, and agreed Queen's Speech,
together with an equally sound guarantee that that coalition government
would not seek a dissolution within a reasonable time, then she would
appoint the person agreed upon to be Prime Minister. The Queen should
further stipulate that the package should be endorsed by the relevant parliamentary parties before it was submitted to her so as to ensure that the
leaderships are entirely in tune with their parliamentary colleagues,[75] and
also that the ultimate agreement should be made public. Such intensely
political negotiations on the package would then take place at Westminster
between politicians, not at Buckingham Palace with the Queen. If the
whole agreement on a majority coalition were achieved, then that fact
would be communicated to the outgoing Prime Minister, who would see
the Queen, recommend that she send for the coalition leader, and resign.[76]
Again from caution, the older formula might be used of inviting the coalition leader to form a government and to report back on his success, rather
than then and there appointing him Prime Minister, so that if, despite
everything, he were unable to form a government the embarrassment of
'revolving door' Prime Ministers would be avoided.[77] Alternatively, if after
the party negotiations no such copper-bottomed coalition agreement were
to prove possible, the Queen should accept the outgoing Prime Minister's
resignation and appoint the Leader of the Labour Party as minority Prime
Minister.[78]

Such a process of audiences would, it is submitted, constitute a fair system that could be seen to be following the electorate's choice so far as practicable. It would leave the political responsibilities and decisions to the
party Leaders, who would have to assure the Queen that, in appointing a
coalition rather than a minority government, she would not be embarrassed by any early demise of that coalition or by an early request for
another general election. The cost of such a process would be time: a

---

[75] This point is made by David Steel, *A House Divided: The Lib–Lab Pact and the Future of
British Politics* (1980), pp. 153–4, in which, reflecting on the lessons of the Lib.–Lab. pact, he
stresses that in any future inter-party co-operation the relevant parliamentary parties should be
involved and their positive support achieved. The point was echoed in a joint letter from Mr
Steel and Dr Owen to prospective Alliance parliamentary candidates before the 1987 general
election.

[76] By the Queen acting on the advice of the Prime Minister, potential problems of Her
Majesty acting on party Leaders' advice, rather than ministerial advice, would be avoided.

[77] This formula was last used in 1963. See Lord Home, n. 48 above, p. 185.

[78] If a *minority* coalition could be formed which had more seats than the largest single party,
it would be entitled to form a minority government.

44   CONSTITUTIONAL PRACTICE

coalition agreement could take several weeks to conclude. That prompts the question of how effective administration could be continued during such a hiatus.

A caretaker government

The British post-election experience is that the defeated Prime Minister will resign and his successor will be appointed the day after the poll.[79] The electorate is used to television pictures of furniture vans in Downing Street the day after the election, moving out one head of government so as to make way for his successor. The formation of a coalition government from a hung Parliament, however, could be a lengthy process, but I suggest that a development of the use of caretaker governments would ensure continuity of administration. The governmental system, through what are in fact (though very rarely in name) caretaker governments, has regularly coped with succession uncertainties caused both by dissolutions and by resignations of Prime Ministers from governments which are to continue in office.

The operations of government are regularly suspended in large part for about three weeks from the announcement of a general election until after the result of it is known.[80] Those periods of suspension have not caused the heavens to fall, and it is difficult to see why a longer period during which coalition negotiations were held after the return of a hung Parliament would invite catastrophe. The *period* itself is scarcely crucial: in 1979, for example, the suspension lasted five weeks from the fall of the Callaghan government to the return of its Conservative successor, and during that time the Labour government acted as a caretaker administration, introducing a minimalist Budget and Finance Bill after discussions with the Opposition. And in 1945 Churchill formed a caretaker Conservative government on the break-up of the war coalition which governed for two months until the overseas election results were declared. A closer analogy is in the six-week interregnum between the 1923 general election and MacDonald's appointment in 1924. In all three cases necessary

[79] Was this expectation partly responsible for the opinion that Mr Heath's delayed resignation in 1974 was in some way 'unconstitutional'? See Lord Crowther-Hunt's letter to *The Times*, 4 March 1974. No one else thinks that Mr Heath acted other than with complete propriety.

[80] At the start of the 1997 general election campaign the Cabinet Office published detailed guidance for civil servants covering all aspects of their work during the election campaign: *1997 General Election Guidance* (Cabinet Office, 1997).

administration continued. The other situation of suspension occurs when a Prime Minister wishes to resign so as to make way for a successor from his government. For example, the Wilson–Callaghan transfer in 1976 took three weeks,[81] and the Wilson government remained throughout effectively as a caretaker.

Thus a Prime Minister whose authority is in question by virtue of a dissolution or his impending retirement (whether voluntary or otherwise) has been entirely able to preside over routine matters of government. All that would need to be accepted after the return of a hung Parliament and during any lengthy political negotiations would be that the defeated administration should stay in office as a caretaker government until the succession was settled.[82] The defeated Prime Minister would merely see the Queen to inform her of the political situation.[83] This would be a non-novel solution,[84] and indeed caretaker governments have worked well in Britain,[85] although we have not tended to recognize caretaker governments as such, rather as Monsieur Jourdain spoke prose most of his life without knowing it.

The second dissolution[86]

The election of a hung Parliament could set a constitutional time bomb ticking in that a resulting minority government might be defeated on a vote of confidence, or a coalition government might disintegrate, so that another general election might be sought, perhaps within a very short time of the inconclusive poll. Could—and would—the Prime Minister's

[81] The Conservative process in 1990 (on which see Chapter 2) took about two weeks; Mrs Thatcher had insisted that the election procedures be speeded up. She did not, of course, wish to resign. I have explained above that, if a Prime Minister, perhaps through sudden illness, had to resign before the secret ballot could be conducted, a caretaker from his Cabinet could take temporary charge during the party election.

[82] Of course, if the Prime Minister insisted on resigning he could not be required to stay in office.

[83] As did Mr Heath on the day after the February 1974 general election.

[84] Sir Ivor Jennings has written that 'It is essential to the parliamentary system that a Cabinet should be formed, and the Cabinet must remain until its successors have been appointed': n. 29 above, p. 57.

[85] See Butler, n. 1 above, ch. 4.

[86] On dissolution generally, see B. S. Markesinis, *The Theory and Practice of Dissolution of Parliament* (1972); Eugene A. Forsey, *The Royal Power of Dissolution of Parliament in the British Commonwealth* (1943), especially chs. 3 and 4; H. V. Evatt, *The King and His Dominion Governors* (1935).

request be refused? How could the existence and viability of an alternative administration in the existing House of Commons, the appointment of which might vitiate the need for another election, be tested? How could the Queen be assured that if she were to refuse a dissolution to one Prime Minister she would not be forced quickly to grant one to his successor? In addressing such questions I hope to suggest an approach which would throw most of the burden of responsibility on to the party Leaders.

It is beyond doubt that the Sovereign can refuse a request for a dissolution of Parliament: the difficulty lies in identifying the situations in which such action would be constitutionally appropriate. That identification is made more awkward by the fact that no dissolution has been refused this century, something which could wrongly be seen as evidence that any refusal would become an acceptance if pressed. But this negative fact proves no more than that no Prime Minister has improperly requested a dissolution, and that therefore the Sovereign has had no reason to refuse. George V certainly considered that the granting of a dissolution was not automatic, so that the cardinal convention of the constitution that the Sovereign acts on ministerial advice was subject to this exception at least.[87] That view is underpinned by the weight of opinion of writers,[88] politicians,[89] and a King's Private Secretary.[90] Few today would assert that the Sovereign has no discretion in the matter—although the prudence of normally granting a dissolution rather than refusing is rightly stressed. And three Governors-General have provided dramatic evidence of actual

[87] In November 1910, according to one account, he was thought to have decided to refuse any request for a dissolution but to have changed his mind having discussed the issue with senior Ministers: see Jennings, n. 29 above, p. 424, but cf. Sir Harold Nicolson, n. 22 above, pp. 125–39 and 150. He was also prepared to refuse a dissolution in 1916 if Bonar Law had succeeded Asquith and had sought one: see Nicolson, n. 22 above, ch. 18, sections (1) and (2).

[88] See, for example, de Smith and Brazier, n. 15 above, pp. 123–6; Wade and Bradley, n. 15 above, pp. 265–8; Hood Phillips, n. 15 above, pp. 148–51; Geoffrey Marshall, n. 51 above, pp. 35–44; Lord Blake, *The Office of Prime Minister* (1975), pp. 60–2.

[89] Harold Macmillan has written 'I ventured to impress upon [Her Majesty] that a P.M. had no right to "advise", a dissolution. "Advice", in the long run, the Crown must today accept. The P.M. "asks" for a dissolution, *which the Crown can agree to or not': Riding the Storm*, p. 750, quoting his diary (my italics). Mr Edward Short, as Leader of the House of Commons, wrote a letter, quoted in *The Times*, 11 May 1974, to reject some Labour MP's opinion that the Queen could not refuse a general election, saying, 'Constitutional lawyers of the highest authority are of the clear opinion that the Sovereign is not in all circumstances bound to grant a Prime Minister's request for a dissolution'.

[90] Sir Alan Lascelles, Private Secretary to George VI, writing as 'Senex' to *The Times*, 2 May 1950. A former Cabinet Secretary, Lord Armstrong, was of the same opinion: see *The Independent*, 21 June 1991.

refusal, in Canada,[91] South Africa,[92] and Australia.[93] Apart from the South African case, acute controversy was caused.

Against that background I wish to make three propositions.

(1) If a government continues in office as a minority administration after an inconclusive general election obtained by its Prime Minister and is immediately defeated on an amendment to the loyal address in reply to the Queen's Speech, there is no precedent for such a Prime Minister seeking a second dissolution; rather, there is ample precedent for him to resign. Baldwin resigned in just that circumstance in 1924. Any such request would be improper because it would smack of an attempt to get a recount of the electorate's first decision (a decision recorded at the Prime Minister's asking). If any such request were made, it would rightly be rejected. Such a refusal of ministerial[94] advice could be said to involve the indirect dismissal of the government.[95]

(2) If either a minority or coalition government is formed from a hung House of Commons and the new Prime Minister had not obtained the first dissolution, then a request by him at any time for a general election should be granted—although I will argue shortly that the alternative course of the Queen seeking another administration should not be ruled out. The first part of this proposition can be demonstrated from the 1974 hung Parliament. Harold Wilson clearly assumed that, since he had formed the

[91] In 1926 the Governor-General, Viscount Byng, refused Mackenzie King's (the minority Liberal Prime Minister) request, believing that Meighen, the Conservative Leader, could form a government with a majority. Meighen's new government was defeated four days later on a vote of confidence, and he was granted what Mackenzie King had been denied. The Liberals won the general election.

[92] In 1939 the Governor-General, Sir Patrick Duncan, rejected Hertzog's request for a general election. Hertzog wanted a mandate for South Africa to remain neutral in the Second World War; the majority of his Cabinet, led by Smuts, favoured a declaration of war. Hertzog resigned; Smuts became Prime Minister; war was declared, and Smuts remained securely in office for four years before seeking and obtaining a dissolution.

[93] In 1975 the Governor-General, Sir John Kerr, refused Whitlam's request for a Senate, rather than a general, election. The Governor-General subsequently dismissed Whitlam's government and appointed the Leader of the Opposition as Prime Minister, and he recommended a general election which he won. See further Gough Whitlam, *The Truth of the Matter* (1979); Sir John Kerr, *Matters for Judgment* (1978); Gareth Evans (ed.), *Labor and the Constitution 1972–1975* (1977).

[94] Geoffrey Marshall, n. 51 above, ch. 3, powerfully challenges the assumed right of a Prime Minister alone to recommend a dissolution without Cabinet approval.

[95] By analogy with the events leading to Edward VIII's abdication: if the King had insisted on marrying Mrs Simpson contrary to the government's advice the government would have felt obliged to resign. Might a government which had been refused a general election decide in certain circumstances to accept that refusal and stay in office?

minority Labour government in March 1974, a dissolution was his for the asking at the time of his choosing (and certainly if the opposition parties were to defeat his government on a vote of confidence).[96] That assumption, it is submitted, was entirely right. His predecessor Mr Heath had been granted the February 1974 dissolution, so that Mr Wilson's request would be his first; and Mr Heath and Mr Thorpe had shown in their abortive talks in February that a Conservative–Liberal coalition could not be formed from that House. A Prime Minister in a position similar to that of Harold Wilson would, like him, have a clearer right to a dissolution the longer the hung Parliament were to last, as that Parliament would have done its job for a period and there could be no convincing allegation that he was really seeking an improper recount.[97] Equally, the Queen would not want to look for an alternative government in such a case.

(3) If a Prime Minister of either a minority or a coalition government in a hung Parliament were to ask for a general election, even for his first time, in order to forestall another majority and workable grouping supplanting his administration, then again refusal would be defensible if that alternative grouping in fact existed. Suppose that, after an inconclusive general election, a Conservative–Liberal Democrat coalition were formed but that eventually a disagreement on some central issue arose. Suppose further that the Liberal Democrats threatened to resign and join a willing Labour Party in a new majority coalition in return for an agreed programme. The Conservative–Liberal Democrat coalition Prime Minister might recommend an immediate election to thwart the coup. The Queen would be required to reconcile two conflicting constitutional principles, the one being that she must accept ministerial advice (here, to dissolve), the other being that a person with a parliamentary majority behind him has the right to be Prime Minister (here, the head of the proposed new coalition). In favour of Her Majesty applying the second principle would be the facts that the Prime Minister would be seeking a dissolution with the improper motive of trying to prevent his ouster from office by an adverse parliamentary majority, and also that a new majority government could be installed without the need for a general election. If the Queen were to apply that second principle and refuse a dissolution, the government would resign and the new Labour–Liberal Democrat administration would take office.

Inherent in the second and third propositions is the question of the presence of an alternative majority government in the existing House of

---

[96] See his speech at High Wycombe, 14 March 1974.
[97] In the event the February 1974 Parliament lasted seven months.

Commons. One major reason in favour of the 'automatic theory' of dissolution is the predictable allegation of bias which would be made against the Queen if she were to refuse a general election to the Prime Minister in the mistaken belief that another government could be formed, and could carry on without an election, when in the event that new government were forced to seek, and was granted, the very thing which had been denied its predecessor.[98] I suggest that, as with the primary decision whether to commission a minority government or a coalition on the return of a hung Parliament, those party Leaders who were wanting to form a majority coalition (so as here to remove the need for dissolution) would have to make public an agreed and watertight package concerning the majority government in waiting. Nothing less than that would do if the Queen were to feel sufficiently confident to take the novel course of refusing a dissolution of Parliament and of bringing about a new administration. This would, in a way, be an example not of revolutionary royal interventionism but of the Queen giving effect to the wishes of Members of Parliament— it would once again be the proper recognition of political decisions, politically arrived at.

Events in Ontario in 1985 give significant support for my approach. Ontario has a system of government which, within the Canadian federation, is similar to Britain's. Elections to the 125-seat Legislative Assembly have to take place every four years, but earlier dissolution is possible. The Premier is appointed by the Queen's representative in the province, the Lieutenant-Governor, and is usually the Leader of the majority party in the Assembly: indeed, the Progressive Conservative Party had enjoyed such a majority for decades. In 1985 the Premier, Mr William Davis, asked for a dissolution from the Lieutenant-Governor, Mr John Black Aird, which was granted. The result gave the Progressive Conservatives 52 seats, the Liberals 48, and the New Democrats 25. Mr Davis decided to form a minority government; the Liberals and the New Democrats, meanwhile, formally agreed on a two-year programme of government, including an agreement that there should be no general election within that period. The Conservatives' Speech from the Throne was duly defeated and a motion of no confidence in Mr Davis's government was passed. The Lieutenant-Governor had caused it to be made clear informally that, if the Premier were to ask for a second dissolution, that request would be denied as there was a viable alternative government waiting in the Assembly which, as the result of its public pact, would have a very fair prospect of governing for at

---

[98] As with Viscount Byng: see n. 91 above.

least two years. Not surprisingly, Mr Davis made no such request, but resigned, and the Leader of the Liberal Party was appointed Premier.[99]

This Ontario episode shows, perhaps, in the British context that the 'automatic theory' of dissolution is dead (assuming that it ever lived); that a minority government, having received one dissolution, will not receive another dissolution, if beaten on an early vote of confidence; that a published copper-bottomed party pact on an alternative government can avoid any embarrassment of having to grant a dissolution to one head of government having refused it to his predecessor; and that an informal communication of the Queen's attitude, in response to the published agreement of some party Leaders prepared to take over the government without a dissolution, avoids, among other things, the general embarrassment of the tendering of formal ministerial advice and its formal rejection.

Of course it would be less controversial for the Queen to accept a request to dissolve Parliament than to seek an alternative. I have, however, posed three cases which could arise in a hung Parliament in which a royal refusal would be possible.

Conclusions

I have tried to develop several themes in this chapter. One is that the Queen is ideally placed to moderate between any competing wishes of party Leaders in a hung Parliament, and indeed that she has ample expertise at her disposal to enable her to do so. Another is that procedures which would scarcely be radically new could be followed so as to enhance the neutrality of the head of state and to continue the historical responsibility of politicians to resolve political questions posed by an inconclusive general election. If, for example, they wanted to achieve the unusual results of either a coalition administration, or the refusal of a sitting government's request for a dissolution and the appointment of a replacement government from the existing House, then the burden would be on the party Leaders involved to present the Queen with a public, watertight guarantee of a successful outcome before she would be justified in making such novel constitutional departures. A linked theme is that, in any prolonged succession crisis, it would be part of the politicians' duty through a caretaker government to ensure the efficient discharge of government until that crisis was ended.

---

[99] For the constitutional consequences of the election of a hung Parliament in Tasmania in 1989, see G. Winterton, 'Tasmania's Hung Parliament, 1989' [1992] *Public Law* 423.

Whenever a hung Parliament is elected, prudence, the current attitudes of the Conservative and Labour Leaders, together with potentially misleading precedents might well produce a minority government rather than a coalition, and consent to a requested second dissolution rather than a refusal of it. But new factors (such as significant political opinion in favour of the coalition of parties in a hung Parliament) might combine with old truths (especially that party Leaders are transient and that MPs prefer office to opposition) so as to make different outcomes possible.

4

THE TRANSFER OF POWER

Before a new Prime Minister or government can take office the outgoing Prime Minister or administration must resign. Such resignations will arise in one of a number of ways. First, if a government is unambiguously defeated at a general election and one opposition party is returned with a majority of seats in the new House of Commons,[1] the modern practice is for that government to resign without waiting to meet Parliament. Secondly, a Prime Minister may be forced to quit through illness or old age, or may die in office; or he may voluntarily decide to retire, or he may lose a party Leadership election, there being no question of a change in the party in power. In the last 45 years the Churchill, Eden, Macmillan, Wilson and Thatcher administrations have ended in that way. Lastly, the resignation of a Prime Minister and his immediate reappointment may be used as a device to show that the whole political basis of the government is to change. So in 1915 Asquith resigned in order to form a coalition government, so as to prosecute the war better than his Liberal administration could have hoped to do; in 1931 MacDonald resigned so that he could form the 'National Government' immediately to succeed his minority Labour government, and in 1945 Churchill resigned on the break-up of the war coalition so that a caretaker Conservative government under him could be installed pending the general election.

The constitutional consequences of those three political scenarios are very different. In the first (where the whole government is to resign after electoral defeat) the Prime Minister will obtain an audience of the Sovereign and resign. This carries with it the resignation of the entire administration, and his colleagues will cease to operate as Ministers and will leave their departments as soon as they have cleared their desks. In the second case (where only the Prime Minister, as an individual, is to go) as soon as the procedures for selecting a successor have been accomplished[2] the Prime

---

[1] The consequences of the return of a hung Parliament were considered in Chapter 3.
[2] See Chapter 2.

Minister will see the Queen and resign—but that act does not cause or signal the resignation of any other Minister at that stage. In this context Harold Wilson somewhat misstated matters in a letter to all his former Cabinet colleagues after he had resigned in 1976. He wrote that he had resigned that day, and continued:

as you will know, this carries with it the resignation of the whole of the present Administration. This does not require other Ministers to tender their individual resignations to Her Majesty; but they should, of course, regard their offices as at the disposal of my successor. Meanwhile, I ask all Ministers to carry on the necessary administration of their Departments until a new government is formed.[3]

Mr Wilson's resignation did not, however, carry with it the formal resignation of the whole of his government, as indeed the last sentence of his letter quoted makes clear. Unless they were reshuffled or dropped, all Ministers stayed in the same offices under his successor. Their offices were at Mr Callaghan's disposal in a political sense, certainly: but Ministers did not leave office unless they were actually disposed of, and even then, because all Ministers are appointed by the Queen, they did not cease to be Ministers until they had resigned in the prescribed manner. Most of Mr Wilson's Ministers continued in the same offices under Mr Callaghan and they did not have to be reappointed to office. Similarly, most of Mrs Thatcher's Cabinet remained as members of Mr Major's first Cabinet in 1990. In the third—and unusual—situation (in which the Prime Minister is to stay but the whole basis of his administration is to change) the Prime Minister will resign and be reappointed, but there is no uniform practice on whether all the other Ministers, too, will resign in the first instance. In 1945, after the Labour Party had decided that the war coalition should be dissolved and that a general election should take place, Churchill decided to form a caretaker Conservative government. He resigned at noon on 23 May, and was reappointed at 4 p.m.[4] Churchill had not asked Ministers to place their posts at his diposal or to resign. Many of the Conservative coalition Ministers were in fact confirmed in the new administration, so appointments or reappointments were not needed for them; Labour and Liberal Ministers,

---

[3] Lord Wilson of Rievaulx kindly gave me permission to quote from his letter.

[4] Churchill's romantic view of the royal prerogative ensured this time interval so as to emphasize the King's freedom of choice in selecting a Prime Minister: see Martin Gilbert, *Never Despair: Winston S. Churchill 1945–1965* (1988), pp. 22–3. As the Conservatives had a majority of 180 at the time, Churchill was scarcely risking the loss of his office. He recommended for the same reason that a whole day elapse on his retirement in 1955 before the Queen sent for Eden—even though Eden had been his nominated heir since 1942: Anthony Eden, *Full Circle* (1960), p. 266.

of course, left office. On the other hand, when Asquith was in effect forced in 1915 to accept a coalition so as to stave off a potentially ruinous Conservative attack on the conduct of the Admiralty,[5] the Prime Minister asked for the resignations of all his colleagues.[6] And in 1931 the Labour Cabinet told MacDonald to inform the King that they had placed their resignations in his hands.[7] Clearly if a Prime Minister is to reconstruct the political basis of his administration he does not (like Asquith) need to obtain resignations because all members of the unreconstructed government will regard their portfolios as being at his disposal.

When Ministers are to leave office so as to clear the way for a transfer of power, it is, of course, the substance that excites interest, not the formalities of how and when the resignations of politicians take place. The media will ensure that the public knows, for example, that a government rejected by the electorate in effect removes itself once the Prime Minister has resigned, or that after an ailing Prime Minister has retired his successor will decide which of his inherited pack to keep and which to discard. But how as a matter of law do Ministers cease to hold office?[8] A resignation may be expressed or implied. So a Minister leaving the government will submit a formal letter of resignation, but the resignation of one who is merely being reshuffled is implicit on his appointment to the new post. In the case of those ministerial appointments which require some formal document to give effect to them (a point which will be explained later), that document will include an express revocation of the previous holder's appointment. The Lord Chancellor and the Chancellor of the Duchy of Lancaster alone now retain the right of audience of the Queen to surrender their seals. The earlier practice by which other resigning Ministers who had seals of office would personally deliver them up to Her Majesty has been discontinued, and their seals are simply collected by the Privy Council Office. Private audiences for such Ministers are, however, usually arranged later as a matter of courtesy so that thanks may be offered and farewells made.[9]

---

[5] See Roy Jenkins, *Asquith* (3rd edn., 1986), p. 359.

[6] See J. A. Spender and Cyril Asquith, *Life of Lord Oxford and Asquith* (1932), ii. 164–6.

[7] See David Marquand, *Ramsay MacDonald* (1977), p. 635.

[8] See Rodney Brazier, *Ministers of the Crown* (1997), ch. 16.2. I am most grateful to the then Clerk of the Privy Council, Sir Geoffrey de Deney, for his kind help on the questions how in law and practice Ministers cease to hold, and take up, office. With his permission, a memorandum which he wrote for me appears in a slightly edited form as Appendix C. Its provisions were followed closely when the Labour Party returned to power in 1997; a change of government had not taken place for the previous 18 years.

[9] An account of a farewell audience is in Tony Benn, *Conflicts of Interest: Diaries 1977–1980* (1990), pp. 498–9. For the farewell audiences accorded to Ministers who left office following

The Prime Minister takes office

The Prime Minister is always a Privy Counsellor. Since 1961 every new Leader of each of the main political parties in opposition on or soon after his election as Leader has been admitted to membership of the Privy Council (if not already a member) on the advice of the Prime Minister.[10] And if a Cabinet colleague is to take over a resigning Prime Minister's administration, he too will be a Privy Counsellor by virtue of his membership of the Cabinet. Thus today every person who is likely to assume the office of Prime Minister will normally possess this qualification.[11] When a party Leader receives the sweet summons to Buckingham Palace[12] to take office, he will be orally appointed Prime Minister, and sometimes will kiss the Queen's hand to signify his acceptance and his loyalty: the kissing of hands may be taken as read.[13]

He will have achieved the supreme prize: but other gifts attach to it, namely the offices of First Lord of the Treasury[14] and Minister for the Civil Service.[15] Most Prime Ministers have taken the title of First Lord of the Treasury: indeed, the last not to was Lord Salisbury from 1895 to 1902, when his nephew Arthur Balfour led the House of Commons and held the title of First Lord. In practical terms, the Prime Minister resides at 10 Downing Street as First Lord of the Treasury; and since 1937 no Prime Minister would wish the other office on to someone else unless he wanted his own services to be offered free during his incumbency, because the Ministers of the Crown Act of that year provided an annual salary of £10,000 for the 'Prime Minister and First Lord of the Treasury'. The equivalent (and identical) formulation today is in the Ministerial and other Salaries Act 1975.[16] Despite this statutory recognition of the fact that those two posts will always

the Conservative government's defeat on 1 May 1997 see the Court Circular for 2, 6, and 7 May 1997: the Queen saw both former Cabinet and former junior Ministers.

[10] This may be seen partly as an honour and partly as a means whereby the party Leaders can be briefed by the Prime Minister on defence or other sensitive matters 'on Privy Counsellor terms'—that is, on the understanding that they do not reveal the details of the briefing to others. See further Chapter 8.

[11] The last not to was MacDonald in 1924. Labour had never held office before, and the King formally admitted him to membership some hours before appointing him Prime Minister: Marquand, n. 7 above, p. 304.

[12] Other venues are possible: in 1908 Asquith had to travel to Biarritz where Edward VII was holidaying in order to be appointed Prime Minister.

[13] Harold Wilson, *The Labour Government 1964–1970: A Personal Record* (1971), p. 2. It was taken as read when Mr Major and Mr Blair became Prime Minister. And see Geoffrey Marshall, 'Ministerial Hand-kissing' [1997] *Public Law* 587.

[14] On that office, see Harold Wilson, *The Governance of Britain* (1976), ch. 5.

[15] Another Minister is charged with day-to-day civil service matters.

[16] See s. 1(1) and Schedule 1.

now be combined, a Prime Minister will formally receive the title of First Lord of the Treasury by taking the oath of office as First Lord at a later ceremony at which his first batch of Ministers are sworn in.[17] Since the creation of the Civil Service Department in 1968—and despite its abolition in 1981[18]—the Prime Minister has also taken the title of Minister for the Civil Service. This gives him significant powers and duties in relation to the civil service, and it is unlikely that any Prime Minister, in the absence of further institutional change, would forgo it. In normal circumstances a Prime Minister would today take on no other additional departmental responsibility, given the vast burdens which he must carry as head of the government; there is, however, no legal or conventional reason why he should not take to himself a number of other offices if he wishes. When Prime Ministers have done this in modern times, however, peculiar conditions have persuaded them to do so: thus Asquith temporarily became Secretary of State for War in 1914 during the Curragh crisis;[19] Baldwin retained the office of Chancellor of the Exchequer for five months after becoming Prime Minister in 1923 during McKenna's convalescence;[20] MacDonald was his own Foreign Secretary in 1924 largely because he considered no one else to be qualified;[21] Churchill throughout his war premiership, and from 1951 to 1952, and Attlee for the first 17 months of his premiership in the aftermath of war were both Minister of Defence. The nearest any other Prime Minister has come this century to taking on another department of state was in 1967 when Mr Wilson, in order to strengthen the position of the Department of Economic Affairs, took personal charge of it with a Secretary of State to assist him. In the event, he relinquished that charge the following year and the Department was wound up in 1969.[22]

Matters legal, conventional, and political[23]

Once he has been appointed to office, the first task facing a new Prime Minister is the selection of personnel for his administration. In 1900 the

---

[17] Harold Wilson, *The Labour Government 1964–1970*, n. 13 above, p. 7.

[18] See S.I. 1968 No. 1656; S.I. 1981 No. 1670.

[19] See Jenkins, n. 5 above, ch. 19.

[20] In the event Neville Chamberlain took the post because of insuperable difficulties which McKenna had in finding a seat.

[21] See Marquand, n. 7 above, pp. 299–300. In 1929 he reluctantly agreed to make Henderson Foreign Secretary.

[22] For an explanation of his decision, see 762 H.C. Deb. 1585–8 (11 April 1968).

[23] See R. Brazier, *Ministers of the Crown* (1997), chs. 2–5 for a detailed analysis.

total number of salaried Ministers was 60; by 1950 that number had risen to over 80; today it is 105.[24] Filling all those posts is obviously a major operation (although as will be explained later the formation of a Cabinet is normally straightforward).

The main legal (although in practice not particularly irksome) restraint concerns the total number of MPs who may be appointed Ministers. So as to impose some limit on prime ministerial patronage, by statute not more than 95 MPs may sit and vote in the Commons and hold ministerial office at any one time, whether paid or not.[25] If a Prime Minister wishes to exceed that number of Ministers in the Commons, he must procure the passage of legislation.[26] As far as pay is concerned, it is true that individual Ministers occasionally take office without drawing a salary—as did Lord Young in Mrs Thatcher's Cabinet, and Mr Geoffrey Robinson and Lord Simon of Highbury in Mr Blair's government—but this may be regarded as somewhat exceptional. For all the rest the Ministerial and other Salaries Act 1975 provides[27] that specified salaries may be paid to no more than 105 Ministers at any one time.[28] Should this provision not prove adequate, a Prime Minister could still properly fill additional offices without pay and provided that not more than 95 Ministers were MPs, or he could invite Parliament to legislate afresh. For the rest, the choice of Ministers will be made in deference to convention, politics, and (to a limited extent) the Queen.

By convention, all Ministers must be or must become members of the House of Commons or of the House of Lords;[29] a Minister without a seat

---

[24] On the various ministerial titles, see Chapter 7. There are additionally a number (currently 40) of Parliamentary Private Secretaries, each appointed directly by a Minister from the back-benches of his party. They act as general parliamentary (but not ministerial) assistants. The consequences of acceptance of the job of PPS is to bind the holder by the doctrine of collective responsibility, breach of which can lead to dismissal by the Prime Minister. See Brazier, n. 23 above, pp. 126–7. The total number beholden to the Prime Minister is, as a result, nearly 150.

[25] House of Commons Disqualification Act 1975, s. 2(1). If the limit is exceeded, those appointed in excess may not sit or vote in the Commons until the excess is reduced to 95: ibid., s. 2(2).

[26] As happened in 1964 when the Ministers of the Crown Act 1964 raised the number from 70 (which it had been since 1957) to 91; there was a further increase by the Ministers of the Crown Act 1974, to the present level of 95. As a temporary measure, those appointed in excess could continue as Ministers but not sit or vote in the Commons.

[27] See s. 1(1) and Schedule 1.

[28] Which may be altered (which in practice means raised) by Order in Council: ibid., s. 1(4).

[29] General Jan Smuts was Minister without Portfolio in Lloyd George's war coalition from June 1917 to January 1919 without a seat in either House, but that is explained by the exigencies of war.

may be appointed, but he must obtain a seat in one or other House within a reasonable time or resign. The broad mass of potential Ministers to whom power is to be transferred will have been returned to the House of Commons or will be peers, or could quite quickly be made peers.[30] Problems can, however, occur where the seatless individual concerned is to remain or become a Minister in the Commons. Thus Ramsay MacDonald was Lord President of the Council and his son Malcolm Colonial Secretary under Baldwin at the general election of November 1935, at which they both lost their seats; they remained in office and were returned at by-elections the following February. But there can be a risk in relying on a by-election. Thus Frank Cousins, the general secretary of the Transport and General Workers' Union, was not an MP when in October 1964 he was appointed to the Cabinet in the new post of Minister of Technology; Patrick Gordon Walker had lost his seat at Smethwick at that election but was none the less translated from his shadow post to be Foreign Secretary. Two sitting Labour MPs were persuaded to accept, with some reluctance, life peerages in order to cause by-elections which the new Ministers fought; Cousins was returned at Nuneaton, but Gordon Walker lost Leyton and a government majority of almost 8,000, the electors not responding as kindly as their counterparts further north to such a device.[31] During the life of the 1979 Conservative government two Ministers lost their seats at general elections, Mr Hamish Gray in 1983 and Mrs Lynda Chalker in 1992: both were translated to the House of Lords and remained in office. If a Minister is given a peerage, there can be no guarantee, however, that his former constituents will fill his old Commons seat at the resulting by-election with a member of the government party. So when Mr David Waddington became Leader of the House of Lords in 1990 his former seat fell to the Liberal Democrats at the ensuing by-election.

Two special cases historically have been the Lord Advocate and the Solicitor-General for Scotland. As a result of a shortage of Scottish MPs or peers with appropriate legal and other qualifications, particularly under Labour governments, appointments have been made to those offices from time to time from people outside Parliament. Since 1969, however, the

[30] Mr Blair obtained peerages for Mr John Gilbert, Sir David Simon, Mr Charles Falconer, and Mr Andrew Hardie in 1997 so that they could be appointed Ministers in his new government. Mr Falconer became Solicitor-General—the only time in the twentieth century that a Law Officer has sat in the House of Lords.

[31] Gordon Walker took Leyton at the 1966 general election and returned to the Cabinet as Minister without Portfolio the following year. Sir Alec Douglas-Home was Prime Minister in 1963 without a seat between the disclaimer of his peerages and winning the Kinross by-election.

Lord Advocate, as the senior Scottish Law Officer, has been given a life peerage when not an MP, and from 1974 to 1987 both Ministers were members of one or other House. But what was becoming an expectation that the usual convention of parliamentary membership would apply to both Ministers received a check when Mr Peter Fraser remained Solicitor-General for Scotland despite having lost his seat at the 1987 general election. He was promoted to be Lord Advocate in 1989, with a peerage; his successors as Solicitor-General for Scotland were chosen from outside Parliament. This will cease to be a consideration for British constitutional practice when a Scottish Executive is appointed from the Scottish Parliament, because both those Law Officers will become members of that Executive and will cease to be members of the British government. It remains to be seen whether their replacement, the Advocate-General for Scotland, is a member of one or other House of Parliament.

Again by convention, if the ministerial head of a department is in the Lords then at least one of his ministerial team will be in the Commons to represent him there. So, for example, when Lord Young was appointed Secretary of State for Employment in 1985, the Paymaster General, Mr Clarke (who was also in the Cabinet) was designated as his representative in the Commons (an arrangement which was continued when Lord Young was switched to be Secretary of State for Trade and Industry, and Mr Clarke Chancellor of the Duchy of Lancaster, in 1987). But there is no equivalent rule for the bulk of Ministers who are departmental heads in the Commons: the small band of Ministers in the Lords must do the best they can to put the government's case in the upper house. This can stretch the abilities of even the most able Minister who will have to answer well outside his own portfolio.

This leads to the question, resolved through a mixture of convention, political convenience, and a small dash of law, of which Ministers are required to sit in one House rather than the other. Most Ministers will perforce sit in the Commons. That House is the representative chamber; party political dogfights take place there; the government will need as much persuasive influence as possible from its ranks in the Commons the better to present its case; the Commons has asserted its superiority (at least since 1911) over the Lords (even though the latter body is still, confusingly, referred to as the upper house). In short, political reality will ensure that all (or practically all) sensitive ministerial posts will be held by MPs. The Treasury ministerial team will all be in the Commons, for that House has total control over finance. But what of the Foreign Secretary? The appointment of a peer as Foreign Secretary is always unpopular with the Opposition, but it cannot be said that any convention now subsists (even if it ever existed) which requires the holder of that office to be in the Commons. After all, Lord Halifax was appointed Foreign Secretary in 1938 at a critical time in European affairs;[32] and the appointments of Lord Home from 1960 to 1963 and Lord Carrington from 1979 to 1982 demonstrate that, if a Prime Minister is prepared to withstand Opposition criticism, there is really no substantial reason why the Foreign Secretary should not be in the Lords,[33] especially as appropriate ministerial arrangements are always made in the Commons.[34] Equally, there is no reason why other senior, non-Treasury Ministers like the Home Secretary or the Secretary of State for Defence should not be peers.[35] The Lord Chancellor, by the custom of the ages, will, however, be a member of the House of Lords. This is assumed to be the case by the Ministerial and other Salaries Act 1975[36] which provides that he shall be paid 'at such a rate as together with the salary paid to him as Speaker of the House of Lords' will amount to a specified sum. So if a future government wished to create a new office of Minister of Justice in the Commons with the Lord Chancellor fulfilling that role, legislation would be needed to remove the judicial functions from him[37] and to amend the 1975 Act so as to place his salary on a par with other Cabinet Ministers: obviously he could no longer be paid the amount now provided for the Lord Chancellor as Speaker of the House of Lords. The Prime Minister will need to make other ministerial dispositions in the House of Lords. At least one Cabinet Minister other than the Lord Chancellor will need to be a peer so as to be Leader of the House of Lords, the government's business manager there. Other junior Ministers will also be appointed in the Lords, although

---

[32] Chamberlain was, it is true, largely his own Foreign Secretary, and he took Foreign Office questions in the Commons himself.

[33] A significant advantage for him is the reduced amount of parliamentary work in that House. Other Foreign Secretaries in the Lords this century have been Lords Lansdowne (1900–5), Curzon (1919–24), and Reading (1931).

[34] For example, Sir Ian Gilmour and Humphrey Atkins were both successively the senior Foreign Office Minister in the Commons as Lord Privy Seal under Lord Carrington and were both in the Cabinet.

[35] They have been more rarely than the Foreign Secretary—only Viscount Cave from 1916 to 1919 (Home Secretary), Lord Chatfield for a short period in 1939 (Minister for Co-ordination of Defence), and Lord Carrington (Defence Secretary 1970–74)—although the Service Ministers were not infrequently peers before the creation of the unified Ministry of Defence under a Secretary of State in 1964.   [36] See s. 1(2).

[37] For example, as President of the Supreme Court, ex officio judge of the Court of Appeal, and President of the Chancery Division (Supreme Court Act 1981, ss. 1(2), 2(2), 4(1), and 5(1)); and his ability to sit in the judicial House of Lords and the Judicial Committee of the Privy Council would have to be abolished (Appellate Jurisdiction Act 1876, s. 5 and Judicial Committee Act 1833, s. 1).

the total number of salaried Ministers in that House will rarely exceed 20 out of a total administration of slightly over 100.

Particularly following a general election which produces a change of party government, a new Prime Minister may wish to make alterations in the machinery of government to reflect the introduction of fresh policies.[38] So, for instance, the return of the Labour government in 1964 after 13 years in opposition not surprisingly heralded several changes in the governmental machine—in particular, the introduction of four new departments of state each headed by a Cabinet Minister,[39] one other new department outside the Cabinet,[40] and a number of alterations of status at junior ministerial level.[41] Mr Heath entered office in 1970 also committed to major changes in the machinery of government, especially the merger of a number of ministries into giant departments, and the creation of a Central Policy Review Staff.[42] Not all new Prime Ministers, it is true, succumb to the temptation to make structural changes so as to presage significant alterations in policy from that of their predecessors: after all, no one would deny that Mrs Thatcher made radical changes in policy from that of her predecessor after 1979, but only one department represented in the Labour Cabinet (Prices and Consumer Protection) was abolished by her and no new department was created.[43] Mr Major made some changes after the 1992 general election, including the merger of the Department of Energy into the Department of Trade and Industry, and the creation of the Department of National Heritage. Mr Tony Blair—leading the Labour Party back to office in 1997 after 18 years in opposition—made remarkably few changes to the organization of government departments. The Departments of the Environment and of Transport were merged into a Department of the Environment, Transport and the Regions (with the Deputy Prime Minister as its Secretary of State); a new Department for International Development was created, with a Secretary of State in the Cabinet; but that was all.

[38] See generally Sir Richard Clarke, 'The Machinery of Government' in William Thornhill (ed.), *The Modernization of British Government* (1975), pp. 63–96.

[39] The Department of Economic Affairs, the Ministry of Technology, the Ministry of Overseas Development, and the Welsh Office.

[40] The Ministry of Land and Natural Resources.

[41] For example, the appointment of a 'Minister of Disarmament' (a Minister of State at the Foreign Office); another Minister of State at the Foreign Office was also the Permanent Representative at the United Nations.

[42] See 'The Reorganization of Central Government', Cmnd. 4506 (1970).

[43] The Departments of Trade and of Industry, which had been separated in 1974, were remerged in 1983; the Civil Service Department and the Central Policy Review Staff were abolished, in 1981 and 1983 respectively. The Department of Health and Social Security was divided into two departments in 1988.

An innovative Prime Minister will have advice available to him from the Secretary of the Cabinet. Indeed, in a typically British arrangement in 1964, Harold Wilson as Leader of the Opposition had a secret meeting, with the Prime Minister's approval, with the Head of the Civil Service three months before the general election, during which he outlined some of his ideas for changes in departmental responsibilities, and received helpful comments and advice.[44] This courtesy is now extended routinely to the Leader of the Opposition before each general election; in 1987 it was offered to Dr Owen and Mr Steel as well. In the fifth year of the 1987 Parliament the Secretary of the Cabinet met the Shadow Cabinet on the Prime Minister's authority, at which a confidential briefing was given on civil service matters. This was followed by confidential discussions between Labour shadow Ministers and Permanent Secretaries about Labour's plans on the structure and organization of government departments. This arrangement was described by the then Prime Minister, Mr Major, as a convention, which is designed to allow spokesmen from the opposition parties to have discussions with senior civil servants towards the end of a Parliament. These contacts are made with the authority of the Prime Minister of the day, the party Leaders, and the Head of the Home Civil Service. The purpose is to allow briefings on factual questions to take place concerning departmental changes which opposition parties have in mind or which might result from opposition party policies. Any exchanges are confidential. Such discussions started in January 1996 in the 1992 Parliament.[45]

Within the Cabinet Office there is a permanent machinery of government division which is available to the Prime Minister and the Secretary of the Cabinet for detailed information and advice about any proposed rearrangements. The days are long gone since primary legislation was needed to give effect to such changes. A more efficient procedure was introduced in 1946[46] and today is contained in the Ministers of the Crown Act 1975. An Order in Council may provide for the transfer to any Minister of any function previously exercised by another Minister, or for the dissolution of any government department and consequent transfer of functions;[47] it may make changes in the departments of the office of Secretary of State, or changes in the functions of a Secretary of State;[48] and it may

[44] Harold Wilson, *The Labour Government 1964–1970*, n. 13 above, p. 4.
[45] See 256 H.C. Deb. 835 (written answers 30 November 1995); 260 H.C. Deb. 225 (written answers 24 January 1996); and *The Times*, 15 August 1995.
[46] Ministers of the Crown (Transfer of Functions) Act 1946.
[47] Ministers of the Crown Act 1975, s. 1(1).   [48] Ibid., s. 2.

change the style and title of a Minister. Provision is made for parliamentary scrutiny of such Orders.[49]

A device open to a Prime Minister to allow one of his Ministers to pursue a particular policy or carry out some function without even the use of such subordinate legislation is the deployment of a senior Minister holding a sinecure. Thus the Lord Privy Seal in MacDonald's second government was responsible for unemployment; the Paymaster-General from 1985 in Mrs Thatcher's Cabinet was also unofficially (and more positively) styled Minister for Employment as Commons representative of the Employment Secretary; the Chancellor of the Duchy of Lancaster in both Mr Major's and Mr Blair's Cabinet was in charge of the office of Public Service (until its merger with the Cabinet office in 1998); there are many other examples. It is invariably more controversial when such a Minister holds a party office as well: the Chairman of the Conservative Party is not infrequently a Minister.[50]

The Cabinet chooses itself

The Cabinet today largely selects its own membership. Despite the evolution of prime ministerial government, a new Prime Minister has strikingly little freedom of choice in ordinary circumstances in picking his first Cabinet. Whether this should worry him to any significant degree, however, as possibly restricting the way in which he is able to govern is, as will be explained in the following two chapters, highly doubtful.

Which departments must be represented in the Cabinet? It is possible to identify three distinct periods this century.[51] The first, which may be styled the all-inclusive period, carried over from the nineteenth century up to the outbreak of war in 1914. In that time, filling all the available ministerial offices was to make the Cabinet, as customarily the only offices excluded from it were the Law Officers and the Royal Household appointments.[52] All central government functions could be represented in a Cabinet of up

---

[49] Ibid., s. 5. See further Chapter 7.

[50] This was the usual case during the 1979 Conservative government. The Chairman did not draw his ministerial pay.

[51] See Brazier, *Ministers of the Crown*, n. 23 above, ch. 1.4.

[52] At various times between 1900 and 1915 the Chief Secretary for Ireland or the Postmaster-General or the First Commissioner of Works were also left out. The Law Officers and the holders of Household appointments (who are Government Whips) are not members of modern Cabinets: the Attorney-General was a member from 1912 to 1916 and 1921 to 1928, but not subsequently.

to 20 people—even including some Ministers without departmental responsibilities, such as the Lord President of the Council, the Lord Privy Seal, and the Chancellor of the Duchy of Lancaster. The war made necessary an increase in the number of ministries; the expanding welfare state added others,[53] so that a second, selective period developed in which some offices had to be excluded if the Cabinet were to remain a manageable body. That selection became the more necessary after the return of the 1945 Labour government, with its major extension of governmental responsibilities.[54] This meant that from the First World War up until the 1970s, Prime Ministers had to decide which departments to exclude from the Cabinet. But with the creation of giant departments through the merger of existing ministries which took place from 1968 to 1983[55] there has been a return to an all-inclusive type of Cabinet of from 18 to 24 members. All departments of state since the early 1970s have been included in the Cabinet. Since that time, therefore, a Prime Minister has had only peripheral decisions to make about the exclusion of offices from the Cabinet, really only involving Overseas Development and Transport.[56]

Thus today a Prime Minister must, on the face of it, be concerned not with which departments to include in his Cabinet but with which of his colleagues to ask to join it, although again freedom of action may be illusory. Some people could hardly be left out, by virtue of their position in the government party and experience in office and opposition: it would have been impossible for, say, Mr Whitelaw, Sir Geoffrey Howe, Mr Prior, Mr Pym, or Sir Keith Joseph at least not to be included in Mrs Thatcher's first Cabinet, or, indeed, for most of her Cabinet not to be carried over into Mr Major's administration. The Shadow Cabinet,[57] too, will find itself

[53] Such as Pensions (1916), Labour (1916), and Health (1919).

[54] So in 1945 the Ministries of Civil Aviation, Food, Pensions, National Insurance, Information, Town and Country Planning, Supply, and (from 1946) the three Service Ministries were not included in the Cabinet.

[55] Those giant departments are the Foreign and Commonwealth Office (created 1968), Department of Health and Social Security (1968—divided again in 1988), Department of the Environment (1970—to which was added Transport and the Regions in 1997), and Department of Trade and Industry (1970)—the latter being split in 1974 and remerged in 1983, the Department of Energy having been created from it in 1974, to be remerged into the DTI in 1992. The responsibilities of ten former departments are now carried out in those five.

[56] The Ministry of Overseas Development finally came to rest as the Overseas Development Administration in the Foreign and Commonwealth Office in 1979: it was replaced in 1997 by the Department for International Development. The Department of Transport was merged into the Department of the Environment, Transport and the Regions in the same year.

[57] On which see John Mackintosh, *The British Cabinet* (3rd edn., 1977), pp. 259–61, 536–40; R. M. Punnett, *Front Bench Opposition* (1973); Brazier, *Ministers of the Crown*, n. 23 above, ch. 3.1, and see generally Chapter 8.

transferred into the substantive Cabinet. The Parliamentary Labour Party (PLP) elects a 19-strong Parliamentary Committee each year when in opposition. Four officers of the PLP, the Leader and Chief Whip in the Lords, and a peer's representative are also members *ex officio*, thus giving a total Parliamentary Committee of 26 people. Since 1955 the Leader has added other MPs so as to form the Shadow Cabinet, each member having a particular shadow responsibility. There is a requirement in PLP Standing Orders, section E that all elected members of the Parliamentary Committee be given seats in the Cabinet, and there is an unwritten expectation in the PLP that the other members of the Shadow Cabinet will be included as well. In 1964 and 1974 the entire Parliamentary Committee was given Cabinet office; in 1964 one non-Shadow Cabinet member was brought in, Frank Cousins.[58] When forming his first Cabinet in 1997 Mr Blair left out two elected and two invited members of the Parliamentary Committee.[59] Mr Blair had to do this in order to have a Cabinet of 22, rather than of 26, people. After the 1945 Conservative defeat, Conservative Privy Counsellors were deployed in debates as the occasion seemed to demand: only in a loose sense did particular Privy Counsellors routinely shadow particular Ministers. Members were added to the Shadow Cabinet but never subtracted; formal minutes were not kept. But under Sir Alec Douglas-Home and Edward Heath the Conservative Opposition adopted fully the Labour strategy of having a formal Shadow Cabinet, with each member discharging a specific shadow responsibility. Thus was the modern Shadow Cabinet system settled in the two main parties by 1964. And since 1964 new Prime Ministers have relied overwhelmingly on their shadow team to make up the Cabinet: its members will, after all, usually have had some years' experience in opposition mastering their shadow departmental duties, and there would need to be a pressing reason why someone should receive a portfolio for which he had had no training in opposition. Although the Leader of the Conservative Party has no party rules to bind him about whom to choose for the Shadow Cabinet, his reliance on that team when

[58] In 1964 two members of the Shadow Cabinet were given posts outside the Cabinet, and two peers in the Shadow Cabinet were excluded. 1945 is not comparable, as Labour had not been in opposition during the war. From 1940–45 the PLP had elected an Administrative Committee of 12, plus peers' representatives, none of whom was a Minister. When Labour is in government the Parliamentary Committee consists of its four officers, six back-bench MPs, one backbench peer, and four Ministers chosen by the Prime Minister: PLP Standing Orders, section F.6.

[59] Mr Michael Meacher and Mr Tom Clarke (both of whom became Ministers of State); and Mr Andrew Smith (who also became a Minister of State) and Mr Derek Foster (who was appointed a Minister of State but who resigned two days later).

the Conservatives come to power can be seen by the inclusion in Mr Heath's Cabinet in 1970 of only two people who had not been in the Shadow Cabinet, and in Mrs Thatcher's Cabinet in 1979 of only three.[60] Moreover, although a Labour Prime Minister is not obliged to give a Minister the portfolio which he has shadowed, it is the occasion when this has not happened that has caused surprise. So, for instance, Richard Crossman and Michael Stewart were each appointed in 1964 to the post which the other had shadowed in opposition.[61] But no less than seven people were appointed in the new Labour Cabinet in 1997 to posts which they had not shadowed in opposition.[62] Even under the Conservative system, it has become unusual for shadows to be switched on appointment: Quintin Hogg, for example, had been Shadow Home Secretary before the 1970 general election, and was surprised after it to be given the woolsack by Mr Heath instead of the Home Office.[63]

A Prime Minister taking over a government from a party colleague will find himself a little less circumscribed than if he had just led his party from opposition to power; but he might conclude that widespread changes at what will always be a politically difficult time would not be sensible. Thus the changes made to his predecessor's Cabinet by Eden in 1955 were minimal because he had decided on an early dissolution; Lord Home's had to be a little wider given that two Cabinet Ministers, Enoch Powell and Iain Macleod, refused to serve under him;[64] Mr Callaghan's in 1976 were somewhat more extensive, including the settling of an old score by dropping Mrs Castle[65]—but even so nearly all of Mr Wilson's Cabinet stayed in the new Cabinet. On taking over from Mrs Thatcher in 1990 Mr Major limited his initial changes largely to reshuffling the same Ministers around the Cabinet table: only Mr Cecil Parkinson and Lord Belstead left the Cabinet, and only Mr Michael Heseltine came in.

---

[60] Mr Noble (President of the Board of Trade) and Mr Thomas (Secretary of State for Wales); Mr Walker (Minister of Agriculture), Lord Soames (Lord President), Mr Howell (Secretary of State for Energy). [61] Housing; Education and Science.
[62] Messrs Dewar, Robertson, Dobson, and Smith and Drs Cunningham, Clark and Strang.
[63] See Lord Hailsham, *The Door Wherein I Went* (1975), p. 244. Perhaps the patronage enjoyed by Prime Ministers over Cabinet appointments should be circumscribed by elections conducted by their parliamentary parties: see Rodney Brazier, *Constitutional Reform* (2nd edn., 1998, pp. 111–12.
[64] Harold Macmillan had more room for manœuvre in 1957 as a number of Eden's Ministers wished to retire from politics.
[65] See Barbara Castle, *The Castle Diaries 1974–1976* (1980), pp. 724–5. Mr Callaghan later justified this by the need 'to replace some Ministers in their sixties by younger people': see *Time and Chance* (1987), p. 402.

One special case in which prime ministerial appointments to senior office will have external restraints is on the formation of a coalition government, when the views of the Leaders of the other coalition party or parties plainly must be taken into account. So Asquith had to consult Bonar Law in 1915, as did Lloyd George a year later; MacDonald had to rely heavily on Baldwin and Samuel for men and advice in 1931 when forming the 'National Government' (as only nine National Labour men joined him in the entire new administration), and although Churchill in 1940 told Attlee the names of four of the latter's senior colleagues whose services in the government were immediately required, he also asked Attlee for a list of Labour names to consider.[66] Such consultations would be relevant today especially if a hung Parliament were returned and a coalition government were to emerge: any coalition Prime Minister would have to consult and cajole his prospective partner or partners to agree on the disposition of offices. Indeed, prior to the general election of 1992, the Leader of the Liberal Democrats indicated publicly the number of seats in the Cabinet which his party would demand if it were to join a coalition government.

The Sovereign's influence

During the transfer of power the Sovereign has to perform two roles, the one formal, the other influential. Her formal role is to appoint Ministers to office. Ministers are the Queen's Ministers: by virtue of the prerogative they hold their offices at her pleasure. Of course, the prerogative is overladen by convention, but the prerogative gives her the formal legal power to appoint and to dismiss. That formal position was underlined in a characteristically helpful memorandum which George V wrote for MacDonald when he first came to office in 1924: 'No change', he wrote, 'is made in the constitution of the Ministry until the King's approval has been obtained'.[67] Without appointment by the Sovereign, a Minister in charge of a department of state does not hold office.

The Sovereign's influential role is less easy to gauge. A Prime Minister's audiences of the Sovereign take place with no one else present; no record is kept; what passes is confidential between Monarch and Minister, although the Queen's views, if appropriate, will be conveyed to the Cabinet. We have to wait for guarded political autobiographies and biographies

---

[66] See Martin Gilbert, *Finest Hour: Winston Churchill 1939–1941* (1983), p. 315.
[67] See Sir Harold Nicolson, *King George V* (1952), p. 388.

for scraps of information, and even longer for royal biographies.[68] Undoubtedly the Sovereign may express a view about proposed appointments; but it must be stressed that, although the Sovereign appoints and the Prime Minister merely recommends appointments, the Queen must defer in the end to the Prime Minister's advice. That follows from the cardinal convention of the constitution that the Queen must act on ministerial (and usually prime ministerial) advice.[69] If, unthinkably, she were implacably to resist a particular appointment and the Prime Minister were to refuse to give way, the only (and unreal) alternative open to her would be to dismiss him and to find a more congenial replacement. Constitutional monarchy has come too far for such a retrograde lunge into a mid-Victorian view of royal power.[70]

In exercising her undoubted rights to be consulted, to encourage, and to warn, however, the Queen does comment on proposed ministerial appointments, if only by way of approbation. Harold Macmillan has described the Queen's reaction to the list of his proposed Cabinet in 1957.[71] '[She] seemed to approve the changes. She is astonishingly well informed on every detail. She particularly liked the decision about the Foreign Office[72] and was interested in what I told her about Percy Mills.'[73] On the other hand, while giving way in due course to the Prime Minister's wishes, the Sovereign may require him to justify a nomination. There are three documented instances of this. In 1918, Lloyd George, in reconstructing the coalition after the December general election, submitted the name of F. E. Smith, then Attorney-General, to be Lord Chancellor. George V demurred. He caused his Private Secretary to write to the Prime Minister inviting him to reconsider, on the grounds that Smith was only 47 and had only been Attorney-General for three to four years, so that his appointment would come 'as somewhat of a surprise to the legal profession'. Lloyd George replied that many distinguished Lord Chancellors had attained the office between 30 and 40, and pressed the appointment: the King replied that 'in the circumstances he could only follow your advice'.[74]

---

[68] It is known that the Queen writes a personal diary. Perhaps it will be published after her death.   [69] See Chapter 9.
[70] For that reason, examples of Queen Victoria's refusals to accept nominations of Ministers are of interest but of no precedential value today. For them, see Sir Ivor Jennings, *Cabinet Government* (3rd edn., 1959), pp. 62–5.
[71] *Riding the Storm* (1971), p. 189, quoting his diary.
[72] That is, to retain Selwyn Lloyd there despite Suez.
[73] He was an industrialist whom Macmillan brought in as Minister of Power with a peerage.
[74] See 2nd Lord Birkenhead, *The Life of F. E. Smith, First Earl of Birkenhead* (1959), p. 332; Kenneth Rose, *King George V* (1983), p. 233. Rose points out that Smith was actually 46, and

The second example comes from 1940 when Churchill recommended the Canadian Lord Beaverbrook as Minister of Aircraft Production. George VI plainly disliked Beaverbrook, and was moved to write a special letter to Churchill on the very day he had been appointed, so taking up the Prime Minister's time with the matter even when military defeat could have been imminent.

I would like to warn you of the repercussions, which I am sure will occur, especially in Canada, at the inclusion of [Beaverbrook]. You are no doubt aware that the Canadians do not appreciate him, and I feel that as the Air Training Scheme for pilots and aircraft is in Canada, I must tell you this fact. I wonder if you would not reconsider . . . I fear that this appointment might be misconstrued.[75]

Churchill defended his choice, and Beaverbrook was appointed. But there could scarcely be a clearer instance of a royal warning to a Prime Minister over a Cabinet appointment. The final example is both the best known and the least clear. What role did George VI play in suggesting to Attlee in 1945 that Bevin should become Foreign Secretary and Dalton Chancellor of the Exchequer, rather than the other way around?[76] Attlee subsequently denied that the King's advice had moved him;[77] the accuracy of his recollection has, however, been doubted,[78] and Dalton's official biographer devotes a whole chapter to 'the switch' and concludes that it is 'reasonable to suppose that the King's advice was an important factor' in transposing the two nominations.[79]

From these examples it is equally reasonable to conclude that the Sovereign can, and occasionally does, ensure that a nomination to office is reconsidered, thus causing a delay in which a Prime Minister can ponder anew, change his mind, or defend his choice so as to secure the proposed appointment.

---

that the only Lord Chancellor who had held office under the age of 40 was Jeffreys in 1685, aged 37.

[75] Martin Gilbert, n. 66 above, p. 316. Churchill recorded that Beaverbrook was at first reluctant to take the job, and that the Air Ministry disliked losing its supply functions—and 'there were other resistances to his appointment . . . [but] I persisted in my view': *The Second World War*, vol. ii, *Their Finest Hour* (Penguin, 1985), p. 12.

[76] See Sir John Wheeler-Bennett, *King George VI: His Life and Reign* (1958), p. 638. There is support for the view that the King played a crucial role in Robert Rhodes James, *Anthony Eden* (1986), pp. 310–11.

[77] *Observer*, 23 August 1959.   [78] By Tom Driberg (1969) 50 *Parliamentarian* at 165.

[79] Ben Pimlott, *Hugh Dalton* (1985), ch. 24 at p. 415. Beginning with George V the Royal Family had disliked Dalton—George VI said that he could not abide him—and that dislike has been suggested as a reason why George VI did not want him as Foreign Secretary: ibid., pp. 414–22.

Ministers take office[80]

The appointment of over a hundred people to a new administration will always take a few days. If there is urgency in the transition, such as the financial crisis in October 1964, the Prime Minister may secure the appointment of the most senior members of his Cabinet quickly and before the others; otherwise, the whole Cabinet will be selected first, followed by the other Ministers.

Junior Ministers[81] are those who are not in charge of a department of state. Given the all-inclusive nature of modern Cabinets the term 'junior Ministers' today encompasses almost all Ministers outside the Cabinet. Whether a particular junior Minister is actually chosen by the Prime Minister or by the ministerial head of the department in which he is to serve varies from one government to another. Attlee, for example, chose all junior Ministers himself, although he consulted senior Ministers about them, because he thought that a senior Minister might not recognize his own deficiencies and that the Prime Minister should construct a departmental team to take account of them.[82] Macmillan followed suit. He has written that the factors which weighed with him were candidates' suitability and merit; the need to represent different parts of the country and different groups of party opinion; the desire to reward loyalty (but not to punish sincere disaffection); and the need to reflect the views of the senior Ministers in whose departments the junior Ministers would work.[83] Mrs Thatcher did likewise in appointing all junior Ministers.[84] By contrast, at least at the formation of his last government in 1974, Harold Wilson gave some Cabinet colleagues, like Roy Jenkins and James Callaghan, a free hand to make their own appointments—even to the extent in Mr Callaghan's case of agreeing to obtain a peerage for an MP who had just lost his seat so enabling him to become a Minister of State at the Foreign and

---

[80] See Brazier, *Ministers of the Crown*, n. 23 above, ch. 5.

[81] See Kevin Theakston (1986) 57 *Political Quarterly* 18—an excellent discussion on junior Ministers—and his *Junior Ministers in British Government* (1987); and Chapter 7, for definitions and discussions.

[82] Quoted in Kenneth Harris, *Attlee* (1982), p. 406.

[83] Harold Macmillan, n. 71 above, pp. 189–91.

[84] So, for example, when James Prior as the new Employment Secretary readily agreed to have Patrick Mayhew as an Under-Secretary of State, Mrs Thatcher was pleased, characteristically adding, 'I'm determined to have *someone* with backbone in your department': see James Prior, *A Balance of Power* (1986), pp. 113–14. See also Margaret Thatcher, *The Downing Street Years* (1993), pp. 29–30.

THE TRANSFER OF POWER

Commonwealth Office.[85] Similarly, Mr Blair allowed the Deputy Prime Minister, Mr John Prescott, the Chancellor of the Exchequer, Mr Gordon Brown, and the Foreign Secretary, Mr Robin Cook, to choose their own junior Ministers when Labour came to power in 1997. The names of new junior Ministers are formally submitted to the Queen; their appointment takes effect forthwith on her formal approval of them. Junior Ministers who took office in the new Labour government in 1997 were received as a courtesy by the Queen on their appointments.[86]

Once his name is approved a new Minister may go at once to his new department.[87] Any formal appointment will come later. There used to be a legal distinction between Cabinet Ministers, who would be sworn of the Privy Council (so as, it was sometimes thought, to apply the Privy Counsellor's oath to them and so ensure the confidentiality of Cabinet proceedings[88]), and other Ministers, who were not. If the Sovereign were advised to admit an individual to the Privy Council, that was tantamount to his joining the Cabinet. That distinction is no longer helpful, because since the 1970s even some Ministers of State have been made Privy Counsellors.

Ministers achieve office in law in a variety of ways.[89] The Promissory Oaths Act 1868, sections 3 and 5, and Orders in Council made under that Act,[90] require that those Ministers specified in Part I of the Schedule (as amended) to it must take the oath of office. Members of the Cabinet take the oath of office before the Queen in Council. To do so, the person concerned must be a Privy Counsellor; if he is not one already, he must be sworn a member of the Council before taking the oath of office:[91] the provisions of the 1868 Act therefore make it a legal requirement that Cabinet Ministers be members of the Privy Council—a case, for once, of law

---

[85] See James Callaghan, *Time and Chance* (1987), p. 294. According to Mr Wilson's former Senior Policy Adviser, in March 1974 many of the other junior appointments were selected at the suggestion of the Prime Minister's personal staff over lunch: see Bernard Donoughue, *Prime Minister: The Conduct of Policy under Harold Wilson and James Callaghan* (1987), p. 48.

[86] *Court Circular*, 8 May 1997.

[87] Assuming that he knows where it is. On being nominated Minister of Health in 1952 Iain Macleod left 10 Downing Street and drove to a telephone box to look up the Ministry's address in a phone book: Nigel Fisher, *Iain Macleod* (1973), pp. 85–6.

[88] The oath was not relied on by the Attorney-General in the Crossman diaries case: *Attorney-General* v. *Jonathan Cape Ltd.* [1976] QB 752, and see Chapter 7.

[89] For the details see Appendix C.

[90] The main one is the Promissory Oaths Order 1939, SR & O. 1939 No. 916.

[91] See Richard Crossman, *Diaries of a Cabinet Minister*, vol. i (1975), p. 29 for an amusing account of the swearing ceremony. Mr Tony Benn has written that 'you do nothing except stand there with your hand raised while [the oath or affirmation] is read to you. You don't even have to assent': *Against the Tide: Diaries 1973–1976* (1989), p. 122.

imitating convention. Having taken the oath of office, the new Cabinet Minister kisses the Queen's hands as a courtesy. Other Ministers, specified in Part I of the Schedule and in an Order in Council,[92] take the oath of office before another senior Minister, usually the Lord President of the Council.[93] Some Ministers receive seals[94] or some other token of their offices; others are appointed by Letters Patent; yet others by a warrant under the sign manual.[95] They do not legally assume office until these requirements have been satisfied. If there are no such requirements in relation to any given office (and junior Ministers fall into that category), the holder of it is legally appointed at the moment when the Queen approves the Prime Minister's list recommending the appointment, and he does not see the Queen in order to assume his office.[96] All Cabinet appointments must be published in the *London Gazette* in order that the Ministers may be paid the appropriate enhanced salaries.[97]

Thus is the administration completed and the Prime Minister may bend himself to his other tasks.

[92] Promissory Oaths Order 1939, SR & O. 1939 No. 916.
[93] The first woman to be appointed to that post was Mrs Ann Taylor in the 1997 Labour Cabinet. She was known simply as the President of the Council.
[94] When Richard Crossman examined the seals which he had received as the first Secretary of State for Social Services in 1968 he discovered that they had been the seals of the newly defunct Commonwealth Office, with sticky tape over them to change their character: n. 91 above, vol. iii (1977), p. 233.
[95] That is, a warrant signed by the Queen. See further Appendix C.
[96] Except for the Government Whips who hold Royal Household appointments— Treasurer, Comptroller, Vice-Chamberlain (in the Commons), Captain of the Gentlemen at Arms, and Captain of the Yeoman of the Guard (in the Lords).
[97] Ministerial and other Salaries Act 1975, s. 1 and Schedule 1.

5

THE PRIME MINISTER

A careful reading of histories and biographies makes me feel that the power of a Prime Minister has steadily grown . . . [T]he very complexity of affairs leads to a concentration of authority in his hands (Harold Macmillan, writing in 1972).[1]

My own conclusion is that the predominantly academic verdict of overriding prime ministerial power is wrong. It ignores the system of democratic checks and balances, in Parliament, in the Cabinet, and not least in the party machine and the party in the country (Harold Wilson, writing in 1976.)[2]

Those conclusions of two former Prime Ministers, the one more or less following the other into office, disclose a divergence of view in the debate about whether Britain has prime ministerial rather than Cabinet government.[3] Both conclusions contain the error which is sometimes made in that debate of offering a final judgement which purports to hold good for the foreseeable future. In practice, however, several variables affect the argument, chiefly the personality of any given holder of the office of Prime Minister. Thus during the long Thatcher years many people proclaimed the final triumph of prime ministerial over Cabinet government. But it was always likely that her successor (whoever he was to be) would revert to more traditional norms, and that is exactly what happened. Any catalogue of a Prime Minister's powers which apparently makes him pre-eminent over his colleagues must always be read with the warning in mind that matters could alter rapidly on a change of Prime Minister.

---

[1] *Pointing the Way* (1972), p. 33.

[2] *The Governance of Britain* (1976), p. 8.

[3] On that debate see (arguing the prime ministerial thesis) Richard Crossman, Introduction to Walter Bagehot's *The English Constitution* (1963)—although he was more ambivalent in his 3-volume *Diaries of a Cabinet Minister* (1975–77); Humphrey Berkeley, *The Power of the Prime Minister* (1968); and see (opposing that thesis) Herbert Morrison, *Government and Parliament* (3rd edn., 1964); Patrick Gordon Walker, *The Cabinet* (revised edn., 1972); Harold Wilson, n. 2 above, Forward and passim; and (for a balanced view) A. H. Brown, 'Prime Ministerial Power' [1968] *Public Law* 28 and 96.

If the Prime Ministers since 1945[4] are considered for a moment, any views as to the supremacy or otherwise of the Prime Minister must take account of very different incumbents: there is no such thing as an 'average' Prime Minister. At one extreme, Winston Churchill from 1951 to 1955 treated Cabinet meetings as great occasions and colleagues with deference, rarely seeking to rely only on his office to obtain his own way in defiance of any contrary majority opinion.[5] Then there have been the relaxed and amusing yet businesslike approaches of Prime Ministers like Harold Macmillan,[6] James Callaghan,[7] and John Major,[8] or the efficient styles epitomized by Clement Attlee or (to a lesser extent) Sir Alec Douglas-Home, both of whom preferred short Cabinet meetings and an absolute minimum of unnecessary talk.[9] Then at the opposite extreme to the peacetime Churchill was Margaret Thatcher, the apotheosis of the imperious style.[10] It is too early to write authoritatively about Mr Tony Blair's style as Prime Minister, although it has been described as being 'presidential'. Future Prime Ministers will bring their own stamps to bear, thus making analysis

---

[4] This chapter is broadly confined to that modern period. For a discussion down to 1951 see Sir Ivor Jennings, *Cabinet Government* (3rd edn., 1959), pp. 177–99, and for an enlightening exposé of Cabinets since 1945 see Peter Hennessy, *Cabinet* (1986).

[5] See Anthony Seldon, *Churchill's Indian Summer: The Conservative Government 1951–1955* (1981), p. 106. Churchill's physical and mental powers were in any case in decline: see Lord Moran, *Winston Churchill: The Struggle for Survival* (1960), chs. 34 ff.; Sir John Colville, *The Fringes of Power: Downing Street Diaries 1939–1955* (1985), Part IV.

[6] For descriptions of Macmillan as Prime Minister, see for example Alistair Horne, *Macmillan 1957–1986* (1989), pp. 12–14; Lord Home, *The Way The Wind Blows* (1976), pp. 191–2; Hennessy, n. 4 above, pp. 58–60; and his own autobiographical version in Macmillan, n. 1 above, ch. 2.

[7] See Phillip Whitehead, *The Writing on the Wall* (1985), ch. 9; Denis Healey, *The Time of My Life* (1989), pp. 447–8; and for his own version, see James Callaghan, *Time and Chance* (1987), chs. 13–17. Mr Callaghan's style was epitomized in the way in which he arranged the discussion of the terms of the International Monetary Fund loan in 1976. He held nine Cabinet meetings over three weeks, during which Ministers in effect convinced themselves that the view of the Prime Minister and the Chancellor that the terms had to be accepted was inescapable, even though initially the government might have broken up over the issue: see Callaghan, above, pp. 427–42.

[8] For a description of Mr Major's prime ministerial style see Anthony Seldon, *Major: A Political Life* (1997), pp. 196–204.

[9] See Kenneth Harris, *Attlee* (1982), pp. 401–18, 427–8, 567: '[H]is object was to get the meeting over as soon as possible' (ibid., p. 403); Hennessy, n. 4 above, p. 64 (interview with Lord Home on his Cabinet style): 'the great thing is to be short. People can't bear [waffle]'.

[10] A number of her former Cabinet Ministers have attested to this: Francis Pym, *The Politics of Consent* (1984), ch. 1; James Prior, *A Balance of Power* (1986), pp. 114–19, and ch. 8; Lord Whitelaw, *The Whitelaw Memoirs* (1989), pp. 262–3; Nigel Lawson, *The View from Number 11* (1992), pp. 124–9; Nicholas Ridley, *My Style of Government* (1991), pp. 24–31. See, for her own perceptions, Margaret Thatcher, *The Downing Street Years* (1993), passim.

even more imprecise. This chapter will, therefore, largely be concerned
with identifying the sources of any Prime Minister's power and then with
those factors which may collectively be termed his weaknesses, and in that
process the nature of the office will be analysed.

The electorate's choice

A Prime Minister has the invaluable political authority of being the choice
(directly or indirectly) of the electorate, an advantage which neither his
party nor any other Minister can claim. A general election is today the
machinery through which a Prime Minister is chosen. Since the 1945
general election at the latest voters have been offered a choice—sometimes
stark—between very different party Leaders: they will vote to keep Mr A
in office, or to put in Mr B in his stead. At some elections the personification of a government in its leader will be stronger (as for instance with
Macmillan in 1959, or Mr Wilson in 1966, or Mrs Thatcher in 1983 and
1987) than at others (as, say, with Sir Alec Douglas-Home in 1964). But
now that general elections are firmly established in the American presidential mould and are projected to a mass television audience it is most unlikely
that any party would now try to win an election by offering a collective
leadership with its Leader buried somewhere in it. No party returned to
power this century could claim with any justice that it had won despite its
Leader—rather, the victorious political parties will acknowledge that,
while the nation's boredom with the late government,[11] perhaps exacerbated by that government's loss of steam,[12] taken with the attraction of the
successful party's alternative policies, all played their parts, the personalities
of the Leaders were vitally important. That concentration of attention on
the successful Leader can clearly be seen in most of the seven general
elections since 1945 at which there was a change of government, and in
the 1970 contest a case has been made that Mr Heath won almost despite
his party.[13] Mr Major, too, may fairly claim much personal credit for

[11] The view that 'it's time for a change' will become stronger the longer a government has
been in office. The Conservatives' fourth consecutive election victory in 1992 was undoubtedly helped by the presence of a new Prime Minister, but the 1997 Labour landslide amounted
to an emphatic rejection of the long Conservative government.
[12] The 1945 Labour government suffered in this way, but it was also physically exhausted
by the Conservative Opposition tactics in the 1950 Parliament of keeping Ministers in the
House late each night: see Harris, n. 9 above, ch. 25: 'Struggling On'.
[13] For example, by *The Economist*, 20 June 1970; Whitehead, n. 7 above, pp. 49–51.

keeping the Conservative government in power at the 1992 general election.

Even when someone becomes Prime Minister by succeeding a resigning colleague or at the formation of a coalition, he can still be regarded as the indirect choice of the electorate, for he must be able to count on the support of the existing House of Commons returned by that electorate. Since 1945 Eden, Macmillan, Sir Alec Douglas-Home, James Callaghan, and John Major did not come initially to office in the wake of electoral victory, but they became accepted quickly by the majority party in the Commons[14] (and both Mr Callaghan and Mr Major had been elected by a majority of their parliamentary parties).[15] From his first moments in office, therefore, a Prime Minister is imbued with authority conferred personally (albeit sometimes indirectly) by the electorate.

Power over Ministers

Patronage in relation to Ministers is the most important political power enjoyed by a Prime Minister, for it establishes his supreme place in the eyes of his government and parliamentary party. No one will achieve ministerial office without his approval; his continuing favour is essential to keep office; the deference which this can cause in many cases is clear. It was noted in Chapter 4 that at an initial transfer of power to a new Prime Minister there are constraints on his freedom of action. But even at that stage it is possible for a Prime Minister who is both exceptionally determined and sure of his power base to set his policy stamp on his government. The outstanding example is that of Neville Chamberlain in 1937 who, when taking over the 'National Government', was ruthless in excluding anyone who might be an uncongenial colleague—in particular, anyone who might want to resist the dictators and to rearm more quickly. Thus men who were to give full-hearted support for appeasement were appointed—Sir John Simon to Chamberlain's old place at the Treasury, Sir Samuel Hoare to the Home Office, the anodyne Sir Thomas Inskip confirmed as an undemanding and largely ineffectual Minister for the Co-ordination of Defence.

---

[14] Eden, Macmillan, and Major successfully fought general elections as Prime Minister. Sir Alec Douglas-Home (narrowly) and James Callaghan lost the only elections they fought as Prime Minister; in Mr Callaghan's case for most of his premiership he had no parliamentary majority, but until the 1979 vote of no confidence no Commons majority was prepared to assert itself so as to bring about a dissolution.

[15] See Chapter 2.

Eden was retained at the Foreign Office, but Chamberlain was always his own Foreign Secretary, directing foreign policy from Downing Street advised by a civil servant;[16] and Eden only lasted nine months, resigning in the end over Chamberlain's insistence on negotiating with Mussolini.[17] Chamberlain summed up his appointments policy in the words, 'I won't have anyone who will rock the boat'.[18] Of course, he was exceptional: most Prime Ministers want to begin with an administration which reflects the various strands of opinion in their party, but Chamberlain showed what can be done; and (as will be seen later) Mrs Thatcher achieved the same result of having an agreeable Cabinet within a couple of years of coming to power.

In making his first appointments to office a Prime Minister will decide on the relative seniority of Cabinet Ministers—the 'pecking order'—and whether to have a deputy. It is not unnatural for Ministers in the Cabinet to wish to be seen as being senior Cabinet Ministers, so as to reflect not only their individual importance but also the importance in the government of the departments which they head.[19] The pecking order can now be seen[20] in the list of Cabinet Ministers published fortnightly in *Hansard*. Occasionally the ranking can stretch credulity, as for example in 1985 when Mrs Thatcher transferred Mr Leon Brittan from the Home Office to the Department of Trade and Industry; this move was regarded by everyone save the Prime Minister and Mr Brittan as a demotion, caused by her desire to bring in new blood to the upper reaches of the Cabinet in the shape of a new Home Secretary, Mr Douglas Hurd: but Mr Brittan remained ranked fifth as he had been as Home Secretary.[21] Some Ministers can be sensitive about their rankings: one such was Michael Stewart in 1966 who, when moved to the Department of Economic Affairs from the Foreign Office to make way for George Brown, insisted on remaining at number three in the

[16] Briefly from January 1938 by Sir Robert Vansittart as Chief Diplomatic Adviser, then by Sir Horace Wilson. On the conflict between Chamberlain and the Foreign Office, see Viscount Templewood, *Nine Troubled Years* (1954), pp. 259–61.

[17] At the crucial Cabinet on 19 February 1938 it is instructive that 14 Ministers supported Chamberlain's proposed initiative and only four expressed any reservations: Robert Rhodes James, *Anthony Eden* (1986), p. 193.

[18] Quoted in R. J. Minney (ed.), *The Private Papers of Leslie Hore-Belisha* (1960), p. 130.

[19] An incidental consequence is that if two Ministers are to meet, the more junior is expected to offer to travel to the other's department: Wilson, n. 2 above, p. 23, n. 1.

[20] It was formerly published in a List of Ministers and Heads of Public Departments published regularly by HMSO.

[21] When Mr Brittan resigned in 1986 following his part in the Westland affair, his successor as Secretary of State for Trade and Industry was ranked bottom of the Cabinet list.

Cabinet.[22] The pecking order is reflected in the seating arrangements at the Cabinet table. The most senior Ministers sit to the Prime Minister's right[23] and left and also directly opposite him, the others being seated further away with the most junior at the ends. A purely practical advantage which this gives to Ministers sitting near to the Prime Minister is that it is easier to catch his eye[24] and to hear and be heard.[25] No doubt this can irritate junior members, but it is a physical reminder of the Prime Minister's ability to put them away from, or near, the centre of authority.

The designation of a Minister as deputy to the Prime Minister[26] has caused some controversy and even denials that any office of Deputy Prime Minister exists.[27] That agitation will be allayed if the reasons for nominating a deputy are more carefully analysed than is usually the case. There are three different reasons why an identified deputy to a Prime Minister may be appointed. The first—and, today, illegitimate—reason could be to indicate that Minister who is recognized by the Prime Minister as the crown prince who would in due course succeed him. Such a designation has become pointless since 1965, which was the year in which the Conservative Party came into line with the Labour and Liberal Parties in establishing a formal election procedure to choose a successor to a resigning Leader. But such a designation must be noted here because it was that sort of attempt to establish a succession which first caused the objections to be voiced that the office of Deputy Prime Minister was 'unconstitutional', and it has clouded the office ever since.

When Churchill returned to Downing Street in 1951 he included in his list of Ministers submitted to the King the name of Anthony Eden as

---

[22] On the other hand a minority of Ministers claim to be unconcerned by the order, and Mr Wilson wrote (n. 2 above, p. 23, n. 1) 'In Attlee's Government I did not even know what my pecking-order position was'.

[23] The Secretary of the Cabinet sits on his immediate right.

[24] Prior, n. 10 above, p. 117. There is some room for prime ministerial manoeuvre: one day Lord Home found the Cabinet Secretary changing the places at the Cabinet table; and he explained that '[t]he Prime Minister cannot stand Enoch Powell's steely and accusing eye looking at him across the table any more, and I've had to move him down the side': Lord Home, n. 6 above, p. 192.

[25] This is why the Cabinet table was altered into a coffin-shape in 1961 so that those at the ends could be a little less out of affairs.

[26] See R. Brazier, 'The Deputy Prime Minister' [1988] Public Law 176. See also the Prime Minister's answer at 263 H.C. Deb. 798–9 (written answers 14 July 1995).

[27] For example, R. A. Butler in the House of Commons stated that 'the office of Deputy Prime Minister is not known to our constitution': 561 H.C. Deb. 1448–9 (6 December 1956); in 1961 Macmillan noted in his diary that '[t]he Queen has in the past rightly pointed out that there is no such official post': At the End of the Day (1973), p. 41. For George VI's objections, see below.

'Secretary of State for Foreign Affairs and Deputy Prime Minister'. George
VI immediately instructed that the second title be deleted on the ground
that the 'office . . . does not exist in the British constitutional hierarchy',
and because it could be seen as an attempt to restrict his prerogative of
choice,[28] especially as it was generally assumed that Churchill would retire
within a short time—he was, after all, 76 in 1951.[29] The King's objection
was sustainable in the days when royal rather than party choice was (at least
in theory) the norm, although even then it should be remembered that
it was George VI who had asked Churchill in 1942 formally to record
whom he should send for in the event of Churchill being killed by enemy
action.[30]

The second reason for nominating a deputy arises in the Labour Party,
where the post of Deputy Leader is recognized by the party's constitution.[31] There will, therefore, always be a Labour Deputy Leader, and he
will naturally be second only to a Labour Prime Minister when the Deputy
Leader is in the government. Thus in Attlee's Cabinet, Morrison was
Attlee's party and ministerial deputy,[32] and in Mr Wilson's first Cabinet,
George Brown was his deputy[33] until Brown resigned from the government in 1968,[34] as were Edward Short and later Michael Foot in the 1974
to 1979 Labour Cabinets.[35] Mr John Prescott, as Deputy Leader of the
Labour Party, was officially gazetted as Deputy Prime Minister (and Secre-
tary of State for the Environment, Transport and the Regions) in the 1997
Labour Cabinet. Given the elective nature of the Labour Deputy Leadership

[28] Sir John Wheeler-Bennett, *King George VI: His Life and Reign* (1958), p. 797.
[29] No one would have predicted a premiership lasting 3½ years. In the event Churchill's
succession by Eden was entirely uncontroversial—'No two men have ever changed guard
more smoothly', was Churchill's assessment, recorded in Eden's *Full Circle* (1960), p. 265.
[30] The King's request had been prompted by Churchill's impending (and scarcely safe)
flight to see Roosevelt in Washington. Churchill had recommended that Eden be sent for in
the event of his death: Martin Gilbert, *The Road to Victory: Winston S. Churchill 1941–1945*
(1986), p. 125.
[31] Labour Party Constitution, cl. VII; Parliamentary Labour Party Standing Orders,
ss. D, F. See Appendix B. The Deputy Leader becomes Acting Leader automatically if the
Leader, for whatever reason, becomes permanently unavailable, and retains that position until
a new Leader is elected at a party conference. This only applies when Labour is in opposition.
[32] As Lord President of the Council and Leader of the House of Commons, and then as
Foreign Secretary 1951.
[33] As First Secretary of State and Secretary of State for Economic Affairs, and then as
Foreign Secretary.
[34] Brown was Deputy Leader from 1960 to 1970. On his resignation from the government
in 1968, Michael Stewart was moved up to number two in the pecking order.
[35] Edward Short was Deputy Leader 1972–76, Mr Foot from 1976–80. Both were Lord
President and Leader of the House of Commons.

it would be difficult to imagine the holder being other than deputy to the Prime Minister.

George VI raised no objection to Attlee receiving the formal style of Deputy Prime Minister in 1942.[36] This is partly explicable[37] as an example of the third reason why a Prime Minister might nominate a deputy: administrative efficiency and convenience. As Churchill's wartime unofficial and later official Deputy Prime Minister, Attlee exercised broad authority in home and economic affairs, leaving Churchill to concentrate on the prosecution of the war. More generally, someone must chair the Cabinet, and Cabinet committees normally taken by the Prime Minister, and answer his questions in the House of Commons,[38] in his absence; perhaps even (according to a Prime Minister's taste) more formally taking charge of the government while he is away. R. A. Butler fulfilled that role from 1955 in a variety of offices in the Conservative government,[39] as did Mr (later Viscount) Whitelaw, and subsequently Sir Geoffrey Howe, in Mrs Thatcher's Cabinet.[40] Mrs Thatcher, however, kept the reins firmly in her hands. She continued to carry out the duties of Prime Minister while abroad, and was rarely ill. Indeed, the existence of instantaneous electronic communications has reduced the need for a deputy to mind the shop while the Prime Minister is away. Yet arrangements which promote efficient continuity of government are plainly beneficial, and no objection can be made to the use of a deputy for such a purpose. Moreover, the nomination of a deputy might make contemporary constitutional sense for a linked reason. He would be able to take temporary charge of the government without controversy if the Prime Minister were killed or injured by terrorist action. Mrs Thatcher, after all, had a lucky escape in the 1984 Brighton

[36] Attlee was first Lord Privy Seal in 1940 in the War Cabinet, then Deputy Prime Minister from 1942 to 1945, being also Dominions Secretary (1942 to 1943), and Lord President (1943 to 1945).

[37] The King had already taken advice about the succession: see n. 30 above.

[38] When Mrs Thatcher's deputy William Whitelaw went to the Lords in 1983, the Leader of the House of Commons was charged with taking her parliamentary questions in her absence.

[39] Lord Privy Seal 1955–59, Leader of the House of Commons and Home Secretary 1957–62, First Secretary of State 1962–63.

[40] Mr Whitelaw had been nominated Deputy Leader of the Conservative Party in 1975 by Mrs Thatcher on her election as Leader, that Deputy Leadership being appointive. He remained Deputy Leader after his resignation from the government in 1988, until 1991. There have only been two other Deputy Leaders, Reginald Maudling (1965–72) and Peter Lilley (1998–). Geoffrey Howe was told in 1989 that Buckingham Palace had 'a little difficulty in accepting the proposed official description of "Deputy Prime Minister" for him, and suggested the formula that he would "act as Deputy Prime Minister" ': Geoffrey Howe, *Conflict of Loyalty* (1994), p. 590. He was formally appointed Lord President of the Council and Leader of the House of Commons.

bombing. Mr Major (who only had a deputy in the last two years of his government) said, however, that there were no standing arrangements for this eventuality.[41]

The actual title accorded to a deputy has varied. Some deputies to the Prime Minister have had to rely on their second place in the pecking order with no distinctive title (such as Lord Whitelaw, first as Home Secretary, then as Lord President of the Council). Only Attlee (from 1942 to 1945), Mr Michael Heseltine (from 1995 to 1997),[42] and Mr John Prescott (1997–) have actually enjoyed the formal title of Deputy Prime Minister: the style which has been used more frequently is that of First Secretary of State, invented in 1962 by Macmillan for Butler. That title denoted Butler's superiority over any other Minister while avoiding the objections which had been raised 11 years earlier to the style of Deputy Prime Minister.[43] On the succession of Sir Alec Douglas-Home in 1963 the office of First Secretary of State was left vacant; on Labour's return to power the following year George Brown, as Deputy Leader, was appointed to the Department of Economic Affairs with the additional rank of First Secretary of State. It was subsequently held by two other Ministers in that Labour government,[44] but then not until Mr Heseltine was accorded it (along with the style of Deputy Prime Minister) from 1995 to 1997.

In summary, the arrangement of a general pecking order of Cabinet Ministers and the singling out of one of them as a deputy to the Prime Minister provide yet another reminder to Ministers that the Prime Minister is chief among them.

As a government ages its personnel will naturally change. Some Ministers will wish to leave for personal reasons, perhaps as the result of illness, or to start or resume another career, or to 'spend more time with their families'.[45]

[41] See 221 H.C. Deb 709–10 (written answers 25 March 1993).

[42] For explanations of Mr Heseltine's role as First Secretary of State and Deputy Prime Minister see 263 H.C. Deb. 496 (written answers 11 July 1995), 750–51 (written answers 13 July 1995). His ministerial office was huge—872 sq. ft.

[43] Butler recorded in his memoirs that 'I was named First Secretary of State and invited to act as Deputy Prime Minister, a title which can constitutionally imply no right to the succession and should (I would advise, with the benefit of hindsight) be neither conferred nor accepted': The Art of the Possible (1971), p. 234.

[44] Michael Stewart 1966–68 while also Secretary of State for Economic Affairs and then as Foreign Secretary, and Barbara Castle 1968–70 as Secretary of State for Employment and Productivity. The title was, however, debased on both occasions as neither was deputy to the Prime Minister.

[45] One example was afforded by James Prior, who retired from Mrs Thatcher's Cabinet in 1984 to become chairman of GEC. Mr Norman Fowler left the Cabinet in 1990 for the reason quoted: he was back as Chairman of the Conservative Party Organization in 1992, presumably having spent enough time with his family.

Additionally, a Minister may need to be moved to another post, possibly because he has become stale; or a Minister may need to be removed from the government because he has ceased to be an asset (although he may be the last to recognize it). Again, a reshuffle may be needed to give the administration a fresher, and perhaps younger, look, and to give promotion to junior Ministers and talented back-benchers. Thus must be played a game of musical ministerial chairs in which some unlucky contestants lose their places. For these reasons a Prime Minister's power over the futures of his colleagues increases as time passes.

In a draft for his Introduction to Bagehot's *The English Constitution* Richard Crossman wrote that a Prime Minister can liquidate the political careers of his rivals as effectively as any Soviet leader.[46] A Minister holds office at the Prime Minister's sufferance: he holds office at the will of the Crown and can be removed at any time on the Prime Minister's recommendation. Yet there are political limits within which any reshuffle must be set: to say with Crossman that the Prime Minister's power in this context is absolute is to overstate the case. Some Ministers are essential to the very continuance of a government, and could not be dropped even if the Prime Minister wanted to do so: thus, for example, the acceptance by Butler of Sir Alec Douglas-Home as Harold Macmillan's successor in 1963 was crucial to the latter's success in forming a government. Butler was guaranteed a place for as long as he wanted it. Michael Foot's personal relationships with trade union leaders throughout the 1970s, too, ensured him office in the 1974 to 1979 Labour government, dependent as it was on its concordat with the unions. And it would have been politically unthinkable for Mr Douglas Hurd, a contender in the succession to Mrs Thatcher, to have been excluded from Mr Major's first Cabinet in 1990. Moreover, at junior ministerial level, no Prime Minister could possibly have personal knowledge of all potential Ministers, and he will have to lean heavily on the Chief Whip, and perhaps the Leader of the House of Commons, for information about candidates' suitability for office, parliamentary performance, particular strengths, and so on. No Prime Minister could begin to reshuffle an administration of over a hundred people from a total pool usually of over 330 government MPs free of such dependency. That advice could deny a Prime Minister the chance to bring in a favourite, whether at Cabinet or junior level. A prime example can be

---

[46] His publishers protested: he cut out the sentence: three years later, after he had been a Cabinet Minister, that deletion was his only regret about the Introduction: John Mackintosh, *The British Cabinet* (3rd edn., 1977), p. 439.

seen in Mrs Thatcher's scarcely concealed desire to restore Mr Cecil Parkinson to her Cabinet as quickly as possible after his resignation from it in 1983: the advice of her deputy Lord Whitelaw and of the Chief Whip not to do so (on the ground that it would encourage the media to give him and thus the government unfavourable publicity) delayed his return until after the 1987 general election.[47] A Prime Minister will also normally need and wish to maintain the political and geographical balance of the Cabinet and administration. Moreover, the complexity of a general reshuffle must be borne in mind: however much a Prime Minister wishes to replace X, move Y, and bring in Z, the pieces at the end must fit. Harold Wilson has described any substantial reshuffle as 'a nightmarish multidimensional jigsaw puzzle'.[48]

Some Prime Ministers have relished and others have dreaded reshuffles: the undoubted power to move colleagues into, about, and out of the administration is subject to the incumbent's attitude towards the task. It was Asquith who first described as a vital attribute of a Prime Minister the ability to be a good butcher, in the sense of being able to remove ineffective colleagues without hesitation. In modern times Attlee has been acclaimed the best butcher. Always a man of few words (for example, when asked during a cinema newsreel interview whether he had anything further to say about the impending general election, he replied 'No'), he was rarely drawn into an explanation for a requested resignation. Once he did bluntly explain that a Minister was going 'Because I don't think you are up to the job';[49] very occasionally he might use a metaphor from his beloved cricket to say that the Minister concerned had had a good innings and it was time to go back to the pavilion and hang up the bat.[50] Mrs Thatcher may now be ranked with Attlee. Her 1979 Cabinet, based on her own choices for the Shadow Cabinet, was a balance between monetarists and non-monetarists, 'one of us' and 'wets'.[51] Yet by the end of 1981 five 'wets' had been shuffled out,[52] leaving only Mr Walker and Mr Prior to represent the

---

[47] See further Chapter 7.
[48] See n. 2 above, p. 34. When planning one reshuffle he found that he had to find an office for a Yorkshirewoman, but the only vacancy was at the Welsh Office, and he had to start again.
[49] Mackintosh, n. 46 above, p. 440.
[50] Quoted in Wilson, n. 2 above, p. 34.
[51] James Prior believes that Mrs Thatcher was responsible 'for pinning this name on her opponents . . . In due course it became a badge of honour, but it was hardly conducive to loyalty in Cabinet': n. 10 above, p. 134.
[52] Lord Soames, Sir Ian Gilmour, Mr St. John-Stevas, Mr Howell, and Mr Carlisle. Lord Carrington and Mr Atkins, who tended to 'wetness', left the government in 1982 over the Falklands: see Chapter 7. On the significance of the 1981 reshuffle in consolidating

liberal Conservative tradition (and by 1984 Mr Prior had retired from politics). Mrs Thatcher's increasing confidence meant that after two years of her premiership she was able to be as ruthless as Neville Chamberlain in excluding possible rockers of the boat. During her long premiership 57 people joined and left her Cabinet. And her style could be as direct as Attlee's in making changes: Mr Pym records that her first words to him after the 1983 general election were, 'Francis, I want a new Foreign Secretary'.[53] Harold Macmillan, on the other hand, would probably not have rejected the title of the worst butcher since 1945. He regarded the duty of asking colleagues and friends to leave the government as very disagreeable;[54] possibly his requests for the resignation of a record seven Cabinet Ministers in 1962 in an attempt to restore the fortunes of his faltering government might never have come to pass had he found it easier to move colleagues more regularly.[55] The title of intermediate butcher could be accorded to Harold Wilson. He seemed reluctant to lose ministerial colleagues entirely, moving them instead from one job to another with the result that Ministers only had an occupancy of any given department of about 18 months. So, for example, from 1964 to 1970 Mr Wilson had three different Secretaries of State for Economic Affairs, four Foreign Secretaries,[56] three Home Secretaries, and six Lord Privy Seals.[57]

Mrs Thatcher's position, see Hugo Young, *One of Us* (1989), pp. 220–1, and Margaret Thatcher, n. 10 above, pp. 129–32, 147–53.

[53] See n. 10 above, p. ix.

[54] *Pointing the Way*, n. 1 above, p. 32.

[55] For his account, see *At the End of the Day*, n. 27 above, pp. 84–98. He concluded that it was a serious error to try to mask the blow to Selwyn Lloyd (who was asked to resign as Chancellor) by combining his resignation with a general reshuffle.

[56] Michael Stewart held the office twice. Mr Wilson lost his first Foreign Secretary, Patrick Gordon Walker, when he failed to win a by-election following the loss of his seat at the general election.

[57] Lords Longford and Shackleton each held the office twice. Richard Crossman wrote in 1968 that 'I am now convinced that one of Harold's greatest mistakes is his constant reshuffling. Too many job changes in three years means a tremendous decline in the power of the politician over the Civil Service machine . . . The truth is that a Minister needs eighteen months to get real control of his Department . . . It's the constant fiddling with Ministers and shifting them round which has undermined the central strategy of this Government', *Diaries of a Cabinet Minister*, vol. iii (1977), p. 78. Colin Turpin in his excellent *British Government and the Constitution: Text, Cases and Materials* (2nd edn., 1990), p. 162, records that from 1918 to 1971, seven leading offices were each held for an average of 27 months; that from 1964 to 1970 the median tenure of office was 19 months; and that of 85 Ministers appointed in 1979, 60 had been moved at least once by 1983. Mrs Thatcher's vigorous reshuffling gave her (by way of example) eight Transport Secretaries and seven Trade and Industry Secretaries. The average Cabinet Minister holds a particular office for under 2½ years: Institute of Economic Affairs, *Inquiry No. 27* (1991).

Now in a reshuffle it is rare for the language of dismissal to be openly employed. If a Minister is to go, he is asked for his resignation. An advantage of this courteous approach is that such a Minister can save face by giving his own reasons for his departure (ill health, a desire to return to private life, and so on). None of Macmillan's 1962 purge was called a dismissal: even Selwyn Lloyd stuck to the euphemistic usage in his resignation letter when he wrote to the Prime Minister, 'You have told me that you would like me to resign and this I willingly do'—a sentence which aptly shows that the line between dismissal and resignation is in some cases a truly fine one.[58] Mr Norman Lamont was, in effect, sacked as Chancellor of the Exchequer in 1993: the Prime Minister's offer of a switch to the Department of the Environment scarcely concealed Mr Major's intention. Dismissals actually so called are, however, rare: Sir Ivor Jennings identifies a number from Victorian times, but none in this century.[59] Two explicit dismissals have occurred since Jennings's last edition. In 1975 Mr Eric Heffer, Minister of State for Industry, broke the terms of the Cabinet's 'agreement to differ' over the referendum on continued membership of the EEC[60] by making a speech in the House of Commons (significantly from the back benches) urging the electorate to vote to withdraw:[61] Mr Wilson immediately wrote to him to say that 'I am . . . informing the Queen that you have ceased to be a Minister'. And in 1981 Mr Keith Speed, a junior Minister in the Ministry of Defence,[62] made a public speech against cuts in naval spending which he knew the Cabinet had approved but which had not been announced. He was sacked.[63] Both dismissals were dramatic demonstrations of the ability of a Prime Minister to dispense with a ministerial colleague who is not prepared to toe the line.

Resignation can, of course, come from a Minister for political reasons: he may decide that he can no longer accept collective responsibility, and leave the government of his own volition, making a parliamentary statement and other explanations of his reasons.[64] The resignation can, in part,

[58] Mr Paul Channon provided another example when he was sacked from the Cabinet in 1989. His resignation letter stated that he understood the need to make changes, 'and so I offer you my resignation'.

[59] See n. 4 above, pp. 209–14.   [60] On which see Chapter 7.

[61] 889 H.C. Deb. 1325–32 (9 April 1975).

[62] He was Parliamentary Under-Secretary of State for Defence for the Royal Navy; a consequence of this episode was the Prime Minister's decision no longer to have junior Ministers representing the three separate Services.

[63] In a letter from Mrs Thatcher of 19 May 1981.

[64] Jennings, n. 4 above, p. 267 asserts a convention that '[a] Minister who resigns from the Cabinet usually desires to make an explanation in Parliament. Since this involves an explanation

CONSTITUTIONAL PRACTICE

be designed to bring about a change in government policy or, at the least, to cause the Prime Minister and government to defend its policy and perhaps cause it embarrassment in doing so. But history shows that such resignations are never fatal to a government, and usually result (after a few days or weeks) in the resigner entering the political wilderness for good. It would, after all, take an exceptional memory that could reconstruct even a partial list of Ministers who have resigned in the last 50 years on policy grounds;[65] most never held ministerial office again, Harold Wilson, Peter Thorneycroft, Enoch Powell, Sir Edward Boyle and Mr Michael Heseltine providing the only exceptions so far. Even the resignations of the Chancellor of the Exchequer and two Treasury Ministers in 1958 because they could not persuade the Cabinet to accept further cuts in government spending could be shrugged off by the Prime Minister as 'little local difficulties'. And the refusal of Iain Macleod and Enoch Powell to join Sir Alec Douglas-Home's administration in 1963 did not affect his ability to form a government: Macleod later became Chancellor of the Exchequer in 1970, but Enoch Powell never held office again.

In the hands of a confident Prime Minister, therefore, the power to appoint, reshuffle, and discard Ministers is, for his ambitious parliamentary colleagues, essential to the inception and continuation of their ministerial lives. It gives the Prime Minister an authority over them which is unrivalled by any other person or body.

---

of Cabinet discussions, he must secure the Queen's consent. For this purpose he asks permission through the Prime Minister'. A similar formulation was given more recently in the Report of the Radcliffe Committee of Privy Counsellors on Ministerial Memoirs, Cmnd. 6386 (1976). I doubt, however, whether this is still the case. Mr Michael Heseltine, for example, made a very full press statement of the reasons for his resignation on 9 January 1986, including details of what had taken place in Cabinet meetings, and made a speech indicating his reasons during a debate on the Westland affair: 89 H.C. Deb. 1098–1107 (15 January 1986). But he has told me in a private letter that he 'was neither aware nor made aware of such a convention'. Mr Nigel Lawson, too, has informed me that he was completely unaware of such a convention when he resigned as Chancellor in 1989. He explained his resignation in an economic debate a week afterwards: see 159 H.C. Deb. 208–10 (31 October 1989). Resignation statements in Parliament are becoming fuller: see, e.g., Mr Lamont's at 226 H.C. Deb. 279–83 (9 June 1993) and Mr Michael Mates's at 227 H.C. Deb. 823–9 (29 June 1993).

[65] A full list can be compiled from David and Gareth Butler, *British Political Facts 1900–1994* (7th edn., 1994), pp. 68–70, and John Mackintosh, n. 46 above, p. 448. To this list must be added the names of Ian Gow (who resigned as Minister of State at the Treasury in 1985 over the Anglo-Irish Agreement), Michael Heseltine (who resigned as Secretary of State for Defence in 1986 over aspects of the Westland affair), Nigel Lawson (who resigned in 1989 over the Prime Minister's refusal to dismiss her part-time economic adviser), Sir Geoffrey Howe (who left in 1990 in opposition to Mrs Thatcher's attitude towards Europe), and David Heathcoat-Amory (who left Mr Major's government in 1996 over the single European currency).

The extent to which any Prime Minister controls Cabinet meetings[66] and decisions will in large part again turn on his disposition and political strength. By custom the agenda for the weekly meeting, normally held on Thursday, is decided by the Prime Minister, and the order of items is fixed by him in consultation with the Secretary of the Cabinet. John Mackintosh believed that this procedure enables the Prime Minister to keep any item which he does not wish discussed off the agenda indefinitely.[67] Harold Wilson, on the other hand, while accepting that in theory that could happen denies that it could take place in practice, because any Minister could raise an issue orally under either of the two standing first items on the regular agenda, namely parliamentary affairs, and foreign and Commonwealth affairs.[68] Those views are not in such conflict as they may seem to be, for a resolute Prime Minister who possesses enough authority could both direct that a particular item be not put on the agenda, and also stop a Minister who tried to raise it orally dead in his tracks; conversely, of course, a less secure chairman might be able to do neither. Take as an illustration the 'great unmentionable' during the early years of the 1964 Labour government, devaluation. No Minister who took the view that the possibility of devaluation ought to be discussed—not even George Brown—could challenge Mr Wilson's implacable determination (fully buttressed by his Chancellor of the Exchequer) that it was not an option open to the government: such a Minister could neither have had the issue put on the agenda nor have raised it orally, for to do so would have invited immediate rebuff and a request for his resignation. That Cabinet's agenda was totally controlled in the sense that such a request or attempt would just not have been made, not in the sense that one was actually made and rejected.[69]

[66] There are descriptions of Cabinet meetings in, for example, Harold Wilson, n. 2 above, pp. 45–62; John Mackintosh, n. 46 above, ch. 21; Patrick Gordon Walker, n. 3 above, chs 2, 6, and 9.

[67] See n. 46 above, p. 449. He cites as evidence (for example) Attlee's refusal to tell the Cabinet about British work on atomic weapons until tests had taken place (an example disputed by Gordon Walker, n. 3 above, pp. 87–91); Chamberlain's attempt to raise House of Lords reform at a meeting in June 1927, which Baldwin thwarted by leaving the room and thus ending the Cabinet; and Hore-Belisha's wish to circulate memoranda in April 1939 advocating partial mobilization, which Chamberlain forbade (although later he allowed him to raise the issue orally). See also Jennings, n. 4 above, pp. 245–9.

[68] See n. 2 above, pp. 47–8. A. H. Brown agrees with Mr Wilson on the ground that no Minister whom he had interviewed could recall a suggested item being kept off the agenda: [1968] Public Law at 51.

[69] Mr Wilson allowed a discussion of devaluation as one economic option in July 1966. A majority of the Cabinet supported his opposition to it, and the topic was again closed. See Barbara Castle, The Castle Diaries 1964–1970 (1984), pp. 148–50; Denis Healey, n. 7 above, p. 334.

A more recent analogy might be that of a member of Mrs Thatcher's Cabinet who might have wished to have debated an alternative economic or industrial strategy, plainly at odds with that of the Prime Minister and a clear majority of her Cabinet: it would have been pointless—perhaps politically fatal—for him to have tried to do so. On the other hand, a Prime Minister who saw that support for a particular policy of his was ebbing away simply could not take such an autocratic view and would find it increasingly difficult to block discussion.

Naturally, the lower down the agenda an item might be the less likely it is that sufficient time would be available to take it; that knowledge will obviously weigh with a Prime Minister in approving the order of business. Cabinet Ministers are absurdly overworked people[70] and they will have other pressing matters to get to (including lunch); the nearer the clock moves to 1 p.m. or 1.30 p.m. the more amenable they will be to a suggested adjournment. Equally, a Prime Minister would be pushing his luck too far if an important matter appeared very low on the agenda, was deferred, and reappeared in the same place at a subsequent meeting.

It does not tell us very much about the position of a Prime Minister in relation to his Cabinet to note that only the former has the authority to summon a meeting of the latter, and that without the Prime Minister's consent no meeting of Ministers is able to make Cabinet decisions,[71] for if enough Cabinet colleagues were to insist on a meeting it would be inconceivable that their chairman would refuse to call one. But a *consequence* of that authority is of great importance, namely a Prime Minister's decision on the frequency with which the Cabinet should have regular meetings. In the premierships of Attlee and Churchill the Cabinet regularly met twice a week during the parliamentary session.[72] At the latest by 1969 those regular meetings had been halved to one a week, and that remains the frequency

---

[70] Exhaustion is frequently referred to in the Crossman and Castle diaries.

[71] When an emergency Privy Council meeting was summoned late at night on 14 March 1968 to approve an Order in Council proclaiming a bank holiday during a gold crisis, George Brown (who did not know what was going on) arranged a meeting of Ministers and asked the Prime Minister over the telephone to join them. The Prime Minister retorted that if a Cabinet meeting was wanted 'they should come over to No. 10 for a properly convened one', which they did: Harold Wilson, *The Labour Government 1964–1970: A Personal Record* (1971), pp. 508–9. George Brown, *In My Way* (Pelican, 1972), ch. 9. Brown resigned over the incident.

[72] Peter Hennessy, n. 4 above, pp. 99–100. The Secretary of the Cabinet refused to give him statistics on the frequency of Cabinets since 1955. Gordon Walker notes that the Conservative Cabinets from 1951 to 1959 met twice a week, but that Harold Wilson reduced the regular meetings to once a week: n. 2 above, p. 101.

today. Now the pressure of government business has not slackened so as to permit fewer Cabinet meetings—indeed, the amount of business has at the very least remained the same as it was from 1945 to 1955. The reason for the cut in the number of Cabinet meetings is the increased use of Cabinet committees and *ad hoc* groups of Ministers. That development is best explained in the context of a full examination of the Cabinet as an institution, which will be undertaken in the next chapter.[73] Here it must be stressed that that development for two reasons represents a significant expansion of prime ministerial power. First, the fewer Cabinet meetings held, the fewer opportunities there will be for Ministers to raise and to discuss issues that the Prime Minister would prefer not to be raised and discussed: the occasions are fewer at which the Prime Minister may have to justify and defend his actions (or inactions). Secondly, the use in particular of informal, *ad hoc* groups allows a Prime Minister to select colleagues who would be likely to further his preferred solutions. An example has been reported of the way that Mr Heseltine's attempt to get additional spending for the inner cities after the 1981 riots was thwarted by the use of a packed *ad hoc* group of Cabinet Ministers. Prime Ministers have altered the machinery of government so that Cabinet government has about half as many opportunities to represent an irritant or even a challenge to the Prime Minister as was the case 35 years ago.

A Prime Minister's ability to influence discussion and decisions at Cabinet meetings will, yet again, vary according to his character and his personal authority. The various styles since 1945 were indicated at the beginning of the chapter.

Votes may be taken at Cabinet meetings on minor procedural matters but not normally otherwise: rather, the Prime Minister sums up and states what he takes the Cabinet's decision to be.[74] A Prime Minister, however, could scarcely use a summing up, however skilful, to disguise by sleight of hand a Cabinet opinion one way as a decision in the opposite sense. There can, though, be a little more leeway in the compilation of the

[73] See especially the second section of that chapter.

[74] Clement Attlee, 'The making of a Cabinet' in Anthony King (ed.), *The British Prime Minister* (1969); Harold Wilson, *The Governance of Britain*, n. 2 above, p. 55; Edward Heath, the *Listener*, 22 April 1976 (who, speaking for his premiership and for those of Eden, Macmillan, and Douglas-Home, in whose Cabinets he had sat, confirms this statement). Writing of Mrs Thatcher's Cabinet, Mr Norman Tebbit noted that 'Cabinet is not a place for votes although if a decision is finely balanced the Cabinet Secretary keeps a tally of views for the Prime Minister's summing up'; a formal count was taken on whether to send the task force to regain the Falkland Islands in 1982: see *Upwardly Mobile* (1988), p. 194; Margaret Thatcher, n. 10 above, pp. 180–1.

minutes.[75] The main responsibility for drafting the minutes lies with the Secretary of the Cabinet or his deputy, who bases them on notes made by him at the meeting. The minutes are promptly circulated to Cabinet Ministers. Harold Wilson has written that the Prime Minister does not see them before that circulation, and that the Prime Minister will only be consulted at the drafting stage in cases of doubt over what had been decided.[76] But Richard Crossman is not entirely alone in asserting that the minutes may bear only a loose relationship to what was actually said or concluded.[77] Mr Michael Heseltine objected that the Secretary had not recorded his protest at a Cabinet meeting over the cancellation of a Cabinet committee which he had understood was due to take place to discuss an aspect of the Westland affair.[78] As a result, the Secretary issued a brief correcting note, but in the minutes 'as finally issued' there was still no reference to his protest.[79] This was not a minor matter, as the cancellation of that committee meeting was an important factor in Mr Heseltine's resignation as Defence Secretary; but when those Cabinet minutes are made public there will, presumably, be no reference in them to that protest and a little piece of history will have been rewritten by the Cabinet Secretary, who could have understood the Prime Minister's wishes without consulting her at all.

Through his authority over the Cabinet agenda, the frequency of Cabinet meetings, the use of Cabinet committees and *ad hoc* groups of Ministers, his chairmanship, and to some extent through his influence over the minutes, a Prime Minister is able to guide the decision-making of the Cabinet.

The highest profile; patronage; dissolution

A Prime Minister's power is greater than the sum total of his powers, and a significant reason for this is that his profile is higher than any other Minister's. In Parliament, he answers Prime Minister's Questions every Wednesday, whereas other Ministers have a chance to shine only once every three to

---

[75] The formal term is 'Cabinet conclusions'. Mr John Redwood has commented that the minutes of Mr Major's Cabinet meetings were 'very bland' and 'will tell historians little about the Major years': quoted in Seldon, *Major: A Political Life*, n. 8 above, p. 208.

[76] Harold Wilson, *The Governance of Britain*, n. 2 above, p. 56.

[77] See *Diaries of a Cabinet Minister*, vol. i (1975), pp. 103–4.

[78] See Chapter 7.

[79] He made this point in public statements explaining his resignation. For an earlier dispute about the recording of dissent, see Tony Benn, *Against the Tide: Diaries 1973–1976* (1989), p. 262.

five weeks.[80] His skill at such frequent gladiatorial contests can enhance his prestige with Ministers and back-benchers—and, through television and radio coverage, with the general public. The Prime Minister will also decide when to intervene in debates, unlike all other Ministers who will normally only speak in debates touching their departmental responsibilities—although such prime ministerial interventions are infrequent. In that sense a Prime Minister has no portfolio and every portfolio and can put his personal prestige behind an issue or a particular Minister. In the country, the Prime Minister can frequently be news: his visits and speeches, carefully arranged into photo opportunities for newspaper photographers and television cameramen, concentrate attention on his doings and sayings. If he wishes to make an announcement over television or radio by ministerial broadcast, he can do so. Abroad, Prime Ministers have represented the country in personal attempts to improve international relations, a development started with Chamberlain's visits to Hitler and accelerated by the onset of easy air travel. During his premiership Harold Macmillan clocked up a tour of the Commonwealth, a visit to Moscow, meetings with Presidents Eisenhower and Kennedy, and the 1960 Paris summit. Mrs Thatcher visited 55 countries, flew over half a million miles, attended 32 European Councils, 12 annual economic summits of the Group of Seven industrialized nations, and seven Commonwealth heads of government conferences. Today, if the Prime Minister wants to discuss an issue at length with the President of the USA, it is taken for granted that he will fly to see him. At the many regular international gatherings, too, the Prime Minister will represent the United Kingdom. Additionally, important visitors from abroad are received personally by the Prime Minister.[81] The electorate must be forgiven if it concludes that the Prime Minister *is* the government, a conclusion which the Prime Minister might not wish to correct.

It is, of course, important to a Prime Minister that his pre-eminence be appreciated by the public, and to that end he controls his party's public relations. To Attlee and Churchill in the pre-television age[82] any such notion as public relations would have seemed entirely foreign. Eden's suspicion of

[80] When he came to office Mr Blair ended unilaterally the previous arrangement for Prime Minister's Questions (which had been taken on Tuesdays and Thursdays for 15 minutes on each day) in favour of one 30-minute session on Wednesdays.

[81] The greatest coup in this respect was when Macmillan persuaded President Eisenhower to appear in a live television broadcast from 10 Downing Street in which the President gave him his personal endorsement shortly before the 1959 general election.

[82] A film was shown during the television programme 'Television and Number 10' on 12 November 1986 of the only television screen test to which Churchill agreed. It was appalling.

the BBC led to television being kept at arm's length during his premiership. Macmillan was the first Prime Minister to appreciate the need to communicate his policy and to project himself to the voters through television. He also appointed the Minister without Portfolio in his Cabinet to co-ordinate government information from the various departments. Edward Heath took responsibility for this into Number 10, employing Donald Maitland, a career diplomat, as head of his Press Office.[83] It has been said that the 1997 Labour government took the presentation of policy to new heights through very careful control of how information was released. Mr Alistair Campbell (Chief Press Secretary to the Prime Minister) co-ordinated 'spin doctors' in that endeavour. The Prime Minister can control which Ministers appear on the media to put the government's case and also which journalists are favoured to receive personal guidance over and above his Press Secretary's briefings 'on lobby terms'.[84] General elections have increasingly been fought through the medium of television, the last three contests being totally geared by all the main parties to the communication of image through photo opportunities and televised party rallies. Labour's election campaign in 1987 was generally agreed to have been its most effective ever, and even better on television than that of the Conservative Party. That the government still convincingly won the election shows that policies remain vital, but Prime Ministers will clearly have to communicate to the best possible effect through television if they are to succeed electorally.

The Prime Minister's supremacy is also marked out by his unique relationship with the Sovereign. That relationship will be explored in Chapter 9: here it will suffice to note that his right of audience enjoyed once each week during the parliamentary session is not shared by any other Minister.

Another area of a Prime Minister's power concerns patronage and honours. In 1977, Mr Callaghan listed in a written answer in *Hansard* those public appointments which were either in his gift, or which he recommended, as Prime Minister. The reply exceeds four columns[85] and even then excludes ecclesiastical appointments, the choice of Ministers of

[83] All Prime Ministers since MacDonald in 1929 have had a Press Secretary (save for Churchill during his wartime premiership). See generally Robert Harris, *Good and Faithful Servant* (1990), ch. 5.

[84] This is the cosy system under which journalists accredited to the Westminster Lobby receive whatever information the government's spokesman (frequently the Prime Minister's Press Secretary) wishes to give out; the *quid pro quo* is that the source be not exactly identified.

[85] 932 H.C. Deb. 232–6 (written answers 19 May 1977). See also Mr Major's list of appointments made by the Queen on the Prime Minister's advice at 248 H.C. Deb. 917–19 (written answers 31 October 1994).

the Crown and certain civil service appointments. At a Prime Minister's effective disposal is a dazzling range of jobs. That range must entail the seeking of advice about possible candidates—he could not know them all—but, having received that advice the patronage is his alone.

His patronage in relation to Ministers has already been discussed.[86] Senior civil servants—Permanent Under-Secretaries of State[87] and other senior officials—need his approbation for their appointment and promotion. In the judiciary[88] the Lords of Appeal in Ordinary, Lords Justices of Appeal, the Master of the Rolls, the Lord Chief Justice, the Vice-Chancellor, and the President of the Family Division are all appointed by the Queen on his advice[89]—although the importance of the Lord Chancellor's view should not be underestimated.[90] In the Church, 384 appointments are made by the Crown on the Prime Minister's advice when vacancies arise.[91] Other appointments include the Chairman and governors of the BBC, the Comptroller and Auditor-General,[92] the Parliamentary Commissioner for Administration,[93] the Chairman of the Police Complaints Authority,[94] the Regius Professors, and so on. All this patronage can clearly encourage the deference shown to any Prime Minister.[95] Formally, the Queen is the fountain of honour and all peerages and honours are conferred by her. But (with a few exceptions[96]) those grants are made on ministerial advice.[97] Appointments to honours from peerages down to the humblest MBE

---

[86] See Chapter 4.

[87] 'Permanent Secretaries' if their Minister is not a Secretary of State.

[88] For the details, see Chapter 12.

[89] It fell to Mrs Thatcher to recommend the appointment of all the Law Lords except one, the entire Court of Appeal, the Master of the Rolls, and the Lord Chief Justice.

[90] Lord Hailsham of St Marylebone LC has written that 'in practice the Lord Chancellor greatly influences [the Prime Minister's] decision': *The Door Wherein I Went* (1975), p. 254. The Home Affairs Select Committee has questioned the Prime Minister's role in these appointments on the ground that he is not better informed than the Lord Chancellor. See 3rd Report from the Home Affairs Committee, *Judicial Appointments Procedures* (H.C. 52 (1995–96)).

[91] I am grateful to the Secretary for Appointments at 10 Downing Street for help on this point. He is puzzled by the figure of 700 given by Jennings, n. 4 above, p. 453, which is more than double the current number.

[92] National Audit Act 1983, s. 1(1): he is appointed by the Queen on an address from both Houses, the motion requiring to be moved by the Prime Minister with the consent of the chairman of the Public Accounts Committee.

[93] Parliamentary Commissioner Act 1967, s. 1(2).

[94] Police and Criminal Evidence Act 1984, s. 83 and Schedule 4.

[95] See also Tony Benn (1980) 33 *Parliamentary Affairs* 7.

[96] Appointments to the Orders of the Garter, the Thistle, the Royal Victorian Order, and the Order of Merit are in the Queen's hands.

[97] Report of the Royal Commission on Honours, Cmd. 1789 (1922), vol. ii, p. 99.

are made on the Prime Minister's advice.[98] To some, honours are very important, and to them the Prime Minister's patronage will be important, too.[99]

The Prime Minister's ability to dissolve Parliament is often described as an important element in his personal power. I think that this is misleading. The legitimacy of the Prime Minister's sole right to recommend a dissolution, rather than any recommendation being the collective advice of the Cabinet, has been challenged.[100] But that right is now so generally accepted by Ministers of all parties that only the acceptance by a future Prime Minister of a most unlikely self-denying ordinance could possibly restore the pre-1918 position[101]—and even then it would be hard to see how that would bind his successors. Of course, the ability to choose an election date strengthens the Prime Minister's hand in relation to the opposition parties, for ideally he will opt for a time when he is most likely to win. But is anyone really taken in by the claim that the dissolution power strengthens the Prime Minister in relation to his Cabinet and party? That claim has it that, because the Prime Minister has the personal right to recommend a dissolution, then he can threaten to obtain a general election so as to bring to heel the rebellious in his administration and his parliamentary party; and government MPs with vulnerable majorities would be restrained from voting so as to bring about an early election, just as turkeys would never vote for an early Christmas. He could *threaten*, certainly, just as Mr Wilson threatened in January 1968 at a PLP meeting,[102] and as Mr Major did in confidence debates in the Commons in 1993 and in 1994; but the weapon would never be fired, for the electorate would see the unattractive picture of a government in disarray, its Leader in open warfare with his own troops. The opposition parties would enjoy a field day, and electoral victory would be likely for them. The notion of a 'penal dissolution' should be forgotten.

Although 16 Prime Ministers since Lloyd George have enjoyed the power which he assumed to recommend a dissolution off his own bat, the

---

[98] Or on the Foreign and Commonwealth Secretary's advice for appointments to the Order of St Michael and St George in the Diplomatic Service.

[99] The Political Honours Scrutiny Committee reports on the suitability of persons to be recommended for titles and honours at CBE level and above (whether for political or any other services), and it was highly critical of some of the recommendations in the Wilson Resignation Honours List in 1976. Mr Major's changes to the honours system in 1993 did not reduce the Prime Minister's patronage at all.

[100] Notably by Geoffrey Marshall, *Constitutional Conventions* (1984), ch. 3.

[101] Namely, that a request to dissolve came from the Cabinet collectively.

[102] Gordon Walker, n. 3 above, p. 82; Mackintosh, n. 46 above, pp. 606–7.

more modern practice[103] has been for the Prime Minister to consult senior Ministers and party officials both to help to pick a date *and* to involve them in collective responsibility for it. Mrs Thatcher's approach to this matter was typical of recent Prime Ministers. Before the announcements of the 1983 and 1987 dissolutions she conferred with a group of senior Cabinet Ministers and the Chief Whip; the discussion led to a 'provisional' decision, on which the Prime Minister slept; a full Cabinet was summoned the following day to be informed of her final choice (which confirmed the provisional date); the Prime Minister saw the Queen and a public announcement from Downing Street followed. (In 1992, by contrast, Mr Major did not consult widely about the timing of the general election, possibly because by law it had to be held that year. Nor were there wide consultations leading up to the 1997 dissolution.[104]) If a Prime Minister, alone, chooses a date and wins, well and good for him; but if he loses, having chosen the wrong date,[105] or the wrong issue,[106] or the wrong campaign[107] (or all three), he could inflict a wound on himself from which he might never recover. It is, therefore, far better for him to rely on his right of personal choice but also to involve at least some senior colleagues—his potential rivals—in the decision so that they are implicated if all goes wrong. Such a practical consideration must detract from the idea that a Prime Minister has unrestricted personal power in the matter, for if he were in a minority in that consultation it would be risky to press ahead despite the opposition: if electoral defeat resulted, the silence of his colleagues could not be guaranteed over the manner in which the decision had been made. This is not to deny that as the decision is the Prime Minister's and as the announcement

[103] See Marshall, n. 100 above, pp. 51–3. According to James Prior, n. 10 above, p. 149, when Mrs Thatcher was deciding on the date of the 1983 general election she consulted the Cabinet in small groups. For a detailed description of the choice of date in 1983, see Norman Tebbit, n. 74 above, pp. 202–4; and for the Prime Minister's approach in 1983 and 1987, see Margaret Thatcher, n. 10 above, pp. 281–5, 569–75.

[104] Seldon, *Major: A Political Life*, n. 8 above, pp. 256–9, 693–4, 703.

[105] One example was, perhaps, Mr Heath's timing in 1974 (in which the entire Cabinet concurred: see Lord Hailsham, n. 90 above, p. 298). Another was, certainly, Mr Callaghan's: he had consulted the Cabinet in August 1978 about the date of the election, and according to one eyewitness account a majority of Ministers favoured a dissolution that autumn, but the Prime Minister and his closest colleagues were opposed to that: see Bernard Donoughue, *Prime Minister: The Conduct of Policy under Harold Wilson and James Callaghan* (1987), pp. 160–3. Mr Callaghan delayed into 1979, by which time the 'winter of discontent' had destroyed any chance of his being returned: for his account, see Callaghan, n. 7 above, pp. 514–18.

[106] Such as Baldwin in 1923—protection. He was back in office as Prime Minister in 1924 and again in 1935.

[107] Like Mr Wilson's of 1970.

one way or the other comes from him,[108] attention will yet again naturally be focused on him when an appeal to the country seems near.

The direction of departments

A Prime Minister's authority reaches into every department of state. In an ideal administration a Prime Minister will leave his colleagues to get on with running their departments within the framework of the government's policies. As head of the government he has the natural right to intervene if necessary to ensure that decisions are carried out, in a way that no other Minister outside his department may do. If, like Eden, he fretfully interferes, too much and at inconvenient times,[109] it will do him no good in the long run. According to one account[110] Mrs Thatcher would really have liked to run at least the major departments herself, and (even though that would have been impossible) presumably her presence was felt in them. On the other hand, if like Macmillan or Harold Wilson[111] a Prime Minister takes charge of a particular matter for a time because his authority needs to be brought to bear, well and good. Prime Ministers who always sit in the back seat, however, can upset Ministers as much as the compulsive driver. Baldwin favoured long weekends at Chequers, refused to have papers sent there, and made little attempt to control his colleagues. He was accessible, loyal, and friendly, but neither intervened in departmental matters nor was much help when Ministers sought his advice.[112] A typical example occurred when Austen Chamberlain was working towards the Locarno Pact and took certain fundamental issues to Baldwin, who listened attentively and then replied, 'Well, Austen, do what you think fit and I will support you'.[113] What Chamberlain wanted was a second opinion from his chief, not a gratifying expression of loyalty.

The Foreign and Commonwealth Office is in a special position because

---

[108] Such as Mr Callaghan's television broadcast on 7 September 1978 announcing that there would be no dissolution recommended until 1979.

[109] As R. A. Butler put it, 'I was . . . at the receiving end of those innumerable telephone calls, on every day of the week and at every hour of the day, which characterized his conscientious but highly strung supervision of affairs': n. 43 above, p. 184.

[110] Pym, n. 10 above, p. 17.

[111] Macmillan had to take over the writing of a White Paper on incomes policy in 1962 as a result of delay by the Chancellor and Treasury: At the End of the Day, n. 27 above, p. 89. Mr Wilson took personal charge of the Department of Economic Affairs for a time from 1967–68.

[112] Keith Middlemas and John Barnes, Baldwin (1969), pp. 482–3.

[113] This incident was recounted by Chamberlain to Jennings, n. 4 above, p. 189.

of the frequency with which politically important matters occur: the Prime Minister and the Foreign Secretary must be left to implement Cabinet policy without constant references to other Ministers. Some Prime Ministers—like Lloyd George, MacDonald, Chamberlain, Eden, Macmillan, and Thatcher—have taken a keen personal interest in international affairs and some of them have tended to treat the Foreign Secretary as their own Under-Secretary. Mrs Thatcher, obviously, was concerned in particular with Anglo-American relations and certain European matters. If a Prime Minister has the will to do so, then (unless the Foreign Secretary is strong enough to resist) he himself can direct major Foreign Office policies. Such close direction of home departments is much less common (save, as already indicated, on a single issue). Here, as in other areas, the office of Prime Minister is what the individual is willing and able to make it.

In order to enjoy the fruits of his office to the full a Prime Minister must have adequate information. He has in fact at his disposal a machine so responsive to his needs that, although it is not in a unified organization or styled such, he has in effect a Prime Minister's department.

A major part of that organization is the Cabinet Office,[114] headed by the Secretary of the Cabinet. He may be likened to a Permanent Secretary to the Prime Minister.[115] As well as servicing Cabinet meetings the Cabinet Office and Secretary in theory service all Cabinet Ministers, but Ministers naturally tend to rely principally on their departmental civil servants, whose first loyalty is to their departments and to their Ministers for the time being; in the result it is for the Prime Minister primarily (and certain Ministers without Portfolio)[116] that the Cabinet Office and Cabinet Secretary work. The Office can get whatever information the Prime Minister needs from the departments: any request made in his name will obviously be given priority. The Prime Minister's Private Office at Number 10 is his inner sanctum of advisers, dealing with his immediate needs.[117] It is small, with three or four civil servants seconded from the major departments to act as Private Secretaries to the Prime Minister. A primary task for the Private Office is to sort out essential items for the Prime Minister to see from the

---

[114] See Chapter 6.

[115] Especially, perhaps, Sir Robert Armstrong under Mrs Thatcher.

[116] Thus Mr Tebbit as Chancellor of the Duchy of Lancaster from 1985 to 1987 was based in the Cabinet Office: see 105 H.C. Deb. 39 (written answers 17 November 1986). Mr Peter Mandelson, too, as Minister without Portfolio (1997–98) was based in that Office.

[117] For a description, see Callaghan, n. 7 above, pp. 405–6; Bernard Donoughue, n. 105 above, pp. 17–26; Margaret Thatcher, n. 10 above, pp. 19–20; Seldon, *Major: A Political Life*, n. 8 above, pp. 142–6.

mass of paper which daily threatens him. The Private Office also co-ordinates the Prime Minister's engagements, assembles materials for speeches, ensures that he is properly briefed before meetings, liaises with Ministers' Private Offices, acts as a link with the Queen's Private Secretary, and as a filter for visitors. The Policy Unit[118] in Downing Street was created by Harold Wilson in 1974 to advise him on all matters, and it has been continued by his successors. Its staff are not civil servants but individuals who are in tune with the Prime Minister's political ideology. It is thus party political, supplying the Prime Minister with systematic policy analysis. It is that political counterbalance to civil service advice which Prime Ministers have found invaluable over the past 20 years. Mr Callaghan considered that the information with which the Unit supplied him enabled him to test and challenge departmental proposals, especially from the Treasury, much more effectively than otherwise would have been possible.[119] The Political Office at Number 10[120] is made up of party members, again not civil servants, paid for by funds which the Prime Minister or his party must find. Its functions vary according to which party is in power: a Labour Prime Minister, for example, will use the Political Office to maintain contact with the National Executive Committee of the Labour Party, with constituency parties, and with the trade unions. No Prime Minister has tried formally to establish a Prime Minister's Department because he already receives all the help he can use through existing structures, especially from the Cabinet Office.[121]

A Prime Minister's weaknesses

The trappings of power and the prestige of the office of Prime Minister ensure that ministerial colleagues and back-benchers acknowledge the

---

[118] See Mackintosh, n. 46 above, pp. 517–21; Callaghan, n. 7 above, pp. 404–5; Donoughue, n. 105 above; Hennessy, n. 4 above, p. 194, who asserts that, with the abolition of the Central Policy Review Staff in 1983 Mrs Thatcher's Policy Unit was expanded 'into a shadow Whitehall with each of its members . . . covering a clutch of subject areas'.
[119] See Callaghan, n. 7 above, p. 404.
[120] See Callaghan, n. 7 above, p. 406.
[121] Mackintosh, n. 46 above, p. 520; Harold Wilson, n. 2 above, p. 82. See also Sir Kenneth Berrill, 'Strength at the Centre: The Case for a Prime Minister's Department' (Stamp Memorial Lecture, 1980), and (for a case against) Sir Douglas Wass, *Government and the Governed* (1984), pp. 32–4. Mr Callaghan decided against such a department partly on the ground that it would duplicate existing machinery and would add an unnecessary layer of administration: see Callaghan, n. 7 above, p. 408.

Prime Minister's supremacy through the deference shown to him. When (as is usually the case) the Prime Minister has a parliamentary majority behind him his political power will be the envy of dictators. But there is another aspect to consider, namely what might be collectively termed a Prime Minister's weaknesses. These will now be briefly sketched.

An unavoidable weakness of every Prime Minister and government in Britain is that they are temporary (although, as Mrs Thatcher has shown us, some are less temporary than others). However complete may be his superiority in the Cabinet and party the Prime Minister must in peacetime face a general election no more than five years in the future, and his tenure of office may be abruptly ended (as was seen, for example, in 1997 when Mr Major and his colleagues were rejected by the electorate). And Prime Ministers and administrations do not only leave office after rejection at the polls: a Prime Minister's ill health may force resignation;[122] governments occasionally break up (as in 1931); a Prime Minister may be required to make way for a coalition (as in 1916 and 1940). Prime Ministers come and go for a variety of reasons, and statistical averages on lengths of tenure are accordingly meaningless. They are, however, salutary reminders for any Prime Minister of the transience of power. The longest continuous premiership this century was Mrs Thatcher's which, at 11½ years, eclipsed all records since Lord Liverpool's in the nineteenth century.[123] Six Prime Ministers have held office for less than three years,[124] with Sir Alec Douglas-Home achieving one year and Bonar Law only seven months. The average period of office since 1902 has been some five years.[125] On that record a Prime Minister will be exceptional if he enjoys more than seven or eight years in office—less than two full Parliaments.

If the governments over the last 40 years are considered, it is possible to formulate the maxim that a Prime Minister will be relatively strong when things go well, but that when affairs go badly his authority will wane and perhaps come under challenge, and if his luck deserts him he may well be finished. Such a statement may be objected to as being too uncertain, but a number of examples illustrate that it is fundamentally correct.

Sir Anthony Eden, Churchill's golden crown prince, popular, respected, a major figure in diplomacy, succeeded Churchill in 1955 and speedily

---

[122] As it has this century with Campbell-Bannerman, Bonar Law, Eden, and Macmillan.

[123] The longest interrupted totals this century are those of Churchill (8 years 8 months) and then Wilson (7 years and 9 months).

[124] Callaghan, Chamberlain, Campbell-Bannerman, Eden, Sir Alec Douglas-Home, Bonar Law.

[125] Aggregating all separate terms where individuals held the office more than once.

consolidated his position at the general election of that year, increasing Churchill's majority of 16 to one of 60. Eden's authority was such that critical decisions over Suez were taken by him and the small Egypt Committee of the Cabinet.[126] But the divisions which the invasion of Egypt caused in the Conservative Party and in the country, and the collapse of his health (rarely strong since a surgical misfortune in 1953),[127] brought about the end of his premiership in January 1957 after only 21 months, after he had been Churchill's heir for 13 years.[128] His successor Harold Macmillan achieved a remarkable feat in so restoring the Conservative government's morale and political fortunes that at the 1959 general election Eden's parliamentary majority was increased to almost 100. 'Supermac' was ascendant from 1957 to 1962, when many things started to go wrong—security lapses, by-election reverses, the 'night of the long knives' in 1962, failure of the initiative to join the European Community, the Profumo scandal, and Macmillan's illness and resignation. Harold Wilson, elected as Leader of the Labour Party in 1963 partly as a direct contrast to Macmillan, was to achieve two general election victories in a row, with the second increasing his Commons majority—a first for this century.[129] Enforced devaluation in 1967 in flat contradiction of three years' toil to maintain the parity of the pound, and repeated financial and economic crises, sapped his credibility as an astute Prime Minister; his 1970 general election strategy was a misjudgement of the electorate's mood in offering a Baldwinesque 'safety first' campaign. True, he was back in office four years later, but the personification of a government in its head in the 1964 Labour administration was seen to be an electoral asset of uncertain value. Edward Heath's government, whatever its successes, was finished by the 1973–74 miners' strike and three-day working week, and possibly by a mistiming of his appeal to the electorate.[130] In James Callaghan the Labour Party had a Prime Minister who could do business with the trade unions which had in effect ruined Mr Heath—a conciliator who had built up close relationships with trade union leaders over the years, who had opposed 'In Place of Strife'[131] (and who

[126] See Robert Rhodes James, n. 17 above, pp. 459–62, 496 ff.

[127] Rhodes James, n. 17 above, pp. 361–9.

[128] Whatever his health, Eden could not have survived the Suez débâcle. The Cabinet urged him on 17 December 1956 not to resign—but then they had to make the best of things, and, when the dust had settled, he would have been pushed out.

[129] Mrs Thatcher repeated the achievement in 1979 and 1983, and surpassed it in 1987.

[130] Prior, n. 10 above, pp. 91–3.

[131] That is, the 1969 White Paper introduced by the Labour government as the basis for legislation (which was ultimately withdrawn).

reminded everyone of it on becoming Prime Minister by dropping its author Mrs Castle from the government). Yet the great inflation of the 1970s and the 'winter of discontent' of 1978–79 with its damaging public-sector strikes seemed to show that his touch had deserted him; and his attempt to last to the end of the October 1974 Parliament without a majority proved fatal. Even Mrs Thatcher—the personification of a strong Prime Minister, victor of three consecutive general elections—in the end could not survive a party coup.[132] Mr Major's position did not recover from his government's enforced decision to withdraw the United Kingdom from the European exchange rate mechanism in 1992; several of his Ministers had to resign at various times, having become embroiled in sleaze of a sexual or financial character; his parliamentary majority disappeared in 1996 through by-election defeats and defections; the Conservative Party was bitterly divided over Europe; the Conservative loss of the 1997 general election to a transformed Labour Party seemed inevitable.

Each of those Prime Ministers might have thought in the early months of their governments that, with luck, a long and successful administration lay ahead. Yet as much as anything it was luck which deserted them, and that annoyingly unquantifiable ingredient must be set in the balance to weigh against any theory of supreme prime ministerial authority.

The Cabinet is not a body of 20 or so politicians unquestioningly committed to the Prime Minister's success. At any time there will be up to five overlapping elements in the Cabinet which can weaken a Prime Minister's authority.

There will be, first, the potential successors who must demonstrate their own departmental successes and (within the limits of collective responsibility) distance themselves from the Prime Minister in anything which smacks of political failure. Sometimes the number of potential successors will be greater than at other times, so that, for example, in the last Wilson Cabinet from 1974 to 1976 there were several, whereas in his first 1964 Cabinet there had been initially none (if previous ministerial experience and position in the party were taken as the main criteria). Secondly, there will be those who will never themselves be contestants for the premiership but who will none the less put the success of the party above the unquestioned continuance of any particular Prime Minister. Such a grouping is easier to discern in the Conservative Party—the grandees, or the 'magic circle'. Thirdly, some senior members of any Cabinet will owe their

[132] See Chapter 2.

membership of it not to the Prime Minister's patronage but to their position in the party or to their indispensability to the Prime Minister. Thus the Deputy Leader of the Party in a Labour Cabinet, defeated rivals in a Party Leadership contest, and senior figures in a Cabinet of any colour could not realistically be excluded, and none of them necessarily owes any personal loyalty to the Prime Minister. Fourthly, some members of a Cabinet will have a different political philosophy or will represent a different strand of party opinion from the Prime Minister. They may believe that the Prime Minister's time will eventually run out and that their time will come—not necessarily through a particular individual succeeding to the premiership but perhaps by means of their political position once more becoming mainstream government philosophy. It is for instance clear that Mrs Thatcher's 1979 Cabinet was a coalition in economic policy terms, of monetarists and the so-called 'wets'. The latter might have hoped that their outlook would carry the Cabinet, but in that particular case the monetarists were triumphant by the time of the 1981 reshuffle.[133] Lastly, there will be those—probably a majority of every Cabinet—who want to survive politically, so that as long as things go well they will support the Prime Minister to the limit; but if things go wrong, if the Prime Minister starts to lose his grip, or if the opinion polls swing away from the government and stay away, they will become the more ready to question and on occasion challenge the Prime Minister. The events of late 1990 have shown how that group may react when the Prime Minister is perceived as being an electoral liability. Those five groups will thus usually give a Prime Minister conditional support at best. They will be prepared when it is in their interests to do so to act to overrule the Prime Minister on particular issues[134] or to force a change of style of government.[135] The Cabinet in that case will assert itself: Cabinet government, at least for a time, may again rival government by Prime Minister.

Any Prime Minister who has a small or no majority in the House of Commons will necessarily appear feebler than one with a comfortable majority, partly because there may be a general expectation of an early reference to the electorate, partly because he will have no guarantee that his

[133] Another example might be those members of the 1974–79 Labour Cabinet who favoured an alternative economic strategy, a 'siege economy'.

[134] Gordon Walker, n. 3 above, pp. 91 ff. and Harold Wilson, *The Labour Government*, n. 71 above, pp. 184, 269, 396, and 513 cite examples.

[135] For example, in July 1966 Mr Wilson conceded that too much economic policy was being decided by too few Ministers, and established a more widely-based Cabinet committee on the subject; and in 1986, in the immediate aftermath of the Westland affair, there was some evidence of a move back towards collective Cabinet government for a time.

government's legislation will pass. Since 1900 governments have had no majority, or one in single figures, for a total of 20 years. In the first hung Parliament of this century, returned at the January 1910 election, the Liberal government depended on the Irish members for its continued existence; in the last hung Parliament from 1977 until 1978 the Labour government depended on the Lib.–Lab. pact for its life;[136] and that government either lost legislation entirely or obtained it in a form which was far from ideal from its point of view. Clearly, such a Prime Minister, and indeed a Prime Minister presiding over a coalition, will be less effective than one with a homogeneous majority, as (say) James Callaghan, Lloyd George, and John Major found to their costs at the end of their premierships.

The potential vulnerability of a Labour Prime Minister under the Party's 1981 constitution was noted in Chapter 2, in particular (a) the danger that Labour's electoral college might choose a Leader who was unacceptable to the PLP, (b) the possibility of a Labour Prime Minister being challenged for the Leadership, and (c) the possibility that he might be denied his seat. These remain theoretical weaknesses—thus far. But Prime Ministers *have* been removed from office, by party vote (as in Mrs Thatcher's dramatic eviction), but more usually by more subtle pressures exerted by their parties and in Parliament. Both world wars produced such casualties, Asquith and Chamberlain. Those might be dismissed as being special to wartime, but there are other examples which show how vulnerable a Prime Minister can be when he is seen as a liability. Churchill was, in effect, levered out in 1955, by which time his advanced old age and increasing infirmity had become major political disadvantages. No one seriously asserts that, had Eden been fully fit, he would have continued in office after the Suez débâcle: the efforts which had been brought to bear on his predecessor would have been deployed more quickly and ruthlessly to show Eden that he no longer had the confidence of the Conservative Party as a whole or of the government. So a removal *can* occur even in peacetime; it would be unusual, certainly, but the threat is there to remind any Prime Minister that he relies ultimately on his parliamentary party.

Conclusions

Through this analysis of a Prime Minister's strengths and weaknesses both generally, and particularly in relation to his Cabinet and parliamentary

[136] See Chapter 10.

party, the main features of the office have become clear. His authority can make him, in theory, an elective dictator. The powers actually exercised certainly give him a superior role in British central government, undoubtedly transcending that of the Cabinet. Some Prime Ministers since 1945 have been more superior than others; even the mightiest, however, have succumbed to forces some of which are no less real for being irritatingly imprecise.

6

THE CABINET

No one writing a book about the practice of British central government today would entitle it (as Sir Ivor Jennings did his work) *Cabinet Government*. Although opinions are not unanimous about the nature of the modern Cabinet, all agree that the Cabinet as a body is not what it once was. The two principal reasons behind the change in its position are the enhanced powers of the Prime Minister,[1] and the increased decision-making outside Cabinet meetings which has taken place at least since the Second World War (whether by the Prime Minister consulting a few ministerial colleagues, or by Cabinet committees, or by informal ministerial groups). It is that second aspect to which particular attention will be paid in this chapter.

Some topics which traditionally appear under the heading of the Cabinet are treated elsewhere in this book. Thus, for example, the choice and composition of the Cabinet were dealt with in Chapter 4; the Cabinet's agenda, procedure, and minutes as they relate to the Prime Minister's authority were examined in the previous chapter; and ministerial responsibility will be looked at in the next chapter, as that notion does not vary according to whether a Minister is or is not a member of the Cabinet.

Cabinet business

Six years after the Cabinet Office had been established Bonar Law contemplated its abolition.[2] But he soon realized that during that time the Cabinet Office had shown its value in making central administration more efficient, and it is indeed astonishing to think today of the amateur way in which the Prime Minister and the Cabinet governed Britain and the

---

[1] On which see Chapter 5.
[2] He originally thought that it was an undesirable relic of Lloyd George's War Cabinet, and planned its abolition—or at least a radical reorganization—after the 1922 general election.

Empire before 1916.[3] The Cabinet would meet without a written agenda; no one acted as secretary and no minutes were taken—indeed, in some Cabinets, Ministers were forbidden to take notes in an attempt to maintain secrecy.[4] The only official account of deliberations was contained in the letter which the Prime Minister sent to the Sovereign, keeping his own copy. Not surprisingly Ministers were not always at all clear what had been decided, a situation aptly encapsulated in the well-known letter from Lord Hartington's Private Secretary to his opposite number at 10 Downing Street in 1882:

Harcourt and Chamberlain have both been here this morning and *at* my Chief about yesterday's Cabinet proceedings. They cannot agree about what occurred. There must have been some decision, as Bright's resignation shows. My Chief has told me to ask you what the devil *was* decided, for he be damned if he knows. Will you ask Mr G. in more conventional and less pungent terms?[5]

That method of doing business continued into Asquith's coalition, but ended abruptly in 1916 with the advent of Lloyd George. He used the Secretariat of the Committee of Imperial Defence as the basis for his new Cabinet Office and Secretariat,[6] with that Committee's Secretary, Colonel Maurice Hankey, becoming Secretary of the Cabinet. Lloyd George's wartime organization of the Office was approved by the Haldane Committee on the Machinery of Government[7] and its functions have broadly remained the same ever since.

The five secretarial functions of the Cabinet Office are (a) to compile the agenda for the Cabinet (under the Prime Minister's direction) and for Cabinet committees (under the direction of their chairmen); (b) to summon members to meetings; (c) to take and circulate Cabinet and Cabinet

---

[3] See generally Lord Hankey, *Diplomacy by Conference: Studies in Public Affairs 1920–1946* (1946), pp. 52, 62–9.

[4] Such a ban existed under Lord Salisbury and under Asquith: see Lady Gwendolen Cecil, *Life of Robert, Marquess of Salisbury* (1921), ii. 223; Lord Oxford and Asquith, *Fifty Years of Parliament* (1928), ii. 197.

[5] Quoted by Viscount Hailsham during a House of Lords debate on the disclosure of Cabinet secrets: 86 H.L. Deb. 529 (21 December 1932).

[6] On which see Sir Ivor Jennings, *Cabinet Government* (3rd edn., 1959), pp. 242–5; Patrick Gordon Walker, *The Cabinet* (revised edn., 1972), pp. 47–55; John Mackintosh, *The British Cabinet* (3rd edn., 1977), pp. 517–21; R. K. Mosley, *The Story of the Cabinet Office* (1969); S. S. Wilson, *The Cabinet Office to 1945* (1975). The organization of the Cabinet Office under the 1974–79 Labour government is described in Bernard Donoughue, *Prime Minister: The Conduct of Policy under Harold Wilson and James Callaghan* (1987), pp. 26–30.

[7] Report, Cd. 9230 (1918).

committee minutes,[8] and to draft reports of those committees; (d) to circulate memoranda and other documents for the Cabinet and its committees; and (e) to file and maintain Cabinet papers and minutes. As was indicated in the previous chapter, the Cabinet Office serves all Cabinet Ministers, but it is really a vital part of what was termed in that chapter the Prime Minister's 'department' and thus of his personal authority, providing him with information and advice; the Secretary of the Cabinet has claim to the unofficial title of Permanent Secretary of the Prime Minister.[9] The Cabinet Secretary is the most important member of the civil service,[10] and, since 1981, has been the Head of the Home Civil Service as well.[11] During the Wilson and Callaghan administrations the Cabinet Secretariat each week issued the Secretary of the Cabinet with its proposals for Cabinet and Cabinet committee business for the following fortnight. Each Thursday the Private Secretary of the Cabinet Secretary discussed it with the Prime Minister's Private Secretary: this constituted the provisional programme of Cabinet and Cabinet committee business for the following two or three weeks. From it the Cabinet Secretary produced a forward programme of business which, when approved by the Prime Minister, became the specific arrangements for government business in the following week.[12]

Of the three functions of the Cabinet identified by the Haldane Committee in 1918,[13] one remains an accurate description of the Cabinet's main role today, namely the final determination of the policy to be submitted to Parliament. Meeting only once a week for a couple of hours with a full

---

[8] For information about how those minutes are taken, and what happens to the notebooks in which they are first written, see 551 H.L. Deb. 103–4 (written answers 3 February 1994); 238 H.C. Deb. 804–5 (written answers 3 March 1994); 239 H.C. Deb. 813 (written answers 17 March 1994).

[9] A title suggested by Gordon Walker, n. 6 above, p. 54.

[10] Sir Robert Armstrong, Cabinet Secretary 1979–87, was perforce brought into the public eye more than his predecessors had been through his roles in the Westland helicopter affair in 1985–86 (on which see Chapter 7), and in the action brought in the Australian courts in 1986–87 by the British government to prevent the publication of the memoirs of a former MI5 spy, Peter Wright.

[11] This combination of office has caused some controversy. The Commons Select Committee on the Treasury and Civil Service recommended that the posts should in future not be held by the same person: see 7th Report from the Treasury and Civil Service Committee, Civil Servants and Ministers: Duties and Responsibilities, H.C. 92 (1985–6), para. 5.44. The government rejected that view in its response: Cmnd. 9841 (1984), para. 42; the Committee persisted in its view: see 1st Report from the Treasury and Civil Service Committee, H.C. 62 (1986–7), para. 3.1; the Prime Minister later announced that the next Cabinet Secretary, Robin Butler, would hold both posts.

[12] See Bernard Donoughue, n. 6 above, pp. 27–8.

[13] Cd. 9230 (1918), p. 5.

agenda, and being composed overwhelmingly of Ministers with heavy departmental responsibilities, the Cabinet could not possibly now be the forum either for the close control of the activities of government or for the co-ordination of the departments of state (essentially the other two functions ascribed to it by the Haldane Committee). As will be seen, much detailed work on policy matters is done outside Cabinet meetings; the Cabinet will consider decisions referred to it by extra-Cabinet decision-makers; its role perforce is largely to ratify or to disapprove decisions taken elsewhere. In that way perhaps the Cabinet has developed another function: to provide the personnel for those Cabinet committees and similar bodies which make up the contemporary Cabinet system.[14]

It would obviously be a profitless exercise to try to list all those matters which in theory could be discussed by the Cabinet. It is, however, instructive to consider those issues which as a matter of practice are not normally taken by the Cabinet, and to note exceptional cases.

In his memoirs Asquith recorded three topics which in his day were not discussed by the Cabinet. These were recommendations concerning the exercise of the prerogative of mercy, the personnel of the Cabinet, and patronage.[15] This was incorrect, however, even when written. The prerogative of mercy is exercised by the Sovereign on the Home Secretary's recommendation, and the Home Secretary acts more judicially than politically in making any recommendation.[16] Partly to underscore that role it is understood that he would not usually take such a question to the Cabinet, where the discussion would tend to be more political than legal. Exceptionally, however, cases under review will have political implications. So, in 1916, the question of whether to recommend a reprieve for Sir Roger Casement was discussed at four Cabinet meetings;[17] and, in the late 1950s,

---

[14] Although that statement is not entirely satisfactory because Ministers outside the Cabinet are also appointed to full membership of Cabinet committees.

[15] Lord Oxford and Asquith, n. 4 above, p. 194.

[16] In Scotland and Northern Ireland recommendations are made to the Sovereign by the relevant Secretary of State. The phrase 'the prerogative of mercy' encompasses pardon and remission of sentence as well as reprieve: it is not, therefore, of historical interest only. See A. T. H. Smith, 'The Prerogative of Mercy, the Power of Pardon and Criminal Justice' [1983] *Public Law* 398, and *R. v. Foster* [1985] Q.B. 115. For a former Home Secretary's account of his task in reviewing death penalty cases see Lord Butler, *The Art of the Possible* (1971), pp. 201–2.

[17] Roy Jenkins, *Asquith* (3rd edn., 1986), pp. 403–4. The Cabinet decided against recommending a reprieve. Jenkins comments that 'There can be few other examples of a Cabinet devoting large parts of our meetings to considering an individual sentence—and then arriving at the wrong decision'.

the Cabinet may well have debated the death sentences passed on a number of Cypriots during the struggle for independence, because executions would have affected both world opinion and negotiations about the island's future.[18] Today, it would be entirely right that the Cabinet (or at least a committee of it) rather than any single Minister should decide any question about the use of the prerogative to free prisoners in response to a terrorist ransom demand or to reprieve anyone convicted of treason, for the political connotations would warrant decisions at Cabinet level. Asquith was also incorrect to write that the personnel of the Cabinet (in the sense of who should be members) is a matter not discussed by it. Of course, such questions are pre-eminently for the Prime Minister.[19] But again there are exceptions, many during Victoria's reign when Prime Ministers consulted ministerial colleagues over whether to give office to individuals,[20] but also this century, such as Baldwin's acceptance in 1923 of his Cabinet's opinion that neither Birkenhead nor Austen Chamberlain should be brought in, whether as Ministers without Portfolio or in any other capacity.[21] Should a Prime Minister wish to consult the Cabinet collectively about possible Cabinet appointments there is no reason why he should not do so. Asquith was, however, right that patronage (in the sense of recommendations for non-ministerial jobs, honours, and so on) traditionally remains for the Prime Minister,[22] although again only as a matter of practice.[23]

Three other areas may be identified in which, again, the modern Cabinet normally has no role. Just as the prerogative of mercy at the end of the criminal process is not usually an issue for the Cabinet, nor is the decision to prosecute at the beginning of that process. That decision today lies initially with the police and, if they feel that there is evidence to justify a prosecution, they will refer the case to the Crown Prosecution Service.[24] The Director of Public Prosecutions is head of that Service; the Attorney-General's role is limited to appointing the Director, to determining his salary (with Treasury approval), and to the 'superintendence' of the Director.[25] The Attorney-General's consent is required before certain prosecutions

---

[18] Mackintosh, n. 6 above, p. 415.   [19] See Chapter 5.
[20] Jennings, n. 6 above, pp. 66–8.
[21] Keith Middlemas and John Barnes, *Baldwin* (1969), p. 174.
[22] Or the Foreign and Commonwealth Secretary for the Diplomatic List.
[23] In a House of Lords debate on the Report of the Royal Commission on Honours, Cmd. 1789 (1922), Lord Curzon went so far as to say that 'the idea that [the Prime Minister] should bring before the Cabinet the question of honours is one utterly foreign to our whole constitutional procedure': 53 H.L. Deb. 286–7 (7 March 1923).
[24] Prosecution of Offences Act 1985, Part I.   [25] Ibid., ss. 1(1)(a), 2(1), (3), 3(1).

may be started;[26] he may also enter a *nolle prosequi* to stop any prosecution. He is expected to exercise an independent judgement in all these matters, not dictated by his colleagues in the government, although naturally he may seek their views on any case which has implications which exceed the legal or judicial and which enter the political arena. So, for example, when the War Cabinet purported to give Sir Frederick Smith instructions about certain prosecutions during the First World War he vigorously protested at the impropriety of this action;[27] on the other hand, Sir Gordon Hewart properly consulted the Home Secretary in 1919 over a prosecution for sedition.[28] The danger inherent in the Cabinet exercising any influence over prosecution policy was manifest in the Campbell case in 1924, where it was assumed that the Attorney-General, Sir Patrick Hastings, had bent to Cabinet pressure in withdrawing a prosecution for sedition against the editor of the *Workers' Weekly*;[29] as a result a vote of censure was carried against the government.[30] The decision in 1985 to prosecute Mr Clive Ponting under section 2 of the Official Secrets Act 1911 for leaking confidential information about the sinking of the warship *General Belgrano* during the Falklands conflict aroused much controversy, but the Attorney-General was able to assert that it was his decision, not the Cabinet's.[31] Similarly, the Attorney-General's decision to request the Director of Public Prosecutions to investigate possible breaches of the Official Secrets Act 1911 arising out of a *New Statesman* article in 1987 on the background to a secret British intelligence satellite, 'Project Zircon', led to controversial searches of the

---

[26] For example, for offences under the Official Secrets Acts 1911 and 1989, the Prevention of Terrorism (Temporary Provisions) Act 1989, and the Public Order Acts 1936 and 1986.

[27] 177 H.C. Deb. 614–15 (8 October 1924).

[28] 177 H.C. Deb. 598–9 (8 October 1924), described by the then Attorney-General Sir Patrick Hastings.

[29] See J. Ll. J. Edwards, *The Law Officers of the Crown* (1964), chs. 10 and 11, and *The Attorney-General: Politics and the Public Interest* (1984), ch. 11; David Marquand, *Ramsay Mac-Donald* (1977), pp. 364–77, 385.

[30] 177 H.C. Deb. 581–704 (8 October 1924).

[31] See 73 H.C. Deb. 737–830 (18 February 1985). Mr Ponting was acquitted: *R. v. Ponting* [1985] *Criminal Law Review* 318; Clive Ponting, *The Right to Know* (1985). The decision not to prosecute Mr Chapman Pincher under the same section following publication of his book *Their Trade is Treachery* was, oddly, not taken by the Attorney-General, who insisted in 1986 that that fact be made publicly known. Sir Michael Havers—the longest-serving Attorney-General (1979–87) in modern times—was also reported in a colourful phrase to have threatened to 'send the police into No. 10 Downing Street' if there were no inquiry into the leak to the press of the Solicitor-General's letter to Mr Heseltine in 1985—a good example of an Attorney-General's independence from his ministerial colleagues. There was such an inquiry: see further n. 118 below and Chapter 7.

responsible journalist's home and of BBC headquarters in Glasgow, where a programme about 'Project Zircon' had been made. Questions were also raised about who in the government had asked or instructed whom to do what in the affair.[32] The prudent course for a Cabinet must be to leave responsibility for initiating and abandoning prosecutions to the Attorney-General, and to be reticent in offering him advice even if he asks for it.

Perhaps the best-known topic which is routinely and regularly handled so as to provide as little opportunity as possible for Cabinet discussion is the Budget. The Chancellor of the Exchequer's proposals are of major political importance, but they are only disclosed to the Cabinet on the morning of the day on which they are to be presented to the House of Commons;[33] for practical purposes, the Budget is presented to Ministers as a *fait accompli*. Indeed, the time at which the Cabinet is informed has changed so as to allow for only a minimum of Cabinet influence over the strategy and details of the Budget: by 1936 on average four or five days elapsed between the Budget Cabinet and the Chancellor's delivery to the Commons[34]—short enough, but better than today's delay of a few hours. The reason advanced to support this apparently cavalier treatment of the Cabinet is the need for secrecy: a practical effect is to put the government's economic and financial policy in the hands of the Chancellor of the Exchequer and the Prime Minister. Thus it is said that the less time there is between a Cabinet Minister hearing these secrets and the publication of them, the less chance there will be of a damaging leak, and it could be argued that since J. H. Thomas's regrettable lapse in 1936[35] no Cabinet Minister (other than the Chancellor himself, Hugh Dalton, in 1947)[36] has admitted to leaking any Budget secret. Would it be too cynical to ask what is so unique about Budget facts as to make Cabinet Ministers untrustworthy of them? Does anyone fear that Ministers will either openly leak any of them (for were they to do so

[32] See 109 H.C. Deb. 330 (written answers 29 January 1987), and the emergency debate on the matter at 109 H.C. Deb. 815–62 (3 February 1987). The Home Secretary said in that debate that 'questions of prosecutions are never discussed collectively between Ministers . . . [the Attorney-General] does not consult his colleagues—indeed, he debars himself from consulting his colleagues on any matter relating to a prosecution': ibid., col. 823. That is plainly not correct.

[33] The Chancellor of the Exchequer traditionally dines with the Queen the evening before and outlines his Budget to her. For an account of that dinner see Geoffrey Howe, *Conflict of Loyalty* (1994), p. 133.

[34] Sir Maurice Hankey's evidence to the Budget Disclosure Enquiry, Cd. 5184 (1936), Minutes of Evidence, p. 25.

[35] See Middlemas and Barnes, n. 21 above, p. 934; Gregory Blaxland, *J. H. Thomas: A Life for Unity* (1964), ch. 30.

[36] See Ben Pimlott, *Hugh Dalton* (1985), pp. 520–48.

they would, like Thomas and Dalton, lose their jobs) or use the information for personal financial gain?[37] It is odd that no modern Cabinet seems to have rebelled at a system which calls into question Ministers' honour, especially since the main source of unattributable leaks[38] in recent years has been Treasury Ministers themselves—an assertion for which the evidence is that only through such leaks could the accurate and detailed predictions appear in the media as they do almost routinely several days before each Budget statement. Cabinets have objected, certainly, but have not in the end kicked over the traces. In 1981, for instance, Sir Geoffrey Howe's Budget was rigidly deflationary and therefore highly controversial at a time of recession, but the strategy behind it was not discussed in the Cabinet, being revealed as usual to the Cabinet on Budget day itself, to the dismay of the Cabinet 'wets', whose protests, in the main, did not lead to changes, or to resignations.[39]

Now a number of correctives must be entered in order to avoid drawing a misleading picture about the background to the Budget. First, Cabinets have brought about changes of detail—although published instances are few and far between and do not amount to significant alterations in the structure of the relevant Budgets. For example, Mr James Prior claims that at the 1981 Budget Cabinet he and like-minded colleagues defeated the Chancellor's original proposal not to increase state retirement pensions in line with inflation, although significantly Mr Prior managed to convince the Prime Minister of the rightness of his case, thus making the Chancellor's defeat much easier.[40] Again, in his 1945 Budget, Dalton intended to make a change in the fuel oil tax but the Cabinet refused to accept it and the Chancellor deleted that item,[41] and in 1951 Hugh Gaitskell's idea for a differential fuel tax was dropped in view of the Cabinet's objections.[42] Selwyn Lloyd acceded to the Budget Cabinet's request in 1962 that he

---

[37] And the financing of social security *is* discussed in the Cabinet: see, for example, Richard Crossman, *Diaries of a Cabinet Minister*, vol. i (1975), pp. 34–5. Of course no one could improperly use information about that to influence the money markets or to make a personal financial gain.

[38] These are discussed later.

[39] Francis Pym, *The Politics of Consent* (1984), p. 18. Geoffrey Howe, n. 33 above, p. 133 goes so far as to say that the Budget Cabinet—at least in the early years of the Thatcher government—formed part of the 'dignified' rather than the 'efficient' side of the constitution.

[40] James Prior, *A Balance of Power* (1986), p. 130; Margaret Thatcher, *The Downing Street Years* (1993), p. 138 merely records that '[t]he dissenters in the Cabinet . . . had been stunned by the budget when they learnt its contents'.

[41] Hugh Dalton, *High Tide and After* (1962), p. 25.

[42] Harold Wilson, *The Governance of Britain* (1976), p. 59.

announce the early abolition of the tax on owner-occupiers.[43] Secondly, Chancellors can and do accept changes during the committee stage of the Finance Bill, presenting them as concessions to party opinion and to representations from interested groups: the opinions of their ministerial colleagues could be taken into account then as well as anyone else's. Thirdly, it is of course wrong to imagine that a Chancellor acts entirely outside the government's economic strategy or that he is immune to ministerial opinions offered during the pre-Budget purdah into which he goes some months before the Budget. (That condition was, in any case, liberalized by Mr Kenneth Clarke.) He will naturally frame his ideas within the government's overall policy, and Ministers will naturally speak and write privately to the Chancellor (especially to seek more money for their departments). He may not, therefore, always come to the Budget Cabinet with tablets of stone carved during a period of total deafness towards his colleagues. Fourthly, the disagreement caused by the 1981 Budget produced a procedural change: it was agreed that the Cabinet would in future meet each year for a full discussion on economic policy before the Chancellor went into purdah.[44] Lastly, it is possible—very occasionally—for the House of Commons itself to force a change to the Budget. This last happened in 1994, when the government was defeated by a few votes on the Chancellor's proposed increase in VAT on fuel: some Conservative MPs refused to support the government in the vote.[45] The government accepted the defeat.

The final area usually outside the Cabinet's formal decision-making is the timing of a recommended dissolution of Parliament. This was discussed in the previous chapter.

Cabinet committees and ministerial meetings[46]

There is nothing new in Prime Ministers using a few senior Ministers, rather than the whole Cabinet, to keep a general oversight of the government's progress and to deal with particular questions. In the 1929 Labour government MacDonald held informal weekly meetings with Henderson,

---

[43] D. R. Thorpe, *Selwyn Lloyd* (1989), pp. 333–4.
[44] Prior, n. 40 above, pp. 140–1. For a full description of the whole Budget exercise, see Nigel Lawson, *The View from Number 11* (1992), ch. 26.
[45] See 251 H.C. Deb. 243–7 (6 December 1994).
[46] Jennings, n. 6 above, pp. 255–61: Mackintosh, n. 6 above, pp. 521–9: Gordon Walker, n. 6 above, pp. 38–47; Wilson, n. 6 above, pp. 62–8.

Thomas, Snowden, and Clynes to discuss parliamentary business and Labour Party affairs,[47] and in the 'National Government' after Snowden's resignation in 1932 until MacDonald's retirement in 1935 the Prime Minister relied heavily on Thomas, Simon, Runciman, Baldwin, and Chamberlain.[48] During 1936 Baldwin kept four colleagues informed of the progress of his audiences with Edward VIII about the King's plans to marry.[49] In the following year his successor Chamberlain used the Foreign Policy Committee of the Cabinet, made up of nine or ten Ministers, to advise him on his approaches to the dictators; by 1938 he abandoned that Committee in favour of discussions with Halifax, Simon, and Hoare, the 'guilty men' of Munich.[50]

It is entirely natural that a Prime Minister should talk to those Ministers whom he finds particularly congenial about issues facing the government, sometimes formally as to an inner Cabinet[51] (like, for example, Harold Wilson's Parliamentary Committee of the Cabinet[52]), sometimes informally, perhaps late at night over a drink. It seems that, rather like Mrs Thatcher, Mr Blair prefers to deal directly with Ministers individually or in small, informal meetings. Such ways of doing business, however, raise important questions. One concerns the ability of a Prime Minister to divert decision-making away from the full Cabinet to a few selected Ministers, either leaving the Cabinet entirely out of account or presenting it with a decision which, for practical purposes, it can only ratify. As was indicated in the previous chapter and will be explained shortly, this has greatly enhanced the Prime Minister's authority over his Cabinet. Another question concerns the status of decisions arrived at outside the full Cabinet compared with decisions of that body, for that question of status has been frequently relied on to justify the astonishing secrecy which has shrouded Cabinet committees and other extra-Cabinet groups. And then there is the matter of definition: what exactly is a Cabinet committee, as distinct from any other ministerial meeting? It is that question which will be explored first.

The essential qualities of a Cabinet committee properly so called are that it is a committee of Ministers (which may include non-Cabinet and junior

---

[47] Marquand, n. 29 above, pp. 489–95.   [48] Marquand, n. 29 above, p. 737.

[49] As Baldwin was to tell the Commons: 318 H.C. Deb. 2180 (10 December 1936).

[50] Jennings, n. 6 above, pp. 241–2. Chamberlain did not consult that group or the Cabinet or any Cabinet committee before signing the Munich declaration in 1938.

[51] For a discussion of the terms 'inner' and 'partial' Cabinets, see Gordon Walker, n. 6 above, pp. 37–8, 88–91.

[52] This is considered below.

Ministers) established by the Prime Minister (whether or not chaired by him), with formal procedures and servicing by the Cabinet Secretariat. No grouping of Ministers will be a Cabinet committee unless (as with a Cabinet meeting) it is set up by the Prime Minister: there must be prime ministerial authority for a committee's existence. Cabinet committees follow procedures which are as formal as those of the Cabinet itself: each has a member of the Cabinet Secretariat assigned to it to be its secretary, and papers are circulated in the same way as for Cabinet meetings; minutes are kept, and if a committee's function is to report to the Cabinet, the chairman will do so, usually in writing. There is a further mark of recognition accorded to a Cabinet committee by the civil service: inclusion in the Cabinet Committee Book maintained by the Secretary of the Cabinet.

Three separate types of committee may be distinguished, ministerial, official, and mixed, only the first being a Cabinet committee proper. The ministerial committees are, in turn, of two sorts, standing and *ad hoc*. The best example of a standing ministerial committee is the Defence and Oversea Policy Committee,[53] which is concerned with defence and external affairs. It is standing in the sense that it exists on a permanent basis throughout any given administration and is not dissolved when that government leaves office (although its personnel will, of course, change). The Prime Minister is invariably in the chair because of the Committee's importance, and senior Cabinet Ministers will make up its membership. The Chiefs of Staff are invited to attend as required. Other examples of standing ministerial committees established under all governments will usually include a number on economic affairs (the main one, on economic strategy, normally being chaired by the Prime Minister); one on home affairs (which may take in social policy and education, as well as Home Office matters); legislation (which will consider departmental legislative proposals in principle, and arrange provisional priorities), and security.[54] *Ad hoc* Cabinet committees are established to deal with particular problems, and are disbanded when they have fulfilled the functions given to them: it is reasonable to assume that any important issue which falls for governmental

---

[53] The existence and usual composition of the Committee were announced in the White Paper 'Central Organization for Defence', Cmnd. 2097 (1963). Originally the Prime Minister, First Secretary of State, Home Secretary, Chancellor of the Exchequer, Secretary of State for Commonwealth Relations, and Secretary of State for Defence were envisaged as members: ibid., para. 16.

[54] There is a chart in Gordon Walker, n. 6 above, pp. 174–5 indicating the main standing ministerial committees from 1914 to 1964. Mackintosh, n. 6 above, pp. 521–9 gives some examples of such committees.

decision may be referred to an *ad hoc* committee if there is no relevant standing committee. Examples of these are legion.[55] Because all *ad hoc* committees are dissolved when a government resigns, inevitably to be replaced by its successor with another elaborate set, they are for ease of identity designated in one administration 'Gen' (for 'General') and then 'Misc' (for 'Miscellaneous') in the next. They are currently 'Misc'.[56] Then there are official committees, which consist of civil servants either to shadow ministerial committees or to do preparatory work for ministerial committees.[57] There will be at least as many official as ministerial committees. Lastly, there may be mixed committees of both Ministers and civil servants. These were tried in particular by Mr Heath during his premiership, but were largely dissolved by Mr Wilson. A well-publicized mixed committee, dubbed 'The Seminar', was used by Mr Callaghan from 1977 to 1979 to discuss sensitive and major decisions on interest rates and the level of sterling; it was made up of a few Cabinet Ministers and senior civil servants under the Prime Minister, and effectively took all the main decisions on those matters. Probably one of the few mixed committees still in existence is the Civil Contingencies Unit, which comes into play during industrial disputes which may threaten the essentials of life.[58]

There are sound machinery-of-government reasons which explain the growth of the Cabinet committee system. The full Cabinet cannot adequately cope with all questions which must be addressed by any government: pressure of business has required that a more efficient method of working be developed. Small committees of Ministers can settle preliminary issues so as to leave only fundamental points (or points of disagreement) for higher authority. Again, even with the merger of departments into the modern structure, problems do not always fall within the remit of any given department of state: it would be pointless to seek to tackle them within the four walls of one department: a committee of Ministers from several departments will frequently be needed. In short, good government requires a network of Cabinet committees.

That network has changed in various ways since 1945. Attlee inherited a complex scheme of committees on coming to power, and used it to help to implement Labour's programme. An attempt in 1946 to rationalize and

---

[55]   Examples are given in Mackintosh, n. 6 above.

[56]   Mr Blair gave limited details about four such committees at 307 H.C. Deb. 811 (written answers 6 March 1998).

[57]   Richard Crossman thought that it was through these official committees that 'Whitehall ensures that the Cabinet system is relatively harmless': n. 37 above, i. 198.

[58]   David Bonner, *Emergency Powers in Peacetime* (1985), pp. 29–35.

to reduce the number of committees was not very successful: by 1951 there were 148 standing and 313 *ad hoc* committees.[59] Lord Hunt of Tanworth has described Attlee's administration as 'government by committee—hundreds of them—rather than government by Cabinet'. He added: '[t]he system worked remarkably smoothly'.[60] Thus the general use of extra-Cabinet decision-making is not a recent phenomenon: it is at least 50 years old. Churchill, with his traditional view of Cabinet government, disliked working through bodies inferior to the Cabinet, apart from the Defence Committee.[61] He authorized an assault on Attlee's structure, as a result of which the number of standing committees was cut and the number of *ad hoc* committees halved.[62] Only with the premiership of Harold Wilson were any significant innovations made in the Cabinet committee system. He established the Parliamentary Committee of the Cabinet in 1968, presided over by him and consisting of some 10 Cabinet Ministers. (It was reduced to seven the following year.) It was serviced by the Cabinet Secretariat in the same way as any other Cabinet committee, but its terms of reference were vague: its declared purpose was to consider general political and parliamentary problems in a way that the whole Cabinet, through pressure of work, could not.[63] The Committee was not, however, continued in 1970 by Mr Heath, and there is no evidence of any subsequent resuscitation. Another alteration in procedure initiated by Harold Wilson was a rule that Cabinet committee papers could not be circulated to the full Cabinet if any dispute remained in the committee over facts. On the face of it a move to save Cabinet time, it actually had at least one political consequence: Douglas Jay's paper written as President of the Board of Trade asserting that British trade would suffer if the United Kingdom were to enter the European Economic Community was kept away from the Cabinet because some Ministers on the committee which was considering entry disputed some of Jay's facts.[64] The last of Mr Wilson's changes, again introduced in the spirit of greater efficiency, came towards the end of the 1964 government. In a 1970 'Minute on Cabinet Committee Procedure'[65]

---

[59] Peter Hennessy and Andrew Arends, *Mr Attlee's Engine Room: Cabinet Committee Structure and the Labour Governments 1945–51* (1983), Strathclyde Papers on Government and Politics, No. 26.

[60] Quoted in Peter Hennessy, *Cabinet* (1986) p. 38.

[61] Anthony Seldon, *Churchill's Indian Summer: The Conservative Government 1951–1955* (1981), p. 117.

[62] Hennessy, n. 60 above, p. 50.   [63] Gordon Walker, n. 6 above, pp. 45–6.

[64] Mackintosh, n. 6 above, p. 528. The rule still exists: see *Ministerial Code* (Cabinet Office, 1997), para. 4.

[65] Quoted by Crossman, n. 37 above, iii. 861.

the Prime Minister decreed that if a Minister on a committee were dissatisfied with a committee decision, then he could only take the dispute to the Cabinet with the consent of the committee's chairman. Mr Wilson thought that far too many 'appeals' had been conducted and he believed that the chairmen, as experienced Ministers, would know when a disagreement was so politically sensitive that consent should be given, and the rule survives today.[66] In his turn Mr Heath reduced the number of Cabinet committees[67] and also designated some committees 'task forces' so as to allow senior civil servants full membership without disturbing the traditional Whitehall concept of Cabinet committees. So, for example, on the introduction of a prices and incomes policy, a 'task force', not a Cabinet committee, was established to supervise it, consisting not only of the Prime Minister and four senior economic Ministers, but also of Sir William Armstrong of the Civil Service Department and Ronald Mackintosh of the Treasury.[68] Too much should not be made of this development, for the line which divides civil servants who are merely invited to attend Cabinet committees for particular items from persons enjoying full membership may be more apparent than real, and the Chiefs of Staff have attended the Defence and Oversea Policy Committee as required (which could mean for most of the time).

It is generally assumed that Mrs Thatcher significantly downgraded the status of the full Cabinet. What is the evidence? Her Cabinet met only once a week, but that has been the case since the 1960s.[69] More importantly, we have it on the authority of Lord Howe that there were very few discussions of government decisions by the full Cabinet.[70] According to Peter Hennessy the number of standing Cabinet committees was reduced by Mrs Thatcher to between 30 and 35, and ad hoc committees to about 120: under Attlee the corresponding figures were 148 and 313.[71] Clearly the extent of governmental responsibility cannot have declined to the extent that weekly Cabinets and the smallest number of Cabinet committees since before the Second World War could efficiently discharge it. It is reasonably clear that Mrs Thatcher made much greater use of discussions in small, informal groups of Ministers—not Cabinet committees, and without civil

[66] Wilson, n. 6 above, pp. 65–6; see *Ministerial Code*, para. 5.
[67] An indication of some of his committees was published in *The Times*, 3 May 1973.
[68] Mackintosh, n. 6 above, p. 516.   [69] See Chapter 5.
[70] Interview in the *Daily Mail*, 6 February 1984. Almost 30 years before W. J. M. Mackenzie and J. W. Grove had written that 'Much Cabinet business is now almost formal'; *Central Administration in Britain* (1957), p. 339.
[71] Hennessy, n. 60 above, p. 101.

service presence—and that Ministers in general used direct interdepartmental correspondence to seek opinions and to arrive at decisions
outside any more formal machinery.[72] An example of that method of
working cited by Mr Hennessy[73] concerns Mr Michael Heseltine's minute
'It Took a Riot' in 1981, in which he urged greater government investment in the inner cities after the riots of that year. Mrs Thatcher convened
an informal ministerial group, with a majority of members chosen by the
Prime Minister who would be unsympathetic towards Mr Heseltine's
proposals. The extra spending which was ultimately authorized was on
nothing like the scale urged by Mr Heseltine.[74] Now although it is generally
acknowledged that Mr Major reverted to a more collegiate and traditional
system of government, it remained open to him and his successors to use
Mrs Thatcher's methods if it suited them, and indeed Mr Blair appears to
have done so.

All this directly raises the question of whether and if so how the increase
in extra-Cabinet decision-making has enhanced prime ministerial power.
Richard Crossman was convinced that the Cabinet committee system, particularly ad hoc committees, allowed the Prime Minister to get his own way
more than he would through the full Cabinet. Thus he wrote in 1970 that
the device of setting up hundreds of ad hoc committees to deal with specific
problems, bypassing the relevant standing Cabinet committees, was important in helping Mr Wilson obtain decisions acceptable to him, primarily
because he packed those committees with Ministers having views similar to
his own.[75] Crossman also thought that the position of individual Ministers

---

[72] Lord Hailsham has testified to Mrs Thatcher's use of such groups. He believes that her
manner of working 'undermines the collegiate character of the Cabinet', and that it is 'handy'
for her because it 'reduces the discussions' in the Cabinet: see (1987) 1 *Contemporary Record* 58.
He developed his views in the Granada Guildhall Lecture 1987. Mr Prior goes so far as to say
(n. 40 above, p. 133) that, since 1982, 'she has adopted ad hoc groups as one of her main methods
of government . . . [T]he formal Cabinet committees were very much downgraded and she
began to operate very much in small groups dominated by her cronies . . . This had obvious
advantages for those few on the "inside track", who came to regard meetings with their other
colleagues as increasingly unnecessary and time-wasting. But it is not at all good for the many,
including Cabinet Ministers, who are on the outside and who believe ad hoc groups can be
weighted against them in the way Cabinet cannot': ibid., pp. 132–3. Mr Norman Fowler
averred that 'most of the Government's decisions on future policy were taken at committee
level. All the proposals then went to the full Cabinet, but it was difficult for anyone not on the
relevant committee successfully to challenge the policy': see *Ministers Decide* (1991), p. 120.

[73] Hennessy, n. 60 above, p. 102.

[74] Crucial decisions on Falkland Islands policy, the banning of trade unions at Government Communications Headquarters, and the American request to use British bases from
which to bomb Libya, were also taken by Mrs Thatcher and small groups of Ministers.

[75] Crossman, n. 37 above, iii. 860–1. Ministers generally had little idea of the scope or

had been weakened by the 1970 rule limiting appeals from committees to the Cabinet.[76] The use of committees (especially the *ad hoc* variety) must certainly entail advantages for a Prime Minister over his Cabinet. First, it is the Prime Minister who has virtually absolute power over Cabinet committees. He alone decides whether to establish a particular committee at all. If he decides to do so, he decides on membership and who is to be its chairman,[77] within the limits of political prudence excluding those who might not further his own preferred solutions. He alone can decide on the terms of reference. He can (like Mr Wilson) lay down rules which restrict access from committees to the Cabinet. He can give a committee executive powers. He alone decides whether to wind up a committee. Secondly, the use of committees and informal ministerial meetings will in certain circumstances reduce the power of the Cabinet. Decisions taken by such bodies may be tantamount to a final Cabinet decision even if that decision goes to the Cabinet for approval. After all, the issue will have been examined minutely, frequently with access to expert official advice; those Ministers on the committee will often have relevant departmental expertise so that respect will naturally be accorded to their views by the rest of the Cabinet; the committee or group will strive to be unanimous, for if it cannot compromise the Cabinet would be unlikely to either; a Minister who sought to hold up the smooth running of a Cabinet meeting by insisting on a return to the first principles of an issue could not count on being popular, and a non-member of the committee or group might want to give its recommendations a clear run so that, when his turn came, the proposals of his committee or group might be accorded an equally clear run.

Now such assertions have been denied. Harold Wilson has described this view of prime ministerial power exercised through Cabinet committees as being, for two reasons, 'facile'.[78] A Prime Minister, he wrote, could not try to go against a unanimous decision of a Cabinet committee of seven or eight Ministers. That, however, sidesteps the Prime Minister's life-giving power over such committees already outlined, especially the fact that he chooses whom to put on the committees in the first place. Harold Wilson

---

indeed the existence of Cabinet committees: see Tony Benn, *Conflicts of Interest: Diaries 1977–1980* (1990), pp. 338–9.

[76] Ibid. Gordon Walker, n. 6 above, p. 44, viewed the 1970 change merely as a way to relieve pressure on the Cabinet.

[77] During Mr Callaghan's administration the Cabinet Energy Committee was chaired by the Secretary of State for Industry, Mr Varley, rather than the Secretary of State for Energy, Mr Benn: *New Statesman*, 21 July 1978.

[78] Wilson, n. 6 above, p. 65.

also prayed in aid Lord Blake to underline the benign nature of the committee system: Lord Blake had written that it 'strengthens—by making more efficient—the Cabinet itself'.[79] That, in its turn, does not do justice to the ways indicated earlier in which the Cabinet's own decision-making power can be diminished by that system. Gordon Walker made assertions similar to Lord Blake's, but offered no explanation or evidence.[80]

Some of the above is still necessarily speculative. This is because the Cabinet committee system is a holy of holies to which only the Prime Minister and the Cabinet Secretary as its high priests have total access. Before 1992 no official list had been published of even the standing committees, their chairmen, members, or terms of reference. Up to then only two official revelations had been made since 1945 about the mystery. In 1963 the existence and membership of the Defence and Oversea Policy Committee was announced in a White Paper on the reorganization of the Ministry of Defence and the abolition of the three Service Ministries[81]—a curious (though welcome) piece of government openness given that the Committee deals with the most secret matters. Then in 1979 Mrs Thatcher confirmed the existence of four key standing committees,[82] Defence and Oversea Policy, Economic Strategy,[83] Home and Social Affairs, and the Legislation Committee. The rest was silence. Why?

For Jennings the main justification for keeping Cabinet committees more secret than the Cabinet itself was that, if information were made available about particular committees, the responsibility of individual Ministers could be undermined. If the identity of a committee chairman became known, and if (as is usual) he had a number of departmental Ministers in his committee, 'the chairman, and not the departmental Minister, will be regarded as the expositor of Government policy'. Jennings thought that the danger had materialized in Churchill's ministerial overlord experiment.[84] Are there not two difficulties inherent in his reasoning?

---

[79] *The Office of Prime Minister* (1975), p. 53.

[80] See n. 6 above, p. 46.   [81] Cmnd. 2097 (1963).

[82] 967 H.C. Deb. 179 (written answers 24 May 1979), repeated at 45 H.C. Deb. 7–8 (written answers 4 July 1983). The reason which prompted these answers is unclear. The terms of reference of a ministerial group on women's issues were announced in 1990: see 178 H.C. Deb. 276 (written answers 25 October 1990); the existence of a ministerial group on the environment was disclosed in Cm. 1200 (1990).

[83] Mr Prior says that he won approval for his step-by-step approach to trade union reform in the Economic Strategy Committee, against the views of the Chancellor of the Exchequer, Sir Geoffrey Howe, who preferred a return to the wholesale approach which had been taken in the Industrial Relations Act 1971.

[84] Jennings, n. 6 above, p. 256. On the overlords, see Chapter 7.

First, the Minister who will carry the can for the committee's decisions will be the one who has to defend it in Parliament: *that* is where the responsibility of a particular Minister will bite, not against whoever might have been the committee chairman. Secondly, Jennings's view of committees is too narrow; many committees straddle several departments, and there could at the committee stage be no obvious departmental Minister who would bear primary responsibility for conclusions. For Sir Burke Trend, giving evidence as Cabinet Secretary to the Franks Committee on section 2 of the Official Secrets Act 1911,[85] the justification for secrecy turned not on individual but on collective responsibility: it was essential that a government's decisions were perceived as being those of the Cabinet as a whole, not merely those of a group of Ministers. So if, for instance, it were known that a certain decision had been taken in a committee, then the impression could be created that named Ministers not on the committee were dissociated from it, or on the contrary that Ministers who had been on the committee were especially and closely associated with it.[86] It is hard to see why that objection would not be met by official confirmation of the obvious—that modern governments must work through Cabinet committees if administration is to be efficiently carried out, and that whether committees act for the Cabinet, or whether their recommendations are ratified by the Cabinet, the result is policy for which the whole Cabinet is responsible. The Trend worries seem based on the belief that the interested citizen would be unable to grasp that simple fact.

The most comprehensive prime ministerial statement of the reasons for secrecy over Cabinet committees is contained in Mr Callaghan's personal minute of 1978, *Disclosure of Cabinet Committees*.[87] Those reasons may be summarized in nine points; brief comments will be offered on each. (a) 'The manner of deciding policy questions is essentially a domestic one for any government.' This is a singularly unconvincing, if not coy, reason because Cabinet committees and the like attract legitimate interest as vital aspects of the machinery of government. As Gordon Walker put it,[88] the

---

[85] Report, Cmnd. 5104 (1972), Minutes of Evidence, iii. 324–6.

[86] Memorandum from the Cabinet Office to the Franks Committee, para. 5. This justification was also given by Mrs Thatcher as Prime Minister to the Commons: see 974 H.C. Deb. 450 (written answers 26 November 1979).

[87] This was leaked and published in the *New Statesman*, 10 November 1978. It is published in full in Colin Turpin's *British Government and the Constitution: Text, Cases and Materials* (2nd edn., 1990), pp. 174–5. It is not insignificant that there is no mention of Cabinet committees in Mr Callaghan's memoirs.

[88] See n. 6 above, p. 45.

public has a right to know at least the organization of the Cabinet and Cabinet committee system given their central role in the way the public is governed. (b) 'The status of a decision could be disputed if it were acknowledged to have been reached by a committee rather than by the full Cabinet.' That is essentially Sir Burke Trend's reason already doubted above. (c) 'The existence of some committees could not be disclosed for reasons of national security.' Within an understanding of national security somewhat narrower than that promulgated by the government in recent years, that must be right.[89] (d) 'The absence of a committee on a particular subject, such as poverty, does not mean that the government attaches no importance to it;' (e) 'the existence in particular of ad hoc committees should not be disclosed because they are ephemeral'. Both those points could be fully met by official explanation—and, in relation to the former, by a government's deeds in relation to the subject-matter. (f) 'Disclosure could reveal that sensitive things were under discussion,' and (g) 'that something was in train about which the government was not ready to make an announcement'. Now both points are really indirect ways of saying that publicity would be inconvenient for a government, as MPs and others might want to contribute to the arguments before a policy was agreed. (h) 'Disclosure of standing committees alone would give a misleading picture.' That could, again, be met by explanation, or by disclosure of all committees (national security permitting). (i) 'Any departure from the convention of non-disclosure would be more likely to whet appetites than to satisfy them.' That phrase encapsulates the regrettable view adopted by civil servants and Ministers down the decades that secrecy is the norm, information and explanation the exception.

Happily, Mr John Major greatly improved matters in 1992. Following a manifesto commitment, he authorized the publication of a list of Cabinet committees[90] and of the document *Questions of Procedure for Ministers.*[91]

[89] The definition of the term 'national security' as understood by the Prime Minister in 1988 was taken 'to refer to the safeguarding of the state and the community against threats to their survival or well-being': 126 H.C. Deb. 7 (written answers 25 January 1988). Some sensitive economic matters would also require that the existence of any *ad hoc* committee on them would not be acknowledged.

[90] Ministerial Committees of the Cabinet: Membership and Terms of Reference (Cabinet Office, 1992). See also 208 H.C. Deb. 110–18 (written answers 19 May 1992); 218 H.C. Deb. 46–7 (written answers 1 February 1993); 250 H.C. Deb. 89–96 (written answers 22 November 1994); 263 H.C. Deb. 1005–1012 (18 July 1995). Mr Major later announced the setting up of a further standing committee (on Public Expenditure), and of an *ad hoc* ministerial group (on refugees from former Yugoslavia): see 218 H.C. Deb 46–7 (written answers 1 February 1993, and 237 H.C. Deb. 405–13 (10 February 1994).

[91] 208 H.C. Deb. 394 (written answers 2 June 1992).

According to that list there were 15 standing Cabinet committees (dubbed Ministerial Committees[92]) and nine sub-committees. The former included committees on Economic and Domestic Policy, Defence and Oversea Policy, Northern Ireland, Home and Social Affairs, Queen's Speeches and Future Legislation, Legislation, and Environment. The latter group embraced sub-committees on European Questions, Eastern Europe, Terrorism, London, Drug Misuse, and so on. So far, so good. But the published terms of reference were bland and uninformative, and the list is far from complete: it leaves out the many *ad hoc* committees which are so important in shaping government policy. And the Prime Minister subsequently announced that he would not publish details of the topics discussed by individual committees, the timing of meetings, or their proceedings. Mr Blair followed that policy on coming to power in 1997. He republished *Questions of Procedure for Ministers* as the *Ministerial Code*, and he published a list of the Cabinet committees which he had set up, along with their terms of reference and membership.[93] There were 13 Cabinet committees and eight sub-committees in his first government: the former included the Defence and Oversea Policy Committee, and committees on Constitutional Reform, Home and Social Affairs, the Queen's Speeches and Future Legislation, and on Legislation.[94]

Confidentiality of proceedings and papers[95]

Obviously the Cabinet and its committees must be able to deliberate in private and with some certainty that neither their proceedings nor their papers will be made public immediately. They could not function on any other basis. What are the main legal and conventional means by which that position is maintained?

It used to be thought that the Privy Counsellor's oath[96] was a legal check

---

[92] The term 'Ministerial Committee' might have been adopted in preference to 'Cabinet committee' to indicate that specified non-Cabinet Ministers are full members.

[93] 295 H.C. Deb. 302–310 (written answers 9 June 1997); *Ministerial Code*, paras. 3–5, 8–18.

[94] The list is on the Cabinet Office website.

[95] See generally R. Brazier, *Ministers of the Crown* (1997), ch. 17.2.

[96] The relevant part of that oath is set out in the Report of the Radcliffe Committee on Ministerial Memoirs, Cmnd. 6386 (1976), para. 21. See also Rodney Brazier, *Constitutional Texts* (1990), p. 294. Oddly, in 1994 the then Lord President of the Council refused to publish the oath in a parliamentary answer on the basis of a convention that the terms of the oath are confidential: see 238 H.C. Deb. 59 (written answers 21 February 1994). That error was corrected by his Labour successor.

preventing disclosure by Ministers of what happened in the Cabinet.[97] In part the Privy Counsellor swears (or affirms) in terms established in Elizabethan times that he 'will keep secret all matters committed and revealed unto [him], or that shall be treated of secretly in Council'. But a literal interpretation of those words does not support that earlier belief, for the Cabinet is not the Privy Council, nor a committee of it: as the Radcliffe Committee on Ministerial Memoirs acknowledged, the Cabinet is a body distinct from the Privy Council.[98] Nor was the oath relied on by the Attorney-General in the Crossman diaries case in seeking to restrain their publication.[99] Before its repeal in 1989, the Official Secrets Act 1911, section 2,[100] probably could not have been used either to prosecute Cabinet Ministers who disclosed Cabinet proceedings.[101] Mr Crossman originally thought that, if he were to persist in his plan to publish revelations about his ministerial life after his resignation, he might be prosecuted under section 2; but the Prime Minister and the Cabinet Secretary told him in 1969 that their legal advice was that section 2 could not be used in that way.[102] The Radcliffe Committee, in a one-sentence paragraph,[103] recorded that no Minister or former Minister had been prosecuted under the Official Secrets Act and clearly considered that fact to have legal significance. The reason for this ministerial immunity seems to have been that, as the Franks Report on section 2 of the Official Secrets Act put it, 'Ministers are, in effect, self-authorizing. They decide for themselves what to reveal'.[104] Section 2 made

---

[97] For example, by Jennings, n. 6 above, pp. 228–9: although he wrote by reference to other factors which produce ministerial discretion, he clearly thought that the oath itself had some legal effect.

[98] Cmnd. 6386 (1976), para. 22.

[99] *Attorney-General* v. *Jonathan Cape Ltd*. [1976] Q. B. 752.

[100] In summary, s. 2 made it an offence, punishable with up to two years' imprisonment, to retain without permission, or fail to take reasonable care of, information obtained as a result of one's present or former employment under the Crown or a government contract; or to *communicate* information so obtained, or entrusted to one in confidence by a person holding office under Her Majesty, or obtained in contravention of the Act, to anybody other than a person to whom one was authorized to convey it or to whom it was one's duty to impart it in the interests of the State; or to *receive* such information, knowing or having reasonable cause to believe that it had been given in contravention of the Act.

[101] Others who received information from a Minister could have been prosecuted, although this happened only rarely. For example, Edgar Lansbury was prosecuted under s. 2 for publishing memoranda which had been submitted to the Cabinet by his father George Lansbury (who had been First Commissioner of Works in the 1929 Labour Cabinet): George Lansbury was not prosecuted: Sir William Anson, *The Law and Custom of the Constitution* (4th edn., 1935), ii. 122.

[102] Crossman, n. 37 above, iii. 898–9.   [103] Cmnd. 6386 (1976), para. 26.

[104] Cmnd. 5104 (1972), para. 18. Former versions of *Questions of Procedure for Ministers* indicated that Ministers were invited soon after appointment to sign a declaration that they had

it an offence (among 2,323 other crimes)[105] to communicate information to anybody other than a person to whom one was authorized to convey it; and Ministers were assumed to have been able to authorize themselves to do so. (Assuming that to have been a correct view of the law, it is not easy to see why anyone who had resigned office might have authorized himself to disclose information, unless, perhaps, the very generous view was taken that as he had been authorized to communicate lawfully while in office, then there was no reason to deny him that facility out of office.)

The Official Secrets Acts 1989 might, unlike its 1911 predecessor, inhibit publication by former Ministers. Section 2 of the 1911 statute was repealed by the 1989 Act. That Act (so far as relevant here) permits disclosure of information covered by its terms where such disclosure is made by a Minister (as a Crown servant) 'if, and only if, it is made in accordance with his official duty.' Disclosure in accordance with that duty would constitute a defence to any prosecution brought under the Act.[106] Now, however those provisions may affect a Minister in office,[107] a *former* Minister is not a Crown servant and has no official duty by virtue of which he could disclose information acquired while in government. Indeed, the Act refers in places[108] to a person 'who is or has been a Crown servant', and where the Act does so an ex-Minister would clearly be at risk of prosecution for disclosure in appropriate cases. Such a situation might well never arise:[109] but a former Minister who chooses not to submit a manuscript to the Cabinet Office would be in danger that he might commit a criminal offence if he were to make a 'damaging disclosure' (as the Act puts it) on (say) defence or international relations of which he had knowledge while in office. Perhaps the Official Secrets Act 1989 has added a new terror to publishing, and ex-Ministers will have to be careful to see that their literary efforts do not contravene the Act.

---

read the relevant provisions of the Official Secrets Acts. The reason for this is rather obscure in the light of the Radcliffe and Franks Reports, and no mention was made of it in the 1992 version of *Questions of Procedure*, or in the current *Ministerial Code*.

[105] Ibid., Minutes of Evidence, ii. 262 (appendix of evidence of the Bar Council).

[106] See ss. 7(1), 12(1). Information protected by the Act is described in ss. 1–6.

[107] Indeed, what of the leaking, either by a Minister or by a civil servant with his permission, of information to which the Act applies, or 'briefing' about such information (about which see below)? As Ministers of all parties regularly leak and brief, might it be argued that they do so in accordance with their official duty?

[108] See ss. 2 (defence), 3 (international relations), and 4 (crime and special investigation powers).

[109] The police and the Crown Prosecution Service might decide not to start a prosecution, which in any case would need to be conducted by the Attorney-General or with his consent: s. 9.

The principles established in *Attorney-General* v. *Jonathan Cape Ltd.*[110] could, however, be relied on in an appropriate case to prevent by injunction a Minister from disclosing Cabinet and other official discussions. The Lord Chief Justice there held that the courts have power to prevent such publication if it would be a breach of confidence and against the public interest by prejudicing the maintenance of the doctrine of collective responsibility. He also held that a Minister could be restrained, if need be indefinitely, from making any publication which would adversely affect national security.[111] On the facts the Attorney-General was denied an injunction because the first volume of the diaries complained of dealt with events which had taken place 10 years before: the confidential nature of the material had ceased to exist—there would be no breach of confidence—and no issue of national security arose.

The significance of legal restraints, though, should not be exaggerated. Ministers do not keep secrets through fear of injunctions, and indeed, as will be mentioned shortly, they make disclosures regularly while in office. To the extent that they feel bound to keep matters confidential they do so for conventional reasons: the weight of tradition (and the tradition of governmental secrecy is very strong), loyalty to their colleagues, a desire not to inhibit frank discussion, and the ultimate political threat—dismissal. True, there are also the guidelines recommended by the Radcliffe Committee[112] and accepted by the then government,[113] to which the overwhelming majority of Ministers and ex-Ministers have adhered since 1976 (subject to a major proviso about leaking). Those guidelines require that at least 15 years should elapse before certain types of material should be disclosed, and the guidelines continue the practice under which a former Minister wishing to publish material derived from his time in office should submit the full text in advance to the Cabinet Secretary, who will check that it is in line with the Radcliffe guidelines. And the Prime Minister of the day is the final court of appeal over national security and external relations matters, so that indefinite secrecy may be enjoined. Those guidelines have not, however, been followed by a number of former Ministers:[114] the public interest is,

---

[110] [1976] Q.B. 752. See also Hugo Young, *The Crossman Affair* (1976).

[111] Ibid., at p. 770.   [112] Cmnd. 6386 (1976).

[113] The government agreed that legislation on the matter would not be wise and that the obligations should be binding on Ministers as a matter of honour: 903 H.C. Deb. 521–3 (written answers 22 January 1976). According to Mr Wilson's former Senior Policy Adviser, the Cabinet Secretary tried to persuade the Prime Minister to insist that Ministers bind themselves more restrictively than the Radcliffe Committee had proposed. See Bernard Donoughue, n. 6 above, pp. 123–4.

[114] Notably by Crossman's literary executors, and by Barbara Castle, *The Castle Diaries*

perhaps, also served by the full inside story of any administration coming into the public domain sooner rather than later, and publishers are eager that such accounts should do so.

In all this there is a wide gap between constitutional myth and political reality. The myth is that for conventional (and perhaps legal) reasons Ministers maintain a discreet silence about all government secrets, so that problems over disclosure do not arise until they wish to publish memoirs after registration. But the reality is that Ministers—and Prime Ministers—'brief' and 'leak' while in office. Attention will now be turned to that issue.

From time to time Ministers will want their views publicly known so as to distance themselves from any Cabinet decision with which they do not agree: they may thus let their supporters know their views, and perhaps mobilize opinion against that decision: to do so they make an 'unattributable leak', they 'brief'—it comes to the same thing.[115] This has taken place for decades. For such a leak to happen a journalist will be given information on the condition that he does not reveal its source. The Minister's purposes are served and the journalist gets his story: it is a symbiotic relationship which has the advantage that the public is better informed than otherwise might be the case. Two well-known examples may be briefly cited. After the devaluation of the pound in 1967 there were several press stories showing how the Cabinet had divided over the consequent economic cuts; and in the early years of Mrs Thatcher's government the economic 'wets' made sure that their case was known outside the Cabinet even if (or especially because) they were to lose the argument there. Prime Ministers have

---

1974–1976 (1980), and Hugh Jenkins, *The Culture Gap* (1979). Mr James Prior felt that the contents of his *A Balance of Power* 'did not justify submission' of the text to the Cabinet Secretary—although it is a book of memoirs. Mr Pym's *The Politics of Consent* was not submitted as it is 'a treatise on politics'. Mr Callaghan's memoirs were, however, vetted. I am grateful to those last three named authors who kindly answered my queries about this. Lady Thatcher resisted some of the suggested cuts to her memoirs. See also the exchanges at 562 H.C. Deb. 341–3 (2 November 1989); Brazier, n. 95 above, ch. 17.2. Thirteen former Ministers submitted manuscripts to the Cabinet Secretary in the two-year period 1989–91: see 194 H.C. Deb. 16–17 (1 July 1991).

[115] As Mr Callaghan helpfully explained, 'Briefing is what I do and leaking is what you do': evidence to the Franks Committee, Cmnd. 5104 (1972), Minutes of Evidence, iv. 187. Crossman recorded in his diary in 1969: 'People brief against each other, letting malicious stories out about who does what. There is a difference between these malicious and damaging announcements and the things I do, which are all designed to put the Government in a decent light': Crossman, n. 37 above, iii. 583. No doubt his tongue was firmly in his cheek. There was notorious competitive leaking during the Westland affair in 1985–86 by Ministers, the majority of whom favoured an American rescue of the helicopter firm, the minority favouring a European solution. See also J. A. G. Griffith and M. Ryle, *Parliament: Functions, Practice and Procedures* (1989), pp. 79–80.

become past masters of the game: the appointment after the Second World War of a Press Officer at Number 10 Downing Street 'made the leak in a sense normal and almost official'.[116] The process developed further under Mrs Thatcher at the hands of her Press Secretary Mr Bernard Ingham.[117] For according to Mr James Prior she was the most adept Prime Minister at handling the press since 1945,[118] and in Mr Francis Pym's view, '[t]he notorious leaks have emanated as much from Downing Street as from anywhere else. The press receives a very good service from Number 10, which is perhaps why so much of it is so uncritical'.[119] Prime Ministers work with the Westminster Lobby system, to which journalists are accredited and through which the Downing Street Press Secretary can twice a day put the Prime Minister's version of events on an unattributable basis. (Mr Blair's Chief Press Secretary, however, conducts some parts of his briefings on an attributable basis.) This is 'briefing', the more respectable form of 'leaking'—after all, the Lobby is formally organized, has rules, and even officers, keeping sources secret on their words as gentlemen.

A day rarely passes without some item in the newspapers giving details of Cabinet or Cabinet committee business which could only have been obtained by a leak. Leaking is periodically and hypocritically condemned by Prime Ministers and Ministers; sometimes leak inquires and set up under the Cabinet Secretary; civil servants and Ministers are questioned; usually nothing comes of them.[120]

In this examination of Cabinet confidentiality Cabinet papers call for separate treatment. Such papers include Cabinet and Cabinet committee agendas, memoranda, minutes, and reports, and papers originating from departments with Ministers' views and civil service advice.[121] The special issues to be canvassed here are the restraints which exist on publication of

---

[116] Gordon Walker, n. 6 above, p. 31. As the Lord Privy Seal was to put in 1988, 'unattributable briefings are one of the techniques widely employed in this country and elsewhere to communicate information': 502 H.L. Deb. 667 (8 December 1988).

[117] Mr Prior claims that she even leaked against her own Cabinet and quotes an example from a newspaper which resulted from it: 'Premier Margaret Thatcher routed the "wets" in her Cabinet yesterday in a major showdown over public spending. She waded into the attack . . .': Prior, n. 40 above, p. 135. See generally Bernard Ingham, *Kill the Messenger* (1992).

[118] Prior, n. 40 above, p. 134. See also Michael Cockerell, Peter Hennessy, and David Walker, *Sources Close to the Prime Minister* (1984).

[119] Pym, n. 39 above, p. 18.

[120] An exception was the Cabinet Secretary's inquiry into the leak to the Press Association of parts of the Solicitor-General's letter to Mr Heseltine in 1985 during the Westland affair, which eventually caused Mr Brittan to resign from the government.

[121] In 1977, 1,800 such papers were circulated to all members of the Cabinet. I am grateful to Mr Tony Benn for that fact.

such papers additional to those already mentioned, the access which former Ministers have to papers which they saw when in office, and whether a government has any right to see its predecessor's papers.

Cabinet documents are the property of the Crown. Anyone who wishes to reproduce any part of them when they are still in copyright is subject to the Copyright, Designs and Patents Act 1988, so that publication of Cabinet papers could be actionable as being in breach of the Crown's copyright. As far as former Ministers refreshing their memories are concerned,[122] they will have been asked on leaving office to leave for their successors Cabinet documents needed for current administration and to return all others to the Cabinet Office.[123] They may, however, at any time thereafter have access in the Cabinet Office to Cabinet papers issued to them while they were in office, although they may not retain them.[124] This sensible arrangement allows former Ministers to write and broadcast more authoritatively, subject to the limitations already noted. Access to one government's papers by a successor is governed by understandings explained by a former Cabinet Secretary, Lord Hunt of Tanworth.[125] They are that (a) Ministers may not see the Cabinet papers of a previous government of a different party, because they may wish to use them for party political capital; (b) Ministers may normally see the papers of previous administrations of the same party, provided the need to do so arises out of normal ministerial duties; and (c) in any case the current Prime Minister seeks the approval of the former Prime Minister concerned (or, if he is not available, the current Leader of the relevant party) for access to the papers of the previous government. Classes of papers excluded from these understandings include documents deemed to be in the public domain (such as Ministers' letters to MPs), papers sent to foreign governments (for example, concerning bilateral negotiations), and Law Officers' opinions (which are not political documents).[126] Those excluded papers may be seen freely by successor governments regardless of party. In all this the object of the civil service is to judge what papers may properly be shown to Ministers without causing political embarrassment to former Ministers.[127]

---

[122] See generally Lord Hunt of Tanworth, 'Access to a Previous Government's Papers' [1982] *Public Law* 514.

[123] *Ministerial Code*, para. 19, and Brazier, n. 95 above, ch. 17.2.

[124] The rule used to be that such papers could not be removed from the Cabinet Office. But two former Prime Ministers, Sir Edward Heath and Lady Thatcher, have been allowed to take their papers home for consultation while writing their memoirs, and to return them in due course.

[125] See n. 122 above.   [126] Lord Hunt, n. 122 above, p. 516.

[127] Cabinet documents may also be protected from disclosure in litigation by a claim that such disclosure would be contrary to the public interest.

Conclusions

In the previous chapter it was postulated that the Prime Minister's power has increased in relation to the rest of his colleagues. In this chapter it has been explained how that process has been accelerated by the development of ministerial decision-making away from the Cabinet as a whole. The Cabinet in its classical form as the supreme organ of administration, executing policies prescribed (or acquiesced in) by Parliament, has become a dignified element in the constitution; the structure of Cabinet committees and *ad hoc* ministerial groupings which occasionally in name and sometimes in effect decide government policy is the efficient part. It is true that from time to time the Cabinet may assert itself as of old to seek to restrain, or to limit the damage done by, the unacceptable exercise of prime ministerial power. It is also true that, as the style and authority of Prime Ministers vary, so the Cabinet as a whole will occasionally move nearer to the centre of the political stage, as it did under Mr Major. Perhaps for both those reasons developments since 1945 should not cause undue concern.

7

MINISTERS AND DEPARTMENTS

Ministerial titles[1]

The titles enjoyed by Ministers in the British government must baffle foreigners (and a few Britons). Some titles are very old and give no clue to the holders' present ministerial responsibilities, such as the Lord Privy Seal or the Chancellor of the Duchy of Lancaster. The ministerial head of a department of state may be called a Secretary of State or (rarely, nowadays) a Minister; his deputy may occasionally have a quaint title, such as Chief Secretary to the Treasury, or Paymaster General, or he may be styled Minister of State (sometimes with an informal title as well, like Minister for Local Government); the most junior Minister in a department may be called the Parliamentary Under-Secretary of State, or simply the Parliamentary Secretary. And most ministerial styles are more of a mouthful today than they were in former times—for instance, the Minister of Defence as was is now the Secretary of State for Defence; the Parliamentary Secretary, Ministry of Health, is now the Parliamentary Under-Secretary of State, Department of Health; and so on.[2] Now none of this matters very much, but ministerial nomenclature requires systematic explanation if it is to be understood at all clearly.

The statutory definition of a Minister of the Crown is 'the holder of any office in Her Majesty's Government in the United Kingdom'[3]—but that is hardly pellucid. A more helpful description of a Minister is a Member of Parliament or peer who is a member of the party (or one of the parties) which forms the government of the day and who is appointed to and removed from

---

[1] See generally R. Brazier, *Ministers of the Crown* (1997), ch. 1.

[2] Mr Edward Heath probably had the longest collection of titles as Secretary of State for Industry, Trade and Regional Development and President of the Board of Trade, in 1963–64, followed by Mr John Prescott currently as Deputy Prime Minister and Secretary of State for the Environment, Transport and the Regions.

[3] Ministers of the Crown Act 1975, s. 8(1).

political office by the Sovereign on the Prime Minister's advice (or, in the case of a junior Minister, by the Prime Minister directly). The various ranks of Minister may, for convenience, be placed in different groups.

The first group is made up of the historical offices—the First Lord of the Treasury (a post always held today by the Prime Minister[4]); the Chancellor of the Exchequer; the Lord Chancellor (whose predecessors go back to the reign of Edward the Confessor); the Lord President of the Council (an office dating from 1497); the Lord Privy Seal[5] (which can be traced back to the fourteenth century); the Chancellor of the Duchy of Lancaster; and the Paymaster General.[6] The last three offices involve few departmental duties,[7] and in a modern administration will have tasks allotted to their holders by the Prime Minister on an *ad hoc* basis. The office of Prime Minister needs no further elaboration here.[8] The only other very old title, however, that of Secretary of State,[9] does require full consideration, because Secretaries of State now head nearly all the most important government departments. Up to 1782 there was only one Secretary of State. In that year his responsibilities were divided between two Secretaries of State, one for domestic and colonial matters, the other for foreign affairs, thus marking the beginning of the offices of Home Secretary and Foreign Secretary. A Secretary of State for War was appointed in 1794; other Secretaries of State were added as governmental responsibilities expanded; today there are 14.[10] In legal theory there is only one Secretary of State,[11] and lip-service is still paid to that theory by the parliamentary draftsman who insists in legislation on using the word 'the' or 'a' Secretary of State, not describing which one he means, even when it is obvious which one is in his mind.[12] Again,

---

[4] See Chapter 4.

[5] Neither the Lord President of the Council nor the Lord Privy Seal need be a peer. The Lord President is always charged with Privy Council Office matters. On her appointment in 1997 Mrs Ann Taylor styled herself simply 'President of the Council'.

[6] The title of Chief Secretary to the Treasury sounds old, but in fact it was invented in 1961 to give further ministerial support to the Chancellor of the Exchequer, and is usually held by a member of the Cabinet.

[7] The Chancellor of the Duchy of Lancaster is responsible for the general administration of the Duchy; the Paymaster General, however, has only nominal departmental tasks because his duties are entrusted to an Assistant Paymaster General, who is a civil servant.

[8] See Chapters 5 and 6. The post of Deputy Prime Minister was considered in Chapter 5.

[9] See Sir William Anson, *The Law and Custom of the Constitution* (4th edn., 1935 by A. B. Keith), ii. 172–84.

[10] The highest number ever was 15 in the 1974 Labour Cabinet.

[11] Unhelpfully, the phrase 'Secretary of State' is defined in the Interpretation Act 1978, s. 5 and Schedule 1 as 'one of Her Majesty's Principal Secretaries of State'.

[12] An exception is in the Defence (Transfer of Functions) Act 1964, s. 2, which refers to the Secretary of State for Defence.

although the office of a Secretary of State can be created by an act of prerogative, it is the usual modern practice to legislate for any new Secretary of State, to make him a corporation sole, and to provide for his duties and powers.[13] The total number of paid Secretaries of State cannot now exceed 21,[14] and a Secretary of State heads every major department except the Treasury, the Lord Chancellor's Department and the Ministry of Agriculture.

As the ministerial heads of all the main departments are usually now in the Cabinet, I suggested earlier[15] that it is permissible to classify all Ministers outside the Cabinet as junior Ministers. (Should a ministerial office now in the Cabinet be excluded from that body, the holder of it would not under this classification thereby become a junior Minister, because he would still be the ministerial head of a department; but it is unnecessary to think of a separate term for such a Minister just to accommodate what will now be a fairly infrequent occurrence.)[16] So in my formulation the expression 'junior Ministers'[17] covers the bulk of the government—the Law Officers, Ministers of State, Parliamentary Under-Secretaries of State, Parliamentary Secretaries, and Government Whips. The number of junior Ministers has increased dramatically, from a total in 1900 of some 30 ministers outside the Cabinet, to just under 70 in 1950, and to some 85 in 1999. Two reasons account for this growth: the general increase in governmental obligations, and (since the 1960s) the merging of departments which has reduced the number of Ministers as heads of departments but which has required a related increase in the number of junior Ministers in those departments. The different types of junior ministerial office may now be considered.

Each government has had four Law Officers as its chief legal advisers, the Attorney-General and Solicitor-General, and the Lord Advocate and the Solicitor-General for Scotland.[18] The Attorney-General deals with

[13] Through a statutory instrument made under the Ministers of the Crown Act 1975, ss. 2, 3. See, for example, the Transfer of Functions (International Development) Order 1997, S.I. 1997 No. 1749.

[14] Ministerial and other Salaries Act 1975, s. 1(1)(a), Schedule 1, Part V, para. 2 (a).

[15] See Chapter 4.

[16] The phrase 'Minister of Cabinet rank (not in the Cabinet)' was used for some years after 1945 to classify such a Minister, but that phrase is meaningless.

[17] See generally Kevin Theakston, 'The Use and Abuse of Junior Ministers' (1986) 57 Political Quarterly 18; Junior Ministers in British Government (1987).

[18] See J. Ll. J. Edwards, The Law Officers of the Crown (1964); The Attorney-General: Politics and the Public Interest (1984). A former Conservative Attorney-General has written, with regret, of the politicization of the Law Officers: Lord Rawlinson, A Price Too High (1989), pp. 4, 237–8, 241. Under the Scotland Act 1998 those last two Law Officers will become

questions of law arising on Bills, and with issues of legal policy, and he is concerned with all major international and domestic litigation involving the government. He has statutory duties in relation to the Crown Prosecution Service.[19] The Solicitor-General handles matters delegated to him by the Attorney-General. They both used to answer in the House of Commons for the Lord Chancellor's Department, an unsatisfactory arrangement which has been superseded by the appointment in that House of a Parliamentary Secretary to the Lord Chancellor's Department.[20]

The next rank of the junior Ministers is that of the Ministers of State.[21] A Minister of State was first appointed in 1941—Lord Beaverbrook, who, having left the Ministry of Aircraft Production, stayed in the War Cabinet and began the task of creating a Ministry of Production. The title was subsequently held by a succession of Ministers, in effect as the equivalent of Ministers without Portfolio. In 1950 the Minister of State was put into the Foreign Office as an additional junior Minister. Since then the number of Ministers of State has increased sharply to 27 by 1999,[22] and almost all departments now have at least one Minister of State.[23] No doubt a contributory factory in this increase is that 'Minister of State' sounds grander than the titles of the other junior Ministers, such as Parliamentary Secretary, and so could be more impressive particularly in international negotiations. All Ministers of State take charge of a particular section of a department, and are also given particular tasks by their ministerial chief. Their exact duties (and indeed those of all other Ministers) are published from time to time by the Cabinet Office in the pamphlet 'List of Ministerial Responsibilities'. In

---

members of the Scottish Executive and will cease to be members of the British government. A new officer, the Advocate-General for Scotland, will advise that government on Scottish legal questions.

[19] See Chapter 6.

[20] In the 1974 Labour government a Parliamentary Secretary to the Law Officer's Department was appointed, although the post lapsed subsequently.

[21] The statutory definition for purposes of the House of Commons Disqualification Act 1975, s. 9(1) is 'a member of Her Majesty's Government in the United Kingdom who neither has charge of any public department nor holds any other of the offices specified in Schedule 2 to this Act or any office in respect of which a salary is payable out of money provided by Parliament under s. 3(1)(b) of the Ministerial and other Salaries Act 1975'.

[22] Including the Financial Secretary and the Economic Secretary to the Treasury, who are of Minister of State rank.

[23] The Lord Chancellor's Department and the Law Officers' Department are the main exceptions in having no Minister of State; the Foreign and Commonwealth Office has four. Dr Gavin Strang was appointed 'Minister of Transport' in the 1997 Labour Cabinet, but his formal rank was that of Minister of State. No replacement was made in 1998 when he was dropped from the government.

order to make the individual duties of the Ministers of State clearer, the custom developed in the 1970s, and continues, of describing certain Ministers of State by informal, or 'courtesy', titles, as Mrs Thatcher aptly dubbed them.[24] So in Mr Blair's government a Minister of State at the Department of Health holds the courtesy title of Minister for Public Health; in the Department of the Environment, Transport and the Regions there are Ministers for the Environment, for Local Government and Housing, and for the Regions, Regeneration and Planning; in the Department of Trade and Industry there are Ministers for Trade, for Trade and Competitiveness in Europe, and for Science, Energy and Industry; and so on. The use of the phrase 'Minister for' discloses the exact status of the holder: they are merely Ministers of State, but in name they represent a reversion to simpler days before the major departmental amalgamations.

At the bottom of the departmental ministerial hierarchy are the Parliamentary Under-Secretaries of State (if the ministerial head is a Secretary of State) or Parliamentary Secretaries (if the Minister in charge is not a Secretary of State: the only Parliamentary Secretaries today are in the Ministry of Agriculture and in the Treasury).[25] A Parliamentary Secretary has been statutorily defined as including 'a person holding Ministerial office (however called) as assistant to a Member of Her Majesty's Government in the United Kingdom, but not having departmental responsibilities'.[26] Some give parliamentary and departmental help directly to a Minister of State; most are themselves given responsibilities for particular areas—so that, for example, the Parliamentary Under-Secretary of State at the Home Office in Mr Blair's government deals with numerous matters ranging from the police to animal welfare, all subject to a Minister of State and the Home Secretary. Parliamentary Secretaries will naturally hope that they so conduct themselves as to earn promotion up the ministerial ladder.

Every modern administration will have about 12 Whips in the House of Commons and a further seven in the Lords. The Government Chief Whip in the Commons is the Parliamentary Secretary to the Treasury (who has no Treasury duties, and indeed no room in it; he and his fellow Whips use Number 12 Downing Street). Under him are six Government Whips with

---

[24] See 106 H.C. Deb. 419 (written answers 1 December 1986). There are internal rules about the conferment of such titles: see *Ministerial Code* (Cabinet Office, 1997), para. 38.

[25] The civil service follows suit: the official head of a department is styled either the Permanent Under-Secretary of State or the Permanent Secretary.

[26] House of Commons Disqualification Act 1975, s. 9(1).

various formal titles[27] and five Assistant Whips. Apart from their main functions of conveying the views of government back-bench MPs to the government, and vice versa, and of issuing the weekly whip (and administering discipline for breaches of it), arranging pairs, obtaining names of MPs to serve on parliamentary committees, and helping to manage government time in the House, the Commons Whips, through the Chief Whip, are a vital source of intelligence for the Prime Minister as to potential Ministers from the back-benches—and the Number 12 Whips' Office itself provides a separate pool from which ministerial promotions are made.[28] In the Lords all the Whips have notional appointments in the Royal Household and suitably fine titles to mark them out.[29] Party allegiances not being so vigorously policed in the Lords, some Whips are additionally designated government departmental spokesmen there. No equivalent status is ever accorded their Commons counterparts, who have to take a vow of silence.[30]

Two other forms of parliamentary and political life must be distinguished from what has gone before. A Minister may appoint a Parliamentary Private Secretary (or Secretaries) from the ranks of government back-benchers.[31] A PPS acts as a general dogsbody, advising his Minister on the state of parliamentary opinion, acting as a two-way channel of communication between MPs and his Minister, and generally helping the Minister with whatever parliamentary work he requires. PPSs are not Ministers; they are not paid; they have no official departmental status—but they are bound by collective ministerial responsibility[32] and as a consequence swell the maximum 'ministerial' vote in the House of Commons to some 150.[33] In return for their labours PPSs will obtain experience of ministerial life and, all being well, ministerial office one day. Since the 1970s Ministers have also taken to appointing one or two personal advisers.[34] These now fall

---

[27]   Treasurer of Her Majesty's Household and Deputy Chief Whip; Comptroller of HM's Household; Vice-Chamberlain of HM's Household; and three Lords Commissioners of the Treasury.

[28]   All Chief Whips since 1951 have gone on to be Cabinet Ministers, and Edward Heath (Chief Whip 1955–59) became Prime Minister.

[29]   Captain of the Honourable Corps of Gentlemen-at-Arms (Chief Whip—who may be a woman: Baroness Llewelyn-Davies was so appointed in 1974); Captain of the Queen's Bodyguard of the Yeomen of the Guard (Deputy Chief Whip); and five Lords (or Baronesses) in Waiting.

[30]   Save in moving the terms of formal motions.

[31]   See Brazier, n. 1 above, pp. 126–7; R. K. Alderman and J. A. Cross, 'The Parliamentary Private Secretary' (1967) 48 *Parliamentarian* 75; P. Norton, 'The Constitutional Position of Parliamentary Private Secretaries' [1988] *Public Law* 233; *Ministerial Code*, paras. 44–7.

[32]   This is considered below.   [33]   Currently 41 PPSs and 105 Ministers.

[34]   See Brazier, n. 1 above, ch. 8.4; Sir John Hoskyns, (1983) 36 *Parliamentary Affairs* 137 at

into two separate groups. First, they may be political advisers, brought in from outside Whitehall to give the Minister help with implementing that part of the government's election programme for which he has direct responsibility. Political advisers are paid from party funds and are not civil servants. Secondly, special advisers may be engaged by a Minister to give independent, non-party political, advice. They are given terms of appointment similar to those of civil servants. All personal advisers leave the department with the Minister.[35] The view that Ministers must have strong, effective support in implementing party policy has gained ground in all the political parties, and, although the presence of personal advisers can cause friction between them and established civil servants, there is no doubt that they are here to stay.[36]

I turn now from ministerial titles to the government departments in which their holders will work.

Departments[37]

A working definition of a department of state is that it is headed by a Minister, is staffed by civil servants, and is charged, through the Minister, with recommending policies to the Cabinet and Cabinet committees; and when those policies have been approved there (and perhaps by Parliament) the department then has the task of implementing the details of those policies.[38]

Until the late nineteenth century all the duties of government could be discharged by the holders of the historical offices. Up to that time, if new responsibilities were assumed, additional Secretaries of State were appointed: thus, for example, the Colonial Office was created in 1768, the War Office in 1794, and the India Office in 1858, each headed by a Secre-

---

146; Harold Wilson, *The Governance of Britain* (1976), Appendix V. Harold Wilson gives two reasons for this development: the pressure of work on Ministers, and the need for the civil service to remain non-party political. For special advisers in the Labour government see 295 H.C. Deb. 96–9 (written answers 2 June 1997).

[35] See Joan Mitchell, (1978) 56 *Public Administration* 87; Mr Callaghan's explanations at 939 H. C. Deb. 913 (written answers 25 November 1977), 951 H.C. Deb. 142 (written answers 20 June 1978), and Mrs Thatcher's at 58 H.C. Deb. 155–6 (written answers 10 April 1984).

[36] In the 7th Report from the Treasury and Civil Service Committee, Civil Servants and Ministers: Duties and Responsibilities, H.C. 92 (1985–6), para. 5, the Committee took the idea of personal advisers further and recommended the creation of policy units for Ministers, staffed by non-civil servants.   [37] See Brazier, n. 1 above, ch. 2.

[38] For a different formulation, see D. N. Chester and F. M. G. Willson, *The Organization of British Central Government 1914 to 1964* (2nd edn., 1968), p. 391.

tary of State. As the functions of government expanded, the Privy Council was used to provide new machinery of government, Boards of the Privy Council being established with a President as the Minister responsible. Thus the Board of Trade was revived in 1786, the Local Government Board[39] was set up in 1871, the Board of Education in 1870 and the Board of Agriculture in 1889.[40] That nomenclature ceased to be fashionable after the turn of the century, and the first Ministry so called, the Ministry of Munitions, came into being in 1915, to be followed rapidly by others such as Pensions, and Labour, in 1916, and Agriculture,[41] Health, and Transport in 1919. (Only one Ministry so called, with a Minister so called at its head, has survived to the present day—Agriculture, Fisheries and Food.) In 1964 the style changed again: from that year many new ministries were dubbed 'Departments',[42] beginning with the Department of Education and Science, to be followed later in the same year by the Department of Economic Affairs, and in subsequent years by the Departments of Health and Social Security, the Environment, Energy, and Prices and Consumer Protection. (Three 'Offices', headed by Secretaries of State, were also created from 1964—the Welsh Office, the Foreign and Commonwealth Office, and the Northern Ireland Office.) There is no legal significance in whether a department of state is designated a Board, Office, Ministry or Department; but since 1964 the descriptions Office and Department and the style Secretary of State have been reserved for the most politically important units.[43]

Prime Ministers will want to change the structure of government departments for various reasons—to establish a new department to implement a new government's policy;[44] to create machinery to cope with matters which can no longer be dealt with adequately within existing

[39] The Board became the Ministry of Health in 1919.

[40] There had been a Vice-President of the Committee of the Privy Council for Education since 1857.

[41] Succeeding the Board of Agriculture.

[42] Exceptions (also created in 1964) were the Ministries of Overseas Development, of Technology, and of Land and Natural Resources. (In subsequent Conservative governments responsibility for overseas development was discharged through the Foreign and Commonwealth Office by a junior Minister. Mr Blair, however, appointed a Secretary of State for International Development in 1997.)

[43] Two oddities may be noted. When the Service Ministries were merged in 1964 into an expanded Ministry of Defence under a Secretary of State for Defence, the new department could logically have been styled the 'Department of Defence', or the 'Defence Office'. Possibly the old appellation was kept in 1964 because 'Department of Defence' might have sounded too Americanized. Then again, when the Department of Health and Social Security was created in 1968, the Secretary of State was styled 'Secretary of State for Social Services', not 'for Health and Social Security'.

[44] In 1964, for example, the new Labour Prime Minister created five new departments. In

structures;[45] to abolish departments whose usefulness has passed,[46] or which have ceased to represent a governmental responsibility;[47] or to merge departments; or to change the titles of Ministers or departments to mark a fresh approach. Frequent departmental changes are, however, disruptive and costly, and that price may not always be set against the benefit which the Prime Minister thinks will be achieved at that cost.[48] Not surprisingly, changes in the machinery of government have tended to be greater under Labour than under Conservative governments.

The Ministers of the Crown Act 1975[49] provides the means of hatching, matching, and dispatching departments and ministerial titles. An Order in Council may provide for the transfer to one Minister from another of any function, or dissolve any government department and distribute any of its functions to another Minister or Ministers, or direct that any Minister's functions will be exercisable concurrently with another Minister (or cease to be so exercisable).[50] An Order in Council may effect changes in relation to Secretaries of State and their departments.[51] If, however, the Prime Minister wishes to create a new department (rather than merely transfer existing functions to it from elsewhere) with a 'Minister' at its head rather than a Secretary of State, the 1975 Act does not apply and a fresh statute must be passed for the purpose. Thus in 1964 the Ministries of Land and Natural Resources, of Overseas Development, and of Technology

---

1997 Mr Blair confined himself to creating a new Department for International Development and a combined Department of the Environment, Transport and the Regions.

[45] So, the Northern Ireland Office was set up in 1972 because the Home Office could no longer adequately deal with the province's problems, and the Department of Energy was established in 1974 after the escalation in the price of oil and during the emergency caused by a miners' strike. The Department of National Heritage was created in 1992, with responsibility for the heritage, sport, broadcasting, and the National Lottery: it was restyled the Department for Culture, Media and Sport in 1997.

[46] A large number of wartime departments were abolished after both world wars; the Department of Economic Affairs and the Ministry of Land and Natural Resources were merged into existing departments in 1967.

[47] Such as the Irish offices after the creation of the Irish Free State, and the abolition of the office of Postmaster-General when the Post Office became a public corporation in 1969; and the merger of the Department of Energy into the Department of Trade and Industry in 1992, all of the energy industry except coal having been privatized.

[48] Of the 28 departments created between 1960 and 1979, 13 had been wound up by 1981: see Christopher Pollitt, 'The Civil Service Department: A Normal Death?' (1982) 60 *Public Administration* 73.

[49] The original statute was the Ministers of the Crown (Transfer of Functions) Act 1946.

[50] Ministers of the Crown Act 1975, s. 1(1). Other consequential provisions are contained in s. 1(2).

[51] Ibid. s. 2(1). Property rights are dealt with in s. 3.

required such an Act.[52] This is a pointless complication: the 1975 Act should be amended to allow the creation of any new department (however called) and any new Minister (however styled) by Order in Council.[53]

The use of non-departmental Ministers [54]

Traditionally, the holders of offices such as Lord President of the Council, Lord Privy Seal, Chancellor of the Duchy of Lancaster and Paymaster General have been allotted particular tasks by the Prime Minister on an *ad hoc* basis within their own very small departments. So, for example, Harold Macmillan charged Charles Hill (as Chancellor of the Duchy of Lancaster) with general government publicity, and Lord Hailsham (as Lord President of the Council) to try to reduce unemployment in the north-east. As the importance of Cabinet committees grew, so non-departmental Ministers were given heavier loads of committee work, and such Ministers will always be a prime source of Cabinet committee membership. In Mrs Thatcher's government, Lords Whitelaw and Wakeham in turn fulfilled that role to the full.

There are, additionally, three other modern uses of non-departmental Ministers. First, the Lord President of the Council and the Lord Privy Seal will usually be the Leaders of the two Houses: this was the case throughout the Wilson, Heath, and Callaghan governments, for most of Mrs Thatcher's,[55] throughout Mr Major's government, and (so far) Mr Blair's. The Leaders of the two Houses have major responsibilities in ensuring the progress of government business in Parliament,[56] and in practice two members of any Cabinet will have most of their time taken up as Leaders of the House of Commons and of the House of Lords.[57] Secondly, the Chairman of the Conservative Party Organization since 1951 has frequently been appointed as a non-departmental Minister with a seat in the Cabinet.[58] The Opposition has routinely objected to this: the fact that the Ministers

[52] Ministers of the Crown Act 1964, ss. 1, 2(1)(a). Their *abolition* was effected by Order in Council.
[53] Especially as s. 5 of the 1975 Act subjects Orders in Council made under it to parliamentary scrutiny.
[54] Brazier, n. 1 above, pp. 20–21.
[55] Although the Leader of the House of Commons from 1979–81 was the Chancellor of the Duchy of Lancaster.
[56] See Chapters 10 and 11.
[57] They are unlikely to be also departmental Ministers, as was the case in (say) the 1950s.
[58] Mr Norman Tebbit was Chancellor of the Duchy of Lancaster in the Cabinet from 1985–87 and Chairman of the Conservative Party: he remained Chairman for a few months

involved have drawn a reduced, or no, ministerial salary has not assuaged them. In recent years such Ministers have spent about a quarter of their time on ministerial duties, and the rest on party work.[59] Thirdly, some Ministers holding traditional titles have been used since 1970 as deputies to departmental Ministers, or have been given a major responsibility within a department. So in 1970 the Chancellor of the Duchy of Lancaster was put in charge within the Foreign and Commonwealth Office of negotiating terms for the United Kingdom's entry into the European Economic Community; from 1979 to 1982 the Lord Privy Seal was placed in the Foreign and Commonwealth Office and the Cabinet as deputy to the Foreign Secretary, who was in the House of Lords; and in 1985 the Paymaster General was brought into the Cabinet and the Department of Employment as number two (and 'Minister for Employment') to the Secretary of State, who was a peer: the same two individuals were transferred to the Department of Trade and Industry in the 1987 reshuffle, as Chancellor of the Duchy of Lancaster and Secretary of State respectively.

Should the four traditional non-departmental offices not be enough for a Prime Minister's purposes, he may designate a colleague (or colleagues[60]) as Minister without Portfolio. The 1951 Conservative government had a Minister without Portfolio from 1954–64, and the 1964 Labour and 1970 Conservative governments for the whole of their lives; Mrs Thatcher, on the other hand, had only one Minister without Portfolio, for about a year,[61] Mr Major had two in succession from 1994–97, and Mr Blair had one for the first year of his government.

Winston Churchill experimented with the use of non-departmental Ministers as co-ordinating Ministers or 'overlords', from 1951–53.[62] Three peers were so used: Lord Cherwell (Paymaster General) co-ordinated scientific research and development; Lord Woolton (Lord President of the

after his retirement from the government in 1987. Lord Thorneycroft, however (Chairman 1975–81), was not given ministerial office in 1979; Mr Gummer (Chairman 1983–85) was made a Minister, but outside the Cabinet. During Mr Major's government a Minister without Portfolio in the Cabinet also held the party chairmanship.

[59] See, for example, 188 H.C. Deb. 603 (25 March 1991). It is unlikely that a Cabinet Minister heading a department would now be given the Chairmanship. One of the last Ministers to do so has described the arrangement as 'bad': Lord Carrington, *Reflect on Things Past* (1988), pp. 259–60. See also Norman Tebbit, *Upwardly Mobile* (1988), pp. 241, 243.

[60] In 1963, 1964–66, and 1967–68 there were two Ministers without Portfolio.

[61] Lord Young, 1984–85. He was made Secretary of State for Employment in 1985 and then for Trade and Industry in 1987.

[62] See Sir Ivor Jennings, *Cabinet Government* (3rd ed., 1959), pp. 78–81; Anthony Seldon, *Churchill's Indian Summer: The Conservative Government 1951 to 1955* (1981), pp. 102–6.

Council) oversaw the Ministries of Agriculture and Fisheries, and of Food, and Lord Leathers (the first—and last—Secretary of State for the Co-ordination of Transport, Fuel and Power) superintended the Ministries of Transport, of Civil Aviation, and of Fuel and Power. The relevant departmental Ministers were not made members of the Cabinet. These arrangements were criticized in Parliament[63] on the grounds that they blurred the responsibility to Parliament of the departmental Ministers, giving some responsibility (or none of it: this was never satisfactorily explained)[64] to the 'overlords'.[65] The system was allowed to lapse in 1953.[66] (Strangely, a significant motive behind the experiment has been understood to have been to reduce the size of the Cabinet. Churchill's Cabinet was smaller by one than Attlee's, but this was in fact achieved by Churchill being Minister of Defence and by the exclusion of the Chancellor of the Duchy of Lancaster.) Co-ordination by a single Minister of the work of two or more departments can, however, be very successful if it is the intention to merge those departments. In 1968 Richard Crossman as Lord President of the Council was given the task of merging the Ministries of Health and of Social Security, which was achieved later that year when he became the inaugural Secretary of State for Social Services.[67]

Ministers' conduct

The three aspects of ministerial conduct which now fall to be considered are collective responsibility, individual responsibility, and rules relating to Ministers' personal financial affairs.

[63] They were never supported by Sir Norman Brook, the Cabinet Secretary, or Sir Edward Bridges, Permanent Secretary to the Treasury: Seldon, n. 62 above, p. 102.

[64] Lord Woolton denied that he had *any* ministerial responsibility to Parliament: 176 H.L. Deb. 474–7 (30 April 1952).

[65] For Churchill's explanations, see 500 H. C. Deb. 188–96 (6 May 1952): in essence, he believed that the departmental Ministers remained individually responsible, while the co-ordinating Ministers shared in the collective responsibility of the whole government.

[66] There was a Cabinet reshuffle in September 1953: Lords Leathers and Cherwell left the government and their 'overlord' functions were not continued. Lord Woolton had left the Cabinet in 1952. Sir John Colville, Churchill's Principal Private Secretary, thought that the experiment had proved unsuccessful: see *The Fringes of Power: Downing Street Diaries 1939–1955* (1985), p. 633. Sir Douglas Wass, a former Permanent Secretary to the Treasury, has, however, referred with approval to a possible 'overlord' scheme: *Government and the Governed* (1984), pp. 27–30.

[67] The Department of Health and Social Security was divided into two departments 20 years later. Duncan Sandys was appointed Secretary of State for Commonwealth Relations in 1960, and was also made Secretary of State for the Colonies in 1962. Separate Secretaries of

Bye the bye, there is one thing we haven't agreed upon, which is, what are we to say? Is it to make our corn dearer, or cheaper, or to make the price steady? I don't care *which*: but we had better all tell the same story.[68]

The essence of Lord Melbourne's cynical observation holds good today. For the doctrine of collective ministerial responsibility[69] requires that all Ministers, and usually Parliamentary Private Secretaries, must accept Cabinet decisions,[70] or dissent from them privately while remaining loyal to them publicly, or dissent publicly and resign, unless collective responsibility is waived by the Cabinet on any given occasion. If a Minister does not resign over an issue of policy or procedure he will be collectively responsible for it, in the sense that he will have to support it publicly through his votes in Parliament and through his speeches. It will be no defence or excuse for him to say that the decision was taken without his knowledge (because, for example, he was a mere Parliamentary Under-Secretary of State not privy to Cabinet discussions, or because he was absent from the relevant meeting), for the doctrine binds all members of the government from the lowest to the highest: it is for that reason misleading to refer to it as collective *Cabinet* responsibility. There are many examples of Ministers of all ranks resigning or being required to resign because they could not accept collective responsibility for some decision or other—Cabinet Ministers,[71] Ministers of State,[72] Chief Whips,[73] and Parliamentary Secretaries.[74]

State were appointed in the new Labour government in 1964, but the two offices were merged into a new Commonwealth Office in 1966.

[68] Lord Melbourne, after his Cabinet had been deliberating on the Corn Laws, quoted in Spencer Walpole, *Life of Lord John Russell* (1889), i. 369.

[69] See generally S. A. de Smith and R. Brazier, *Constitutional and Administrative Law* (8th edn., 1998), pp. 195–202; E. C. S. Wade and A. W. Bradley, *Constitutional and Administrative Law* (12th edn., 1997), ch. 7; Jennings, n. 62 above, pp. 277–89; John Mackintosh, *The British Cabinet* (3rd edn., 1977), pp. 531–6; Geoffrey Marshall, *Constitutional Conventions* (1984), pp. 55–61; D. Woodhouse, *Ministers and Parliament: Accountability in Theory and Practice* (1994); the Scott Report, H.C. 115 (1995–6); 2nd Report from the Public Service Committee, *Ministerial Accountability and Responsibility*, H.C. 313 (1995–6).

[70] And Cabinet committee decisions taken executively on the Cabinet's behalf.

[71] For example, Mr Heseltine as Secretary of State for Defence in 1986, Mr Nigel Lawson as Chancellor of the Exchequer in 1989 (on which see his *The View from Number 11* (1992), pp. 930–3, 952–71), and Sir Geoffrey Howe in 1990.

[72] For instance, Mr Ian Gow, Minister of State at the Treasury, resigned in 1985 because he could not defend the government's conclusion of the Anglo-Irish Treaty with the Republic of Ireland. Mr David Heathcoat-Amory resigned as Paymaster General in 1997 because he wanted the Major government to take a more hostile stance towards the euro.

[73] Attlee's Chief Whip in the Lords described the government's handling of a dock labour dispute in 1949 as 'absolutely crazy', and had to resign.

[74] For example, Dr Jeremy Bray, Parliamentary Secretary, Ministry of Technology, in the 1964 Labour government wanted to publish a book on economic management and the

If a Prime Minister wishes, he may extend (and since 1945 usually has extended) the doctrine to Parliamentary Private Secretaries as well. Although it is individual Ministers who appoint their own PPSs, the consequence of accepting appointment is that they may be bound by collective responsibility, and may be dismissed by the Prime Minister if they fail to give the government the loyalty which he thinks it deserves. This is as it should be. True, they are not Ministers and they are not paid; but they are necessarily very close to Ministers and public dissent by a PPS could be taken as a sign that the Minister himself dissents. In 1967 the PPSs to the President of the Board of Trade and the Minister of Agriculture campaigned vigorously against possible entry into the European Economic Community, and were correctly seen as surrogates for their ministerial chiefs.[75] Early in the life of Mr Blair's government five PPSs resigned or were dismissed because they would not support the Cabinet's decision to cut lone parent benefit.

Now it is wrong to view collective responsibility either as a notion which ensures ministerial solidarity of almost former Soviet proportions or as a weapon which the Prime Minister can use in deadly fashion if faced by a recalcitrant colleague. In order to preserve the essentials of the doctrine at all a number of safety valves have been developed in it. Of these the unattributable leak[76] is the life-saver of collective responsibility. A Minister puts his views in the Cabinet or Cabinet committee; it turns out that he is in a minority and the decision goes against him; the Minister can accept neither defeat nor the end of his ministerial career, so he stays in the government and briefs the press as to his opposition. The result is that all the world knows that he opposes the policy, just as if he had resigned, but by using an unattributable leak the façade of collective responsibility is maintained and Minister, press and Prime Minister are happy. The citizen, however, will be left rather puzzled. But the leak has also had another general and beneficial side effect. Ministerial solidarity involves the stifling of open dissent: it thereby contributes to secrecy in government, for although questions

---

machinery of government: Mr Wilson refused him permission, saying that as Prime Minister he had to uphold 'the collective responsibility of the Administration', and Dr Bray resigned: see *The Times*, 26–9 September 1969. Mrs Elizabeth Peacock was sacked in 1992 after she had voted against the government's plans to close certain coal mines. Mr Malcolm Chisholm resigned as a junior Scottish Office Minister in 1997 rather than support the Labour government's decision to cut lone parent benefit—the first ministerial resignation from Mr Blair's administration on grounds of collective ministerial responsibility.

[75] Mackintosh, n. 69 above, p. 532.

[76] See Chapter 6.

may be strongly contested between Ministers, solidarity requires that they are not aired in a way that would enable public opinion to be expressed before decisions are reached. The argument 'goes on behind the screen of collective responsibility'.[77] The leak will, however, occasionally draw that screen to one side.

A second safety valve consists in the ability of a Minister to run very close to the boundary between ministerial solidarity and open dissent in the hope or knowledge that the Prime Minister will do precious little to rein him in. Frank Cousins, the trade union general secretary temporarily turned Minister of Technology and MP in the 1964 Labour government,[78] publicly expressed his 'delight' when his union voted to condemn both the government's prices and incomes policy and its attitude to the Vietnam war.[79] In 1969, the Home Secretary, James Callaghan, spoke in the NEC against the government's proposals for industrial relations legislation contained in the White Paper 'In Place of Strife'; his dissent was (as he would have wished) leaked; but the only penalty imposed was exclusion from the Parliamentary Committee of the Cabinet. Then again, during the contest for the Leadership of the Labour Party in 1976 on Harold Wilson's retirement, Tony Benn, Secretary of State for Energy, publicly advocated policies which ran counter to the government's actual or likely policies. A similar phenomenon occurred in the 1990 Conservative Leadership contest after Mrs Thatcher had withdrawn. I argued in Chapter 2, however, that Leadership contests represent a special case. What was *not* in any sense special was Mr Benn's dissociation in the NEC from the Cabinet's policies which produced a rebuke from the Prime Minister and a minute to Ministers reminding them of the obligations imposed on them by collective responsibility—but no other sanction.[80] And during Mrs Thatcher's administration Mr Peter Walker was widely regarded as using 'coded' public speeches, such as his Harold Macmillan Lecture in 1984, to advocate 'wetter' economic and social strategies than those being collectively pursued by his colleagues. These and similar occurrences amply show that near or actual breaches of collective responsibility provoke no automatic penalty: much will turn on the particular Minister's political strength, his ability to brazen out any demands for his resignation, and the attitude of the Prime Minister.

---

[77] Colin Turpin, *British Government and the Constitution: Texts, Cases and Materials* (2nd edn., 1990), p. 187.

[78] See Chapter 4.   [79] Mackintosh, n. 69 above, p. 532.

[80] He had to repeat the exercise in 1974: see Wilson, n. 34 above, Appendix I.

A somewhat different safety valve may allow a Minister, or the Prime Minster, publicly to go beyond and extend the agreed policies of the government without prior authority; the result can be a falling into line behind the Minister concerned.[81] As Prime Minister, Lloyd George occasionally made policy in this way, one of the most notable examples being his announcement in 1916 to a journalist (an American journalist at that) of the strategy of the 'knock-out blow' against the Axis powers—a vast commitment of men to overwhelm the enemy—without prior consultation of any Cabinet colleague.[82] Minsters have even announced departures during parliamentary debates: for instance, Sir William Joynson-Hicks, the Home Secretary, replying to a debate on a Private Member's Bill in 1927, startled the Prime Minister and indeed the whole House by committing the government to introduce its own Bill to reduce the age at which women would get the vote.[83] The Cabinet had taken no such decision, but rather than drop his Home Secretary, Baldwin adopted the proposal as the lesser evil.[84] Mrs Thatcher, a past master at the television interview, has been judged to have developed policy in that medium, for example on immigration: but then what can a modern Cabinet do other than acquiesce in such things, at least outwardly?[85]

The last and uncommon and derided but in my view attractive device for holding a government together is the agreement to differ. The only three examples of such agreements this century are well known and will not be rehearsed in any detail here.[86] They were the National Government's agreement to differ in 1932 over the introduction of a general tariff (without which four free-trade Cabinet Ministers would have resigned);[87] the Labour Cabinet's decision to suspend collective responsibility 'in the unique circumstances' of the 1975 referendum campaign (on whether the United Kingdom should continue to be a member of the European Economic Community) so that Ministers who dissented from the Cabinet's

---

[81] A number of examples this century are given by Jennings, n. 62 above, pp. 287–8.

[82] See Lloyd George, *War Memoirs* (1933), ii. 856–7.

[83] Lord Birkenhead, *Life of the First Earl of Birkenhead*, vol. ii (1934), pp. 291–2.

[84] The qualifying age for women to vote had been set at 30 in 1918. The Representation of the People Act 1928—the result of Joynson-Hicks's pledge—reduced it to 21. Joynson-Hicks went into honourable retirement in 1929 as Viscount Brentford.

[85] In 1990 Mrs Thatcher surprised the government by announcing, in a speech to party workers, an outline manifesto and several new and radical domestic policies: see *The Independent*, 25 June 1990.

[86] See Jennings, n. 62 above, pp. 278–81; David Marquand, *Ramsay MacDonald* (1977), pp. 709–13; Wilson, n. 34 above, pp. 75–6, 194–7; D. L. Ellis, 'Collective Ministerial Responsibility and Collective Solidarity' [1980] *Public Law* 367 at 383–9.

[87] Including the leading Liberals Sir Herbert Samuel and Sir Archibald Sinclair.

recommendation to vote to remain in could say so publicly—although outside Parliament;[88] and the further suspension in 1977 so that Ministers who could not support the introduction of direct elections to the European Assembly could vote against the second reading of the European Assembly Elections Bill.[89] These suspensions are usually regarded as some sort of affront to our system of government, not to be spoken of in polite society. Sir Ivor Jennings, for instance, wrote that the 1932 agreement was a 'strange device', but that 'no harm was done by the precedent of 1932 provided that it is not regarded as a precedent'.[90] MacDonald's resort to an agreement to differ is usually described as a failure. Now, partly no doubt because of their rarity, agreements to differ look bad. The contrast between government A, which keeps its disagreements discreetly private, and government B, which openly announces a disagreement, is sharp and provides political ammunition for the latter's opponents. And James Callaghan's announcement at the time of the 1977 suspension—'I certainly think that the doctrine [of collective responsibility] should apply, except in cases where I announce that it does not'[91]—was seen by some as a cynical exploitation of prime ministerial power. I find these objections unimpressive. The 1975 and 1977 suspensions were not only undoubted successes for the governments concerned—the two administrations held together, which is the main aim of the exercise—but also the issues before Ministers and the country (particularly in 1975) were more fully aired and argued than otherwise would have been the case. Even the 1932 experiment bought the coalition government an extra eight months of continued free-trade support (both National Liberal and National Labour) which it otherwise would have forfeited, at a time when the maximum national solidarity was desirable.[92] More fundamentally, why in a mature democracy do we still insist on the maintenance of the fiction that all Ministers are agreed on everything all the time—or at least that they all loyally fall in unreservedly behind majority decisions? That they do not is eloquently attested to by

---

[88]   See Mr Wilson's explanation at 884 H.C. Deb. 1746 (23 January 1975) and 889 H.C. Deb. 351 (written answers 7 April 1975); *The Governance of Britain* (1976), pp. 194–7. Mr Heffer spoke *inside* the House of Commons against continued membership and was dismissed as Minister of State for Industry: see Chapter 5.

[89]   See Mr Callaghan's statement at 889 H.C. Deb. 1307 (23 March 1977).

[90]   Jennings, n. 62 above, pp. 279, 281. Even Wade and Bradley, n. 69 above, p. 116 consider that this 'short-lived departure from the principle of unanimity has generally been regarded as demonstrating the virtues of that principle and justifiable, *if at all* [my italics], only in the special circumstances of a coalition government formed to deal with a national crisis'.

[91]   933 H.C. Deb. 552 (16 June 1977).

[92]   Nine free-trade Ministers eventually resigned in September 1932 over imperial preference.

leaks—themselves an accepted but dishonest ruse, more objectionable in my view than an occasional and open agreement to differ. Governments should be readier to announce majority decisions and should use suspensions of the obligations of collective responsibility more often. The electorate would see more of the reality of political life, and there would be some increase in public debate of major issues. Naturally, there would have to be limits: every government must officially hold together on essentials—monetarism rather than traditional liberal Conservative orthodoxy in the 1980s, for example; and too many suspensions could be politically dangerous. Subject to that, I accept Dr Geoffrey Marshall's injunction in the same spirit in which it is offered, that 'Those who now esteem open government ought perhaps to encourage open disagreements, openly arrived at'.[93]

Despite the safety valves (which could alternatively be described as the weaknesses in the doctrine of collective responsibility) some Ministers will reach a point of unavoidable departure from the administration. The Westland affair is instructive.[94] The Westland company supplied helicopters to the Ministry of Defence and other NATO countries, and in 1985 was in urgent need of financial reconstruction. Two reconstruction programmes emerged, one supported by the American-backed Sikorsky-Fiat group, the other by a consortium of European manufacturers. Mrs Thatcher has always maintained that her government's policy was to leave the decision about which to take up to the Westland company; Mr Michael Heseltine, the then Secretary of State for Defence, maintained throughout that both she and Mr Leon Brittan, the then Secretary of State for Trade and Industry, consistently urged the Sikorsky-Fiat scheme on Westland, whereas he believed that the European option should have been chosen.[95] The two sides, as they may fairly be described, did not subsequently agree on other important details, for example, whether the issues were ever fully

---

[93] Marshall, n. 69 above, p. 58.

[94] On which see Geoffrey Marshall, 'Cabinet Government and the Westland Affair' [1986] *Public Law* 184; Magnus Linklater and David Leigh, *Not With Honour: The Inside Story of the Westland Scandal* (1986); Lawson, n. 71 above, pp. 675–81; Margaret Thatcher, *The Downing Street Years* (1993), pp. 423–37; Dawn Oliver and Rodney Austin, 'Political and Constitutional Aspects of the Westland Affair' (1987) 40 *Parliamentary Affairs* 20; Defence Committee, Westland PLC: The Government's Decision-making, H.C. 519 (1985–6)—and the government's response, Cmnd. 9916 (1986); Treasury and Civil Service Committee, 7th Report, Civil Servants and Ministers: Duties and Responsibilities, H.C. 92 (1985–6)—and the government's response, Cmnd. 9841 (1986).

[95] His account was given fully in a public explanation of his resignation on 9 January 1986—a statement not previously offered to the Prime Minister for clearance, on which aspect see Chapter 5.

considered by the Cabinet, and whether a meeting of an important Cabinet committee about Westland had been arranged and whether the Prime Minster had ordered its cancellation. Meetings of Minsters summoned by Mrs Thatcher had always, apparently, left Mr Heseltine in a minority, and at a Cabinet meeting on 12 December 1985 she refused him permission to raise the Westland issues.[96] On 9 January 1986 it was accepted by the Cabinet that all ministerial answers to queries about Westland should be referred to the Cabinet Office for clearance; Mr Heseltine could not accept that procedure, and resigned.[97] He variously described his reason for resigning as being the attempted censorship through the Cabinet Office clearance procedure, or as the 'breakdown of constitutional government'.[98] Throughout the saga the two sides heavily leaked: not even that safety valve, fully opened, could keep the government together, because Mr Heseltine considered the points of disagreement to be too vital, and none of the other safety valves described earlier could be resorted to.

Attention may now be turned to individual responsibility.[99] Broadly, each Minister is individually accountable for (a) his private conduct, (b) his general conduct of his department, and (c) acts done (or things left undone) by civil servants in his department. Responsibility for (a) and (b) is somewhat clearer than for (c).

It remains the case that a higher standard of private conduct is required of Minsters than of others in public life, a major reason for this today being that the popular press and the investigative journalism of its more serious rivals will make a wayward Minister's continuance in office impossible. The Profumo affair[100] in 1963 shows that a Minister who deliberately lies to the House of Commons cannot remain in the government. Mr John Profumo was Secretary of State for War, and his extra-marital affair with Miss Christine Keeler, who was also sharing her sexual favours with a Soviet naval attaché (in reality, a Soviet intelligence officer), additionally raised for some people possible security questions—certainly for the Opposition, which did not wish to found its attack openly on the morality of his sexual behaviour.[101]

---

[96] The Prime Minister's ability to control what is discussed in the Cabinet was examined in Chapter 5.

[97] The Westland company subsequently adopted the Sikorsky-Fiat package.

[98] See his article in the *Observer*, 12 January 1986.

[99] See generally de Smith and Brazier, n. 69 above, pp. 190–5; Wade and Bradley, n. 69 above, pp. 120–7; Marshall, n. 69 above, pp. 61–6 and ch. 6.

[100] On which see Marshall, n. 69 above, pp. 95–101; Harold Macmillan, *At the End of the Day* (1973), ch. 13; Lord Denning's Report, Cmnd. 2152 (1963).

[101] Lord Denning thought that the danger had been in Profumo's susceptibility to blackmail; Christine Keeler denied that she had ever asked him about national security matters.

Mr Profumo denied in the Commons that there had been any impropriety between him and Miss Keeler:[102] he could not stand the strain caused by that lie, and later resigned.[103] Lord Lambton's[104] resignation as a Minister and MP 10 years later, when it was revealed that he had used the services of prostitutes—of which encounters photographs and tape recordings existed—could again be linked to a possible national security risk: after all, he was Parliamentary Under-Secretary of State for Defence for the RAF at the time. The resignation the following day of Earl Jellicoe, the Lord Privy Seal and Leader of the House of Lords, who owned up to having done the same thing, had no obvious security aspect,[105] but he clearly thought that he had fallen below the standard of personal conduct required of a Minister. Ten years later still Mr Cecil Parkinson resigned as Secretary of State for Trade and Industry. Into the public domain had come the fact that his former secretary was expecting his child, together with her assertion that twice he had promised to obtain a divorce and to marry her, and had failed to try to do so. At first the Prime Minister strongly maintained that this was an entirely private matter which had no bearing on Mr Parkinson's ministerial life, but the press cared nothing about his ministerial life and so hounded him about the affair that he could no longer function effectively as a Minister, and resigned. He was summoned back to the Cabinet in 1987. The tabloid press played a key role in the eventual resignation of Mr David Mellor as Secretary of State for National Heritage in 1992. His extramarital affair was exposed, and subsequently allegations were made that he had not followed rules about gifts received by Ministers (in his case, of free holidays). Although he denied that allegation, and although the Prime Minister fully supported him for some months, he remained embarrassingly in the news before he resigned. In a way the press has made it unnecessary to judge the morality of Ministers in such a position. Indeed, Mr John Major's government was beset by criticism of individual Ministers for aspects of their personal behaviour. Usually they clung to office until media, back-bench, and constituency opinion forced them to

---

[102] For his personal statement, see 674 H. C. Deb. 809–10 (21 March 1963).

[103] He also left the House of Commons and asked for his name to be removed from the list of Privy Counsellors.

[104] This was a courtesy title: he was an MP at all material times.

[105] The Security Commission reported that there had been no danger to security in Lord Jellicoe's case (because he had entertained the girls in his own flat where there was no danger of photographs being taken, and he had used a false name); Lord Lambton, however, had taken cannabis during his sessions with prostitutes and there was a risk that he could have inadvertently revealed secret information: see Cmnd. 5367 (1973).

resign.[106] By contrast, the revelation in 1997 that Mr Robin Cook, the new Labour Foreign Secretary, had been having an extra-marital affair received a muted public and media response, and there never seemed to be any question of him having to resign.

In summary, if a Minister lies to Parliament, or so conducts himself as to raise an arguable case that national security could have been thereby compromised,[107] or conducts his financial affairs other than with scrupulous care,[108] or—though doing none of those things—through his behaviour makes it impossible for him to carry out his departmental duties because of the attentions of the media, then (regardless of how loyal the Prime Minister may be) he will have to go.

A Minster is responsible for the general conduct of his department: more precisely, he may have to pay the price for political misjudgement within it. What amounts to misjudgement may be a matter of opinion, and guidance can be difficult to formulate. A marginal case is provided by the preliminaries to the Falklands conflict. The Foreign Secretary, Lord Carrington, and two of his ministerial colleagues, Mr Atkins and Mr Luce, felt compelled to resign in 1982 after the Argentinian invasion of the Falkland Islands because they considered that the Foreign and Commonwealth Office had not adequately judged Argentina's intentions. The Prime Minister did not want to accept their resignations, but the three Ministers persisted and left the administration.[109] The subsequent wide-ranging inquiry by a committee of Privy Counsellors[110] exonerated them: no blame could be attached to any individual (or to the government collectively). The three Ministers' belief that a fresh Foreign Office ministerial team was desirable from the onset of the invasion had provided them with an impetus for resignation which any misjudgement alone perhaps would not have done. A clearer case from earlier in the same year involved the Solicitor-General for Scotland, Mr Nicholas Fairbairn, who gave his reasons for not

[106] For a catalogue see Brazier, n. 1 above, ch. 15.1, 15.2, and the Prime Minister's answers at 256 H.C. Deb. 365–6 (written answers 13 March 1995), 288 H.C. Deb. 14–17 (written answers 13 January 1997).

[107] In that second case, a Prime Minister could allow the Minister concerned leave of absence while the allegations were investigated. This has never been done, but it was urged as an alternative in the Profumo case by the First Secretary of State: see Anthony Howard, *RAB: The Life of R. A. Butler* (1987), pp. 298–9.

[108] Lord Brayley, Parliamentary Under-Secretary of State for Defence for the Army, had to resign in 1974 after an inquiry into his former business interests.

[109] See Carrington, n. 59 above, pp. 368–71. The Secretary of State for Defence, Mr John Nott, also offered to resign but his resignation was refused on the ground that the Ministry of Defence had not been responsible for policy on the Falkland Islands or Argentina.

[110] 'Falklands Islands Review', under the chairmanship of Lord Franks, Cmnd. 8787 (1983).

agreeing to a prosecution in a dreadful rape case to the press before going to answer questions about it in the House of Commons. He thereby offended the sensitivities of that House, and resigned. Mr Leon Brittan, the second Cabinet casualty of the Westland affair, has provided a further example of ministerial misjudgement within a department leading to resignation.[111] In January 1986 the Solicitor-General wrote a letter to Mr Michael Heseltine indicating some material inaccuracies in a letter which Mr Heseltine had sent to a merchant bank about Westland. Selective parts of the Solicitor-General's letter, damaging to Mr Heseltine, were soon telephoned to the Press Association by Miss Colette Bowe, Mr Brittan's director of information at the Department of Trade and Industry. There had been prior consultation between her and officials in the Prime Minister's office, and it was decided to use that rather curious method to put the Solicitor-General's views as quickly as possible into the public domain, in time for an important meeting of the Westland board. The Solicitor-General, however, had not been consulted, and was furious: not only are Law Officers' letters not leaked, but it is also a long-settled practice that even the fact of their opinions having been offered is never disclosed. The Cabinet Secretary was directed to conduct a leak inquiry. Mr Brittan was taken to have tacitly approved an inexpedient and improper leak; Mrs Thatcher agreed that, had she personally been asked for her view at the time, she would not have approved the precise form used to leak the Solicitor-General's views. Mr Brittan lost support among Conservative backbenchers, and resigned.[112]

The extent to which a Minister will carry the can for the errors of his civil servants is bound up with the aim of preserving the anonymity of civil servants, for only by making them reasonably secure from (and their political masters open to) public censure can they give frank advice to successions of Ministers. At one extreme a Minister's responsibility for his officials could be formulated as involving total responsibility for all the acts of his officials, however junior and even if he did not know of their existence. Thus on that view the resignation of Sir Thomas Dugdale as Minister of Agriculture in 1954 over the Crichel Down affair[113] was entirely correct

---

[111] See G. Marshall [1986] *Public Law* 184.

[112] Some of the claims made by or on behalf of the Prime Minister and the Secretary to the Cabinet in this episode lend great weight to Mrs Thatcher's statement (in a television interview on Westland) that 'Truth is often stranger than fiction'. Leon Brittan later publicly named Charles Powell (one of Mrs Thatcher's Private Secretaries) and Bernard Ingham (her press secretary) as having approved the leak: *Guardian*, 6 April 1989.

[113] On which see Turpin, n. 77 above, pp. 428–32, and references cited therein. Lord

even if he had had no knowledge of the maladministration of his senior civil servants—the better view being, however, that he had been personally involved in that maladministration and had failed to organize his department efficiently. At the opposite extreme, simple justice and the improved administration which could result from the rooting out of incompetent civil servants would require that individual officials be publicly named and disciplined for misconduct. Thus the judicial inquiry under the Tribunals of Inquiry (Evidence) Act 1921 into the collapse of the Vehicle and General Insurance Company in 1972[114] was, according to such a view, correct in blaming named civil servants in the Department of Trade and Industry for failing to set in motion a timely investigation of the company's affairs, and in exonerating the responsible Ministers. As far as ministerial responsibility in these matters is concerned, the middle way is normally taken, ignoring the two extreme paths. So the further the Minister was, geographically or hierarchically, from the people or events complained of, the less he will generally be expected to take the blame for mistakes and resign.[115] Or—to put it in the language used by Conservative Ministers during the 1980s and 1990s—Ministers are responsible for policy, while others (such as prison governors) are responsible for the operation of that policy; and for operational matters Ministers may have no responsibility. Such approaches explain a number of ministerial non-resignations, from that of the Colonial Secretary, Mr Lennox-Boyd, in 1959 over the killing of 52 people by the security forces in Nyasaland[116] (were they not, to borrow Neville Chamberlain's phrase, a far away people of whom Mr Lennox-Boyd knew nothing?), to that of Mr William Whitelaw as Home Secretary in 1982 after an intruder had confronted the Queen in her bedroom (for how could Mr Whitelaw know about or direct security measures at Buckingham Palace?),[117] to Mr Prior's and Mr Scott's as Secretary and Parliamentary Under-Secretary of State for Northern Ireland following the mass escape of 38 prisoners from the Maze Prison in

---

Carrington was Parliamentary Secretary at the Ministry of Agriculture at the time: for his account, see Carrington, n. 59 above, pp. 90–3.

[114] H. L. 80, H.C. 133 (1971–2).

[115] That was the view of the 1979 Conservative government. As the Lord Privy Seal put it in 1991, the doctrine of ministerial responsibility 'does not mean that Ministers must take all decisions, or take the blame for wrong decisions of their subordinates of which they know nothing or could be expected to know nothing': 532 H.L. Deb. 51 (written answers 18 November 1991).

[116] See Report of the Nyasaland Commission of Inquiry, Cmnd. 814 (1959); Harold Macmillan, *Riding the Storm* (1971), pp. 733–8.

[117] See Lord Whitelaw, *The Whitelaw Memoirs* (1989), pp. 211–13.

1983 (for how could they be expected to control day-to-day prison security throughout the province?).[118] The policy/operations defence was relied on especially by two Conservative Home Secretaries, Mr Kenneth Baker and Mr Michael Howard, who insisted that responsibility for prison escapes rested with the relevant prison governor or the Director-General of the Prison Service, and not with them.[119]

Failure adequately to discharge an aspect of a Minister's individual responsibility will not lead inexorably to loss of office. The Opposition may overreact in its criticism, perhaps putting down a motion of censure: then the government may well decide to close ranks around the unfortunate Minister and stand or fall with him. Mr Henry Brooke was so placed as Home Secretary from 1962 to 1964, and survived. And despite criticism of Mr William Waldegrave and Sir Nicholas Lyell (the Solicitor-General) by Sir Richard Scott in his judicial inquiry into the 'arms to Iraq' affair, the government and Conservative MPs closed ranks around them and voted down an Opposition attack on them in the House of Commons.[120] The Prime Minister in particular may stand firmly beside the Minister, defying the Opposition to defeat them—and government MPs not to support them. Sir Geoffrey Howe as Foreign Secretary was thus defended in 1983 when the Foreign and Commonwealth Office was discovered to have no more knowledge of the American invasion of the Commonwealth state of Grenada than the man in the street. Conversely, of course, if the Prime Minister decides that the Minister's position is untenable, he will be finished: thus Baldwin realized that Sir Samuel Hoare's conclusion on his own initiative of the Hoare–Laval Pact in Paris in 1935, which would have given the Italian invaders of Abyssinia part of that country, was ultimately indefensible.[121] And, despite the Prime Minister's full support for her Secretary of State for Trade and Industry, Mr Nicholas Ridley, after he had

---

[118] Mr Prior's offered resignation was refused: James Prior, *A Balance of Power* (1986), p. 232. Also refused, in 1992, was Mr Peter Brooke's resignation as Secretary of State for Northern Ireland. He had sung on a television chat show hours after terrorists had killed seven people in the province. See generally Rodney Brazier, *Constitutional Texts* (1990), pp. 378–84.

[119] For a prime example of Mr Howard's approach see 252 H.C. Deb. 31–4 (10 January 1995).

[120] For the Scott Report see H.C. 115 (1995–6); for the debate and vote see 272 H. C. Deb. 589–689 (26 February 1996).

[121] On being summoned by George V to receive the seals of office in succession to Hoare, Eden wrote that he was told by the King: 'I said to your predecessor: "You know what they're all saying, no more coals to Newcastle, no more Hoares to Paris" '. The King added that (not surprisingly) 'The fellow didn't even laugh'. The veracity of Eden's recollection has, however, been disputed: see Kenneth Rose, *King George V* (1983), p. 400.

apologized for using derogatory remarks in a magazine interview about
Germany's ambitions within the European Community, back-bench support for him collapsed. He resigned a few days later. Alternatively, the
Minister may be saved from resignation by being reshuffled to another
post, or he may resign following his transgression but return to a less
exposed and perhaps less important job when the dust has settled.[122] As
Professor Finer has observed, an enforced resignation will usually only
follow if the Minister is compliant, the Prime Minster willing to let him go,
and the party insistent that he should resign.[123]

Some Ministers have to decide matters which will have an effect
on industry, business, and the money markets. There are therefore sensible
rules which are designed to ensure that no conflict arises between the conduct of their ministerial offices and their private financial interests.[124]

The rules now in force were set out in an Annex to a Memorandum by
the Secretary of the Cabinet to the Royal Commission on Standards of
Conduct in Public Life.[125] The rules were subsequently codified in *Questions of Procedure for Ministers*, and are now in its replacement, the *Ministerial Code*. The main rules about financial interests are as follows.[126]
(a) Ministers must order their affairs so that there is no conflict between their
private interests and their public duties. They must not take an active part
in any undertaking which may have contractual or other relations with any
government department. This could arise not only if the Minister had a
financial interest in such an undertaking, but also if he were associated with
any body (even of a philanthropic character) which might have dealings or
disputes with the government. More precisely, (b) on assuming office
Ministers must resign *all* directorships which they hold in *any* company,[127]
as well as any directorships or offices held in any philanthropic undertaking

[122] Thus Dalton resigned as Chancellor of the Exchequer after his Budget leak in 1947, but
returned as Chancellor of the Duchy of Lancaster the following year; Hoare came back as First
Lord of the Admiralty in 1936; Mr Parkinson returned as Secretary of State for Transport in
1987.
[123] S. E. Finer, 'The Individual Responsibility of Ministers' (1956) 34 *Public Administration*
337 at 393–4.
[124] See Brazier, n. 1 above, ch. 7.
[125] The Parliamentary Clerk at Number 10 Downing Street kindly supplied me with a
copy of the Memorandum. It recorded that Campbell-Bannerman, Neville Chamberlain, and
Winston Churchill had all made parliamentary statements on the matter, the latter formulation still being the basis for the current rules: see 496 H. C. Deb. 702–3 (written answers 25
February 1952). Rules added since 1952 include those on partnerships, 'names' at Lloyds, and
pension arrangements.
[126] *Ministerial Code* (Cabinet Office, 1997), paras. 111–29.
[127] Excluding directorships in private companies established to maintain private estates.

if there is any risk of conflict arising through such an undertaking. (c) Ministers who are partners in professional firms, such as solicitors or accountants, must on taking office cease to play any day-to-day part in their firm's affairs—although they do not need to dissolve the partnership or let any practising certificate lapse. (d) Ministers are not expected to dispose of all their investments, but if they hold a controlling interest in a company a conflict of interest could then arise similar to those attaching to a directorship, and such a controlling interest should be disposed of. If shares are held in any company which could have dealings with the Minister's department, then, again, there could be a conflict of interest and those shares should be sold. (Mr Basil de Ferranti had to resign as Parliamentary Secretary, Ministry of Aviation, within a few months of his appointment in 1962 because it proved impossible for him to divest himself of shares in his family business which had major contracts with that Ministry.) In less clear-cut cases it might be appropriate for Ministers to place shares in the hands of trustees, that is, in a blind trust. (This was done by Lord Cockfield in 1982 after his appointment as Secretary of State for Trade: he deposited the share certificates of a company in which he had a small investment at his bank and directed the bank not to deal in those shares as long as he was a Minister.)[128] (e) No Minister should accept a gift or services which would place him under an obligation to a commercial undertaking. (John Belcher, Parliamentary Secretary, Board of Trade, fell badly foul of this rule by accepting small gifts knowing that in return speedy and favourable licensing decisions were expected from the Board of Trade.)[129] In any case of doubt about any of these rules, Ministers should consult the Prime Minister, who will be the final judge, advised by the Secretary of the Cabinet.

The House of Commons maintains a Register of Members' Interests.[130] Ministers who are members of that House have to make returns as MPs: most Ministers, having followed the rules already explained, have nothing to register. On leaving office, Ministers are free to put their expertise to work wherever they can, as company directors or otherwise. But checks now exist which are similar to those which apply to senior civil servants who wish to leave government service for the private sector. Normally a former Minister must wait three months (and can be required to wait two years) before taking up certain employment.[131]

---

[128] See also 34 H.C. Deb. 955–62 (22 December 1982).
[129] Report of the Lynskey Tribunal of Inquiry, Cmd. 7616 (1948).
[130] See Chapter 10.
[131] *Ministerial Code*, para. 129; Prime Ministers had consistently refused to lay down rules

Other, related rules are contained in the *Ministerial Code*. Ministers may not publish books relating (even if only loosely) to the work of their departments.[132] They may, however, publish fiction while in office (as Mr Douglas Hurd has voluminously demonstrated)[133] or books on historical,[134] scientific, or philanthropic matters. Ministers may not write regular newspaper columns, although occasional contributions on any matter are permissible.[135]

Ministers' pay and conditions

Ministerial salaries are prescribed by Order in Council made under the Ministerial and other Salaries Act 1975, section 1.[136] Under that Act (as amended) ministerial salaries are increased by the same annual percentage rise as that awarded to a civil servant at the mid-point in the senior civil service pay band. The Act provides for *maximum* salaries, and less may be paid:[137] so for example Mrs Thatcher and Mr Blair as Prime Minister and Lord Hailsham as Lord Chancellor[138] chose to draw only the same as their Cabinet colleagues, rather than the higher amounts which attached to their offices. Another consequence of that statutory provision is that the House of Commons may still in theory lawfully exercise its traditional right to

---

restricting former Ministers: see, for example, 667 H. C. Deb. 999–1000 (20 November 1962) (Macmillan); 766 H. C. Deb. 171 (written answers 20 June 1968) (Harold Wilson). Several Ministers who had been instrumental in the privatization programme during the 1980s were criticized by the Opposition for taking senior posts in privatized companies after they had left the government. For example, Mr Norman Tebbit was criticized by Labour back-benchers for accepting a directorship in British Telecom when he ceased to be a Minister and Chairman of the Conservative Party because, as a Minister, he had helped to privatize the company. See also Brazier, n. 1 above, pp. 300–301. The procedures indicated in the text were implemented following the 1st Report of the Committee on Standards in Public Life, Cm. 2850 (1995).

[132] As Dr Bray discovered in 1969: see above.

[133] He published a number of political thrillers in the 1970s and 1980s while holding various ministerial offices.

[134] Baldwin sanctioned the publication by his Chancellor of the Exchequer Winston Churchill of *The World Crisis*, vols. 1–5 (1923–28).

[135] Such as book reviews: the Secretary of State for Energy, Mr Peter Walker, for example, published a review of his former colleague's, Mr Michael Heseltine's, book *Where There's A Will* (1987) in *The Independent*, 11 March 1987.

[136] As amended by the Ministerial and other Salaries Act 1997.

[137] 1975 Act, s. 4.

[138] His salary is fixed at £2,500 a year more than that of the Lord Chief Justice: Ministerial and other Pensions and Salaries Act 1991, s. 3.

reduce a Minister's salary as a censure upon him.[139] The current maximum salaries for Ministers sitting in the Commons[140] are as follows.

Prime Minister	Lord Chancellor[141]	Cabinet Minister	Minister of State	Parliamentary Secretary
£60,000	£151,000	£45,000	£32,000	£24,200

Additionally, Ministers who are MPs are entitled to the parliamentary salary, currently £45,000. Even so, able people may be deterred from accepting office given the financial rewards which, compared with those of other callings, are limited.[142]

Some Ministers have the use of official residences, Number 10 Downing Street and Chequers for the Prime Minister, Number 11 Downing Street and Chevening for the Chancellor of the Exchequer, Number 1 Carlton Gardens and Dorneywood for the Foreign and Commonwealth Secretary, and Admiralty House.[143] Ministers have chauffeur-driven cars from the government car pool for use on official business. On leaving office Ministers receive a pension achieved through contributions from their ministerial salaries made to the Parliamentary Contributory Pension Fund.[144] None of these arrangements could be fairly described as excessive, or even generous.

[139] This last happened in 1976 when government whips prematurely released some of their MPs in the belief that the day's divisions had ended: the Opposition then carried a motion to cut the Secretary of State for Industry's salary by £1,000. Another vote restored it a few days later. See 905 H.C. Deb. 461–527 (11 February 1976) and 1133–1204 (17 February 1976).

[140] Cabinet Ministers in the Lords are currently entitled to a ministerial salary of £78,000. Ministers in the Lords now receive a parliamentary allowance in addition to their salaries: Ministerial and other Pensions and Salaries Act 1991, s. 5.

[141] Fourteen per cent of that pay is received as Speaker of the House of Lords.

[142] See Tony Benn, *Against the Tide: Diaries 1974–1976* (1989), p. 115.

[143] For the details see 586 H.L. Deb. 78–9 (written answers 23 February 1998). According to James Callaghan (who has been Chancellor of the Exchequer and Prime Minister) the living accommodation at No. 11 Downing Street is superior to that of No. 10: see *Time and Chance* (1987), p. 229. Harold Wilson did not live at No. 10 during his last premiership. Because he has three children, Mr Blair and his family live in the accommodation in No. 11, while the Chancellor of the Exchequer, Mr Gordon Brown, lives in the flat over No. 10. The Prime Minister and the Home, Foreign, and Northern Ireland Secretaries also have constant Special Branch protection. This can scarcely be classed as a benefit.

[144] Former Ministers who sat in the Commons will also have contributed part of their MP's pay towards an MP's pension. Severance pay is also available: Ministerial and other Pensions and Salaries Act 1991, s. 4. Former Prime Ministers and Lord Chancellors receive a pension of one half the annual pay payable in respect of those offices at the time they left them; ibid., s. 1. Former Prime Ministers may also claim an allowance to meet their continuing office costs; they are also provided with an official car: see 188 H.C. Deb. 428 (written answers 27 March 1991); 260 H.C. Deb. 125 (written answers 16 May 1995).

8

THE OPPOSITION

The main party out of power organizes itself for opposition, but the arrangements which it makes have far-reaching and perhaps unforeseen consequences for the shape and membership of its government when that party comes to power. The purpose of an Opposition is to oppose, but the Leader of the Opposition will be invited by the Prime Minister to co-operate with him from time to time, and the Opposition will be expected to co-operate with Ministers daily in the conduct of parliamentary business. Such constitutional paradoxes need to be explored and explained. The constitutional rights and duties of the Leader of the Opposition and of the Opposition as a whole, the similarities and differences in the composition and functions of Conservative and Labour Shadow Cabinets, and the consequences of dispositions made in opposition for the transfer of power between one party and another, must all be analysed in order to get a complete picture of the parliamentary Opposition in the United Kingdom.

The Leader of the Opposition

There is usually no doubt as to the identity of the person who is to be Leader of the Opposition.[1] A party Leader will assume that office in one of two ways. If a Prime Minister resigns having lost a general election, but remains at least for the time being in the House of Commons as Leader of his party (as most do and all have done—with one exception[2]—since

---

[1] Very little has been written about the place of the Leader of the Opposition in the constitution. For an exception see Sir Ivor Jennings, *Cabinet Government* (3rd ed., 1959), pp. 32–40, 43, 46, 51–7, 500–1. On the Opposition's role in the House of Commons, see J. A. G. Griffith and M. Ryle, *Parliament: Functions, Practice and Procedures* (1989), ch. 9.

[2] After the Labour Party's landslide victory in 1997 Mr John Major announced that he would resign as Conservative Leader as soon as a successor was elected, as Mr William Hague was in the following month. Mr Major remained as an MP.

1945), he will automatically be Leader of the Opposition if his party is the largest in the House in opposition to the government. Alternatively, if the Leader of the Opposition ceases to be Leader of his party, his successor as party Leader will succeed to the leadership of the Opposition. Only if two or more opposition parties had similar numbers of seats would there be any difficulty over which MP was Leader of the Opposition.[3] In any dispute, the Speaker has the duty of deciding the issue. That duty was given to him in 1937, when for the first time the Leader of the Opposition was accorded a salary by statute. The Opposition Leader was (and remains) defined as 'the Leader of that party in the House in opposition to Her Majesty's Government having the greatest numerical strength in the House'.[4] There has been no dispute since that provision was made.

The paramount constitutional duty of the Leader of the Opposition is to be ready to take office as Prime Minister. All his actions in opposing the government are taken with the aim of being required to assume that duty, which is characterized by a number of rights and obligations. First, after a general election in which his party has secured an overall majority of seats in the House of Commons, the Leader of the Opposition is entitled to be appointed Prime Minister on the resignation of the outgoing Prime Minister. That entitlement is so absolute that the transfer of power is as well-drilled as the changing of the Guard. In that clear case, it is the Leader of the Opposition's right to succeed to power forthwith, with no delay either from the defeated Prime Minister or from the Sovereign.[5] No Prime Minister since Baldwin in 1924 who has been defeated at the polls has waited to meet Parliament to have his fate sealed there. Procrastination by him would be pointless, because party disciplines are such that the accumulation of seats under each party's banner at the polls can be guaranteed to be

---

[3] Of the parties outside Lloyd George's coalition following the 1918 general election, Sinn Fein had 78 seats, Labour had 63 seats, and the Asquithian Liberals 28. Sinn Fein had the best *prima facie* claim to provide the Leader of the Opposition, but Labour objected on the ground that all Sinn Fein seats were in Ireland. Mr Speaker Lowther compromised by allowing the Chairman of the Parliamentary Labour Party and the acting Leader of the Asquithian Liberals to take turns in asking business questions and in opening and closing major debates for the Opposition. See Lord Ullswater, *A Speaker's Commentaries* (1925), vol. 2, pp. 251–2.

[4] See Ministers of the Crown Act 1937, s. 5; Ministers of the Crown Act 1975, ss. 2(1), (2). He is currently paid £101,500 a year, and is provided with a car from the government car pool. For details of other official assistance given to the Opposition in Parliament, see 310 H.C. Deb. 724–6 (written answers 24 April 1998).

[5] A slight pause may result if the principal actors have to return to London. After the 1970 Conservative victory, for example, the Queen was not advised to cut short a visit to Ascot races in order to return to Buckingham Palace and accept Mr Wilson's resignation and to appoint Mr Heath as his successor.

translated into firm party arithmetic in the new House of Commons. No Sovereign would seek to delay the fruits of victory to the Leader of the Opposition. He must not be put even to the theoretical risk of exclusion from power by the Sovereign taking advice before sending for him. If she were to consult anyone else in this clear parliamentary situation it could only be for the purpose of thwarting the Leader of the Opposition. No modern monarch would contemplate trying to put the clock back to Queen Victoria's occasional attempts to circumvent the will of the electorate.[6] Secondly, and by contrast, on the return of a hung Parliament the Leader of the Opposition has no automatic expectation either of the Prime Minister's immediate resignation or of his own summons to form a government.[7] So, for example, Mr Edward Heath acted perfectly properly in February 1974, after the general election had produced a hung Parliament: he stayed in office as Prime Minister for a few days to try to negotiate coalition with the Liberal Party. The then Leader of the Opposition, Mr Harold Wilson, subsequently acknowledged the propriety of Mr Heath's course of action.[8] When Mr Heath's attempt at coalition-making failed, he resigned—four days after the election—and Mr Wilson was appointed to succeed him, forming a minority Labour government. Lastly, in the different case of the resignation or retirement of the Prime Minister, or of his death, leaving a majority government, the Leader of the Opposition has no constitutional task to perform. The government party will elect a new Leader, and the Queen will appoint him Prime Minister.[9]

Most of the daily burden on a Leader of the Opposition does not, of course, consist of taking part in the transfer of power, but in leading his party in Parliament and in the country. It is inappropriate to dilate here on the party political duties of the Leader of the Opposition. Through his questioning of the Prime Minister in the House of Commons every Wednesday afternoon, in leading for his party in major debates, in harrying the government, and in seeking to portray the strengths of himself and of his party in the House of Commons, on television, and up and down the country, he is in part discharging his duty of preparing himself and his colleagues to take over the government by working for the electoral defeat of their opponents.

[6] For the Victorian examples, see Jennings, n. 1 above, pp. 33–7.

[7] Jennings, n. 1 above, pp. 32ff., in discussing conventions about the Leader of the Opposition, gives insufficient thought to the consequences of the return of a hung Parliament, and fails to qualify the Opposition Leader's rights in that case.

[8] See Chapter 3.

[9] As on the last occasion, in 1990, when Mr Major succeeded Mrs Thatcher.

Plainly a major purpose of an Opposition is to oppose. But the Leader of the Opposition occasionally has to decide whether to set aside that purpose so as to offer limited co-operation to the Prime Minister, when the Prime Minister offers him access to confidential official information, or invites him to enter into consultations on government policy. To what extent is the Leader of the Opposition obliged to give that co-operation? There is no reason why the head of government and the head of the Opposition should not meet informally and privately. Their respective positions do not require them to carry their party differences to the extreme of avoiding one another outside the chamber of the House of Commons. Naturally, some holders of these offices have got on better personally than others: Harold Macmillan and Harold Wilson, for example, enjoyed a drink together at the House of Commons from time to time without compromising the intense political rivalry between them, as did John Major and John Smith, whereas others (such as Mrs Margaret Thatcher and Mr Neil Kinnock) disliked each other so much that personal contact was avoided as much as possible. On a more formal level, any Leader of the Opposition (perhaps together with one or two senior colleagues) may be offered briefings and consultations on Privy Counsellor terms, that is, on condition that information communicated is not revealed to others.[10] A government's motives in making such offers may be very mixed. Ministers may think that certain important information should be known to the person who might be Prime Minister one day; or they may hope that, once the Opposition Leader realises the constraints within which Ministers must operate, he will understand that government policy is not as indefensible or wrongheaded as he might otherwise allege; or even that, once he knows all the facts, he might be reduced to silent acquiescence. Whatever may be the rhetoric of the party dogfight, constitutional history shows that consultations between Prime Ministers and Leaders of the Opposition have been extensive. Such talks have taken place in particular in two areas of public policy, constitutional affairs, and foreign affairs and defence.[11]

There are numerous examples of meetings on Privy Counsellor terms about constitutional matters. The Ulster crisis produced negotiations

---

[10] A new Leader of the Opposition, if not already a Privy Counsellor, will be made one. This is partly to make briefings on Privy Counsellor terms possible, partly so that he may be given precedence in being called by the Speaker, and partly as an honour. During the 1992 Parliament a number of Labour Shadow Cabinet members were made Privy Counsellors on the nomination of the Leader of the Opposition.

[11] Consultations on economic affairs have been rare. The events leading up to the formation of the National Government in 1931 provided an exception.

between Asquith and Bonar Law, although little was achieved either in producing a better mutual understanding of Liberal and Unionist positions or (even less) in working towards any common policy.[12] Such consultations were entirely in keeping with the gravity of the crisis. The future government of India, too, caused inter-party talks to take place, for example before the Simon Commission was established in 1927.[13] Baldwin consulted MacDonald on what the Labour membership of the Commission should be, and obtained agreeable nominations from him.[14] During the abdication crisis, Baldwin was able to deploy a subtle blend of statesmanship and political cunning: he met the Leader of the Opposition, Clement Attlee, the Leader of the Liberal Party, Sir Archibald Sinclair, and Winston Churchill as a group, to keep them informed but also to ensure that, if his advice to the King about his proposed marriage to Mrs Simpson were rejected, none of them would be prepared to form a government. If it was to prove to be a matter of the King's abdication or of Baldwin's resignation (as it did so prove), these talks can be said to have settled that issue.[15] Again, at various times during this century attempts to reform the House of Lords have led to negotiations between the Prime Minister and the other party Leaders, sometimes to be continued by surrogates but always with the most important points being agreed to (or dissented from) by the Prime Minister and his opposite number.[16] And since the 1970s the Prime Minister and the Leader of the Opposition have sought to maintain a degree of all-party agreement on Northern Ireland through face-to-face talks.[17] Important

---

[12] Asquith suggested that he and Bonar Law meet in October 1913. Two further meetings followed, in November and December, after which they acknowledged that a bipartisan approach was out of the question. With the Prime Minister's permission, the Leader of the Opposition made it known publicly that the talks had taken place. See Roy Jenkins, *Asquith* (3rd edn., 1986), pp. 287–8.

[13] Kenneth Harris, *Attlee* (1982), pp. 75–84.

[14] Including the man who was ultimately to secure the passage of independence legislation for India, Clement Attlee. See Harris, n. 13 above, pp. 76–7.

[15] Keith Middlemas and John Barnes, *Baldwin* (1969), p. 999; Harris, n. 13 above, pp. 132–4. Attlee consulted none of his colleagues before giving Baldwin the assurance he wanted to hear from the Leader of the Opposition.

[16] This last happened during the 1964–70 Labour government, when all-party talks nearly reached full agreement on reform. Macmillan consulted Gaitskell on the form of what became the Life Peerages Act 1958; for that, and other talks between them, see Alistair Horne, *Macmillan 1957–1986* (1989), pp. 83, 96, 180–1, 185, 366–7. And for discussions between Macmillan and Wilson, ibid. pp. 156–7. In 1998 talks about Lords reform took place between the Leader of the House of Lords and the Leader of the Opposition in that House. They were unsuccessful.

[17] Indeed, in 1998 the Prime Minister, the Opposition Leader, and the Leader of the Liberal Democrats worked publicly together to promote the Northern Ireland Good Friday agreement (Cm. 3883 (1998)).

statements by the Prime Minister touching the Queen or the royal family will invariably be shown to the Leader of the Opposition in advance, and there may also be discussions on the underlying issues with him in private before any statement is made.

These were all matters of high constitutional importance and occasionally drama. But there are also regular contacts between the Prime Minister and the Opposition Leader in more mundane constitutional matters. So, for example, a list of new working peers is drawn up from time to time, consisting of people who will be expected to take a full part in the parliamentary work of the House of Lords, and who will take a party whip there.[18] Again, a Dissolution Honours List is issued early in the life of each new Parliament, primarily to honour former Ministers and MPs of all parties who did not seek re-election. The Prime Minister will have consulted the other party Leaders about it.[19] More generally, whenever the main Opposition party is to provide members of investigative bodies such as Royal Commissions or committees of Privy Counsellors,[20] possible names will be put up by the Leader of the Opposition to the Prime Minister.

Consultations in foreign affairs and defence have had a similar history throughout this century. Thus in 1908 Balfour accepted the Prime Minister's invitation to join the Committee of Imperial Defence—a remarkable display of bipartisanship and the most formal arrangement for contacts between a Prime Minister and a Leader of the Opposition up to then and since.[21] During his first premiership when he was also Foreign Secretary, MacDonald often sent Foreign Office papers to Baldwin in an attempt to reduce the differences between the parties on foreign policy.[22] He also consulted Baldwin over Ireland. Throughout the European crisis from 1938 to 1939, and into the war, Chamberlain kept the Opposition leaders informed of his negotiations with the dictators and about the progress of the war.[23] And there are several other instances of discussions on foreign policy and defence throughout the century.[24] During times of armed conflict, the government will be careful to keep Opposition leaders informed about the fighting.[25]

---

[18] Other party Leaders are not always consulted in this process.

[19] See further Chapter 11.

[20] An example of the latter would be the inquiry by six Privy Counsellors into British policy on the Falkland Islands leading up to the Argentinian invasion.

[21] Jennings, n. 1 above, p. 267.   [22] Middlemas and Barnes, n. 15 above, p. 268.

[23] Jennings, n. 1 above, p. 501.   [24] Jennings, n. 1 above, pp. 500–3.

[25] See for example David Steel, *Against Goliath* (1989), p. 232 (the Falklands conflict in 1982); Anthony Seldon, *Major: A Political Life* (1997), pp. 155–6 (the Gulf conflict in 1990–91).

This catalogue shows that such discussions are almost a common feature of the constitution. But is the Leader of the Opposition under any obligation to enter into talks with the Prime Minister if they are offered, and, if he does, what are the limitations on the use to which he may put information received during them? Clearly such an offer may be very tempting to an Opposition Leader because, by accepting it, he may appear statesmanlike (to his own satisfaction, at any rate). But on the other hand by receiving information which is only available to the government he may well restrict his freedom to attack Ministers, because without the Prime Minister's consent neither the fact that a meeting took place nor what passed in it may be communicated to others: that is the effect of the gentlemen's agreement which is implicit in a meeting on Privy Counsellor terms. It is for that reason that a Leader of the Opposition may properly refuse an offer from the Prime Minister. A rejected overture which was made in 1958 illustrates the point well. Macmillan approached Hugh Gaitskell as Leader of the Opposition with a proposal that they should hold joint talks on defence policy.[26] Gaitskell declined. Apart from the political difficulties which such discussions would almost certainly have caused him within his own party, it was also suggested (and possibly Gaitskell accepted the suggestion) that such an arrangement would be incompatible with the Opposition's constitutional function of criticizing the government; for if Gaitskell had received secret information this would have inhibited him when his party pressed him to attack the government's policy. Conversely, it was also suggested[27] that the Opposition had a duty to the Crown which could not be properly discharged if information which would help it in its duties were refused. That last point is, however, old-fashioned and vague—for what is the Opposition's duty to the Crown? Indeed, it could be said that because the Opposition's principal duty is to be ready to assume office, anything which would tend to blunt the Opposition's attack on the government (and thus make its accession to power even marginally less likely) should be resisted. The Leader of the Opposition must make a political judgement, rather than apply some constitutional precept, in deciding whether there would be any advantage in agreeing to offered talks. Perhaps for that reason the Labour Opposition refused an offer of talks from the Secretary of State for the Environment in 1990 on possible reforms of the poll tax.[28] That view might,

[26] Geoffrey Marshall and G. C. Moodie, *Some Problems of the Constitution* (5th edn., 1971), p. 138.

[27] By Professor Max Beloff, letter to *The Times*, 29 April 1958.

[28] For the offer, made to all the parties, see 184 H. C. Deb. 318 (5 December 1990).

perhaps, be subject to an obligation to confer on matters of exceptional national gravity, although even that might not be beyond dispute.

Because these discussions are held in secret and are rarely acknowledged publicly at the time, the extent to which a Prime Minister and a Leader of the Opposition conduct them cannot be ascertained. Discussions on routine matters go on through surrogates behind the Speaker's chair, but how often those two Leaders meet on matters of high national concern is unknown.[29]

A remarkable overture to an opposition party was made by Mr Blair in 1997. He formed a Joint Cabinet Consultative Committee with the Liberal Democrats, on which sat Mr Paddy Ashdown and four of his parliamentary colleagues. A major purpose of the committee was to continue Labour and Liberal Democrat co-operation on constitutional policy, but other matters of mutual interest were discussed as well.

Constitutional duties of the Opposition

The ways in which an Opposition prepares itself politically to win power— by developing policy, by portraying its leaders as people eminently fit to govern, and (perhaps of greatest importance these days) by showing the party to the electorate on television as being competent and desirable—are outside the scope of this chapter. But the parliamentary duties and powers of the Opposition are of central relevance.

The principal parliamentary duty of the Opposition is to oppose. Through attacks on the government as a whole and on individual Ministers, inadequacies are exposed, ministerial responsibility to Parliament is made real, and the Opposition's status as the alternative government is set out. At the same time, because the Opposition is loyal to parliamentary democracy, the duty to resist is taken to embrace the acknowledgement that the government has a right to govern and (in the main) to get its legislation through.[30] Accordingly, all-out obstruction of parliamentary business is very rare:[31] normally, it has no part in an Opposition's repertoire.

---

[29] Mrs Thatcher was asked in the House of Commons what the arrangements were for briefing the Leader of the Opposition on security matters. In a written reply she said that 'as a matter of normal practice I do not propose to confirm or deny whether briefings on security matters are envisaged or have taken place': 143 H. C. Deb. 345 (written answers 9 December 1988).

[30] The precedence of government business in the House of Commons in recognized in its standing orders: see S. O. No. 14(1).

[31] The action of Irish MPs in the 1880s was the last sustained example.

The Opposition will challenge, question,[32] debate, divide the House: but, in the end, the government's majority will inevitably carry it through,[33] and the Opposition would be foolish if it failed to accept the facts of parliamentary life and embarked on a doomed attempt to stop the government's legislative programme in its tracks. Parliamentary realities and constitutional duty in this sense go happily hand in hand.

The parliamentary co-operation which is essential to ensure that the House of Commons functions efficiently (so as to get government business through) but with due regard to the proper role of the Opposition (so as to enable it to carry out its parliamentary tasks adequately) manifests itself in several ways. Government and Opposition Whips are in daily contact behind the Speaker's chair to try to reach agreement on a range of matters—the avoidance of guillotine motions (which are frequently not avoided), the timing of adjournments, the dates of recesses and the timing of, and subjects for, debates. The Opposition has a completely free choice of subject on Opposition days;[34] it chooses (after discussion through the usual channels) the subjects for debate on the address in reply to the Queen's Speech. Governments accord Oppositions other rights, too.[35] Otherwise, however, the government has control of the timetable of the House of Commons, although Opposition Whips will seek to persuade government business managers to be flexible and to meet Opposition requests about the arrangement of the order paper. Through co-operation and compromise parliamentary business can be conducted to the benefit of both sides of the House.

A rather different form of co-operation with Ministers may take place outside the chamber of the House and the committee rooms. In the same way that the Prime Minister and the Leader of the Opposition may confer on Privy Counsellor terms, so on occasion Ministers may wish to consult Shadow Ministers. Such contacts are subject to the same considerations as attach to talks between their chiefs.

---

[32] The Leader of the Opposition questions the Prime Minister every Wednesday, and is allowed up to six questions—more than any other party Leader; he may also put Private Notice Questions to Ministers—although his question to the Chancellor of the Exchequer in 1988 was the first from a Leader of the Opposition to a departmental Minister for 34 years: see 140 H.C. Deb. 21–7 (7 November 1988). See also Chapter 10.

[33] Although even governments with large majorities are vulnerable to occasional defeat, as the loss of the second reading of the Shops Bill in 1986 showed.

[34] See Chapter 10.

[35] Opposition MPs chair important select committees, such as those on Public Accounts and the Parliamentary Commissioner for Administration; and the Opposition provides the chairmen for about half the departmental select committees.

If, however, the Opposition at any time considers that it cannot co-operate with the government—because, say, it feels that Ministers have behaved in a high-handed or unfair or improper fashion—what can it do? It may ask for government time to debate a censure motion, either one of no confidence in the government (for which time is usually found by Ministers),[36] or one to reduce a Minister's salary (for which time will normally, but not invariably, be found by the government).[37] Rarely will either motion be carried. The Opposition could go further if it considered that government actions had absolved it from the duty of co-operation, and refuse discussions about business through the usual channels. Deliberate obstruction of business, through repeated points of order, interventions during government MPs' speeches, refusing to co-operate in standing committees or in the work of departmental select committees, would constitute inconvenience for any government. In the end, however, it will amount to no more than an inconvenience, because Government Whips can ensure victories in the division lobbies to carry (for example) the closure and the guillotine. Perhaps as a result deliberate obstruction is a course upon which Oppositions do not often embark.[38]

Because any Shadow Cabinet wants to look like an alternative government, and because a Leader of the Opposition wishes to be seen to be in command of a united team, all Opposition spokesmen willingly accept a duty to be bound by an obligation of collective responsibility—at least on first appointment. That collective responsibility applies to all Opposition spokesmen from the Shadow Cabinet down to the most junior spokesman on the least important aspect of government activity.[39] Some commentators have said that this is one of the most significant developments in the position of the Shadow Cabinet during this century.[40] The doctrine is easier to embrace in opposition than in government, simply because it is rather less onerous. Dissent is less likely to lead to dismissal or resignation from the shadow team, because while a government must maintain the impression of unity, an Opposition is obviously not constrained by the doctrine of

[36] See Erskine May, *Parliamentary Practice* (21st edn., 1989), p. 272.
[37] In 1988 the Opposition put down an early-day motion to reduce the Chancellor's salary by £1,000. The Cabinet discussed the request for government time to debate it, and rejected it on the ground that the Opposition could use an Opposition day in the following and imminent parliamentary session for the purpose.
[38] For a rare modern example, see 984 H. C. Deb. 114 (6 May 1980).
[39] See R. Brazier, *Ministers of the Crown* (1997), ch. 3.2.
[40] See D. L. Ellis, 'Collective Ministerial Responsibility and Collective Solidarity' [1980] *Public Law* 366 at 392; R. K. Alderman and J. A. Cross, *The Tactics of Resignation* (1967), p. 69.

ministerial responsibility. The pressure for collective action and speech is less. Shadow Ministers do not head real departments, and so there can be no question of their resignation following ministerial or official miscon- duct in any department.[41] And decisions in opposition do not have to be as clear-cut or as final as is required in government: the opportunities for glossing over differences are greater.

In the last resort resignation or dismissal is the sanction for an inability to accept the policies of the Shadow Cabinet. In its 13 years of opposition from 1951, it is true, only two people resigned from the Labour Shadow Cabinet following fundamental disagreements on policy.[42] But, by con- trast, Labour's years in opposition from 1979 to 1997 witnessed several cases of dismissal of Opposition spokesmen[43] for refusals to go along with party policy,[44] as well as a resignation of a member of the Shadow Cabinet of his shadow portfolio because of disagreement over his Leader's style and lack of consultation over the policies within that portfolio,[45] and also resignations of Opposition spokesmen who could not accept Shadow Cab- inet tactics over legislation.[46] Mr Kinnock took a very strict view of the

[41] A Shadow Cabinet member's personal conduct might fall below the standard which his parliamentary colleagues and his Leader thought was required, and any resignation would be similar to a Minister's resignation for breach of the obligations of individual responsibility. A junior defence spokesman resigned in 1993 after being convicted of being drunk and disor- derly and assaulting a police officer. He was appointed nonetheless as a junior Minister in 1997.

[42] Aneurin Bevan in 1954 over the party's attitude to the creation of the South East Asia Treaty Organization and American policy in South East Asia; and Anthony Greenwood in 1960 over Gaitskell's leadership.

[43] They were junior Opposition spokesmen, not elected members of Labour's Shadow Cabinet who cannot be dismissed from it.

[44] For example, in 1982 Mr Michael Foot dismissed three junior spokesmen who had voted in a debate on the Falklands crisis contrary to the advice from the Shadow Cabinet; in 1986 Mr Neil Kinnock sacked Mr Norman Buchan as arts spokesman because he refused to accept the party's policy on future ministerial arrangements for broadcasting; and in 1988 Ms Ann Clwyd was dismissed as a junior education spokesman for voting against the defence esti- mates after the Parliamentary Labour Party had decided to abstain. In 1989 Mr Kinnock sacked Mr Austin Mitchell as a trade and industry spokesman for taking a job as a television interviewer, which Mr Kinnock thought might have led to breaches of collective responsi- bility when Mr Mitchell interviewed other Labour spokesmen.

[45] Mr Denzil Davies resigned as Shadow Defence Secretary in 1988 (but not from the Par- liamentary Committee) because he thought that Mr Kinnock was developing the party's defence policy in media interviews without consulting him.

[46] Ms Clare Short and Mr Andrew Bennett refused to go along with the Shadow Cabinet's decision to abstain on the second reading of the Prevention of Terrorism (Temporary Provi- sions) Bill in 1988, and resigned their junior spokesmanships. Mr Jim McAllion resigned in 1996 as a junior Scottish affairs spokesman rather than accept Labour's policy of holding a ref- erendum about a Scottish Parliament.

obligations of collective responsibility. During his nine years as Leader of the Opposition, several Labour spokesmen either resigned, or were sacked, for failing to toe the Shadow Cabinet line.[47] Conservative Shadow Cabinets, by contrast, have been much more cohesive affairs. Mr Enoch Powell's notorious 'rivers of blood' speech in 1968 on the consequences of immigration policies was a spectacular exception which prompted the Leader of the Opposition to dismiss him. Mrs Thatcher's period of opposition from 1975 to 1979 was characterized by traditional Conservative solidarity, although Mr Winston Churchill was dismissed as a junior defence spokesman after he had voted (contrary to a Shadow Cabinet decision) against the annual renewal of the Southern Rhodesia Sanctions Order in 1978.[48] Mr William Hague lost his shadow Minister of Agriculture, Mr David Curry, in 1997: he opposed the Shadow Cabinet's policy towards the euro. This Conservative unity and occasional Labour disunity can be explained, perhaps, by the loyalty of Conservative MPs and spokesmen to the Leadership (which is only overborne in extreme cases), and by the omnipotence of the Conservative Leader in both the creation of policy and in the appointment to shadow or actual office. As will be seen later, the Leader is much freer than his Labour counterpart to shape policy in his own image, and to choose entirely congenial colleagues who will follow the party line.

The shadow government

With the development of the party system in Parliament, particularly during the mid- and late nineteenth century, the need for the party out of power to decide its parliamentary tactics and policies was increasingly satisfied by the members of its previous Cabinet—by the ex-Cabinet, or, in a term which came into fashion in the 1880s, the Shadow Cabinet.[49]

[47] For example, four spokesmen were sacked (and Mr John Prescott was reprimanded) in 1991 for refusing to accept Labour's policy towards the Gulf conflict. Mr Tony Blair dismissed two junior spokesmen in 1995 after they missed important House of Commons business while on an unauthorized overseas trip. Mr John Smith lost Mr Bryan Gould from the Shadow Cabinet in 1992 over Labour's European policy.

[48] Mr John Biggs-Davison (a junior Northern Ireland spokesman) resigned over the same issue.

[49] For the historical background see D. R. Turner, *The Shadow Cabinet in British Politics* (1969), chs 1–5; R. M. Punnett, *Front Bench Opposition* (1973), pp. 36–73; John Mackintosh, *The British Cabinet* (3rd edn., 1977), pp. 259–61, 530–41; Sir Ivor Jennings, *Parliament* (2nd edn., 1957), pp. 81, 181–2. And see generally on the shadow government Brazier, n. 39 above, ch. 3.1.

The Conservative Shadow Cabinet[50] has always enjoyed three characteristics which distinguish it from its Labour equivalent. It has never been the subject of formal rules; its members have always been chosen at the personal discretion of the Leader of the Conservative Party; and its methods of working have largely depended on the personality and wishes of the Leader. After the 1906 electoral débâcle, Balfour was content that the members of the former Conservative Cabinet should constitute the Shadow Cabinet, and it was not until four years later that he added new members, including F. E. Smith. Baldwin, as Leader of the Opposition in 1924 and from 1929 to 1931, summoned a Shadow Cabinet which met regularly and formally, and which was serviced by the Conservative Research Department. He styled this body the Leader's Consultative Committee, a title which has been kept formally to this day to underline whose committee it is, and what is its function. Churchill called a Consultative Committee to weekly meetings after Labour's 1945 landslide (with, typically of Churchill, fortnightly lunches at the Savoy Hotel).[51] At first it consisted of 15 members, but Churchill added new members from time to time without discharging any existing member, so that it eventually grew to a body of over 25 people. All Conservative Privy Counsellors sat on the Opposition front bench; individuals were not charged with shadowing any particular department. In keeping with that rather informal approach, no minutes were kept of meetings. As will be seen later, those loose arrangements were to be significant in Churchill's Cabinet-making in 1951. When the Conservatives went back into opposition in 1964, changes were made in the workings of the Shadow Cabinet which were to affect (among other things) the choice of Ministers and the machinery of government decided upon by subsequent Conservative Prime Ministers.

In stark contrast, Labour's dispositions out of government have always been more formal, being based on the party's constitution and, more recently, on the Parliamentary Labour Party's standing orders. These provide for elections to the Shadow Cabinet and leave the Labour Leader with much less choice of his colleagues. Labour's internal arrangements became of general constitutional interest in 1922, when for the first time in its history the party became the second largest group in the House of Commons. MacDonald, as Leader of the main party in opposition to the Conservative government, became Leader of the Opposition. The Parliamentary Labour

---

[50] And, indeed, the Liberal Shadow Cabinet in the nineteenth and early twentieth centuries.

[51] On Churchill's Shadow Cabinet arrangements, see Martin Gilbert, *Never Despair: Winston S. Churchill 1945–1965* (1988), pp. 163, 227, 529; Robert Rhodes James, *Anthony Eden* (1986), pp. 316–18; Harold Macmillan, *Tides of Fortune* (1969), pp. 43–6.

Party (PLP) elected an Executive Committee, whose title was changed in 1950 to the Parliamentary Committee to avoid confusion with the National Executive Committee of the Labour Party. The formal title of Labour's Shadow Cabinet remains that of Parliamentary Committee. From 1923 to 1981 the Parliamentary Committee consisted of 12 MPs elected by the PLP (together with *ex officio* members); in 1981, PLP standing orders were amended to increase that number to 15, and subsequently to 18, then to 19.[52] Those 19 members are elected at the beginning of each parliamentary session.[53] Seven people are members of the Parliamentary Committee *ex officio*,[54] making a total membership of 26 directly and indirectly elected members. Another change made in 1981 was that the Parliamentary Committee would continue in being when Labour is in government, although with a different membership.[55] A Labour Leader of the Opposition may, at his discretion, invite two other colleagues to attend meetings of the Parliamentary Committee, although they do not thereby become members of it. He may, for example, want the expertise of a member of the parliamentary party at his disposal during Shadow Cabinet deliberations, even though that person had failed to be elected to membership. Examples of this device have included the confirmation by Mr Kinnock of Mr Martin O'Neill as Shadow Defence Secretary and of Mr Kevin McNamara as Shadow Northern Ireland Secretary, even though neither secured election to the Shadow Cabinet in the autumn of 1988; and Mr Blair's appointment of Dr Jack Cunningham as shadow National Heritage Secretary in 1995 despite his failure to be re-elected to the Shadow Cabinet. A Labour Leader is, therefore, largely although not entirely constrained by the wishes of the PLP as to who should be his principal advisers and party spokesmen—and who should be senior Ministers when the party comes to government.[56] Not only the membership, but also the functions, of the Parliamentary Committee are provided for by PLP standing orders.[57] It is the executive

[52] See PLP Standing Orders, s. F.6. In voting for the Parliamentary Committee, each Labour MP must cast at least four votes for women candidates.

[53] For the detailed election procedure, see PLP Standing Orders, s. I; R. M. Punnett, *Front-Bench Opposition* (1973), pp. 110–18. Any casual vacancy on the Committee is now filled by a by-election: see Standing Orders, s. F.11.

[54] The Leader, Deputy Leader, Opposition Chief Whip, Chairman of the PLP, Leader of the Labour peers, Chief Whip in the Lords, and one peer elected by Labour peers: Standing Orders, s. F.6.

[55] Standing Orders, s. F.1. The membership in government is: the four officers, six back-bench MPs (elected by back-bench MPs), one back-bench peer (elected by back-bench peers), and four members of the government selected by the Prime Minister.

[56] This point will be elaborated below.

[57] PLP Standing Orders, ss. F, I.

authority of the PLP and (for example) must ensure proper liaison between the parliamentary party and the National Executive Committee, must discuss the forthcoming business of the House, and (when the party is in power) must maintain a channel of communication between the government and back-benchers in both Houses. To do so, it must meet weekly.

There are thus major differences between the Shadow Cabinets of the two main parties. The Conservative Shadow Cabinet was, historically, based on ex-Cabinets: the formation of a Shadow Cabinet was a consequence of losing ministerial office. Labour's Parliamentary Committee was provided for in opposition, for opposition, rather than as a consequence of losing power. A Conservative Leader has an unfettered discretion in choosing his Shadow Cabinet:[58] he can appoint, reshuffle and discard spokesmen at will. The large majority of a Labour Shadow Cabinet is, on the other hand, elected or is there *ex officio*: there is, accordingly, no guarantee that a Labour Leader will find the Parliamentary Committee congenial either as to personalities or as to policies. He cannot dismiss elected members of the Parliamentary Committee—although he can reshuffle shadow portfolios. These differences have consequences for the patronage powers of the party Leaders when they choose the members of a government.

The smaller parties have not usually gone in for full-blown Shadow Cabinets. Any attempt to do so by a party with only a handful of MPs would be pretentious and perhaps silly. For one special purpose—the Lib.-Lab. pact of 1977 to 1978—the Liberal Leader did, however, nominate an entire 'shadow administration', which contained a large number of peers.[59] The Liberal Democrats, who currently have 46 MPs, are able to field spokesmen in the Commons, supplemented by Liberal Democrat peers.

At the turn of the century, Lord Salisbury's government consisted of some 60 Ministers. By the time of Churchill's return to power in 1951, the total administration numbered over 80. Today a government will have over 100 members. The size of the Cabinet has ranged throughout the century (except in wartime) at between 18 and 24. If an Opposition is to be able to discharge its parliamentary functions efficiently—by putting questions to Ministers, by opening and winding up debates, by having an official spokesman on standing committees, and so on—there must exist not just a Shadow Cabinet but also an entire shadow administration. This trite proposition was, however, first acted on only some 45 years ago. In 1955 Clement Attlee announced two major changes in his Opposition

---

[58] Including whether or not to nominate a Deputy Leader.
[59] For the arrangements, see David Steel, *A House Divided* (1980), Appendix 4.

arrangements. First, members of the Parliamentary Committee and other Opposition spokesmen were to cover specific policy areas, and thereby were to have shadow portfolios.[60] Secondly, in order to ensure that there would always be a party spokesman available for all Opposition parliamentary activities, a total of 39 members of the PLP were appointed as spokesmen, in addition to the members of the Shadow Cabinet. Each Parliamentary Committee member would have a small team of spokesmen beneath him and subject to his leadership.[61] The junior spokesmen were appointed by the Leader. Some opposed these changes,[62] but they had substantial advantages: the Opposition could be more effective, as a result of specialization; everyone could see clearly who was likely to take charge of which Ministry in the event of a Labour government; enough spokesmen would be available to meet the demands of appearances in the constituencies and (increasingly) on television. Limits were set later on the Labour Leader's increased patronage by PLP standing orders which require that the list of spokesmen be submitted to the PLP 'for its approval', and that the total number of Opposition spokesmen should be 'of the order of one-fifth of the PLP'.[63] Nine years after Attlee's changes, the Conservative Leader was to flatter Labour by imitating that system when the Conservatives left office, and it has remained the pattern for Oppositions of both colours ever since. In the result, a Leader of the Opposition will have a Shadow Cabinet, junior spokesmen, Opposition Whips, and party spokesmen in the House of Lords. Mr William Hague's shadow administration in the Commons currently numbers 60 people.[64]

The increase in the number of Opposition spokesmen way beyond a Shadow Cabinet has created potential friction within any Opposition party in the Commons between its front bench spokesmen and its backbenchers. Anyone who is entitled to sit on the Opposition front bench has precedence in being called by the Speaker.[65] During the last century the convention developed that the seats on the front bench to the Speaker's left

[60] See Punnett, n. 53 above, pp. 59–65.

[61] The Opposition front bench team became 45-strong. The present PLP Standing Orders, s. G.2(iii) state that 'non-elected Front benchers should not depart from the policy line of the senior spokesman for the area'.

[62] Herbert Morrison, for example, attacked them on the ground that they increased the patronage of the Opposition Leader: see *Government and Parliament* (1959), p. 350.

[63] PLP Standing Orders, s. G.1. What would be the consequence if the PLP did not approve? As will be seen shortly, the PLP now claims a similar veto over junior ministerial appointments.

[64] There is also a full complement of Conservative spokesmen in the Lords.

[65] See Erskine May, n. 36 above, p. 367.

were for Opposition MPs who were Privy Counsellors. If the Leader of the Opposition wanted an MP to become a member of his Shadow Cabinet and to speak from the Opposition front bench, he would need to procure a Privy Counsellorship for him if he were not already a member of the Privy Council. This presented no great difficulty when the Conservative and Liberal Parties alternated in office, because the outgoing Cabinet would simply move to the Opposition front bench. When Labour formed the Opposition for the first time in 1922, however, very few of Mac-Donald's colleagues were Privy Counsellors: the Speaker ruled that in the circumstances his Shadow Cabinet could all occupy the Opposition front bench, thus resolving that technical difficulty.[66] But Attlee's creation of an entire shadow government in 1955 created another problem: were all his spokesmen to occupy the front bench, with the advantage in catching the Speaker's eye which went with such seating? That was, indeed, to be the case, but the PLP later adopted a standing order to strike a balance between the rights of Labour back-benchers to contribute in the House, and the rights of the 80 or so Opposition spokesmen to speak for the party there. Thus, at Question Time, or after a ministerial statement, or during debate, when more back-benchers wish to contribute than would otherwise be able to, a 'non-elected Front Bencher' should not try to put a supplementary question (unless he had put the original question), or intervene, unless he has a compelling constituency or regional interest.[67] Conservative MPs have no parliamentary standing orders, and there is no equivalent rule to help Conservative back-benchers—although no doubt timely complaints to the Whips would be made if Conservative Opposition spokesmen were to try to hog parliamentary occasions. The conventions of the House require that Opposition spokesmen who are neither Shadow Cabinet members nor Privy Counsellors should sit on the back-benches, and only move to the front bench while exercising their official Opposition functions in the House.

Shadow into substance[68]

The Leader of the Opposition becomes Prime Minister through the operation of the political process and by an exercise of the royal prerogative.

---

[66] Privy Counsellors on the Opposition side who are not party spokesmen do not sit on the Opposition front bench.

[67] PLP Standing Orders, s. G.2(iii).   [68] See Brazier, n. 39 above, ch. 3.3.

Others receive ministerial office at his hands as Prime Minister: the Queen will appoint to office anyone recommended by him. A new Prime Minister has patronage extending over more than 100 ministerial jobs. What is sought to be shown now, however, is that a Prime Minister's hands are largely tied while still in opposition over who should be in the Cabinet, and at which departments represented in it. This is quite apart from the general constraints on anyone who forms a government for the first time. At the same time he has a much freer hand over the choice of the 80 or so Ministers who are not to be in the Cabinet—although in Labour's case the PLP has a role to play in relation to such junior Ministers.

It was noted earlier that the bulk of a Labour Shadow Cabinet is elected as the Parliamentary Committee, while others are members *ex officio*, and that the Leader of the Labour Party is bound by that election and that he cannot remove any elected member. All Shadow Cabinet members will be allotted a portfolio to shadow, or will be given a specific task to discharge. These arrangements affect the formation of any Labour Cabinet. By the time of Labour's electoral victory in 1964, the party had been in opposition for 13 years. Harold Wilson had few colleagues at his disposal who had held Cabinet or other ministerial office in the Attlee government. He formed a Cabinet of 23 Ministers. All except Frank Cousins had been in the Shadow Cabinet.[69] But five members of the Shadow Cabinet were not given Cabinet office.[70] When Mr Wilson returned to office in 1974 after a break of less than four years, he included all his Shadow Cabinet in the actual Cabinet.[71] The next Labour Prime Minister was *required* to give all elected Parliamentary Committee members seats in the Cabinet because of the provisions of PLP Standing Orders, s. E. This reads:

When the Party is in Office, the Cabinet shall continue to be appointed by the Prime Minister. On taking office as Prime Minister, the Leader shall appoint as members of his Cabinet those who were elected members of the Parliamentary Committee at the Dissolution and have retained their seats in the new Parliament.

This standing order was adopted in 1981, and was a manifestation of greater accountability of the parliamentary leadership to the party as a whole, represented in this case by the PLP.[72] The standing order recognizes the

---

[69] He had been General Secretary of the Transport and General Workers Union.

[70] Three were given posts outside the Cabinet; two (both peers) received no office.

[71] The 1964–70 period of Labour government had vastly increased the pool of those with ministerial experience.

[72] See Dawn Oliver, 'The Constitutional Implications of the Reforms of the Labour Party' [1981] *Public Law* 151.

constitutional authority of the Prime Minister to appoint the Cabinet.[73] But what is the nature of the obligation cast on him by that standing order?[74] Clearly a new Labour Prime Minister would not be bound to include in his Cabinet those spokesmen whom he had added to the Parliamentary Committee at his discretion, because they had not been elected. As to the majority of that Committee who had been elected, however, the PLP would expect the standing order to be implemented. But what would be the sanction if it were not? A new Labour Prime Minister would be under a moral and political duty to carry out the spirit of the standing order, and no doubt would wish, in the main, to do so. The Sovereign would take no account of whether a Prime Minister had followed the internal rules of his party in submitting his list of Cabinet appointments for approval. Her constitutional obligation is merely to consider that list and to offer whatever comment seems appropriate. If she were to remark that a Parliamentary Committee member did not feature in the Cabinet list, she would have to confirm the list as drafted if that remained the Prime Minister's advice: for it is the cardinal convention of the constitution that the Sovereign accepts ministerial advice.[75] A disappointed member of the Parliamentary Committee would have to look to the PLP for help, but the PLP would be unlikely to take any formal action over the matter. After all, following the 1945 election victory, Herbert Morrison tried to insist that Attlee seek re-election as Leader of the Labour Party before he accepted the King's commission to form a government. The party's Administrative Committee and the PLP refused to inquire into that claim, and Attlee became Prime Minister without a party election.[76] On forming his first Cabinet in 1997 Mr Tony Blair left out two elected Parliamentary Committee members, Mr Michael Meacher and Mr Tom Clarke; they were made junior Ministers. Neither appears to have troubled the PLP with a grievance.

[73] Strictly, to recommend such appointments to the Queen.

[74] If any elected member of the Parliamentary Committee lost his Commons seat at the general election, the Labour Leader would be under no obligation to him under the standing order.

[75] The Sovereign may object to any proposed appointment (and did, in relation to F. E. Smith in 1918, Beaverbrook in 1940, and Dalton and Bevin as Foreign Secretary and Chancellor respectively in 1945: see Chapter 4); but if the Prime Minister persists in his recommendation, the Sovereign must follow the convention that ministerial advice must be accepted in the end.

[76] See Harris, n. 13 above, pp. 262–3; Harold Wilson, *The Governance of Britain* (1976), p. 24. The standing order would not seem to apply at all when a Labour Prime Minister takes office otherwise than after a general election victory. So if a Labour Prime Minister were to retire and were succeeded by a Cabinet colleague, his successor would seem to have a free hand.

How long does the obligation in the standing order last? In the past, Labour Prime Ministers have felt free to drop original members of the Cabinet after a while and to bring in new blood.[77] The standing order implicitly accepts that that authority should continue, perhaps in recognition that a Prime Minister should not be forced to retain anyone who has proved inadequate. Moreover, while the Parliamentary Committee is no longer dissolved when the party is in government, on the first elections to it in a new Parliament its membership is very different from that in opposition, and only a minority of those who had been nominated to the Cabinet from it will be eligible to be on the new Committee. That also seems to recognize the Prime Minister's authority to make Cabinet changes when he thinks fit, without regard to what the composition of the Parliamentary Committee had been when he first formed a government.

The PLP also claims power over non-Cabinet ministerial appointments. PLP Standing Orders, s. G.1 (headed 'Junior posts in government and front bench spokespersons in Opposition') reads:

Junior Posts and Front Bench Spokespersons shall be appointed by the Leader but the list shall be submitted to the PLP for its approval and any change effected by the Leader shall be notified to the PLP at the earliest available opportunity. The total number of Front Benchers shall be of the order of one-fifth of the PLP.

This imposes a novel restriction on a Labour Prime Minister. Although inelegantly drafted, it purports to give the PLP a veto over the Prime Minister's initial appointment of 80 or so junior Ministers, and also over any changes made throughout the life of the government. Even the least important Parliamentary Secretaryship would be subject to PLP ratification. The same considerations over whether a Labour Prime Minister would be bound by it, and what sanctions might exist in case of breach, apply as in the case of the choice of a Labour Cabinet.[78] In 1997 the first item of business at the first PLP meeting in the new Parliament was the formal approval of all ministerial appointments, which was done on the nod.

---

[77] Harold Wilson's first Cabinet reshuffle came 14 months after he had taken office in 1964. He dropped Tom Fraser, the Minister of Transport, from the Cabinet. Mr Blair followed the same timetable, dropping Harriet Harman, David Clark, Gavin Strang and Lord Richard from his Cabinet in 1998.

[78] The restriction on the number of 'Front Benchers' probably refers to 'Front Bench Spokespersons' *in opposition*. If it were read as meaning that a Labour Prime Minister's patronage were to be limited, a Labour government with a one-seat majority would consist of no more than 75 Ministers (one-fifth of 376)—a reduction of 25 to 30 in the size of any government since 1945. The PLP would need to be *500* strong to permit a government of 100 Ministers.

Churchill's loose parliamentary arrangements for opposing the Attlee government were described earlier. The significance for Churchill's Cabinet-making in 1951 was that he was able to appoint to particular offices more or less anyone whom he thought fit (except that Eden had a reversion on the Foreign Office). No one (except for Eden) had an obvious claim to any particular department. So, for example, R. A. Butler was surprised to be given the Treasury;[79] Harold Macmillan (who had established himself as a principal spokesman on industrial and economic matters in opposition, and who had frequently spoken on foreign affairs) was taken aback when offered the Ministry of Housing;[80] Iain Macleod's appointment as Minister of Health was so unexpected that he had no idea where the Ministry was;[81] the new Secretary of State for Commonwealth Relations, Lord Ismay, had no reason to think that he would be in the government at all.[82] Churchill even felt able to invite the Leader of the Liberal Party, Clement Davies, to join the Cabinet as Minister of Education.[83] Rarely could a Prime Minister have had such an unfettered discretion. No Prime Minister was to enjoy it again. Sir Alec Douglas-Home's disposition of his Opposition team when the Conservatives lost office in 1964—arrangements which have been followed by both of the Conservative Leaders of the Opposition since—ended that Churchillian exercise of power. He appointed a shadow Minister for every government department, including the new departments freshly created by Harold Wilson and which were to be abolished when the Conservatives returned to power in 1970. Some of the members of the late Conservative Cabinet were given fresh shadow responsibilities:[84] there was to be no continuation of the old, informal habit of former Ministers automatically shadowing their former departments. Specific, efficient shadowing and criticism of the new government, and preparation for the next Conservative government, were to be the orders of the day.[85] Edward Heath maintained that opposition pattern, and when he formed his

[79] See Lord Butler, *The Art of the Possible* (1971), p. 156; Anthony Howard, *R.A.B.: The Life of R. A. Butler* (1987), pp. 178–80.

[80] 'I knew nothing whatever about the housing problem except that we had pledged ourselves to an enormously high figure, generally regarded by the experts as unattainable': Alistair Horne, *Macmillan 1894–1956* (1988), p. 332.

[81] See Nigel Fisher, *Iain Macleod* (1973), pp. 85–6.

[82] Gilbert, n. 51 above, pp. 653–4.

[83] He was tempted to accept, but the other Liberal MPs were against it and Davies rejected the offer.

[84] For example, the former Minister of Transport, Ernest Marples, became Shadow Minister of Technology.

[85] For his own account, see Lord Home, *The Way the Wind Blows* (1976), pp. 217–18.

Cabinet in 1970 he left out only two members of his Shadow Cabinet (although both were made Ministers of State),[86] and he included in it only two who had not been in the Shadow Cabinet.[87] Similarly, Mrs Thatcher took the same approach as Leader of the Opposition, and when she came to power left out only three Shadow Cabinet members from her actual Cabinet (two becoming Ministers of State[88] but one receiving no office),[89] and brought in only three non-members.[90] Since 1964 new Prime Ministers of both parties have overwhelmingly given members of the Shadow Cabinet the same real portfolios as those which they had shadowed in opposition. Indeed, it has been the occasions when this has not happened which have caused comment—the switch in 1964 of Richard Crossman to the Ministry of Housing and Local Government (after he had shadowed education) and Michael Stewart to the Department of Education and Science (after he had shadowed housing), or making Quintin Hogg Lord Chancellor in 1970 when he had been Shadow Home Secretary. Mr Blair was much more adventurous in 1997. Mr Donald Dewar (who had been Opposition Chief Whip) was appointed Secretary of State for Scotland; Mr George Robertson (Scotland) became Secretary of State for Defence; Mr Frank Dobson (environment) went to the Department of Health; Dr Jack Cunningham (national heritage) became Minister of Agriculture; Mr Chris Smith (health) became National Heritage Secretary; Dr David Clark (defence) was appointed Chancellor of the Duchy of Lancaster; and Dr Gavin Strang (agriculture) became Minister of Transport. But, in general, a translation of shadows into substance is entirely sensible: after all, Shadow Cabinet members will usually have had several years' experience in mastering their shadow departmental responsibilities, and there would need to be a pressing reason to appoint someone to a ministerial portfolio for which he had had no training in opposition. For those reasons in making his shadow appointments a Leader of the Opposition is in fact ensuring that, if he forms a Cabinet, it will largely choose itself as to members and who goes to which department. He will be freer in appointing junior Ministers.

An observer in the public gallery of the House of Commons looking down on the Opposition benches might consider the Opposition as representing at one and the same time several different aspects of parliamentary

[86] Lord Balniel and Mr Joseph Godber.
[87] Mr Michael Noble and Mr Peter Thomas.
[88] Mr Tom King and Mrs Sally Oppenheim.   [89] Mr John Peyton.
[90] Lord Soames, Mr Peter Walker and Mr David Howell. See Margaret Thatcher, *The Downing Street Years* (1993), pp. 25–9.

government. If he casts his mind back, he might view the Opposition as the party which had been rejected by the electorate at the last general election. Or, as he watches the day's proceedings unfold, he might see the Opposition benches made up of people with daily tasks to perform, some important, some insignificant, many tedious, but all necessary to make parliamentary democracy work. Or he might look ahead, and see the Opposition as the future government if the voters were to decide next time that they had made a mistake last time. Such thinking would in fact encapsulate the functions of the Opposition in today's constitution.

9

CONSTITUTIONAL MONARCHY

The Queen is a symbol of national identity, a focal point of national loyalty, transcending political partisan rivalry. She personifies the state and the nation, their history and continuity. Coronations, royal weddings and funerals, and an investiture of a Prince of Wales are great national occasions. The Queen is also the supreme governor of the Church of England and an exemplar of family life. Wide legal powers are vested in the Queen or Her Majesty in Council. A great many formal acts have to be done by her in a traditional manner and require her personal signature or approval. She also presides at Privy Council meetings and reads the Queen's Speech at the opening of each new Parliament or parliamentary session. She receives letters of credence from ambassadors and Commonwealth High Commissioners, receives homage from new bishops, and holds some two hundred formal audiences each year.[1]

The Queen additionally has a part to play behind the political scenes. The extent to which a particular Sovereign may have a major impact on public affairs will depend on the number and gravity of the political problems of his or her reign. It was not till near the end of his life that Edward VII was faced with a serious constitutional issue, the dispute about the proper relative powers of the two Houses. George V, on the other hand, not only inherited that problem but his reign also saw the Home Rule crisis of 1912 to 1914, the trauma of the First World War, the choice of Baldwin or Curzon to succeed Bonar Law in 1923, the first (and minority) Labour government in 1924, the General Strike, the economic depression, and the events of the summer of 1931. His handling of these, and many less weighty, issues set the pattern for modern constitutional monarchy. Edward VIII's was a single-issue reign: the whole of his kingship may now be seen as a preparation for his leaving of it. George VI was required to be

---

[1] S. A. de Smith and R. Brazier, *Constitutional and Administrative Law* (8th edn., 1998), pp. 129, 134. See also R. Brazier, *Constitutional Texts* (1990), ch. 8; *Constitutional Reform* (2nd edn., 1998), ch. 7; V. Bogdanor, *The Monarchy and the Constitution* (1995).

a symbol for a nation at war for survival, and had to supervise a critical decision in 1940: fortunately, the choice between Halifax and Churchill as Chamberlain's successor was made for him. The Queen has been unavoidably involved twice in the succession to the office of Prime Minister, in 1957 and in 1963; otherwise political questions since 1952 have been answered by politicians. By 1999 she had experienced 34 years of government by the Conservatives and 13 by Labour—slightly more of the latter variety than the aggregate under all of her predecessors. Although we must wait for the authorized biography to be published after her death for reliable information about her conduct as a constitutional monarch, the indications are that she has matched her father and grandfather as an exemplary head of state.

Some matters have been considered elsewhere in this book and so will not be further rehearsed here, such as the Sovereign's role in the choice of a Prime Minister,[2] her influence and function in the formation of a new government,[3] and the circumstances in which she might exercise her right to refuse a requested dissolution of Parliament.[4] Rather, what may be called her usual powers to advise, to encourage, and to warn her Ministers will be examined in this chapter, as will her reserve powers (any of which would, if exercised, involve the rejection of ministerial advice), followed by the legal rules which ensure the smooth operation of monarchy when the Sovereign is in some way incapacitated, and which regulate the succession to the throne.

The Queen's usual powers

The Queen normally exercises her formal legal powers on ministerial advice.[5] Asquith admirably summarized matters in a minute to George V in December 1910:

The part to be played by the Crown . . . has happily been settled by the accumulated traditions and the unbroken practice of more than seventy years. It is to act

---

[2] See Chapters 2 and 3.   [3] See Chapter 4.   [4] See Chapter 3.

[5] Two routine exceptions are her Christmas Day broadcast to the Commonwealth and her Commonwealth Day message, neither of which are prepared or delivered on ministerial advice as they are made in her capacity as Head of the Commonwealth—a title which imports only a symbolic function, not a legal or constitutional one: see R. W. Blackburn, 'The Queen and Ministerial Responsibility' [1985] *Public Law* 361. The text of the Christmas Day broadcast is shown in advance to the Prime Minister. Abnormal situations in which the Queen might act *contrary to* ministerial advice will be considered later.

upon the advice of the Ministers who for the time being possess the confidence of the House of Commons, whether that advice does or does not conform to the private and personal judgement of the Sovereign. Ministers will always pay the utmost deference, and give the most serious consideration, to any criticism or objection that the Monarch may offer to their policy; but the ultimate decision rests with them; for they, and not the Crown, are responsible to Parliament.[6]

The Queen's usual powers are customarily encapsulated in the formula that she has the rights to advise, to encourage, and to warn Ministers.[7] These rights must be employed with scrupulous impartiality in relation to governments of different party colours: the Sovereign must be totally even-handed, colour-blind as between the parties. Royal biographies and political autobiographies show that these powers are routinely exercised and are generally welcomed by Ministers, so that the Sovereign may have a marginal but beneficial influence on governmental decisions. It is convenient to look first at the Sovereign's right to encourage a Prime Minister and Ministers who are in difficulty or who need a little help, for that right will be exercised in uncontroversial circumstances.

It is impossible to read the official biography of George VI[8] without perceiving how Neville Chamberlain must have been heartened by the King's letters and audiences, particularly in relation to the policy of appeasement[9]—or without understanding the equal succour which Chamberlain's successor received to help him prosecute the total opposite of Chamberlain's policy: indeed, George VI and Churchill developed a close, comradely relationship during the war.[10] The King's third and last Prime Minister, Attlee, and the post-war Labour Ministers were accorded similar friendly help and a good working relationship was soon established.[11] After the 1950 general election, at which Labour held on by a tiny majority and after which the Conservative Opposition did its best to grind down weary Ministers[12] by keeping them late in the House of Commons every night,

---

[6] Quoted in Colin Turpin, *British Government and the Constitution: Text, Cases and Materials* (2nd edn., 1990), p. 99. Asquith wrote in a similar vein three years later, but on that occasion emphasized that it was the King's *duty* to point out any objections he might have and to suggest alternatives: see Sir Ivor Jennings, *Cabinet Government* (3rd edn., 1959), p. 336.

[7] Bagehot's actual formulation was 'the right to be consulted, the right to encourage, the right to warn': Walter Bagehot, *The English Constitution* (1963 edn., with Introduction by Richard Crossman), p. 111. The ways in which the Queen is consulted were described in Chapter 3.

[8] Sir John Wheeler-Bennett, *King George VI: His Life and Reign* (1958).

[9] Ibid., Part III, chs. 3 and 4.   [10] Ibid., Part III, chs. 6–9.

[11] Ibid., pp. 650–4; Sarah Bradford, *King George VI* (1989), pp. 380–2.

[12] Many Labour Ministers had been continuously in office since 1940.

the King was sympathetic (although not at the price of seeking to defer the inevitable second election). Occasionally, the Sovereign may offer encouragement to an individual Cabinet Minister, rather than to the Prime Minister or the government as a whole. An instance has been revealed which took place in 1976. In that year James Callaghan as Foreign and Commonwealth Secretary was contemplating an approach to the regime which had made an unlawful declaration of independence in Rhodesia in 1965, and he mentioned this to the Queen at a dinner. The following day Mr Callaghan received a letter from the Queen's Private Secretary stating Her Majesty's view that, despite the clear difficulties in the way of success, she thought that an approach along the lines indicated to her by the Foreign and Commonwealth Secretary would, in her opinion, be worthwhile. Fortified thus by such 'an authority on the Commonwealth', the initiative was made.[13] Any Minister will be gladdened by a sympathetic hearing and helpful words from someone above the party battle, with no political axe to grind, and who (in the Queen's case) has seen it all—or nearly all—before.[14]

It is when a Sovereign chooses to advise or to warn that necessarily a Prime Minister may hear things which he finds uncongenial. Although George V greeted the first-ever Labour Prime Minister fairly and in a friendly way,[15] and through an early memorandum[16] and through other means[17] helped the Labour Party to adjust to the responsibilities of government, none the less at MacDonald's very first audience the King told him that he objected to some of Lansbury's remarks about the Court, that the combination of being both Prime Minister and Foreign Secretary was too much for one man, that he hoped he would never have to receive a representative of the Soviet government which had murdered his cousin and the Tsar's family, and that he wished the Labour Party would stop singing the 'Red Flag'.[18] Baldwin, in his turn, was urged in 1924 'to really close and

[13] James Callaghan, *Time and Chance* (1987), pp. 378–82. Like so many other attempts by governments of both parties to negotiate with the regime, it failed.
[14] Queen Victoria once gave Gladstone information which Wellington had given her about Pitt. It would be interesting to learn if the Queen has had occasion to give any of her Prime Ministers information which (say) Churchill had given her about Asquith.
[15] '[The King] has been considerate, cordially correct, human and friendly', MacDonald wrote in his diary: Kenneth Rose, *King George V* (1983), p. 329.
[16] It is set out in Sir Harold Nicolson, *King George V* (1952), p. 502.
[17] '[F]rom the moment Labour took office, the King seized every opportunity to demonstrate his trust both in public and in private; and when old friends presumed on their intimacy to commiserate with him on the affliction of a socialist Government, they were sharply snubbed for their pains': Rose, n. 15 above, p. 328.
[18] Nicolson, n. 16 above, pp. 497–9.

powerful grips with such questions as housing, unemployment, the cost of food and education',[19] and was later warned against the dangers of undue provocation by the government during the General Strike. The best-known—and ultimately heeded—royal warning was that issued by George VI to Churchill in 1944: it was just short of a command that Churchill should not view the hostilities at the D-Day landings.[20] It took two letters from the King (with some arguments suggested by his Private Secretary Sir Alan Lascelles)[21] and an explanation from the Navy of the dangers which would be involved before Churchill abandoned his plan: 'I must defer to Your Majesty's wishes and indeed commands', as the Prime Minister put it in a letter to a relieved King.[22]

A constitutional monarch will remember, before voicing either advice or warning, that however long may be her experience she does not have to preside over what may be a far from compliant Cabinet; she does not have to defend herself to the public through the media; she does not have to manage the House of Commons, or eventually face the electorate. What may be seen as an ideal policy from Buckingham Palace may simply not be practical politics in the view from Downing Street. The Sovereign will understand, too, that some of the obligations owed to her may also be minor irritants or inconveniences from time to time: a hard-pressed Prime Minister may wish that ideally his weekly 30-minute or hour-long audience could be missed in deference to other pressures on him (but it is neverthe-less rare for that audience not to take place while Parliament is sitting).

Some obligations also affect other Ministers: Richard Crossman, when Lord President of the Council, regularly recorded his annoyance in his diary[23] that he and three colleagues had to travel for Privy Council meet-ings to the Queen at Balmoral when she was on holiday there, rather than the Queen break her holiday and return to London so as to save four busy Ministers perhaps a night and a day away from their offices.[24] (It is difficult

[19] Nicolson, n. 16 above, p. 520.

[20] Wheeler-Bennett, n. 8 above, pp. 601–6; Sir Winston Churchill, *The Second World War*, vol. v (Penguin edn., 1985), pp. 546–51.

[21] Including the point that the King himself had wanted to go too, and yet he had been prevailed upon not to.

[22] A convention may still exist which requires the Sovereign's consent for the Prime Minister to leave the United Kingdom, although Churchill implicitly denied it in that letter. Cabinet Ministers are required by a rule in the *Ministerial Code* ((Cabinet Office, 1997), paras. 69, 70) to seek the Queen's approval as well as the Prime Minister's for any absence from the United Kingdom (other than to European Union states).

[23] Richard Crossman, *Diaries of a Cabinet Minister* (1975), vol. ii, pp. 44, 194, 490, 512; vol. iii, pp. 39, 52, 132.

[24] Three Privy Counsellors constitute a quorum.

to understand why Privy Council business could not be wholly conducted in writing during the Queen's absence from London.) In all these matters, therefore, the Sovereign needs an acute appreciation of her Ministers' circumstances and a deftness of touch so as not to cause antagonism in her dealings with them.

The existence of the rights to advise and to warn must mean that the Queen will have personal views about some political issues which will not coincide with those of the Prime Minister and the Cabinet. Indeed, the opinions of the Queen and of her government *could not* always be the same unless she were to undergo a very odd change of heart and mind on the main issues of the day with every change of party government. The Sovereign may urge her view on the Prime Minister, especially at the weekly audience (at which the two are alone and no formal record is kept)—but in strict confidence, and in the end normally deferring to any contrary view persisted in by the Prime Minister. Any public revelation of disagreement could be damaging to the existing and future relationship between head of government and head of state, for obviously if it became known that the Queen had criticized government policy, she might be taken to be biased against that government and to be in favour of another. In 1986 someone in Buckingham Palace (generally assumed to be the Queen's Press Secretary Mr Michael Shea) allowed the *Sunday Times* to publish a story[25] that the Queen was 'dismayed' by 'an uncaring Mrs Thatcher': the source had agreed with suggestions from that newspaper that the Queen disapproved of several major government policies. The Queen's Private Secretary Sir William Heseltine intervened in a rare letter to the press.[26] He made three points which must be correct. (a) The Sovereign has the right and duty to counsel, encourage and warn her government. She is thus entitled to have opinions on government policy and to express them to the Prime Minister. (b) Whatever the Queen's personal opinions may be, she is bound to accept and act on the advice of her Ministers.[27] (c) The Sovereign is obliged to treat communications with the Prime Minister as entirely confidential. Sir William totally denied that any member of the Queen's household

[25] *Sunday Times*, 27 July 1986. See Geoffrey Marshall, 'The Queen's Press Relations' [1986] *Public Law* 505.
[26] *The Times*, 29 July 1986. Rare, but not unprecedented. Sir Alan Lascelles had written under the pseudonym Senex about when a dissolution of Parliament could be refused: *The Times*, 2 May 1950, and see Chapter 3.
[27] Sir William did not digress into the situations in which the Queen might be justified in using her reserve powers contrary to Ministers' wishes—an understandable omission in the circumstances.

would reveal the Queen's private views, and concluded that Her Majesty enjoyed 'a relationship of the closest confidentiality with Mrs Thatcher', emphasizing that reports purporting to be the Queen's opinions on government policies were 'entirely without foundation'. The *Sunday Times* stood by its story; Mr Shea left the Palace in March 1987 for a job in industry. Now whether the Queen actually held the views ascribed to her is unimportant, but the episode does amply demonstrate the complete truth of her Private Secretary's three points, especially that the Sovereign can only exercise her rights, and a political consensus will only remain in favour of her continuing to do so, if complete confidentiality is observed by both Buckingham Palace and Number 10 Downing Street.

The Queen's reserve powers

Prime Ministers and governments do not routinely request dissolutions of Parliament in circumstances in which the Sovereign feels constrained to refuse; the Sovereign does not insist on a general election when her government does not advise one; royal assent to legislation is not withheld; governments do not decline to leave office having lost a general election, or behave in any other outrageous or illegal way so that the Sovereign is moved to dismiss them from office. These things just do not happen in Britain: rather, the players observe the rules of the game. That the Queen however possesses in law what I term her reserve powers[28] which would enable her to behave in these ways is not disputed.[29] Analysis of them is, however, made rather unreal through the difficulty of proposing hypothetical facts which would not be brushed aside as fanciful, thus causing doubt whether those powers could ever be used. Still, that analysis must be tried, for it would be a very strange constitution which endowed a head of state with certain rights but which did not allow of any indication of the circumstances in which they might be used and the consequences of their use.

   All the reserve powers share a common attribute: the deployment of any of them would involve the setting aside of the cardinal convention of the constitution that the Queen must act on ministerial advice; for in all cases what the Sovereign would be moved to do (or not to do) would run

---

[28] Termed, less happily, by Jennings, n. 6 above, ch. 13, her 'personal prerogatives'; see also Geoffrey Marshall, *Constitutional Conventions* (1984), ch. 2.

[29] Save (at least in part) by those few who still adhere to the 'automatic theory' of dissolution, dismissed above in Chapter 3.

counter to that which her Ministers advised. One of the reserve powers—refusal of a recommended dissolution—has been discussed in Chapter 3. So let the first reserve power to fall for consideration here be the Queen's right to insist, contrary to the government's wishes, that Parliament be dissolved. The Queen not only has the legal power to dissolve Parliament: Parliament cannot be dissolved without her intervention, for dissolution requires an exercise of the royal prerogative. The main circumstance customarily and correctly offered as a case in which the Queen would be justified in insisting that a general election take place is where a government has lost a vote of confidence in the House of Commons yet refuses either to recommend a dissolution or to resign; but then no government in Britain would ever behave in such an astonishing fashion. Another case sometimes and again correctly suggested would be where a government wished improperly to postpone a general election beyond five years after the previous one,[30] say through fear of rejection by the electors; but, again, it is entirely improbable that would ever be contemplated.[31] It is worth noting, though, that in both hypotheses a forced dissolution would be for the Queen a lesser evil than dismissal of the government, for the electorate, not the politically neutral head of state, would be able to decide the political issue of whether that administration should be replaced.

The only situation in this context which is worth examining in any detail is one which actually came to pass earlier this century. If a government were to advise the Sovereign to create a large number of peers in order to secure the passage of legislation (perhaps legislation to abolish the House of Lords itself), the Sovereign could insist that the government's policy be first approved by the electorate.[32] Peerages are created on the Prime Minister's advice.[33] If the Queen thought that a mass creation was improper,[34] she *could* refuse to make such a creation, but the more prudent course would be

---

[30] Dissolutions were properly postponed with all-party agreement during both world wars. See Parliament and Registration Act 1916; Parliament and Local Elections Acts 1917 and 1918; Prolongation of Parliament Acts 1940 to 1944.

[31] Indeed, assuming that such an errant administration at least stayed within the law to the extent of persuading Parliament to pass a Bill to extend Parliament's maximum five-year term, the Sovereign's role would arise in the context of refusing her assent to that Bill, a reserve power considered later.

[32] For a technical reason to be explained later, however, I doubt whether a request for a mass creation of peers is likely ever to be made again.

[33] Save for two cases: peerages granted to members of the Royal Family (such as the earldom conferred on Princess Margaret's then husband, and the Dukedom of York to Prince Andrew), and the earldoms given to former Prime Ministers: see further Chapter 11.

[34] For example, because a Bill to abolish the House of Lords could be passed, despite the dissent of that House, under the Parliament Acts 1911 and 1949.

not to refuse but rather to follow precedent and require that the government had the electorate's agreement through the ballot box for what was
proposed. In neither of the first two relevant precedents, in 1712 and in
1832, was any reference made to the electorate, but then they arose before
the advent of universal male suffrage.[35] By the time of the latest precedent
in 1910–11,[36] however, such suffrage was in place. Both Edward VII and
George V in turn insisted—and Asquith's government accepted—that
before either would use the royal prerogative to create enough new peers
to ensure the passage of the Parliament Bill[37] (which would reduce the
Lords' absolute veto to a suspensory veto), the electorate must first approve
the government's policy. That approval was achieved at the second,
December, general election of 1910.[38] The House of Lords subsequently
passed the Parliament Bill after the King's conditional guarantee to create
peers was made public. An insistence on a general election[39] on the issue of
creating a large number of peers would plainly be in accordance with the
1910–11 precedent. The reason why the electorate's approval is considered
so important is as apposite today as when the King's Private Secretary Lord
Knollys wrote to Asquith in 1910:

[T]he King regards the policy of the Government as tantamount to the destruction
of the House of Lords, and he thinks that before a large creation of peers is
embarked upon or threatened the country should be acquainted with the particular project for accomplishing such destruction.[40]

It is unlikely since the enactment of the Parliament Acts 1911 and 1949
that any government would ask for a mass creation: it could, perhaps, only

[35] In 1712 Queen Anne created 12 Tory peers to provide the government with a sufficient
majority in the House of Lords (of some 150 members) to approve the Treaty of Utrecht, and
in 1832 William IV reluctantly agreed to create enough Whig peers to carry the Reform Bill:
in the event, however, enough Tory peers abstained to allow the Reform Bill to pass without
fresh creations. See generally Jennings, n. 6 above, ch. 13, section 4.

[36] On which see Roy Jenkins, *Mr Balfour's Poodle* (1954); Nicolson, n. 16 above, chs 9
and 10.

[37] In Roy Jenkins, *Asquith* (3rd edn., 1986), Appendix A is a list of some 250 people whom
it was proposed to approach with a view to the submission of their names to the King if a mass
creation proved necessary. It was probably not a complete list of all those who would have had
to be recommended.

[38] The Liberals and Conservatives obtained 272 seats each, the Irish Nationalists 84, and
Labour 42. In the January 1910 election the equivalent figures had been 275, 273, 82 and 40.
The Irish and Labour generally supported the Liberal government in both hung Parliaments.

[39] Perhaps an acceptable alternative to a general election might today be a referendum. A
referendum is uniquely suited (as a general election never is) to a single issue. A disadvantage
would be that legislation to provide for a referendum would have to be enacted, which the
government might not be prepared to secure.

[40] Quoted in J. A. Spender and Cyril Asquith, *Life of Lord Oxford and Asquith* (1932), i. 261.

occur if a government were not prepared to have any of its legislation held up by the House of Lords for the year allowed under the Acts[41] or if a government in the fifth year of a Parliament did not wish to allow a Bill introduced in that last year to be voted down by the Lords, thus effectively vetoing it in that Parliament. But there is a major, and so far insufficiently appreciated, barrier in the way of a government in a hurry hoping through a mass creation to produce a co-operative House of Lords. Every newly created peer must be introduced into the House of Lords before he may take his seat or vote.[42] However rapidly new peers could be created, the crucial question would be how quickly they could become voting members. The answer to this lies with the House of Lords itself, because it is the total master of its own internal procedures, and those procedures can only be altered (apart from legislation) by resolution of the House. The practice which governs the timing of the introduction of new peers is set out in the authoritative *Companion to the Standing Orders of the House of Lords*,[43] which states that usually 'not more than two introductions take place on any one day'. The maximum rate of introductions under that timing is thus *ten a week*: it would therefore take a long time to get a large number of new peers introduced and therefore able to sit and vote, and indeed the House could always vote to *reduce* the rate of introductions. The current rate is usually adhered to even if more than two newly created peers are awaiting introduction. The House has, however, agreed through the usual channels to exceed that timing on occasion in recent years, notably in 1997 when 50 new peers were waiting to be introduced from a number of lists: three peers were introduced on most sitting days. But such matters are for the House itself. The House of Lords, moreover, would not be likely to alter its internal procedures in order to accommodate a government which it saw as trying to cut legislative corners (and perhaps to abolish the House of Lords itself). Once that introduction procedure becomes more properly understood, the likelihood of any future recommended mass creation would become even more remote. (The shortening of the ceremony of introduction itself which was approved by the House in 1998 does not affect this argument.)

If, for whatever reason, a Sovereign were to insist on a dissolution which the government refused to recommend, the Sovereign would have to dismiss that government in order to achieve that dissolution. This is because

---

[41] One month for money Bills: Parliament Act 1911, s. 1.

[42] See Erskine May, *Parliamentary Practice* (21st edn., 1989), pp. 419–20; Sir John Sainty, *Companion to the Standing Orders of the House of Lords* (17th edn., 1994), p. 5.

[43] Sainty, ibid.

the mechanics of dissolution require the essential participation of the Lord Chancellor.[44] Parliament is dissolved by proclamation under the Great Seal, which is in his custody, and the proclamation is issued by the Queen in Council and announces that she has directed the Lord Chancellor to issue writs to returning officers to cause elections to take place to the new Parliament. If, taking his Prime Minister's line, the Lord Chancellor were to refuse to co-operate, the only way around the impasse would be for the Sovereign to dismiss the government and to find another.

A second reserve power is that of refusal of assent to legislation. Such a refusal would be signified by the Clerk of the Parliaments: when the title of the doomed Bill was read out in the House of Lords for royal assent he would reply 'La Reine S'Avisera'. Royal assent has not been withheld from legislation since 1707; that negative precedent might be wrongly taken to mean that royal assent must always be granted to a Bill which has passed Parliament; but all that it really signifies is that no case has arisen since 1707 in which a Sovereign has felt impelled to refuse. The legal power to refuse certainly subsists. There will, however, be government advice that royal assent be given to every Bill passed by both Houses (or by the Commons alone under the Parliament Acts).[45] That advice will attach to every government Bill as well as to legislation for which it has no responsibility but which has received parliamentary approval, such as a Private Member's Bill or a Private Bill. It follows that one situation in which a refusal of assent might be recommended by the government itself with little controversy would be where a Bill had been introduced by one government and had passed both Houses but a change of government had come about without a dissolution and before royal assent had been sought.[46] If the new government then advised that royal assent be withheld, the Queen would obviously be acting on ministerial advice in refusing. Another example[47] could occur if a Private Member's Bill were to pass both Houses, perhaps on a free vote in the Commons but against the government's advice to Parliament:

[44] A dissolution also requires a Privy Council meeting at which the Queen assents to an Order in Council effecting the dissolution. The Lord President of the Council usually arranges for the calling of such meetings, but this is only customary. For example, during the night of 14–15 March 1967 an emergency Privy Council was summoned by the Prime Minister to authorize a bank holiday, after he had informed the Lord President, who was detained in the Commons during an all-night sitting: Harold Wilson, *The Labour Government 1964–70: A Personal Record* (1971), pp. 506–9. If, in the example in the text, the Lord President refused to co-operate someone at Buckingham Palace (perhaps the Queen's Private Secretary) could on the Queen's behalf summon three non-party Privy Counsellors to a meeting.

[45] Subject to possible special cases to be mentioned later.

[46] With a dissolution all public Bills fall.

[47] Suggested by Marshall, n. 28 above, p. 22.

the government might decide that the Bill was so inimical to the public interest that a royal veto should be recommended.[48] But what of the harder cases: veto in the face of ministerial advice?

(a) If an Act provided for mandatory procedures to be followed before given legislation could be enacted, and legislation were passed at the government's request but contrary to those requirements, then the Queen could claim to be acting as a referee upholding the law by vetoing the resultant defective Bill. So, if a future Bill of Rights Act prescribed special majorities in Parliament or a referendum before it could be amended or repealed, and an amending or repealing Bill were passed notoriously without resort to the prescribed safeguard, the Queen might feel obliged to veto the Bill which had been passed in defiance of the law.[49] I think that such action on her part would, however, be unwise. I suggest that the two Houses of Parliament should themselves attract any public odium for legislating improperly; that the government which had initiated the defective legislation should be forced to take political, and perhaps electoral, responsibility for it; that the Queen should assent to the Bill and thus give the courts an eventual opportunity to decide whether it was a valid Act of Parliament,[50] and that those three consequences would be adequate to meet the case, rather than the Queen precipitating a political crisis through the exercise of her veto (perhaps involving the government's resignation following rejection of its advice that she assent to the measure).[51]

(b) If a government were to procure the passage of a Bill to prolong the maximum life of Parliament for no proper reason the Queen would certainly be acting as the ultimate guardian of the constitution if she were to veto the Bill. The democracy upon which the constitution is built requires regular general elections at the elapse of no more than five years,[52] and unless the country were at war a prolongation Bill would be properly vetoed. But such prolongation—particularly without all-party agreement—would, again, just not be contemplated by any British government.

---

[48] It would be unclear why, if that were the government's view, it would allow a free vote in the first place. Without a free vote it could use its majority to vote down the Bill in the Commons. Perhaps the example given might be more likely to happen in a hung Parliament.

[49] This is another example given by Marshall, n. 28 above, pp. 22–3. He thinks that the Queen might have to use her veto in that case.

[50] The courts would have to decide whether royal assent had cured any procedural defect. For consideration of the relevant issues see de Smith and Brazier, n. 1 above, pp. 87–93.

[51] Of course, a government whose Bill had been vetoed could shrug its shoulders, abandon the Bill, and carry on. We must be careful not to assume that governments are looking for excuses to sack themselves.

[52] Parliament Act 1911, s. 7.

And what on earth would the House of Lords have been doing in failing to use its absolute veto over such a shocking measure?[53]

(c)   A government Bill designed to achieve a permanent subversion of the democratic basis of the constitution[54] could be appropriately vetoed, but there would be problems which suggest to me that the Sovereign would be wiser either to assent (under vigorous private protest) or to insist on a dissolution. So, a Bill might be designed to gerrymander the constituencies in the government party's favour, or to effect some fundamental modification of the electoral system to the same end. But there could be tricky questions of degree which might pit the Queen's judgement against that of her Ministers. What form of gerrymandering would justify the use of the veto? Not, presumably, the Orders in Council under the Parliamentary Constituencies Act 1986,[55] which adjust constituency boundaries to take account of population changes but which are regularly denounced by the Opposition as gerrymandering. What, then, would be a sufficiently offensive modification of the electoral system?[56] Would the attempted introduction of proportional representation, which would enhance the position of a third party in the Commons at the expense of the Conservative and Labour Parties, qualify? Surely not. What is needed is a somewhat more closely drawn formula which would restrict royal intervention to the worst case. That formula, I suggest, could be that if (i) the House of Commons were persuaded to pass a fundamentally undemocratic measure designed irreversibly to affect the electoral system in peacetime, and (ii) the Queen were satisfied that no reasonable person outside the government supported the measure, then she would be justified in rejecting ministerial advice to the extent of insisting on a dissolution[57] so that the electorate could decide the issue.

Legislation is the end product of the political process. As with the choice of Prime Minister, the modern constitution ought to require political decisions, and responsibility for them, to be taken by politicians and (where appropriate) the electorate, not by the head of state. The Queen would, therefore, be justified today in using her legislative veto only over a Bill designed to postpone, without all-party agreement, a dissolution in

[53]   Parliament Act 1911, s. 2(1): Bills to prolong the life of the House of Commons beyond five years are outside the Parliament Acts, and the Lords' absolute veto over them remains.

[54]   This is Jennings's phrase, and the examples which follow are his.

[55]   Formerly the House of Commons (Redistribution of Seats) Acts 1944 to 1979.

[56]   No doubt not the suspension of the right to vote in local government elections (see the Local Government (Interim Provisions) Act 1984, s. 1) or the abolition of a tier of local democracy (see the Local Government Act 1985, s. 1.).

[57]   Or a referendum: see n. 39 above.

peacetime. In all other cases her role should be restricted either to vigorous private protest (but ultimately assenting to the controversial Bill), or to insisting on a dissolution (but assenting to the Bill if passed again in the new Parliament).

The last reserve power to be examined is that of dismissal of a government. Dismissal could arise indirectly, through the Queen's insistence on a dissolution or through her refusal of assent to legislation: the government might take rejection of its advice as a ground for resignation.[58] Direct dismissal is much less likely.

(a) If a government lost a vote of confidence in the House of Commons and refused either to recommend a dissolution or to resign then (because a government's only basis for legitimacy is majority support for it in the House of Commons)[59] the Queen would in theory be justified in dismissing it, and no reasonable criticism could attach to her for doing so. A more cautious reaction, however, might yet again be to bring about a dissolution, so as to put the political question to the electorate. It would be comforting to assume that the electors would not take kindly to a government so blatantly breaking the rules and that it would elect a different administration.

(b) It has already been suggested that a government which procured the passage of outrageously undemocratic legislation should receive the royal reaction of insistence on a general election. A *dismissal* of such a government would be inappropriate because that would involve the Queen attempting to resolve a profoundly political argument.

(c) The circumstances of the dismissal of the Whitlam government in 1975 could scarcely occur in the United Kingdom.[60] The nearest analogy might be a confused political situation in which only minority governments had been formed after at least two general elections, and in which those governments could not persuade the Commons to pass essential Finance Bills. Even assuming that the parties were prepared to put perceived party advantage over the national interest, however, it is difficult to understand what reserve power could be deployed—not dismissal (for presumably any alternative grouping in the Commons which could have coalesced into a stronger alternative government would have done so), and

[58] Or it might not: see n. 51 above.

[59] Or, in a hung Parliament, the absence of any majority against it prepared to vote it down.

[60] Because the House of Lords cannot reject money Bills. On the Whitlam affair, see Sir John Kerr, *Matters for Judgment* (1978); Gough Whitlam, *The Truth of the Matter* (1979); Gareth Evans (ed.), *Labor and the Constitution 1972–1975* (1977); Colin Turpin, n. 6 above, pp. 150–4.

not insistence on a dissolution (for what would be achieved if yet another hung Parliament were returned?). In such a volatile situation the Queen should confine herself to her traditional and usual powers—perhaps urging the possibility of a coalition of some kind being formed.

If, despite everything, a dismissal of a government were ever unavoidable, it would at least be easy to effect. The Queen would simply inform the Prime Minister that he and the government ceased to hold office. From that moment all ministerial posts would be vacant.[61]

The Queen and the Scottish Parliament

The creation of the Scottish Parliament casts new responsibilities on the Sovereign as head of state of the United Kingdom. Some of those responsibilities will be routine in nature, but the discharge of others could cause constitutional problems.[62]

The Scottish Executive (as the Scottish government will be called) should enjoy a relationship with the Scottish Parliament similar to that between the United Kingdom Government and the United Kingdom Parliament.[63] So the Executive will be drawn from the Parliament and will be responsible to it, and will depend on the Parliament's confidence to continue in office. The Parliament will exist for a fixed, four-year term, although in certain circumstances there may be an early dissolution. But a number of matters that are dealt with at Westminster by constitutional convention, or by parliamentary standing orders, will be statutory in Scotland. In particular, the choice of the First Minister will be the subject of statutory rules.

The Scotland Act 1998 attempts to keep the Queen out of the political front line in the selection of the First Minister. The Queen will make an appointment on the nomination of the Presiding Officer,[64] who will act on the recommendation of the Parliament. That Officer will be the main channel of communication between the Parliament and the Queen, and that office may well come to be constitutionally important. Quite unlike the United Kingdom conventional position on government formation, the Scottish Parliament will be under a statutory duty to choose one of its

---

[61] See Chapter 4.

[62] See generally R. Brazier, 'The Scottish Government' [1998] *Public Law* 212, and 'The Scotland Bill as Constitutional Legislation' [1998] *Statute Law Review* 12.

[63] See the government's explanation in *Scotland's Government*, Cm. 3658 (1997), para. 2.6.

[64] On whom see the Scotland Act 1998, s. 19.

members to be First Minister. The Act sets out four events which will trigger the exercise of that parliamentary duty—the holding of a Scottish general election, the First Minister resigning, the office of First Minister becoming vacant (otherwise than in consequence of the First Minister's resignation)[65] and the First Minister ceasing to be a Member of the Scottish Parliament (otherwise than by virtue of a dissolution).[66] This nomination must be made within 28 days.[67] The Presiding Officer in his turn will then be under a duty to recommend the nominee to the Queen. This statutory scheme will place on politicians in the Scottish Parliament the clear responsibility of making a viable nomination, rather than leaving it to the Queen to make a choice in her own discretion (as she does in relation to the Prime Minister, albeit guided by convention). In the British government's view, the nominee will normally be the leader of the party able to command the majority support of the Parliament.[68] Matters are expressed that way because it may be unusual for one party to enjoy a parliamentary majority, given that the Parliament will be elected by the additional member system of proportional representation. Political horse-trading, party pacts, perhaps even formal coalitions, will have their places in the Parliament. But if the 28 days expire without a nomination being agreed the Presiding Officer 'shall propose' a day for holding a general election, and then Her Majesty 'may' by proclamation dissolve the Parliament and require an extraordinary general election to take place.[69] It is unlikely that the Queen would do other than comply with the Presiding Officer's proposal, given the clear and comprehensive statutory framework which will govern dissolutions, and given that the politicians in the Parliament will have failed, over a month, to agree on a First Minister. Nonetheless, it is noticeable that the Bill gives the Queen discretionary powers in such circumstances—she 'may' dissolve the Parliament. If she were minded to dissent from a proposal for an election, it is certain that she would wish to take and rely on advice. This could only come from the Prime Minister.

A person will take up office as a Scottish Minister or junior Minister on appointment by the First Minister, with the prior approval of both the Parliament and the Queen.[70] This requirement for parliamentary approbation will be a novel check which has no equivalent at Westminster. The Scotland

---

[65] That encompasses the appointment of a successor, which vacates his holding of the office (ibid., s. 45(3)), or probably losing his parliamentary seat, which disqualifies from Scottish ministerial office.

[66] Ibid., s. 46(1), (2).   [67] Ibid., s. 46(3), subject to specified exceptions.

[68] *Scotland's Government*, n. 63 above, para. 9.6.

[69] See s. 3(1)(*b*),(2) of the 1998 Act.   [70] Ibid., s. 47(1), (2).

Act does not provide for Scottish Ministers to receive seals or other tokens of office. The First Minister (having been nominated by the Parliament's Presiding Officer) is to be appointed by the Queen. The First Minister will be the Keeper of the Scottish Seal,[71] and it may be that delivery to him by the Queen (and its surrender back) will mark the legal taking up (and leaving) of the office. Where this appointment will take place remains to be seen. Scottish Ministers will be required to take the official oath and the oath of allegiance on appointment, while junior Ministers will take just the oath of allegiance.[72] Again, there is no indication where these oaths will be taken, or before whom. British junior Ministers take no oaths on appointment: they take up office as a matter of law once the Queen has approved their names. The requirement in Scotland, by contrast, that all members of the Scottish administration take the oath of allegiance underlines the constitutional point that their duty is not owed to the Scottish Parliament alone, and that the administration and the Parliament are part of the United Kingdom of which the Queen is head of state. There is, though, a direct reflection of British constitutional practice that all Scottish Ministers will hold their offices at Her Majesty's pleasure.[73] (It will, incidentally, also make reshuffles easier for a First Minister to execute (as it does for a Prime Minister), for no obstreperous Minister could decline to leave office: he could (on the First Minister's advice) be dismissed by the Queen.) These precise statutory provisions for taking office make no mention of Privy Council membership. Membership of the Privy Council could be significant in enhancing the status of the First Minister and other Scottish Ministers and officials, and in underpinning confidentiality both within Scottish government and in relation to United Kingdom Ministers. If Privy Counsellorships are conferred it is possible that the Leader of the Opposition in the Parliament (if there is to be one) will also become a Privy Counsellor, as is the invariable practice in London.[74]

The creation of a Scottish Parliament and Executive will not affect the status of Scotland as an integral part of the United Kingdom. But necessarily the creation of a devolved parliamentary and executive system will raise constitutional questions which will affect the Crown. There will be direct

---

[71] Ibid., s. 45(7). This is Her Majesty's Seal appointed by the Treaty of Union to be kept and used in Scotland in place of the Great Seal of Scotland: ibid., s. 2(6).

[72] Ibid., s. 84(4), (5).

[73] Ibid., ss. 45(1), 47(3), 49(4). The First Minister may at any time tender his resignation to the Queen: ibid., s. 45(2).

[74] This would also allow the practice of talks on Privy Counsellor terms to be copied in Edinburgh.

channels of communication between the Queen and the First Minister, and between the Parliament and the Queen. The Scotland Act confers executive powers on Scottish Ministers: those of the Queen's prerogative and other executive functions that are exercisable on her behalf by a Minister of the Crown will be exercisable in or as regards Scotland by Scottish Ministers, rather than by a Minister of the Crown.[75] That reserves to the Crown (however obliquely) the Queen's personal prerogatives, because functions that are exercisable by her personally will not fall within the functions devolved. The Act gives the Queen additional duties. Those in relation to the appointment of Ministers have been noted already. Scottish Bills, once passed by the Parliament, will require royal assent to become law.[76] That assent will be signified by Letters Patent under the Scottish Seal signed by Her Majesty's own hand,[77] a form of signification that will be similar to that used for United Kingdom Acts. Would that assent ever be withheld? In the United Kingdom the Queen retains the power as part of the prerogative not to assent to legislation (while in Scotland the right of assent or veto will stem from statute). No doubt any possible veto of Scottish legislation would only be considered in the most exceptional circumstances. A possible veto ought not to arise on the grounds that a particular Scottish Bill was *ultra vires* the Parliament, because there will be discrete legal procedures to deal with such questions before the assent stage.[78] A possible veto might arise, therefore, only if the Queen were advised to do so by the Cabinet, and then presumably because the policy in the Bill was repugnant to United Kingdom interests. This would itself be a course of action, were it ever to be embarked upon, which would be resented greatly in Scotland. The Queen might feel constrained to act on the Prime Minister's advice, given that he speaks for the government of the whole United Kingdom of which the Queen is head of state.[79]

The Scotland Act provides that the Scottish Parliament will be dissolved either every four years, or, before that time is up, on a resolution by at least two-thirds of the total membership of the Parliament that it be dissolved, or if the Parliament fails to nominate a First Minister.[80] Given goodwill in the Scottish Parliament, dissolutions outside the fixed timetable may be

---

[75]   See s. 53 of the 1998 Act.   [76]   Ibid., s. 28(2).   [77]   Ibid., s. 28(3).
[78]   Ibid., ss. 29–33, 98–103, Schedule 6.
[79]   Another approach for the Cabinet to take would be to recommend that royal assent be given, but for legislation to be enacted at Westminster to negate the offensive Scottish Act. The Westminster Parliament retains the power to make laws for Scotland (ibid., s. 28(7)), and its ultimate legal sovereignty over Scotland is not removed by the Scotland Act.
[80]   Ibid., ss. 2, 3.

fairly unusual. In general politicians do not act so as to prevent government being carried on, and they certainly do not seek more parliamentary elections than are necessary. As a matter of British constitutional law it would be possible, in rare cases, for the Queen to refuse to accept the Prime Minister's advice to dissolve the Westminster Parliament, or for her to dissolve that Parliament contrary to the Prime Minister's advice. It is unlikely, however, that there will be any such royal action in relation to the Scottish Parliament. It is true that if an extraordinary dissolution were sought following the necessary vote, or failure to name a First Minister, the Queen will have a discretion whether to comply with the Presiding Officer's proposal. It is unlikely that she would do other than comply, for the clear statutory provisions about extraordinary dissolutions ought to cover most foreseeable political circumstances. Moreover, the First Minister would lack any legal power to recommend a dissolution outside those statutory requirements; and it is hard to imagine any case in which the Queen would feel compelled to dissolve the Parliament contrary to the wishes of the Parliament itself. Indeed, she would not have the legal power to dissolve the Scottish Parliament outside the statutory provisions which govern dissolution. That Parliament will be the creation of *statute*, and so she would not possess any *prerogative* powers of dissolution in relation to it.[81]

No Prime Minister has been unambiguously dismissed since 1783. Yet as with their United Kingdom counterparts Scottish Ministers will hold their offices at the Queen's pleasure. Accordingly the Queen would have a clear legal right to dismiss the First Minister or any other Scottish Minister at any time. But that power might never fall to be used, because the Parliament will have statutory powers to vote out the Executive. If a First Minister were to lose a vote of confidence in the Parliament, he will be required by law to resign.[82] The appointment of a new First Minister will vacate the former holder's occupancy of the office.[83] In that case the Presiding Officer would set in train the process of nominating a successor, and the Presiding Officer might have to recommend a premature election if the Parliament could not agree on a nomination. The Queen would be able to act in such circumstances on the advice of the Presiding Officer, rather than

[81] In any event there would be a difficulty over the formalities. The First Minister will have custody of the Scottish Seal, and might refuse to allow it to be used in the dissolution process.

[82] See s. 47(2) of the 1998 Act. Strictly, the Act gives the Parliament the right to resolve that the Scottish Executive, not the First Minister, no longer enjoys its confidence, but if the Parliament wished to get rid of him it would no doubt vote the necessary motion under s. 47(2).

[83] Ibid., s. 45(3).

on her own initiative. If a Scottish Executive were to lose the support of the Parliament, it would be for that Parliament to pass a vote of no confidence in it, thus triggering a change of government or an extraordinary general election. It is very hard to envisage circumstances in which the Queen would be justified in acting on her own initiative to dismiss the First Minister or Executive if the Parliament were content for them to remain in office.

Scottish Ministers will be entitled to tender ministerial advice on devolved matters. Because they will enjoy direct access to the Queen there will be no filter to prevent advice reaching her which conflicts with advice from United Kingdom Ministers. What right will Scottish Ministers have to insist that their advice on devolved matters be taken to the exclusion of any conflicting ministerial advice? In principle, the only source of minister-ial advice on devolved matters should be the Scottish Executive, just as the only source of advice on reserved matters will remain Ministers in London. The risk of conflicting advice being tendered has been reduced by the Act keeping the powers of the Secretary of State for Scotland to a minimum: he will not have a role which would permit ministerial advice to come from him as a member of the British Cabinet which might conflict with that of Scottish Ministers.

Continuity and succession

Because of the tasks entrusted to the Queen in the government of the country, there must be provision for her contribution to be continued if she is personally unable to carry them out. There has been no need for a Regency since 1820; Counsellors of State, on the other hand, have been appointed frequently since provision was first made for them by statute in 1937, and they will be considered first.[84]

The Queen may (and will) appoint Counsellors of State if she intends to be absent from the United Kingdom or if she is suffering from an illness which is not so serious that a Regency is required.[85] Counsellors will have delegated to them by Letters Patent such royal functions[86] as are specified in order to prevent delay or difficulty in the dispatch of public

---

[84] See Wheeler-Bennett, n. 8 above, Appendix A for an historical account of the provi-sions for a Regency and for Counsellors of State.

[85] Regency Act 1937, s. 6(1). None has been appointed during the Queen's reign on account of any illness of hers.

[86] These are defined, ibid., s. 8(2) as including 'all powers and authorities belonging to the Crown, whether prerogative or statutory'.

business.[87] The only legal restriction on the Counsellors is that they cannot dissolve Parliament save with the Sovereign's express approval, and they cannot create peers.[88] Candidates to be Counsellors are Prince Philip (as the Sovereign's spouse), those four persons next in line of succession to the Crown,[89] and Queen Elizabeth the Queen Mother.[90] Prince Charles has acted as a Counsellor of State when required since his eighteenth birthday in 1966, thus giving him useful though strictly limited experience of the role he will one day fulfil alone. By custom, two Counsellors act jointly,[91] together holding Privy Council meetings, receiving people in audience, and so on.

A Regency would be required if (a) the Queen were so ill as to be incapable of performing the royal functions, or if (b) she were for any definite cause not available to perform those functions, or if (c) a Sovereign were under 18 on his or her succession.[92] In cases (a) and (b) a collection of notables[93] would have to certify the existence of the incapacity.[94] The person would then be Regent who was next in line of succession to the Crown, over 18 and not disqualified because a Roman Catholic:[95] that person would today be Prince Charles.[96] A Regent's only legal disabilities are that he cannot assent to any Bill to alter the succession to the throne or which would repeal the Acts which secure the established Church in Scotland.[97]

It would be a worthwhile, though unprecedented, departure for the Queen to request a declaration of a Regency when she next has a lengthy overseas tour, rather than (as has been the invariable custom) to appoint Counsellors of State. By reason of that absence she would, in terms of the Regency Act 1937, be definitely not available for the performance of her royal functions, and there would be a practical advantage that Prince

[87] Ibid., s. 6(1).   [88] Ibid., s. 6(1), proviso.

[89] And who would be qualified to act as Regent (discussed below) and be present in the United Kingdom. The heir to the throne may be a Counsellor of State provided he is over 18: Regency Act 1937, s. 6.(2A) as replaced by the Regency Act 1943, s. 1.

[90] Regency Act 1953, s. 3.

[91] No minimum number is prescribed in the Acts, but the delegated functions must be 'exercised jointly': s. 6(3) of the 1937 Act.

[92] Regency Act 1937, ss. 1, 2. If Prince Charles died after his accession and was succeeded by Prince William while he was still under 18, the Duke of York would be Regent.

[93] That is, any three or more of the Sovereign's spouse, the Lord Chancellor, the Speaker, the Lord Chief Justice, and the Master of the Rolls.

[94] It also declares the termination of the incapacity: Regency Act 1937, s. 2(1).

[95] He must also be a British citizen and be domiciled in the United Kingdom: ibid., s. 3(1), (2).

[96] Had a child of the Queen succeeded when still under 18, Prince Philip would have been Regent: Regency Act 1953, s. 1(1).

[97] Regency Act 1937, s. 4(2).

Charles as Prince Regent would enjoy a period actually doing the job to which he might not otherwise succeed until he was in his 60s. A further development which I offer for consideration is that in several years' time the Queen might seek the passage of a fresh Regency Act to create Charles Prince Regent during the Queen's old age. Some duties might be expressly reserved to Her Majesty, but the more onerous tasks would be devolved to her son. This would both lighten the Queen's load and advance the day when Prince Charles would perform a central constitutional role while at the same time being a more acceptable change than abdication for them both. In any event, the Prince of Wales is being groomed for the throne.[98] Since the early 1990s, for example, he has received privately individual Ministers and Opposition politicians, and has been seeing more official papers.[99]

The succession to the throne is based at common law and in statute on heredity, primogeniture[100] (and not coparceny[101]) and on religious tests (Catholics and persons marrying Catholics[102] are excluded;[103] a Sovereign must also swear to maintain the established Church in England and Scotland and take the Coronation Oath[104]). Thus the succession now is in the line Prince Charles, Prince William, Prince Henry, the Duke of York, Princess Beatrice, Princess Eugenie, Prince Edward, the Princess Royal, Peter Phillips, Zara Phillips—and so on.[105]

---

[98] See R. Brazier, 'The Constitutional Position of the Prince of Wales' [1995] *Public Law* 401.

[99] The Australian Prime Minister was reported in 1998 to have offered the Governor-Generalship of Australia to Prince Charles, who declined it.

[100] The Labour government has undertaken, with the Queen's agreement, to introduce legislation to remove the preference given to males over females in the line of succession to the throne. See 586 H.L. Deb. 916–7 (27 February 1998).

[101] That is, an older daughter succeeds in preference to any younger daughter in the absence of a son.

[102] Prince Michael of Kent removed himself from the line on his marriage to a Catholic in 1978. Their children remain in line because they were baptized and have been brought up as Anglicans. The Earl of St Andrews similarly removed himself in 1988; his children remain in the line for the same reason.

[103] By the Bill of Rights 1689, the Act of Settlement 1701, and the Succession to the Crown Act 1707.

[104] Ibid., and the Accession Declaration Act 1910.

[105] The Duke of York may not be as far away from the throne as the formal line indicates, given the habit of the Prince of Wales of travelling by air with both his sons.

10

THE HOUSE OF COMMONS

Elections, Members, and parties

The maximum life of a Parliament is five years from the day, fixed at the dissolution, on which it was summoned to meet after a general election.[1] Parliament would be dissolved automatically on the expiry of that time, but Parliament never ends in that way: it is, of course, dissolved by the Sovereign on the Prime Minister's advice. Only five Parliaments since 1945 have been allowed by the Prime Minister to approach the maximum span allowed by law;[2] six have been terminated after some four years.[3] The Prime Minister will usually bring about a dissolution in good time before the maximum duration of Parliament and at the best moment as he can judge it for his party to win: this is an unfair advantage for him, but one which the Leaders of the opposition parties in the main[4] hope to enjoy themselves one fine day.

After the Prime Minister has received the Queen's consent for the dissolution the news of it is released through a press notice issued from Number 10 Downing Street. The first the House of Commons itself usually hears of this will be by rumour at Westminster or through news bulletins, a discourtesy which causes a small but justified grievance among Members of that House who are, after all, the most intimately affected by the development.[5]

---

[1] Parliament Act 1911, s. 7.

[2] Those of 1945, 1959, October 1974, 1987, and 1992.

[3] Those of 1951, 1955, 1966, 1970, 1979, and 1983. The Parliaments of 1950, 1964, and February 1974 are left out of account because the government had very small majorities (and in the last case no majority) and the Prime Minister's freedom of choice was therefore more limited.

[4] Though not the Leader of the Liberal Democrats, whose party advocates fixed-term Parliaments.

[5] Ironically, the House of Lords was informed by a Minister of the impending dissolution in 1997 straight after the Prime Minister's announcement. News of that dissolution was given to the Commons a few hours after it had been announced, in a statement re-arranging business.

Parliament will actually be dissolved some seven to 10 days later.[6] Dissolution[7] is effected by a royal proclamation under the Great Seal made by the Queen at a Privy Council.[8] The proclamation recites that Parliament is dissolved and that the Lord Chancellor has been directed to issue writs to individual returning officers to cause elections to a new Parliament to be held. In practice polling day[9] is fixed by the proclamation for about four weeks after dissolution, with the new Parliament being summoned to meet on a date specified in the proclamation some two weeks after the election. In law Parliament need only be summoned to meet once every three years.[10] In fact, whether after a dissolution or otherwise, it will meet in annual session because there is a natural expectation that (recesses apart)[11] Parliament should be at work, because the government needs to procure legislation year in, year out as the lifeblood of its existence, and because some essential laws must be renewed every year.[12]

The newly elected MP[13] receives a fair, but scarcely generous, financial

[6] This delay enables some of the government's legislative programme to be salvaged and passed (especially any Finance Bill) following negotiations with the main opposition party. It would be open to the Opposition to say that, if the government chooses to dissolve Parliament for party advantage during a session, it must take the consequence of losing any remaining Bills. No Opposition has taken that stance, both because the government could respond by securing the passage of guillotine motions to force the legislation through quickly, and because when the Opposition became the government it would not want *its* legislation held up, or lost, before a dissolution: Oppositions and governments subscribe to the maxim that dogs must not eat dogs.

[7] A prorogation ceremony customarily took place before dissolution, formally ending the parliamentary session with a short speech on the Queen's behalf summarizing the work achieved during that session. There was, however, no such ceremony before the 1979, 1983, 1987, or 1992 dissolutions. There was a prorogation in 1997, and the gap between it and dissolution was the longest in living memory. (The end of each annual parliamentary session always has a prorogation ceremony, the main practical effect of which is to cause all public Bills which have not completed all stages to lapse; private Bills may, on application from their sponsors, be suspended over into the next annual session.) See generally R. Blackburn, *The Meeting of Parliament* (1990).

[8] The last time Parliament was dissolved by the Sovereign in person was in 1818, by the Prince Regent on behalf of the King.

[9] The detailed rules concerning the conduct of parliamentary elections are outside the scope of this book. See *Halsbury's Laws of England* (4th edn., 1977), paras. 401–981; Erskine May's *Parliamentary Practice* (21st edn., 1989), ch. 2; R. Blackburn, *The Electoral System in Britain* (1995).

[10] Meeting of Parliament Act 1694.

[11] For summer, Christmas, Easter, and Whitsun. The House of Commons sits for about 165 days each year.

[12] Especially the Armed Forces Act (currently of 1996) (which regulates Army and RAF discipline) and the Naval Discipline Act 1957, which would expire without an annual Order in Council; and legislative authority to raise income tax and corporation tax.

[13] To be elected a person must be 21 or over (Family Law Reform Act 1969, s. 1(4), Schedule 2, para. 4) and a British citizen (which for this purpose includes a citizen of the

settlement. He or she[14] is paid an annual salary of £45,000.[15] He may currently claim up to £30,000 a year as an office costs allowance for out-of-pocket office, secretarial and research expenses; all his travel within the United Kingdom on parliamentary business is either free or qualifies for a car mileage allowance, and his phone calls and postage from the House of Commons are free.[16] He must find his own London accommodation if his constituency is too far away to allow daily commuting.[17] If he expects a room of his own in which to work he may still be disappointed: only rather more than half of all MPs have their own offices; others must share, or use a table in the Library or benches in the corridors. Under the current building programme, however, every Member should have his own office by the year 2000. If he wants a secretary he must find one and pay the agreed salary out of his secretarial allowance. He will, at least, enjoy an excellent Library and Research Division.[18] For some MPs access to the media, particularly television, is a valuable fringe benefit; consultancy, or lobbying, can also bring in cash—although such activities must be entered in the Register of Members' Interests, and are subject to a code of conduct for MPs which was adopted in 1996.[19] The hours of work have been improved during the 1997 Parliament. The House sits in the morning on Wednesdays

---

Republic of Ireland: British Nationality Act 1981, s. 50(1)), and must not be subject to any disqualification (to be explained shortly).

[14] The highest number of women MPs was 121 in the 1997 Parliament.

[15] From 1988 the rate of MPs' pay has been linked to a prescribed percentage of the salary at a specified point on the civil service pay band so that as civil service pay rises, so will that of MPs: see 46 H.C. Deb. 329–52 (19 July 1983); 120 H.C. Deb. 295–341 (21 July 1987). This should avoid the previous embarrassment of legislators voting themselves pay increases; indeed, MPs voted to take no increase at all in 1993. See 231 H.C. Deb. 481 (3 November 1993).

[16] These provisions have effect by virtue of various resolutions of the House. The office costs allowance is indexed to the salary paid to a senior personal secretary in the civil service, so that each annual percentage rise in that salary is reflected in an equivalent increase in the allowance: 120 H.C. Deb. 340–1 (21 July 1987), and 211 H.C. Deb. 1081–110 (14 July 1992). For information about allowances available to legislators in foreign parliaments, see 173 H.C. Deb. 461–4 (written answers 5 June 1990).

[17] MPs who stay in London overnight away from home are entitled to an allowance of about £30,000 a year. If they have an inner London constituency and live there they may draw a London supplement annually.

[18] See M. Rush (ed.), The House of Commons: Services and Facilities 1972–1982 (1983).

[19] The Register is published periodically as a House of Commons Paper. The Register enumerates nine separate classes of financial interests which all MPs should register, including directorships, paid employment, and sponsorships: Erskine May, n. 9 above, pp. 386–90. They must also register any paid lobbying activity in public relations, political and parliamentary advice and consultancy. Some MPs were suspended from the service of the House during the 1992 Parliament for not properly registering all registrable interests.

for private Members' debates, and on other days at 2.30 p.m.[20] (but not at all on 10 'constituency Fridays')[21] and, although the notional time at which the Commons rises is 10 p.m. on Monday to Thursday, late night and occasional all-night sittings are still occasionally unavoidable. It cannot be said fairly that the House has provided lavishly for the reward, comfort, or efficient working of its Members, but any of them who make a reasonable objection face the certainty of being sharply told by someone that there is no shortage of candidates to take their places.[22]

Should an MP wish for whatever reason to quit membership of the House he has to resort to an antiquated device in order to resign. He must seek the office of Steward and Bailiff of either Her Majesty's three Chiltern Hundreds of Stoke, Desborough, and Burnham, or of the Manor of Northstead. These nominal offices are in the gift of the Chancellor of the Exchequer, who gives one on demand to any MP who asks for it, and under the House of Commons Disqualification Act 1975[23] holders of those offices are disqualified and their seats are vacated.[24] Should an MP decide (as of course most do) to stay, he may be involuntarily removed from membership of the House in a number of ways[25]—defeat at the next general

[20] S.O. Nos. 9, 10. (All Standing Orders of the House of Commons referred to are in the 1998 revision: see H.C. 1 (1997–8).)

[21] S.O. No. 12.

[22] No MP is returned unopposed (not even the Speaker seeking re-election), and the number of candidates for the 651 seats must be multiplied considerably to represent the total number who sought selection in the various parties.

[23] Section 4 and Schedule 1. Over 1 million office-holders are disqualified under the Act.

[24] From the late seventeenth century acceptance of a paid office under the Crown was considered to incapacitate an MP from continuing to sit, because an MP receiving a salary from the Crown could not be reckoned to scrutinize independently the actions of His Majesty's government. This disability extended to Ministers so that, on accepting ministerial office, they were disqualified and had to fight a by-election in their former seats; that inconvenient rule was amended by the Re-election of Ministers Act 1919, and was finally abrogated in 1926. The two Stewardships are held either (a) until the Chancellor appoints another applicant, each new appointment expressly revoking that of the previous holder: in that manner 15 Ulster Unionist MPs were able to leave the House of Commons on the same day, 17 December 1985, so as to cause by-elections in Northern Ireland on the issue of the Anglo-Irish Agreement; or (b) by the holder applying for release from it, which he might do if he wished to fight a by-election in his former seat (such as Mr Dick Taverne in 1973). The other ways of voluntarily leaving the House are to accept a disqualifying job so described in the House of Commons Disqualification Act 1975, s. 4 and Schedule 1, or to be ordained into the Church of England or Scotland or Ireland (House of Commons (Clergy Disqualification) Act 1801) or into the Roman Catholic Church (Roman Catholic Relief Act 1829, s. 9); Nonconformist clergy are not disqualified, a discrimination of which the numerous reverend MPs from Northern Ireland take full advantage.

[25] See Erskine May, n. 9 above, ch. 3.

election; inheritance of a peerage;[26] adjudication of bankruptcy which lasts for six months or more;[27] sentence to prison for more than a year, or for life;[28] detention in a mental hospital for six months or more;[29] or expulsion by resolution of the House.[30] On ceasing to be an MP a former Member will be entitled to a pension if he has contributed to the Parliamentary Contributory Pension Fund; if he loses his seat at a general election, he may receive severance pay, known as resettlement grant.[31]

In the regulation of its affairs the House of Commons is firmly wedded to the two-party system, one party (usually with a majority of seats) forming the government, another party (usually with the second largest number of seats) forming the Opposition—entirely regardless of the number of votes which had been cast at the election for them or for other parties represented in the House. The status of Her Majesty's Opposition carries with it numerous advantages, and, in a two-party system, that is as it should be for the Opposition represents the alternative government and it should have certain rights to enable it to act as such. That proposition is, however, a little less self-evident after the last four general elections in which the SDP/Liberal Alliance, and then the Liberal Democrats, polled a significant proportion of the popular vote but were rewarded with a tiny number of seats.[32] Nevertheless, in the present parliamentary system the Leader of the

---

[26] *Acceptance* of an offered peerage must be classed as voluntary (although some are less voluntary than others—such as one urged upon an MP to provide a by-election for a Minister without a seat). The Member is disqualified from the moment of inheritance, and cannot go back into the chamber even to retrieve property: for an illustrative incident see Lord Home, *The Way the Wind Blows* (1976), pp. 100–1.

[27] Insolvency Act 1986, s. 427. Being adjudged bankrupt disqualifies an MP from sitting or voting; that disqualification ceases on discharge, but if bankruptcy lasts six months or more the seat is vacated. The last MP so excluded was Mr C. Homan in 1928.

[28] Representation of the People Act 1981, ss. 1, 2. During a sentence of less than one year an MP may not sit or vote, but he could be expelled on the resolution of the House. Any sentence for treason automatically disqualifies. The Speaker is informed by the court of any MP imprisoned by it, and he informs the House. See, for example, 195 H.C. Deb. 1 (15 July 1991)—Mr Terry Fields, imprisoned for 60 days for non-payment of his poll tax.

[29] Mental Health Act 1983, s. 141. The Speaker must be notified of any MP's detention under the Act: if it lasts six months or more his seat is vacated. The last MP so excluded was Mr C. Leach in 1916.

[30] This can be for any reason, although the House cannot stop the expelled MP from standing at a by-election.

[31] On the pension, see Parliamentary and other Pensions Act 1972; Parliamentary and other Pensions Act 1976; Parliamentary Pensions etc. Act 1984; Parliamentary and other Pensions Act 1987. Resettlement grant is based on age and length of service; it has been available since 1971 by virtue of a number of resolutions of the House. See also 136 H.C. Deb. 313–14 (written answers 30 June 1988).

[32] But the electoral system gave the Liberal Democrats 46 seats at the 1997 general election, based on 17 per cent of the national vote.

Opposition (who is the 'Leader of that party in the House in opposition to Her Majesty's Government having the greatest numerical strength in the House')[33] receives an annual salary of £101,000 (which includes his parliamentary allowance), and is supplied with a car from the government car pool.[34] Other party Leaders receive no salary.[35] The Leader of the Opposition has the opportunity to put six questions at Prime Minister's Question Time every Wednesday, whereas the Leader of the Liberal Democrats is limited to two. Subject to the understanding that the government must be able to get its essential legislation through the House and to the rule that (with exceptions) government business has precedence in the House,[36] the government and the Opposition 'through the usual channels' (that is, the Leader of the House and Government Whips, and their Opposition counterparts) are in regular contact about parliamentary business—the timing of debates on Bills, general debates and divisions, and so on.[37] The other parties are, however, merely informed of the results of those deliberations. In major debates the Leader of the Opposition will be called immediately after the Prime Minister; the other party Leaders are either called next, or must take their chances in catching the Speaker's eye (by which time the lure of the tea room may have proved too great for many Members). The Opposition chooses the subjects for debate on 17 days during the session; the third largest party has that privilege on only three days.[38] If the Prime Minister or other Minister makes a ministerial broadcast, the BBC and ITV will offer the Opposition the right to reply; other parties may or may not be favoured with equal time.[39] In all these ways the standing of the Opposition

---

[33] Ministerial and other Salaries Act 1975, s. 2(1). In any dispute the Speaker decides: s. 2(2). The office was first recognized in a similar statute in 1937.

[34] The Opposition Chief Whip receives a salary of £77,000 a year. See generally Chapter 8.

[35] Opposition parties, however, receive public money to help them with their parliamentary work, calculated on the number of seats and votes won at the previous general election: see 231 H.C. Deb. 613–15 (4 November 1993). This provision is known as 'Short money' after the Leader of the House who introduced the concept. On political funding generally, see the Report of the Committee on Financial Aid to Political Parties, Cmnd. 6601 (1976); M. Pinto-Duschinsky, *British Political Finance 1830–1980* (1982); K. D. Ewing, *The Funding of Political Parties in Britain* (1987). Legislation is expected in the light of a report from the Committee on Standards in Public Life. Additionally, companies and trade unions help fund the Conservative and Labour Parties respectively. Donations to the Conservative Party have proved controversial recently; its refusal to publish details about donations has fuelled that controversy.

[36] S.O. No. 14(1).

[37] Discussions through the usual channels take place 'behind the Speaker's chair', which is figurative rather than strictly geographic, meaning merely that the discussions are held outside the chamber. On these arrangements see Donald Wade, *Behind the Speaker's Chair* (1978).

[38] Opposition days are considered in more detail later.

[39] See generally Alan E. Boyle, 'Political Broadcasting, Fairness and Administrative Law' [1986] *Public Law* 562, especially pp. 575–87. The only regular ministerial broadcast is that of

and its Leader is enhanced in the House of Commons and indirectly in the eyes of the general public, to the detriment of other parties represented there.

All parties in the House organize themselves for maximum efficiency. The Whips are of vital importance, especially to the government and the Opposition. They convey back-bench opinion to the leadership, and vice versa; they keep Members informed of forthcoming business through means of the weekly whip—a document in which business is underlined once, twice, or three times to denote how important attendance is;[40] they supervise pairs with MPs from other parties so that paired absences make no difference to the result of divisions; they make recommendations of back-benchers for promotion;[41] and they help to maintain party discipline. Then again, the parties have parliamentary machinery designed to tap back-bench views. The Conservative Party has its 1922 Committee for that purpose,[42] made up of all Conservative MPs not in the government or the Shadow Cabinet: it is an important focus of opinion and leading Conservative Party figures may defer to its views. All Labour MPs form the Parliamentary Labour Party, which operates similarly to the 1922 Committee but more formally and sometimes more aggressively towards its leadership. The Liberal Democrats have looser arrangements, largely because they have far fewer MPs than the Conservatives or Labour.[43]

---

the Chancellor on the evening of his annual Budget. The Chancellor, the Labour Shadow Chancellor, and the Liberal Democrat economics spokesman each deliver a 10-minute broadcast on successive evenings. Time is given for party political broadcasts and party election broadcasts by both the BBC and ITV in ratios agreed between them and the parties. In recent general election campaigns the broadcasting authorities have given equal time to the three main parties; other news and current affairs time was broadly divided equally between those parties. For an unsuccessful attempt in 1985 to require the Broadcasting Complaints Commission to examine an allegation that the Alliance parties had received unfair treatment in news and current affairs programmes, see *R. v. Broadcasting Complaints Commission, ex p. Owen* [1985] 1 Q.B. 1153.

[40] Technically the whip is claimed by the parties to be an order to attend, but it is acknowledged to carry the implicit instruction (not always obeyed) to vote with the party as well. In 1993 a Conservative MP, Mr Rupert Allason, had the whip suspended temporarily after failing to vote for the government at the end of a confidence debate. It was restored in 1994. In the same year eight Conservative MPs had the whip removed for a similar offence, and a ninth resigned the whip in sympathy with them. All nine whips were restored in 1995. The whip was removed from Mr Peter Temple-Morris in 1997, and he subsequently joined the Labour Party. Such disciplinary action had been rare in the Conservative Party before the 1992 Parliament.

[41] See Chapter 5; and see Cecil Parkinson, *Right at the Centre* (1992), pp. 120–3.

[42] So named from the meeting of Conservative MPs at the Carlton Club in 1922 which decided to end the Lloyd George coalition.

[43] The Parliamentary Liberal Democrats consist of all Liberal Democrat MPs, and they have a Chief Whip.

The Commons and the government

The role of the House of Commons in the system of government has been much analysed. Perhaps five functions, briefly stated, may suffice here. First, it is the House of Commons which gives the government its political legitimacy.[44] A party which secures 330 seats or more at a general election, or a coalition of parties with that representation, is entitled to form an administration. In a hung Parliament a minority government obtains conditional legitimacy from the Commons: it takes up and retains office until that House removes its legitimacy by carrying a vote of no confidence in it. Secondly, the House provides a forum in which a continuing general election campaign may be fought. The pace of that campaign will slacken off after a decisive poll, but will quicken again as the years pass. Through that forum the parties in opposition seek to present themselves as the alternative and preferable government, and the government seeks to prove the opposite. This must be a rather daunting prospect for opposition parties, but then Parliaments cannot last more than five years (and four years is nearer the mark); even governments with very large majorities are only rarely returned by a majority of electors;[45] there is a sizeable floating vote, and only four times this century has a government won three consecutive general elections out of a total of 26 contests.[46] All governments are thus temporary—although as Mrs Margaret Thatcher and Mr John Major have shown us, some are less temporary than others. Thirdly, the House of Commons is the mechanism through which the government will achieve its legislation. A party returned to power at a general election will have commitments to legislation in its manifesto, and will bring forward more as time passes and as exigencies require; on average some 60 to 70 public general Bills will be passed each session, most of which will have been introduced by the government. A government is, by virtue of its majority in the House of Commons, entitled to expect that House to pass its legislation within a reasonable time, assuming that it retains the support of its MPs for it. Fourthly, the House of Commons is a place in which grievances may be ventilated, at Question Time, in debates, by putting down amendments to Bills and 'early-day' motions,[47] and in other ways. The House is, however,

---

[44] Just as appointment by the Queen, or with her approval, gives Ministers their legal status.

[45] In 1997, for example, the Labour Party obtained a majority of 179 even though nearly 56% of the total votes cast went to other parties.

[46] In 1906 and the two elections of 1910; 1951, 1955, and 1959; and in 1979, 1983, 1987 and 1992.

[47] Any MP may put down a motion for debate 'on an early day', knowing that his chances

not very well equipped to *redress* grievances: for that, the citizen may be better advised to ask his MP to write to the relevant Minister or other authority (who might prefer to put the matter right quietly without risking publicity) or to put his complaint to the Parliamentary Commissioner for Administration[48] or the Health Service Commissioners;[49] or to seek justice from the Commissioner for Local Administration;[50] or to conduct an appeal to the courts, or to seek judicial review; or to try to interest the media in his complaint. Fifthly, and just occasionally, the whole House will actually represent the views of and speak for most of the nation, in time of war or armed conflict,[51] or of natural or man-made disaster, or after a terrorist outrage, or on the death of a respected citizen, or at a time of national rejoicing.

No administration governs without being affected by influences outside both Houses of Parliament. Particularly as a general election approaches, evidence that the government is not faring as well as it might hope in opinion polls[52] will present a temptation to trim policies—or, in the more acceptable modern idiom, to improve the presentation of policies.[53] Such pressure will be subtle, but can be just as effective in producing changes in a government's thinking as any efforts by the opposition parties in the House of Commons. By-election results, too, may have the direct effect of bringing the government up with a start and perhaps encouraging shifts of emphasis, even though every government publicly dismisses adverse by-election results as being just by-election results which would not be repeated at the general election.[54] The views of the party loyalists outside Parliament will obviously be taken into account as well. For the Conservative Party this will be informally expressed through local constituency

---

of it being selected for debate are very slim, but so as to allow other MPs to show support for it by signing it. As many as a thousand early-day motions may be tabled in the average session. See further 3rd Report from the Procedure Committee, H.C. 254 (1986–7). (Figures from the 1996–97 session are not considered in this chapter because the dissolution of Parliament made it a short session.)

[48] Parliamentary Commissioner Act 1967.

[49] Health Service Commissioners Act 1993.

[50] Local Government Act 1974, Part III.

[51] Such as during the Falklands conflict in 1982, although not during the Suez invasion in 1956.

[52] A high standing in the opinion polls may clinch the timing of a dissolution for a Prime Minister, as it did in both 1983 and 1987 for Mrs Thatcher.

[53] Involving, perhaps, a Cabinet reshuffle, or the appointment of a new Conservative Party Chairman, or the hiring of a different public relations agency.

[54] This is a fair point. Of the seats lost by the government at by-elections in the last 25 years, a clear majority were retaken at the subsequent general elections.

associations—but not at the annual conference, which is stage-managed to present a united party in the best light to the general public. For the Labour Party, extra-parliamentary party opinion will be voiced through the National Executive Committee,[55] the constituency parties, the trade unions, and through the annual conference, which has a constitutional role in the making of party policy.[56] But Labour's annual conference is as well stage-managed as its Conservative counterpart. For the Liberal Democrats, constituency opinion is important, as is its Federal Policy Committee. Its biannual conference is its sovereign representative body with the power to determine the party's policies which bind its MPs.[57] All governments are pressed, too, by organized pressure groups, although their actual impact as measured through changes in policy or in legislation sponsored by any government may not be very great. International opinion (especially that of allies),[58] international obligations, and the international economic climate[59] will all exert their influences on any government.

It is, however, to the House of Commons that the government will look for its strength and legislation. A government with a majority of seats behind it is, in Lord Hailsham's famous and apt phrase, and with only some exaggeration, an elective dictatorship.[60] No majority government has been unambiguously voted out of office or forced to the polls by the House of Commons since 1895.[61] Such a government could only be put at risk if it

---

[55] On which see Constitution of the Labour Party, ch. 8. The NEC has places reserved for representatives from the trade unions, constituency parties, the Co-operative movement, Young Labour and women, as well as for the Leader and Deputy Leader and Treasurer of the Labour Party.

[56] For example, the annual conference adopts policies for the party which, if approved by a two-thirds majority on a card vote, are included in the 'Party Programme', from which the manifesto is drawn up jointly by the NEC and the Cabinet (or Shadow Cabinet): Constitution, cl. V.

[57] See Constitution of the Social and Liberal Democrats, arts 5–7.

[58] Of which a spectacular manifestation in 1986 was the government's agreement to let the USA use United Kingdom air bases to launch a bombing raid on Libya in response to terrorism.

[59] Consider, for example, how the 1964 Labour government's economic policy was moulded by an initial decision to maintain the international parity of the pound, and by the need to try to correct an adverse balance of payments; or the Conservative government's efforts to keep the pound within the European Exchange Rate Mechanism until it was withdrawn in 1992.

[60] Lord Hailsham, *The Dilemma of Democracy: Diagnosis and Prescription* (1978), pp. 9–11.

[61] In that year Lord Rosebery's Liberal government was defeated on a snap vote to reduce the salary of the Secretary of State for War, Campbell-Bannerman, by £100 because of an alleged shortage of ammunition and cordite, and resigned. Chamberlain's resignation in 1940 was largely brought about by the refusal of over 90 Conservative MPs to support him on the division after the adjournment debate on the conduct of the war.

were to be rent by an internal party split of such vehemence that enough of its supporters were determined to engineer a dissolution. But, as all the years since 1895 have shown, this is unlikely to happen because modern governments and government parties in the Commons are cohesive, being bound both by loyalty and by the knowledge that they sink or swim together. Even the fractitious parliamentary Conservative Party in the 1992 Parliament shrank from that result (although four Conservative MPs crossed the floor). Potentially rebellious government back-benchers know that if by their votes they were to endanger the continuance of the government they could well be denied party endorsement at the general election and thus almost certainly lose their seats: that is a very high price for any MP to be prepared to pay. The endorsement of the Conservatives or Labour or a major third party is usually essential for election to the House of Commons,[62] as independent candidates are but rarely elected (although there is more room for success in the Nationalist cause in Scotland or Wales,[63] or in the sectarian parties in Northern Ireland).[64] The election of Mr Martin Bell as an Independent MP in 1997 was based on a pact in his constituency under which Labour and the Liberal Democrats did not put up candidates, so as to defeat the sitting Conservative MP, Mr Neil Hamilton. Party endorsement is made even more valuable because the national campaigns of the major parties, seen mainly through television, are much more important for the election of individual candidates than the efforts and identities of those candidates in their constituencies. So a majority government controls its MPs and has great power in and over the House of Commons, and it may be likened to the possessor of almost dictatorial powers, albeit powers that are restrained by regular general elections and by notions of what is generally acceptable in a liberal democracy. It has legislative

[62] Selection of candidates is largely a matter for local constituency parties. In the Labour Party, a candidate is chosen locally subject to the endorsement of the NEC (which is not always forthcoming: Mr Kinnock, for example, persuaded the Committee to reject a number of candidates before the 1987 general election, and Mr Blair had one rejected before the 1997 poll). Additionally, every Labour MP must submit to a reselection once in every Parliament, if a majority in his constituency vote for such a procedure. A number of Labour MPs, having been deselected, have indirectly lost their seats. The Conservative Party uses a lighter rein; disagreements between Conservative Central Office and the constituencies over candidates are infrequent, and locally chosen candidates are usually endorsed. The Liberal Democrats have a powerful central candidates' committee which maintains a list of parliamentary candidates approved by it. Each local party chooses its candidate by secret ballot. Liberal Democrat MPs are subject to reselection.

[63] The maximum Scottish National Party presence in the House was 11, and Plaid Cymru four.

[64] Of the 18 Northern Irish MPs, most will be Protestant Unionists.

supremacy in the Commons: its business (subject to exceptions which will be examined later) has precedence at every sitting,[65] and it can invoke the closure[66] and the guillotine[67] to ensure that it gets its legislation. It will suffer adverse votes from time to time, but the mass of its legislative programme will be enacted as it wants despite the best efforts of the opposition parties.

Two correctives need to be added to this description. First, in *very* special cases a Prime Minister may be forced from office directly or indirectly by the House of Commons.[68] The only three examples since 1895, however, have occurred during world war (Asquith's replacement by Lloyd George in 1916, and Chamberlain's by Churchill in 1940) and during a coalition in which the Prime Minister had only a minority of Commons seats and was always vulnerable to the majority party pulling the rug from under him (Lloyd George's ouster in 1922).[69] Secondly, a government backed even by a very large Commons majority may decide that the actual or feared resistance of its own back-benchers requires a change of course—not in relation to its core policies (for that might raise the question of whether the government continued to enjoy the confidence of the House), but in relation to less central matters over which the government may decide to change its mind. Even Mrs Thatcher's administration, whose lowest general election majority was 43 in 1979, altered its policies on a number of occasions, for instance on whether to compile a register of immigrants, the possibility of introducing local referendums, changes in green-belt policy, loans (rather than grants) to students, and the burying of nuclear waste at four planned sites. Changes of mind may thus be brought about by back-bench opinion without the spur of any formal vote.

Minority governments[70] are obviously less certain of the fate of their

[65] S.O. No. 14(1).

[66] S.O. Nos. 36, 37. A Government Whip moves 'That the question be now put' and, unless the Speaker thinks that this is an abuse, that motion is immediately voted on; if it is carried with at least 100 MPs supporting it, the main question under debate is put and decided, so ending debate.

[67] S.O. Nos. 82, 83. The government may move an allocation of time, or guillotine, motion in respect of a controversial Bill, and that motion is debated for up to three hours. The motion will allocate time for the standing committee to spend on each clause of the Bill, and for the time to be spent on report and third reading: as a result, parts of it may not be examined at all in committee. The late Conservative government guillotined three or four Bills each session, although 10 were guillotined in the 1988–89 session.

[68] As distinct from pressures or elections within the government and government party, as with Churchill in 1955 or Thatcher in 1990.

[69] See Chapter 2.

[70] On the parliamentary difficulties of the 1974 minority Labour government, see R. Brazier, 'The Constitution in the New Politics' [1978] *Public Law* 117.

policies and legislation in the House of Commons. They are prone to defeat in the division lobbies at any time. They are liable to the passage of a vote of no confidence (although the opposition parties may not all be ready to precipitate a dissolution too near to the previous one).[71] They may be in difficulty at the committee stage of Bills (for, in nominating standing committees to examine them, regard is had to the party composition of the House,[72] so that the government will be in a minority on those committees). Nevertheless, even minority governments retain the power of dissolution,[73] which can be put to effective use, as the second 1974 dissolution showed.[74]

Every government (whether majority, coalition, or minority) and every House of Commons must know exactly what votes adverse to the government are fatal, in the sense of inevitably leading to a dissolution of Parliament or the government's resignation. Defeat on an unambiguous motion of confidence or of no confidence has been treated as fatal by all governments since 1832. So, when the House of Commons resolved on 28 March 1979 'That this House has no confidence in Her Majesty's Government',[75] James Callaghan immediately told the House that he would seek a dissolution the following day. Now it used to be the case that a defeat on a major matter had the same effect as if an explicit vote of no confidence had carried. Ramsay MacDonald expressed the essence of this to the Commons after he had formed his first minority administration in 1924:

The Labour Government will go out if it is defeated upon substantial issues, issues of principle, issues which really matter. It will go out if the responsible leaders of either party or any party move a direct vote of no confidence, and carry that vote . . . If the House on matters non-essential, matters of mere opinion, matters that do not strike at the root of the proposals we make, and do not destroy fundamentally the general intentions of the Government in introducing legislation—if the House wish to vary our propositions, the House must take the responsibility for that variation—then a division on such amendments and questions as those will not be regarded as a vote of no confidence.[76]

That differentiation between, on the one hand, defeats on substantial issues which really mattered together with votes of no confidence (which were

---

[71] See Chapter 3.   [72] S.O. No. 86(2).

[73] Assuming, as I have argued in Chapter 3, that no other stronger grouping is ready to take over without a dissolution.

[74] The minority Labour government achieved a majority of five at the second 1974 general election.

[75] 965 H.C. Deb. 461–590 (28 March 1979).

[76] 169 H.C. Deb. 749–50 (15 January 1924).

both taken as decisive) and, on the other hand, non-essential defeats (which could be ignored) survived down to the 1970s. During that decade a significant change occurred, perhaps as an understanding that there is no reason why an isolated defeat on even a substantial matter should call in question the government's right to go on. Despite an initial majority of 30 seats Mr Edward Heath's government from 1970 to 1974 suffered six Commons defeats including, for example, the loss of draft Immigration Rules.[77] His successor Mr Harold Wilson made an early statement to the House about the position of the new minority Labour government:

The government intend to treat with suitable respect, but not with exaggerated respect, the result of any snap vote or any snap division . . . In case of a Government defeat . . . the Government will not be forced to go to the country except in a situation in which every Hon. Member of the House was voting knowing the full consequences of his vote. It is a vote of confidence about which I am speaking . . . In other words, we shall provide a recount.[78]

This marked a recognition that what was of account was not whether a particular matter was 'substantial' rather than 'non-essential', but rather whether a particular vote was recognized as being one of confidence in the administration. After this time only a division characterized by the government as a formal vote of confidence would, if lost, involve a general election, and the government would put down a motion of confidence if it suffered some other major loss in the division lobbies. This development had a wider parliamentary effect, because government MPs became readier to show their disapproval of their government's policies through abstentions and votes with the Opposition, a development which was accelerated during the 1974 Labour government.[79] So, in the short Parliament of 1974 the government lost 17 divisions,[80] for example on industrial policy[81] and on an Opposition motion on the rating system;[82] and in the 1974–79 Parliament it suffered 42 defeats before the final vote of no confidence was carried.[83] Those defeats were largely shrugged off by the

---

[77] 846 H.C. Deb. 1343–459 (22 November 1972).

[78] 870 H.C. Deb. 71–2 (12 March 1974).

[79] See generally P. Norton, *Dissension in the House of Commons 1945–1974* (1975), and *Dissension in the House of Commons 1974–1979* (1980).

[80] Norton, n. 79 above (1980), p. 491.

[81] 875 H.C. Deb. 689–769 (20 June 1974). The House resolved to regret the government's damaging industrial policies based on massive nationalization and the control of individual companies.

[82] 875 H.C. Deb. 1750–876 (27 June 1974). The House called on the government to introduce fundamental reform of the rating system.

[83] See Norton, n. 79 above (1980), 491–3.

government, and Ministers implied that if the opposition parties disliked that reaction the remedy was in their hands—to procure the passage of a vote of no confidence.[84] Mr John Major's government had to resort to lay-ing motions of confidence in order to carry a small number of votes towards the end of the 1997 Parliament: those moves were designed to force Conservative MPs to support their own government.

In (say) 1960 the defeat of a government Bill at second reading would have raised the probability of a general election,[85] but no one could still hold that view by 1980. The 1974 Labour government lost several Bills, the main casualties being the Aircraft and Shipbuilding Industries Bill,[86] the Scotland and Wales Bill (which lapsed after the government failed to carry a guillotine motion),[87] the Reduction of Redundancy Payments Bill (which was lost on second reading)[88] and the Local Authority Works (Scotland) Bill (which fell[89] at third reading).[90] Even Mrs Thatcher's gov-ernment, sustained as it was by large majorities, was not immune from actual or anticipated adverse votes in the House. The Protection of Official Information Bill, which was designed to change the law on official secrets, was withdrawn from Parliament in the 1979–80 session after it had received its second reading in the House of Lords: it was clear that the heavy criticism to which it had been subjected meant that its chances of ultimate survival in either House were small.[91] The draft Immigration Rules were defeated in the Commons in 1982.[92] Most spectacularly, the Shops Bill, which would have liberalized the rules on Sunday trading, was defeated at its second reading in 1986 by 14 votes, 68 Conservative MPs

[84] There were three unsuccessful motions of no confidence debated in the 1974–79 Parliament before the fatal one.

[85] '[I]t is now assumed as a matter of course that any defeats in the House of Commons must be reversed or else lead to a Government's resigning or dissolving Parliament': Graeme Moodie, *The Government of Britain* (1964), p. 100.

[86] The Bill lapsed at prorogation in 1976 after Opposition tactics had delayed it in the Commons, and the Lords had insisted on wrecking amendments.

[87] 926 H.C. Deb. 1234–367 (22 February 1977).

[88] 925 H.C. Deb. 1183–9 (7 February 1977).

[89] 935 H.C. Deb. 351–81 (12 July 1977).

[90] A motion on the government's public expenditure plans was also lost by 284:256, which led to a government motion of confidence being debated and carried the following day: see 907 H.C. Deb. 430–576 (10 March 1976); 907 H.C. Deb. 634–758 (11 March 1976). Numerous other provisions in various Bills were lost or amended contrary to the govern-ment's wishes.

[91] For the second reading debate, see 402 H. L. Deb. 608–80 (15 November 1979). The House of Lords does not usually reject a Bill at second reading but it may be emasculated or voted down in committee (customarily a Committee of the Whole House).

[92] 34 H.C. Deb. 355–439 (15 December 1982).

voting against it despite a three-line whip.[93] That government also with-drew the Family Homes and Domestic Violence Bill in the 1994–95 session after its second reading because of the deep opposition to it within the Conservative Party and the tabloid press. These examples show that no government, even with a sound or even huge majority in the Commons, can assume that elective dictatorship will carry all its legislation—although it must be stressed that the number of legislative defeats may well not be large, and the importance of the losses may be quite small.

So what adverse votes are fatal? The passage of a vote of no confidence[94] is always deadly, whether it be formally expressed as such or whether it is some other motion accepted by the government as testing the confidence of the House in it.[95] Defeat on any other major matter may cause the gov-ernment to ask the House to approve a formal motion of confidence,[96] and to recommend a dissolution or to resign if that is lost. Any other adverse vote in the House of Commons will have whatever effect is prescribed by the terms of the vote, but no other.[97]

The real significance of the general requirement that a government retain the confidence of the House of Commons is not in the rare loss of a vote of confidence or in the somewhat more frequent legislative defeat, but rather that it obliges every government to defend itself, explain its policies, and justify its actions, to its own back-benchers, to the opposition parties, and through them to the country as a whole.

Members' influence on the government

The dramatic cases of the House of Commons forcing the government to seek a fresh term from the electorate may now be left to one side. What

---

[93] 95 H.C. Deb. 584–702 (14 April 1986). For details of government Bills from 1958 to 1988 which (for various reasons) did not pass, see 194 H.C. Deb. 95–7 (written answers 12 July 1988).

[94] Or, of course, defeat on a government motion of confidence.

[95] The 1924 Labour government declared the amendments to its motion on the Campbell case (the Liberal amendment, which was successful, demanding a select committee on the affair) to be tantamount to motions of no confidence: see 177 H.C. Deb. 581–704 (8 Octo-ber 1924). What was to become the European Communities (Finance) Act 1995 received its second reading only after the government declared the vote on it to be one of confidence: see 250 H.C. Deb. 932–1034 (28 November 1994).

[96] A spectacular example occurred in 1993, when the government failed to carry a vote which was vital to the ratification of the Maastricht Treaty on European Union. The Prime Minister put down a motion of confidence in the government's policy in the matter which, when carried, amounted to the necessary vote. See 229 H.C. Deb. 627–725 (23 July 1993).

[97] Frequent adverse votes will naturally cause any government embarrassment.

must now be examined are the routine opportunities enjoyed by MPs inside and outside the chamber to exert an influence on and to challenge Ministers and their policies.[98] Those opportunities will be looked at in turn, and it will become apparent that there is a major imbalance of advantage in favour of Ministers and against both individual MPs and the opposition parties, produced by the procedural rules of the House and by the government's ability to achieve its way in the end by deploying its Commons strength.

The parliamentary question[99] is exceptionally popular with MPs. Nearly 50,000 were put down in the 1995–96 session.[100] The attractions of the question for an MP are obvious. It is easy to put one down:[101] any MP (other than a Minister or, by convention, the Leader of the Opposition)[102] may give notice of his question to the Table Office of the House of Commons. The MP putting a question for oral answer is entitled, after the Minister has replied, to put a supplementary question of which no advance notice is given, and in the MP's inventiveness and in the Minister's quick-wittedness parliamentary reputations (so it is said) may be made or damaged. Moreover, more MPs contribute in the chamber by asking questions than otherwise manage to speak there: some 40 to 50 Members will have the chance to shine during Question Time, which is more than will speak during an average debate.

Question Time is, however, more of an entertaining diversion than a method of parliamentary control of or influence over the government. Ministers only answer questions according to a rota which is agreed through the usual channels and in which the more important departments

---

[98] For a good short account of the order of business both during a parliamentary session and on an average day, see T. C. Hartley and J. A. G. Griffith, *Government and Law* (2nd edn., 1981), pp. 204–20.

[99] See Martin Franklin and Philip Norton (eds.), *Parliamentary Questions* (1993); J. A. G. Griffith and M. Ryle, *Parliament: Functions, Practice and Procedures* (1989), pp. 366–74; Erskine May, n. 9 above, pp. 281–97; 1st Report of the Select Committee on Procedure, H.C. 379 (1989–90), and H.C. 178 (1990–91); 178 H.C. Deb. 391–2 (24 October 1990).

[100] At an average current cost of £244 to provide each oral answer and £105 for each written answer. MPs must indicate whether they want oral or written answers: S.O. No. 22(3). Questions for written answer are usually designed to elicit purely factual information. Questions for oral answer which are not reached at Question Time receive written answers.

[101] Subject to it being in order, which is explained shortly.

[102] The Leader of the Opposition uses the private notice procedure under S.O. No. 21(2): a question of an urgent character and which relates to matters of public importance or the arrangement of Commons business may be taken after Question Time provided the Speaker received it before noon, agrees that it satisfies those conditions and is told that the Minister has received notice of the question. Such use by the Leader of the Opposition is rare. The last time he used it was in 1988; the previous occasion was in 1952.

put up a Minister to reply roughly every four weeks.[103] Consequently, Members can only question a particular Minister when his turn in the rota comes round, however anxious they may be to grill him immediately. This is in stark contrast to Question Time in, for example, the Canadian House of Commons, during which any Minister (including the Prime Minister) can be asked any question on any day. (A British Minister who is not due to respond at Question Time may decide to make a statement after questions on an urgent or other matter,[104] and MPs may then question him on it: but if no statement is forthcoming MPs and the Speaker can do nothing about it.) The Prime Minister's rota requires his presence at the dispatch box for 30 minutes every Wednesday. These are occasions which many former Prime Ministers profess to have dreaded, but given the political ability which they must have to carry them to the top office together with previous ministerial[105] and Commons experience,[106] all Prime Ministers have tended to acquit themselves to the satisfaction of their supporters in the Commons.[107] Then again, Ministers have advance warning of the question which will appear on the order paper. A Member must give two clear days' notice of the question to which he wants a Minister to give an oral answer.[108] A Member can put down a question up to 10 sitting days before the Minister is due to answer, but not before that period,[109] a rule designed to prevent the order paper being filled up with questions which are stale by

---

[103] Each major department is allocated to a particular day of the week, together with three or four others. When at the top of the rota, its Minister will be questioned first, and is likely to be questioned for the whole of the time available. In the following week he will be at the bottom of the rota, and in each successive week he rises a place, so that after three or four weeks he is back on top. Thus he can usually expect to answer questions for the best part of an hour once a month. Ministers with special responsibilities, or at the head of minor departments (like the Attorney-General) answer questions for 10 or 15 minutes on a specified day at regular intervals, usually every four weeks.

[104] The Speaker is informed of his intention, but neither his nor the House's leave is necessary.

[105] Ramsay MacDonald and Tony Blair were the only people to become Prime Minister this century with no previous ministerial experience.

[106] Sir Alec Douglas-Home had been in the Lords for 12 years when he became Prime Minister, and an MP again, in 1963.

[107] Even the open question (for example, asking the Prime Minister to state his engagements for the day, followed by a wholly unrelated supplementary) is taken in any Prime Minister's stride. For Mrs Thatcher's approach, see *The Downing Street Years* (1993), p. 41.

[108] S.O. No. 22(6). The private notice procedure (see n. 102 above) circumvents this, but is only of limited use. The requirement of two days' notice has the advantage that the text of the question is printed on the order paper, so that as each MP is called upon to ask his question, he merely states the number of it, rather than reading out the text, thus saving parliamentary time.

[109] S.O. No. 22(5).

the time they come to be answered. But because of the large number of MPs who wish to question Ministers, an MP in practice must give notice on the first possible day to have any chance of his question being reached and given an oral answer. The effect of the rota and rules about notice is that on each day MPs are tabling questions to a particular Minister for a fortnight ahead. This gives the Minister's Private Office more than enough time to assemble all the information that the Minister will need and to work out what supplementary questions are likely to follow: no Minister should, therefore, go to the House to answer questions like a lamb to the slaughter.[110] In the result, as one writer has aptly put it, 'few Ministers are caught napping'.[111]

Moreover, a number of other procedural rules work in Ministers' favour. To be accepted by the Table Office and thus to appear on the order paper at all, a question must (quite fairly) relate to the public affairs with which the Minister is officially connected, to proceedings in Parliament, or to administrative matters for which the Minister is responsible.[112] So for instance the Table Office will not accept questions relating to local authority responsibilities, the Stock Exchange, the banks, the police,[113] or which ask for an opinion on a point of law or for which, for whatever reason, the Minister has no responsibility. Erskine May's *Parliamentary Practice* sets out these exceptions over three pages of small print.[114] Additionally, a Minister will not usually answer any question (even if passed by the Table Office) which concerns confidential exchanges with other governments, or affects national security, or involves commercial confidentiality, or which seeks information about individuals or companies for which he has no responsibility, or which would involve the disclosure of any advice given to him by the civil service.[115] MPs have, therefore, nothing like *carte blanche* to ask

---

[110] 'One evening I found Churchill at the Cabinet table . . . "What are you doing, Prime Minister?" I asked. "Oh, parliamentary questions. Preparing improvisations! Very hard work!" ': Harold Macmillan, *Tides of Fortune* (1969), p. 496.

[111] Sir Norman Chester, *Questions in Parliament* (1962), p. 185.

[112] Erskine May, n. 9 above, p. 289.

[113] The Home Secretary is the police authority for the Metropolitan Police district and can therefore be asked detailed questions about the conduct of that force—save any concerning 'operational matters'.

[114] See n. 9 above, p. 289.

[115] A list of 95 excepted matters is given in Appendix 9 to the Report from the Select Committee on Parliamentary Questions, H.C. 393 (1971–2). See also the Scott Report, H.C. 115 (1995–96), iv, paras. K8.5–K8.14. Although much information has been published officially since 1992 about the Security Service, the Prime Minister will not answer questions about its operational work: see 201 H.C. Deb. 469 (written answers 13 January 1992). Advice to the Queen from the Prime Minister about honours is also excluded: see, for example, 183 H.C. Deb. 175–8 (18 December 1990).

Ministers anything. If a Minister were embarrassed by a question which was in order he could (though rarely does) refuse point blank to answer: he is not obliged to say anything, but there are of course ways of speaking without saying anything, and if an MP is dissatisfied by a reply there is precious little he or the Speaker can do about it (the Speaker not being responsible for the quality of ministerial answers, as she reminds the House rather plaintively from time to time). Alternatively, and just as unhelpfully, the Minister may respond that he will write to the Member. Such a reply is offered periodically. As well as being sent to that MP, the Minister's letter is also made available in the House of Commons Library, indexed under the MP's name, but it is not published in *Hansard*. An MP seeking to joust with a Minister or looking for publicity through his question will be thwarted if the Minister resorts to this formula. Again, Ministers may, and sometimes do, decline to answer on the ground that the information sought could only be assembled at disproportionate cost, currently set at £500.[116] Another recent development has caused MPs further difficulties. Ministers now refer questions on operational (as distinct from policy) matters arising within executive agencies to the relevant chief executive. His letter in reply will be published in *Hansard*. Opposition MPs claim that this practice has diluted Ministers' responsibility and accountability for large numbers of civil servants. Indeed, the new Labour Home Secretary announced soon after taking office in 1997 that questions about the Prison Service would be answered in future by Home Office Ministers rather than the Director-General.

Transcending all of those difficulties in the way of a questioning MP, however, is the imbalance of information and resources available to him, in contrast to the government, which is buttressed by all the resources of the civil service. No MP, however well served by the Research Division of the House of Commons Library or helped though the 'Short money' paid to his parliamentary party,[117] can hope to have at his fingertips the kind of detailed facts which could be deployed so as to make Question Time an effective exercise of parliamentary power. A Member will occasionally make a telling point, a Minister may occasionally stumble,[118] but both the procedural rules and expertise which is available only to Ministers mean

---

[116] 583 H.L. Deb. 159–60 (written answers 2 December 1997).

[117] See n. 35 above.

[118] A Minister who needs factual information which he does not have with which to reply to a question may be helped by civil servants from his department who will be on hand in a special box, technically outside the chamber, and who can pass notes to him. No Minister would want to be seen to be too reliant on that source.

that Question Time is not really much of a method of parliamentary control.

Each day one Member has the opportunity to speak in the adjournment debate.[119] This lasts for 30 minutes and is the final item of business. A ballot is held in the Speaker's office every Thursday, into which goes the name of every MP who wishes to speak on the adjournment together with the topic he wishes to raise.[120] The successful Member may then raise that issue—local or national, helpful to or critical of the government—and he will receive a ministerial reply[121] from a junior Minister (for after all the adjournment debate will take place late at night). The fundamental weakness of the adjournment procedure for the back-bencher who may wish to exert some influence over government policy is that he cannot question or reply to the Minister's speech: it is rather like Question Time without the right to put a supplementary, although sometimes the Minister gives way to interruptions and will then have to answer points made during them. And daily adjournment debates are thinly attended, partly because the matters raised may be of significance only to one constituency, and partly because of the timing.

The government will hear from its attackers and defenders during Opposition day debates.[122] Twenty days[123] during the session are allotted to subjects chosen by the opposition parties, the Leader of the Opposition selecting the subjects on 17 of those days while the remaining three are at the disposal of the Leader of the second largest opposition party in the House.[124] Fitting in those 20 days obviously affects the arrangement of the government's business. (The government must, additionally, find time to debate any motion of no confidence which the Opposition may put down, although the number of such motions has declined over the years.) Now the government will not normally be at risk of defeat on the invariably critical Opposition day motions, but the existence of such days helps parliamentary reputations to be enhanced or diminished and, yet again,

---

[119] S.O. No. 9(2)–(6).

[120] An MP dissatisfied by a ministerial reply to a question sometimes says he will seek an opportunity to raise the matter on the adjournment. The ballot is the means of doing so.

[121] Other MPs do not usually intervene.

[122] The term Opposition day replaced the former (and ancient and latterly misnamed) Supply days in 1982.

[123] The figure had been set at 19 in 1982, but was raised to 20 in 1985: see 79 H.C. Deb. 1246 (23 May 1985).

[124] S.O. No. 14(2). In the 1982 changes, all the Opposition days were given to the Leader of the Opposition; informal talks with the Liberal Party and the SDP ceded a few days to them ad hoc, but in 1985 the rights of the second largest opposition party were written in.

obliges the government to answer criticism and thus provide interested electors outside the House with one more piece of information to weigh at the next general election.

It is in the process of legislation that the impotence of the opposition parties and back-benchers when faced by a cohesive majority government may be seen the most clearly.[125] As already noted, legislative defeats can be inflicted occasionally, but in the main most governments will get their legislation broadly in the form they desire. The Opposition cannot hope in the usual case to vote down a government Bill at second or third reading or on report, for government troops will be ready in the division lobbies to beat off attacks. The Opposition may try to amend the Bill in committee, but the government will have its majority on each standing committee,[126] so that if it does not want to accept any given amendment it can, if pressed, vote it down. In a detailed examination of the fate of amendments moved to government Bills in committee during three sessions of the 1964 Labour government, it emerged that of 3,510 amendments moved by back-benchers in standing committee only 171 carried, whereas of 907 amendments proposed by the government to its own Bills all save one carried.[127] There is no reason to believe that that pattern is untypical. Indeed, it is more accurate to classify the committee stage as an opportunity not for the Opposition to alter the terms of government Bills but rather for the government to incorporate its own second thoughts into its legislation; some of those second thoughts will result from representations from non-governmental quarters, and that is a far cry from a procedure permitting of detailed scrutiny and involving amendment of legislation by back-benchers.

The special public Bill committee[128] should be mentioned briefly here. This is a very useful type of committee[129] which has the power to send for

---

[125] On that process of legislation, see S. A. de Smith and R. Brazier, *Constitutional and Administrative Law* (8th edn., 1998), pp. 270–82; D. R. Miers and A. C. Page, *Legislation* (1982); I. Burton and G. Drewry, *Legislation and Public Policy* (1981); and, for detailed rules, Erskine May, n. 9 above, ch. 21.

[126] S.O. No. 86(2): in nominating MPs to standing committees, regard must be had to the party composition of the House so as to reflect it in the composition of each standing committee. See also 252 H.C. Deb. 158 (11 January 1995).

[127] See J. A. G. Griffith, *Parliamentary Scrutiny of Government Bills* (1974).

[128] S.O. No. 91. See H. J. Beynon, 'The House of Commons' Experiment with Special Standing Committees' [1982] *Public Law* 193; H. Brooke, 'Special Public Bill Committees' [1995] *Public Law* 351.

[129] Such a committee was first established experimentally in 1980: see 991 H.C. Deb. 835–6 (30 October 1980). The 2nd Report from the Select Committee on Procedure, H.C. 49 (1984–5), paras. 11–13 recommended that more use should be made of special standing committees, as virtually all the evidence which it had received about them had been enthusiastic—including evidence from Ministers.

persons, papers, and records during its deliberations on a Bill, and may hold up to four morning sittings, at three of which oral evidence from interested individuals and groups from outside Parliament may be given in public. This horizon-broadening procedure should, I believe, be resorted to more often: it exposes the government not to defeat but to opportunities for wider debate and expertise than is otherwise the case, and thus promotes the emergence of legislation of a higher quality.

In the 1995–96 session 17 Private Members' Bills passed into law. Eighty-nine had been introduced. Although the success rate is always low, some individual back-benchers do see their legislative proposals receive royal assent each year. There are three routes along which such back-bench Bills may progress, although only the first gives much prospect of eventual enactment. On 10 Fridays each session Private Members' Bills have precedence over other business[130]—but in order to introduce a Bill on such a day a Member must be one of the 20 successful MPs in yet another ballot held for the purpose periodically through the session;[131] and he must also be at or near the top of those 20 for there to be sufficient time in the later arrangement of business for the Bill to be fully considered. Fortunately for back-benchers they do not have to indicate in that ballot the nature of the Bill which they want to introduce, for at that stage most have no idea.[132] A second route is through the 10-minute rule procedure,[133] through which a Member may give notice that he will seek the leave of the House to introduce a Bill on a Tuesday or a Wednesday (although only one MP may seek leave on any day, on a first come, first served basis).[134] The Speaker allows a brief explanatory statement from that MP, followed by one brief speech from any MP who opposes it, after which the question is put whether leave be given.[135] In general the use of the 10-minute rule procedure is not a serious attempt to legislate, but rather is a way of drawing attention to the need for a change in the law: only some thirty 10-minute rule Bills have actually been enacted since 1945. The final route—and the one chosen by most aspirant back-bench legislators—is merely to present a Bill after giving notice (but without needing the leave of the House): such a measure will be formally read a first time and will be set down for second reading on a

[130] S.O. No. 14(4).   [131] S.O. No. 14(6).

[132] MPs successful and high up in the ballot are much sought after by pressure groups keen to get them to take up their proposals, and to supply them with draft Bills and other help. See generally David Marsh and Melvyn Read, *Private Members' Bills* (1988).

[133] S.O. No. 23.

[134] S.O. No. 23(2). Such Bills cannot be introduced on Budget day: this rule prevents any MP hogging the limelight just before the Chancellor speaks: see S.O. No. 23(3).

[135] S.O. No. 23(1).

specified Friday.[136] Any Member opposing the Bill—not infrequently a Government Whip—can postpone that second reading on that day simply by calling out 'object'. Even supposing that a Member is successful in the ballot,[137] or in getting leave under the 10-minute rule, or in avoiding an opponent uttering the deadly word, there may still be a major obstruction in his path—not the government using its majority to vote the Bill down, for that is something which governments refrain from doing—but rather that no Private Member's Bill is in order if it has as its main purpose the creation of a charge on public funds.[138] If a Member wishes to do that he must privately persuade the government to agree to a Minister signifying the Queen's recommendation that the Commons approve a financial resolution,[139] which is tantamount to the government adopting the Bill as its own (or to the government vetoing it if it refuses to do so). Large areas of public policy are effectively placed out of bounds to private Members by this rule. By contrast, the government will occasionally smile on a back-bench Bill and even, in a few cases, provide help in drafting it[140] and give up some of its time for it to be considered.[141] That a dozen or so Private Members' Bills become law each session is in the main attributable to luck and the acquiescence of the government—factors which in a wholly rational parliamentary system would not be the determinants for back-bench legislative initiatives.

In 1981 the Select Committee on Procedure (Supply) concluded that 'the House's financial procedures are antiquated and defective and need a thorough overhaul'.[142] Even after the adoption of that Committee's

---

[136] S.O. No. 57.

[137] The top 10 MPs in the ballot may draw up to £200 each to help towards drafting expenses. That sum has not been increased since the grant was introduced in 1971: the equivalent sum in 1995 would have been £1,454: few MPs bother to claim it: see 252 H.C. Deb. 402 (written answers 17 January 1995). Non-lawyer MPs may seek the help of friendly lawyer-MPs with drafting.

[138] S.O. No. 50. The government's use of a three-line whip in January 1988 to defeat Mr Richard Shepherd's Protection of Official Information Bill was unprecedented.

[139] S.O. No. 48; Erskine May, n. 9 above, ch. 29.

[140] For example, the Sexual Offences (Amendment) Act 1976.

[141] A list of Private Members' Bills which have been given extra parliamentary time by the government since 1954 is given at 62 H.C. Deb. 367–72 (written answers 25 June 1984); 62 H.C. Deb. 495–6 (written answers 28 June 1984). Very occasionally the government may have to bow to parliamentary and public opinion and legislate itself as the result of a back-bench initiative. For example, Mr Austin Mitchell's Home Buyers' Bill, designed to end the solicitors' conveyancing monopoly, achieved its second reading and was only withdrawn when the government promised its own Bill with the same objectives; its legislative provision became the Administration of Justice Act 1985, Part II.

[142] H.C. 181–I (1980–1), para. 37.

proposals, and others from the Public Accounts Committee,[143] neither the House as a whole nor individual back-benchers have much real control over the raising and spending of public money. Members of Parliament are the last to hear the Chancellor's Budget which is presented, more or less, as a *fait accompli*,[144] and the Finance Bill which is constructed on it passes into law without even marginal changes having been made to it at the insistence of the House. Members go through the motions of scrutinizing Finance Bills, but amendments are made almost entirely at the request of Ministers. (As already pointed out, there is no examination at all of Consolidated Fund Bills or of Appropriation Bills even though billions of pounds are spent each year by virtue of authority contained in them.) Nor is there any parliamentary control over the government's borrowing, even though this is a major source of any government's revenue. The House oversees the government's estimates as best it can through the three Estimates days on the floor of the House, during which Members debate, and vote on, the details of government expenditure;[145] but the Public Accounts Committee reported in 1987 that 'Parliament's consideration of the annual estimates— the key constitutional control—remains largely a formality'.[146] The Public Accounts Committee[147] itself is better placed. It is composed of 15 MPs, selected to reflect party strengths in the House, with an Opposition MP as its chairman (and who is usually a former junior Minister at the Treasury). The Committee's task is to check that money has been spent according to Parliament's wishes, although it ranges more widely and quite frequently discovers and reports on wasteful and extravagant expenditure and imprudent government contracts.[148] The Comptroller and Auditor-General[149] sits with the Committee, and its reports are treated with respect in White-hall—but an inevitable weakness is that it can only report after money has

---

[143] The Public Accounts Committee recommended (H.C. 115–I (1980–1)) in particular the creation of a National Audit Office in place of the Exchequer and Audit Department. It was through the efforts of Mr Norman St John-Stevas (as a back-bench MP, having resigned from Mrs Thatcher's Cabinet), that that proposal passed into the law in his Private Member's Bill which became the National Audit Act 1983.

[144] See Chapter 6.

[145] S.O. No. 54. This was another 1982 procedural change adopted from H.C. 118–I (1980–1).

[146] 8th Report from the Public Accounts Committee, H.C. 98 (1986–7), para. 2.

[147] See S.O. No. 148.

[148] It was reported in 1986, for example, that the Ministry of Defence had overspent by £938 million on 12 major defence contracts, and had paid out over £200 million in another seven projects which had later been cancelled: 6th Report from the Public Accounts Committee, H.C. 104 (1986–7).

[149] See National Audit Act 1983, *passim*.

been spent. All in all, as the Public Accounts Committee put it in 1987, '[p]ublic expenditure is constitutionally subject to the control of Parliament. At present this control is of doubtful effectiveness'.[150]

Back-benchers scrutinize and influence the government more successfully away from the chamber in the select committees which examine the expenditure, administration, and policy of government departments. These departmental select committees owe their existence to experiments in the 1966 Parliament,[151] the 1978 Report of the Select Committee on Procedure,[152] back-bench pressure, and a reform-minded and determined Leader of the House, Mr Norman St John-Stevas, supported by a commitment in the Conservative Party's 1979 general election manifesto.

The committees[153] oversee 16 major departments.[154] The Lord Chancellor's Department and the Law Officers' Department were originally excluded because of fears that parliamentary inquiries into them might interfere with the independence of the judiciary. Those ungrounded fears were set aside in 1991 when those departments were brought within the system.[155] Members are chosen by the Committee of Selection[156] (which will hear informal advice from the Whips); each committee selects its own chairman[157] (although by custom half the chairmen are from the Opposition); the committees choose what to investigate (subject to the Liaison

[150] 8th Report from the Public Accounts Committee, H.C. 98 (1986–7), para. 1.

[151] The Select Committee on Agriculture (which was allowed to lapse after two years), on Education and Science, on Science and Technology, on Race Relations and Immigration, on Scottish Affairs, and on Overseas Development.

[152] 1st Report from the Select Committee on Procedure, H.C. 588–I (1977–8).

[153] See Dermot Englefield, *Commons Select Committees: Catalysts for Progress?* (1984): Dilys Hill, *Parliamentary Select Committees in Action* (1984); Gavin Drewry (ed.), *The New Select Committees* (2nd edn., 1989); Griffith and Ryle, n. 99 above, ch. 11.

[154] See S.O. No. 152. The committees are: Agriculture; Culture, Media and Sport; Defence; Education and Employment; Environment, Transport and the Regions; Foreign Affairs; Health; Home Affairs; Northern Ireland; Public Service; Science and Technology; Scottish Affairs; Social Security; Trade and Industry; Treasury; and Welsh Affairs. Each has 11 members.

[155] See 195 H.C. Deb. 607–8 (18 July 1991). The departments are within the remit of the Select Committee on Home Affairs which, however (and rightly) cannot examine 'individual cases and appointments and advice given within government by Law Officers'.

[156] S.O. No. 121. The Committee of Selection consists of nine MPs: see Standing Orders of the House of Commons (Private Business), H.C. 130 (1983–4), S.O. No. 109. In nominating the select committees it reflects the party composition of the House—not by virtue of any standing order, but because the House as a whole approves motions to appoint to them and nominations are negotiated reflecting party strengths through the usual channels.

[157] In 1992 Conservative Whips invented a rule which precluded chairmen from being re-elected after 12 years' service. A notable casualty (and the Whips' target) was Mr Nicholas Winterton, an outspoken and independent-minded Conservative back-bencher who had been chairman of the Select Committee on Health. See 211 H.C. Deb. 913–45 (13 July 1992).

Committee which comprises the select committee chairmen and which prevents duplication of inquiries); the Education and Employment, Foreign Affairs, Home Affairs, and Treasury Committees may nominate subcommittees so that each may conduct simultaneous examinations.[158] The formal powers of the committees to send for persons, papers, and records are impressive but have only been used once:[159] an informal invitation usually does the trick. A refusal to comply with a select committee order would be a contempt of the House of Commons, and the committee concerned would refer it to the House to be dealt with.[160] The committees' power to send for persons embraces Ministers (but not Prime Ministers[161]) and civil servants (even the Head of the Home Civil Service and Secretary to the Cabinet). In setting up the committees in 1979 the government promised that Ministers would attend,[162] although the Prime Minister has occasionally directed a Minister to attend other than the one sought; and the Liaison Committee reported in 1982 that the physical attendance of Ministers was satisfactory—although that was before Westland[163] and two other incidents. In the aftermath of the Westland affair the Defence Select Committee wanted to examine named civil servants who had been involved in the improper leaking to the press of the Solicitor-General's letter to a Minister:[164] intense negotiations, at one stage of which the Committee made it clear that it was ready to use its formal powers and to respond to any obstruction by referring the matter to the House as a possible contempt, produced a compromise in which the Permanent Under-Secretary of State

[158] S.O. No. 152(3).

[159] In 1982 when the Energy Select Committee made a formal order against Mr Arthur Scargill summoning him to give evidence before it. The Warrant Officer of the Serjeant at Arms served the order on Mr Scargill, with which he fully complied and gave his evidence, and a similar order was made against the Maxwell brothers in 1993: see n. 180 above. If a committee wants to summon a reluctant MP to give evidence, only the House as a whole can order his attendance.

[160] 1st Report from the Liaison Committee, *The Accountability of Ministers and Civil Servants to Select Committees of the House of Commons*, H.C. 100 (1986–7), para. 2; Erskine May, n. 9 above, ch. 10.

[161] Baroness Thatcher declined to give evidence to the Foreign Affairs Select Committee in 1994 during its Pergau dam inquiry, relying on 'the convention, established since 1945, that Prime Ministers and former Prime Ministers do not give evidence to select committees on specific issues'. Lord Callaghan gave evidence in 1994 to the Treasury and Civil Service Committee (as it then was) on the role of the civil service (which Lady Thatcher characterized as evidence on 'a general issue').

[162] See 969 H.C. Deb. 45 (25 June 1979).

[163] On the Westland affair generally, see Chapter 6.

[164] Mr John Michell, Mr John Mogg, Miss Colette Bowe (all of the Department of Trade and Industry), and Mr Bernard Ingham (Chief Press Secretary to the Prime Minister) and Mr Charles Powell (Private Secretary to the Prime Minister).

at the Department of Trade and Industry and the Cabinet Secretary attended instead.[165] Two years before that the government had refused to allow either the Director of the Government Communications Headquarters at Cheltenham or a trade union official working there to appear before the Employment Select Committee as part of its inquiry into the government's ban on trade union membership at GCHQ.[166] Then again, the Trade and Industry Committee was refused certain documents by the government, and civil servants appearing before it were instructed not to answer certain questions, so preventing it from reaching precise conclusions in its inquiry into the collapse of the tin industry in 1985.[167] At no stage in any of those episodes did the Committees accept any restriction on their ultimate legal powers to obtain whatever witnesses they wished. Now if compromise allows the select committees to get the witnesses they need and permits the government to uphold what it perceives as its legitimate rights, well and good; but if compromise fails the committees should, I suggest, assert their undoubted powers deliberately granted to them by the House of Commons itself in an attempt to redress the balance of advantage between legislature and executive.

It is one thing to establish machinery in order to elicit information more efficiently than through other forms of parliamentary inquiry: it is quite another actually to extract that information from witnesses. Broadly, this has not been a problem, but the government has been extremely cautious about allowing civil service witnesses to give certain kinds of evidence. Standing instructions[168] stress that when attending select committees civil servants remain subject to ministerial orders. In any case civil servants must not give answers about advice given to Ministers,[169] interdepartmental exchanges on policy, advice given by the Law Officers, matters in the field of political controversy (but are not most governmental matters politically controversial?), sensitive commercial information, and sensitive negotiations with other states or with the European Community.[170] These are

[165] 4th Report from the Defence Committee, *Westland plc: The Government's Decision-making*, H.C. 519 (1985–6), paras. 225–33. The Committee recorded that the evidence of those two witnesses was hearsay; and it reiterated that a select committee's power to secure the attendance of witnesses remained 'unqualified': ibid., para. 228.

[166] 1st Report from the Employment Committee, H.C. 238 (1983–4), paras. 6–7.

[167] See 2nd Report from the Trade and Industry Committee, H.C. 305 (1985–6); Government Response, H.C. 457 (1985–6); 1st Report from the Trade and Industry Committee, H.C. 71 (1986–7); debate at 101 H.C. Deb. 72–118 (7 July 1986).

[168] *Departmental Evidence and Response to Select Committees* (Cabinet Office, 1994).

[169] 1980 Memorandum, para. 25.

[170] In its reply to the Defence Committee report on Westland (*Government Response to the*

major exceptions, although in the main they do not seem to have caused too much interference with the committees' work.

The departmental select committees provide a means by which witnesses (Ministers, civil servants, and others) can be cross-examined at length and more thoroughly than in any other way now open to either House; their members have developed expertise and knowledge about the departments; the committees try to achieve, and usually do achieve, unanimous reports, cutting across party lines and thus carrying more weight than would any partisan document;[171] Ministers and civil servants may have to consider the committees' likely reactions to major new policies before they are finally formulated;[172] and the Liaison Committee has stressed that a markedly improved flow of information has been achieved from the departments to the House of Commons, not only through the committees' reports and published evidence but also through the government's responses to them published in White Papers in reply, so that overall the committees have become a valuable feature of parliamentary life.[173] But two drawbacks must be noted. First, only a minority of select committee reports are debated by the House itself. For example, in the four years from 1991 to 1995, 222 reports were so debated, although many others had been relevant to the course of other debates.[174] Gathering information is an important exercise, but unless the House finds the time to debate such

---

3rd and 4th Reports from the Defence Committee, Cmnd. 9916 (1986), para. 44), the government stated that it would instruct civil servants in the future not to answer questions directed to their own or other named civil servants' conduct. The Treasury and Civil Service Committee, in H.C. 62 (1986–7), para. 5, termed that 'unfortunate'; the Liaison Committee considered it to be 'wholly unacceptable', and urged the government to reconsider its position 'without delay': 1st Report from the Liaison Committee, The Accountability of Ministers and Civil Servants to Select Committees of the House of Commons, H.C. 100 (1986–7), paras. 6, 11. The government, however, broadly stuck to its guns: it has directed that, if civil service witnesses are asked questions about the conduct of named civil servants with the aim of allocating individual criticism or blame, those witnesses should reply that such matters are for the relevant Minister; the Minister would then investigate, and report to the committee: Government Response to the 1st Report from the Liaison Committee, Cm. 78 (1987), paras. 9–12 and Annex.

[171] An unusual example of a select committee reporting on party lines was the Foreign Affairs Committee's report on the sinking of the General Belgrano during the Falklands conflict: that report was approved, and a Labour draft report rejected, by six votes to four: see H.C. 11 (1984–5).

[172] A point made by Dilys Hill, n. 153 above, p. 29.

[173] 1st Report from the Liaison Committee, The Select Committee System, H.C. 92 (1982–3); see also 2nd Report from the Select Committee on Procedure, The Working of the Select Committee System, H.C. 19 (1989–90)—a similarly enthusiastic endorsement.

[174] 228 H.C. Deb. 26 (written answers 19 June 1995). But the system, according to the Liaison Committee, remained 'a major, successful parliamentary reform'.

information and conclusions formed from it there is an obvious danger that select committee reports will merely take up shelf space in libraries. Secondly, Ministers and other witnesses are not obliged to answer questions, as Mr Leon Brittan's stonewalling showed during his appearances before the Defence Select Committee in its Westland investigations.[175] This failing must not be exaggerated, but as with Question Time it is an unfair advantage enjoyed by Ministers which the House as a whole has not adequately addressed.[176]

[175] H.C. 519 (1985–6), paras. 203, 204: the Defence Committee records a number of vital questions which it put to Mr Brittan and notes, 'He refused to tell us'. It could be a punishable contempt to refuse to answer select committee questions: Erskine May, n. 9 above, p. 117. Despite that, a former junior Minister, Mrs Edwina Currie, stonewalled while giving evidence to the Select Committee on Agriculture in 1989. And in 1992 Mr Robert Maxwell's two sons refused to answer certain questions before the Select Committee on Social Security on the grounds that to do so could prejudice their anticipated trial. No formal Commons' action was requested in either case.

[176] Possibly again because today's Opposition MPs are tomorrow's Ministers.

11

THE HOUSE OF LORDS

Acquiring and losing membership

At the time of writing the composition of the House of Lords faces radical change. The Labour government has a manifesto commitment to exclude hereditary peers from membership as the first stage towards creating a more democratic second chamber.[1] At the moment, however, membership of the House of Lords consists of the Prince of Wales, hereditary peers, life peers, the Lords Spiritual and the Lords of Appeal in Ordinary.[2] In 1998 there were 767 hereditary peers (including 20 hereditary peeresses) and some 500 life peers (of whom only 88 were women): that potential membership of over 1200 made it easily the largest chamber in any bicameral parliament in the developed world. The hereditary peerage is divided both by rank and by country of origin. Senior by rank are dukes (28 in 1998), followed by marquesses (34), earls (169, plus five countesses in their own right), viscounts (103) and barons (463, plus 14 baronesses in their own right).[3] Such peers are members of the peerage of England or of Scotland if their peerages were created before 1707; after the Union with Scotland, newly created peers became peers of Great Britain; since the Union with Ireland in 1801 newly created hereditary peers have been peers of the United Kingdom. Peers of Scotland whose peerages were created before the Act of Union sit as of right;[4] peers in the Irish peerage cannot sit at all.[5] Female hereditary peers have been entitled to sit in the House of

---

[1] See further the final section of this chapter.

[2] House of Lords Standing Order No. 2, provided they are over 21.

[3] A peeress 'in her own right' is one who holds her own peerage, rather than just having a title because her husband is a peer.

[4] Peerage Act 1963, s. 4. Before 1963 such peers elected 16 of their number to represent them in the House of Lords.

[5] *Re Earl of Antrim's Petition* [1967] 1 A.C. 691; Report of the Privileges Committee, H.L. 85 (1994–5) and 565 H.L. Deb. 1092–1104 (5 July 1995) (barony of Farnham carries no right to sit in the House of Lords because it is in the Irish peerage). Before 1922 peers of Ireland

Lords in their own right since 1963.[6] Members of the royal family may sit only if they have a peerage. Being merely a Prince or Princess of the United Kingdom does not qualify, and so Prince Edward is not a member; the five royal dukes (Edinburgh, Cornwall, York, Gloucester and Kent) may sit, as may Princess Margaret's former husband the Earl of Snowdon, who received his earldom after their marriage in 1961.[7]

Not surprisingly, not everyone who might be willing to join the House of Lords found either the notion of heredity as a qualification or the social stratification inherent in the hereditary peerage acceptable. The Labour Party especially had insufficient people who were prepared to accept such peerages, and so it was conspicuously weak in the House of Lords. The Life Peerages Act 1958 has, however, helped. A life peerage in the rank of baron may be conferred on any person giving him membership of the House of Lords for life: the peerage expires on his death.[8] Even though the Act expressly states that a life peerage may be given to a woman,[9] life barons outnumber life baronesses by more than seven to one.[10] The Lords Spiritual sit in the House of Lords with the right to speak and vote, the Archbishops of Canterbury and York and the Bishops of London, Durham and Winchester being there *ex officio*, and 21 other Anglican bishops according to seniority of appointment to their sees.[11] All Lords Spiritual appointed since 1976 are subject to retirement at 70; on retirement the right to sit and vote is lost[12] and the next *ex officio* appointee or the next most senior bishop takes his place; by custom the Archbishop of Canterbury is given a peerage on his retirement.[13] Lords Spiritual are not peers:[14] it follows that (unlike peers) they may vote in elections to the House of Commons. The

---

elected 28 of their number to represent them in the House; the machinery to elect them ceased to exist in 1922 on the creation of the Irish Free State. Peers of Ireland can, however, be elected as MPs and vote in parliamentary elections: Peerage Act 1963, s. 5.

[6]   Peerage Act 1963, s. 6.

[7]   No other commoner who has married into the royal family since 1961 has taken a peerage.

[8]   Life Peerages Act 1958, s. 1.

[9]   Ibid., s. 1(3).

[10]   The first list struck a slightly better ratio of 10 men and four women.

[11]   But never the Bishop of Sodor and Man: Erskine May, *Parliamentary Practice* (21st edn., 1989), p. 9.

[12]   Retired Lords Spiritual may, however, take full advantage of all the facilities open to peers outside the chamber: 4th Report from the House of Lords' Offices Committee, H.L. 173 (1970–1), para. 4.

[13]   The Lords Spiritual consist of only Anglican clergy. Other clergy are given peerages very occasionally (such as Lord Soper), but peerages are not even given to the heads of other faiths, although there would seem to be every reason from Parliament's point of view why they should be. The Chief Rabbi received a peerage in 1988.

[14]   See S.O. No. 6; see also Erskine May, n. 11 above, p. 8 for the authorities.

Archbishop of Canterbury exercised that right in the 1983 general election and caused a ripple of surprise by doing so.[15] The Law Lords, as they are commonly styled, are made up of two distinct classes. Lawyers who are appointed Lords of Appeal in Ordinary receive life peerages and a salary on appointment and make up the two Appellate Committees of the House of Lords. To qualify for appointment they must hold a Supreme Court quali- fication.[16] In practice Lords of Appeal are appointed from the Court of Appeal. They are subject to a retiring age of 70,[17] but they may sit in the legislative House for life by virtue of their peerages. Up to 12 Lords of Appeal may be appointed.[18] By convention two are always Scottish lawyers. The other class of Law Lord is those peers who hold, or have held, high judicial office,[19] that is the Lord Chancellor,[20] former Lord Chancel- lors,[21] and the Lord Chief Justice (who, though, sits full time in the Crim- inal Division of the Court of Appeal); and any Master of the Rolls, Lord Justice of Appeal, High Court judge, or judge of the Court of Session who holds a peerage[22] (but any who do will actually confine themselves to the work of their own courts). In 1998 there were 20 Law Lords in total from both classes, although the Lords of Appeal in Ordinary make up the active membership of the Appellate Committees, each of which usually sits with five members.[23] The Law Lords can and do intervene in the general

---

[15] See Phillipa Hughes and Stephanie Palmer, 'Voting Bishops' [1983] *Public Law* 393. The government stated in reply to questions in the House of Lords that the issue whether Lords Spiritual were disqualified from voting in parliamentary elections had never been addressed in the courts, but at least by custom they had refrained from doing so. The Bishop of Derby, on behalf of *all* the Lords Spiritual, then announced that no Lord Spiritual would again do as the Archbishop had done: see 443 H.L. Deb. 243 (29 June 1983). The draftsman of the Parliament (No. 2) Bill of 1968–69 (which will be considered later) plainly thought that Lords Spiritual might have been barred by law from voting, as cl. 16 stated that 'A person shall not be disqualified for voting at elections to the House of Commons—. . . (b) as being one of the Lords Spiritual'. This provision was not explained in the accompanying White Paper, 'House of Lords Reform', Cmnd. 3799 (1968), nor in the Commons.

[16] Courts and Legal Services Act 1990, s. 71 and Schedule 10; see also Chapter 12.

[17] If appointed after the coming into force of the Judicial Pensions and Retirement Act 1993, s. 26 and Schedule 5; otherwise 75.

[18] Administration of Justice Act 1968, s. 1(1)(a).

[19] Appellate Jurisdiction Act 1876, s. 25 and Appellate Jurisdiction Act 1887, s. 5.

[20] Lord Hailsham (Lord Chancellor from 1970–74 and 1979–87) frequently sat in the Appellate Committee, and Lord Mackay of Clashfern (1987–97) followed suit. Lord Irvine of Lairg has, so far, sat infrequently. On Lord Chancellors as judges, see R. F. V. Heuston, 'Judi- cial Prosophography' (1986) 102 *Law Quarterly Review* 90 at 90–1.

[21] Of whom there are currently two: Lord Hailsham and Lord Mackay of Clashfern.

[22] Few do. The prefix 'Lord' enjoyed by members of the Court of Session is merely a courtesy title.

[23] The judicial work of the House will not be considered further here. See Louis

legislative work of the House,[24] and are particularly helpful at the committee stage of Bills.

The formal creation of a peerage used to be effected by a writ of summons from the Sovereign to attend the House of Lords followed by the new peer taking his seat,[25] but the modern method is for the Sovereign to issue Letters Patent which actually create the peerage. Those Letters Patent state how the peerage, if it is hereditary, is to descend on death.[26] At the beginning of each new Parliament *all* peers who are entitled to sit receive an instruction to attend (also called a writ of summons). New peers by creation must be formally introduced before they may sit or vote; peers who have inherited their titles merely take their seats.[27] Peerages are created by the Sovereign on the Prime Minister's advice.[28] This is a valuable source of patronage for any Prime Minister:[29] for example, during the Labour governments of 1964 to 1970 and 1974 to 1979 nearly 300 new peers were created; during the Conservative governments of 1970 to 1974 and 1979 to 1997, 362 people joined the House of Lords.[30]

A person will receive a peerage today through one of six entirely separate lists. First, a list of working peers is drawn up, usually once a year, consisting of new peers who are expected to take a full part in the parliamentary

---

Blom-Cooper and Gavin Drewry, *Final Appeal* (1972); Robert Stevens, *Law and Politics: The House of Lords as a Judicial Body 1800–1976* (1979); Alan Paterson, *The Law Lords* (1982).

[24] The Bill which became the Land Registration Act 1988 was introduced by a Lord of Appeal, Lord Templeman. It was uncontroversial and based on a Law Commission recommendation.

[25] See *Halsbury's Laws of England* (4th edn., 1981), vol. XXXV, paras. 820–2.

[26] Usually this would be to male heirs in direct line of descent. A hereditary peerage created by Letters Patent would only descend to a female if they contained a special limitation, which very few do. Older peerages created by writ of summons descend to heirs generally, male or female, lineal or collateral.

[27] S.O. No. 43. This could have an implication for any mass creation of peers: see Chapter 9. Very occasionally a person proves that he is the heir to a peerage which had fallen into abeyance. Thus the Barony of Grey of Condor fell into abeyance in 1496, and was revived in 1989. Sometimes a writ of acceleration is used to put the next in line to an hereditary peerage into the House of Lords during the lifetime of his kinsman. Lord Cranborne was so favoured in 1992: the Prime Minister wanted him in the House as a junior Minister.

[28] Subject to possible minor exceptions noted below.

[29] See Chapter 5. As with other honours, the Prime Minister's recommendations must first be considered by the Political Honours Scrutiny Committee to see whether the intended recipients are fit and proper persons to receive them.

[30] These figures omit the life peerages conferred on Lords of Appeal in Ordinary: see the Lord Privy Seal at 581 H.L. Deb. 151 (written answers 22 July 1997). Details of the 156 peerages recommended by Mrs Thatcher up to early 1987 are given at 120 H.L. Deb. 355–9 (written answers 23 July 1987); equivalent details for peerages awarded on Mr Major's recommendation are given at 576 H.L. Deb. 322–5 (written answers 16 January 1997).

work of the House and who should see their peerages as a means to that end rather than primarily as honours. Such peers belong to a political party and sit with the peers of that party in the House of Lords. The lists of working peers are drawn up by the Prime Minister after inviting the Leader of the Opposition, and usually the Leader of the Liberal Democrats, to make nominations. Mrs Thatcher's lists always contained a majority of Conservative nominations, but Mr Major recommended rather more non-Conservative creations.[31] These annual working peer lists are the largest regular source of new recruits to the Lords. Indeed, in the summer following his party's general election victory Mr Blair recommended a list of working peers which contained 47 names, of whom 31 were Labour supporters. A further 17 Labour life peers were announced in the summer of 1998. Secondly, new peers may be included in the Queen's Birthday[32] and New Year Honours Lists, again on the Prime Minister's recommendation. Inclusion in them signifies mainly the bestowal of an honour, although of course such peers may take part in the proceedings of the House if they choose to do so. Thirdly, a Dissolution Honours List is issued early in the life of each new Parliament, primarily to honour former Ministers and MPs of all parties who did not seek re-election. Former Cabinet Ministers will normally receive a life peerage in that list.[33] The Prime Minister is, again, responsible for the list, and there will be consultations with other party Leaders. If the government changes as a result of the general election the new Prime Minister will take responsibility for his predecessor's list. In the 1992 Dissolution Honours List, by way of example, 21 life peerages were announced; 11 went to former Conservative Cabinet Ministers (and one to Mrs Thatcher), five to former Labour Ministers and MPs, two to former Nationalist MPs, one to a former Leader of the SDP, and one to the former Speaker. Fourthly, when a Prime Minister resigns other than following a

---

[31] From 1975 (when lists of working peers were invented) to 1992 the total numbers of Conservative and Labour peers in those lists were roughly equal: see 158 H.L. Deb. 1056 (17 July 1992). But by the end of the Conservative government in 1997 the party allegiances of new peers created since 1979 were: 165 Conservative, 98 Labour, 23 Liberal or Liberal Democrat, and 71 crossbenchers: see 581 H.L. Deb. 151 (written answers 22 July 1997).

[32] This falls on the second Saturday in June.

[33] Before 1964, retiring Cabinet Ministers received viscountcies and other former Ministers baronies, but now former Cabinet Ministers who are moved to the House of Lords mainly receive life peerages. This change dates from the period 1964–82, when no hereditary peerages were created; the old differentiation could, of course, be revived. Few people who have left the Cabinet and the Commons since 1964 have remained outside the House of Lords. Former Ministers may receive honours other than peerages (because, for example, they may not wish to go to the House of Lords): John Nott was knighted on leaving the Cabinet in 1983, as was Norman Fowler in 1990, and Brian Mawhinney and Malcolm Rifkind in 1997.

general election, he will compile a Resignation Honours List, consisting only of members of his party and others who have served him, which his successor will recommend without amendment. It will normally contain a number of peerages.[34] Fifthly, special creations may be made infrequently and not necessarily on the Prime Minister's advice, though no doubt with his knowledge. Members of the royal family who receive peerages may be so classified—such as Prince Andrew's creation as Duke of York in 1986, or Mr Armstrong-Jones's ennoblement in 1961 as Earl of Snowdon—and so may the peerages customarily conferred on former Prime Ministers. Since 1900 only seven former Prime Ministers have remained commoners.[35] All the rest (apart from four) have received earldoms, the most recent being Attlee in 1955, Eden in 1961, and Harold Macmillan, who became Earl of Stockton in 1984 on his ninetieth birthday, 20 years after he had left the House of Commons. Sir Alec Douglas-Home was made a life peer on his retirement from the Commons in 1974, the only rank of peerage he could by law receive as he had disclaimed his hereditary peerages in 1963.[36] Harold Wilson and James Callaghan were created life peers in the 1983 and 1987 Dissolution Honours Lists respectively,[37] although they might of course both have declined hereditary peerages as they had recommended no such creations while Prime Minister. Mrs Thatcher accepted a life peerage after her retirement from the Commons in 1992, although there had been speculation that she might have become a countess. The attitude of the potential recipient and perhaps the personal intervention of the Sovereign in relation to the rank of peerage offered and accepted may be important,[38] and it seems safe to conclude that a former Prime Minister is entitled to be

[34] Harold Wilson's Resignation Honours List contained eight new peers: it was very controversial: see Joe Haines, *The Politics of Power* (Coronet edn., 1977), ch. 7. Harold Macmillan's List in 1963 contained only one peer; Mrs Thatcher's in 1990 contained 7. Mr Major's Resignation Honours List in 1997 contained 10 peerages. Before the dissolution in that year he recommended a list of 21 peers consisting of MPs who were not to contest the general election. The list was separate from any Dissolution (or Resignation) Honours List; he justified it on the ground that a large number of MPs wished to retire from the Commons.
[35] Campbell-Bannerman, Bonar Law, Chamberlain (all of whom died soon after resigning), MacDonald and Churchill (both of whom declined peerages), Sir Edward Heath and John Major (who are still MPs). Churchill had declined a dukedom: see Sir John Colville, *The Fringes of Power: Downing Street Diaries 1939–1955* (1985), p. 709.
[36] Peerage Act 1963, s. 3(2).
[37] As such their names were recommended by the Prime Minister and strictly their names do not belong in this category.
[38] At his resignation audience the Queen offered Eden an earldom 'when he wished': see Robert Rhodes James, *Anthony Eden* (1986), p. 595. She wrote to Macmillan in 1963 after his resignation that an earldom was his for the asking from her 'on her authority', that is, without ministerial advice: Harold Macmillan, *At the End of the Day* (1973), pp. 517–18.

made an earl or a countess if that is what he or she wishes (although that course would be less attractive if hereditary peers are excluded from the House of Lords). Sixthly and lastly the Prime Minister may recommend a peerage for someone without a seat in either House in order that he may become a Minister. Thus Macmillan procured a peerage for Percy Mills on his being brought into the Cabinet from industry as Minister of Power in 1957, Mrs Thatcher obtained a peerage for David Young on joining the Cabinet as Minister without Portfolio in 1984, and Mr Blair recommended peerages for four people in 1997 so that they could assume junior ministerial posts.

On first becoming Prime Minister in 1964 Harold Wilson decided to recommend no new hereditary peerages.[39] Edward Heath and James Callaghan followed suit, as did Mrs Thatcher for the first few years of her administration, so that between 1964 and 1983 only life peerages were created. A new convention seemed to be emerging that no new hereditary peers would be created, but Mrs Thatcher's recommendations of viscountcies for the former Speaker of the House of Commons, George Thomas, and for William Whitelaw[40] in 1983 showed that if such a convention were emerging it would, like many conventions, contain exceptions.

Disputes over the right to succeed to a hereditary peerage are rare.[41] The House of Lords itself resolves such disputes, invariably by accepting the recommendations of its Committee for Privileges,[42] which is made up for that purpose of up to 16 peers together with three Lords of Appeal in Ordinary.[43] Given the complexity of peerage law it is natural that the Committee should be guided by the Lords of Appeal in Ordinary and that the House should accept the Committee's recommendations.

A peerage carries with it two disabilities: a peer other than the holder of an Irish peerage[44] may not vote in any parliamentary election,[45] and he may

[39] Sir Alec Douglas-Home's Dissolution Honours List was recommended by Mr Wilson: it had six hereditary creations in it, but this was an application of the principle that a new Prime Minister after a general election recommends his predecessor's List without amendment.

[40] He became Lord President of the Council and Leader of the House of Lords, remaining Deputy Leader of the Conservative Party and deputy to the Prime Minister.

[41] There could be no room for dispute over a life peerage.

[42] On which see S.O. No. 72.

[43] The last three claims resolved were the *Ampthill Peerage Claim* [1977] A.C. 547, the *Annandale and Hartfell Peerage Claim* [1986] A.C. 319, and the *Barony of Moynihan Peerage Claim*, *The Times*, 28 March 1997. In the second of those cases the Earldom of Annandale and Hartfell was revived after having been in abeyance for nearly 200 years.

[44] See n. 5 above. No new Irish peers have been created since 1898 when Curzon, not wishing to lose the possibility of returning to the House of Commons, was made a baron in the Irish peerage on his appointment as Viceroy of India: see Kenneth Rose, *Curzon* (1969), p. 331.

[45] The House of Commons resolves at the beginning of each new Parliament that no peer 'hath any right to give his vote in the Election of any Member to serve in Parliament'.

not be elected or sit as an MP. The first disability would have been removed by clause 16 of the unsuccessful Parliament (No. 2) Bill in 1968–69;[46] the second may be cast off by an instrument of disclaimer, a device which was introduced in 1963. Disclaimer may now be considered, together with other ways of losing membership of the House of Lords.

Before 1963 a peer could not divest himself of his peerage. Thanks chiefly to the efforts of Mr Tony Benn, who succeeded to the viscountcy of Stansgate in 1960,[47] Harold Macmillan's government agreed to introduce what became the Peerage Act 1963. Under that Act anyone who succeeds to a peerage[48] may disclaim it for his life by delivering an instrument of disclaimer.[49] A succeeding peer has one year in which to make up his mind whether to keep his peerage; to be effective, any disclaimer must be made within those 12 months (or, if he is under 21 on his succession, within a year of reaching that birthday).[50] If an MP succeeds to a peerage, he has only one month in which to disclaim but he can sit and vote as an MP while he decides what to do.[51] A valid disclaimer makes the peer a commoner: it divests him (and, if he is married, his wife) of all right in and titles of the peerage, and all the disabilities that go with it;[52] the courtesy titles of any children are, however, unaffected[53] and any heir does not succeed to the peerage until the death of the disclaiming peer. There are two limitations. Anyone who agrees to be created a peer cannot later disclaim because he did not *succeed* to that peerage: if he has doubts, he should decline the offer. And if a peerage is disclaimed, no further hereditary peerage may be conferred on the former peer, although he may subsequently

---

[46]   That Bill will be considered later. It was designated '(No. 2)' to distinguish it from a Private Member's Parliament Bill which had already been introduced that session; three other back-benchers' Parliament Bills followed it in the 1968–69 session.

[47]   For his own account, see Tony Benn, *Out of the Wilderness: Diaries 1963–1967* (1987), ch. 1. And see Report of the Joint Committee on House of Lords Reform, H.L. 23 and H.C. 38 (1962–63); Lord Home, *The Way the Wind Blows* (1976), p. 179; Lord Hailsham, *The Door Wherein I Went* (1975), pp. 221–3; *Re Parliamentary Election for Bristol South-East* [1964] 2 Q.B. 257.

[48]   Other than an Irish peerage: but then as it carries with it no practical disadvantage there is no reason why disclaimer should be available.

[49]   Peerage Act 1963, s. 1(1) and Schedule 1.

[50]   Ibid., s. 1(2). Existing peers at the time of the passing of the Peerage Act 1963 had 12 months from the commencement of that Act in which to decide whether to disclaim: s. 1(3).

[51]   Ibid., s. 2(1). A succeeding peer who has been nominated, or is nominated subsequent to his inheritance, as a parliamentary candidate is deemed to succeed immediately after the declaration of his election result and has one month from then to decide whether to disclaim: s. 2(2).

[52]   Ibid., s. 3(1).

[53]   Thus, for example, when the Earl of Durham disclaimed his earldom his heir remained known as Lord Lambton.

receive a life peerage.[54] Only 17 peers from a potential total of some 770 have disclaimed: but the 1963 Act has removed a sense of injustice from a minority; it has allowed one peer to become Prime Minister and an MP (the Earl of Home); it has also allowed another peer to try to become Prime Minister and to be elected an MP (Viscount Hailsham);[55] and through it the most reluctant peer of them all, Mr Benn, was able to return to the House of Commons.

A peer may lose his right to membership of the House of Lords, but not his peerage, in four other ways. Aliens are disqualified:[56] an alien may not receive a peerage, and if a British citizen became a peer and later renounced that citizenship he would have no right to sit. Adjudication of bankruptcy disqualifies a peer from sitting and voting unless and until the adjudication is set aside.[57] A conviction of treason disqualifies from membership until the sentence is served or a pardon is granted.[58] And peers under the age of 21 may not sit.[59] None of the other types of disqualification which affect MPs[60] affect peers, and the House of Lords (unlike the House of Commons) has no power to expel any member.

Now a person may be willing enough to succeed to a peerage while wishing to take no part in the proceedings of the House. Equally, it is right that such a peer, or one who sits rarely, should not turn up, as it were unannounced, and perhaps with others affect the outcome of a vote. This problem of 'backwoodsmen' led to the introduction of leave of absence.[61] At the beginning of each Parliament the Clerk of the Parliaments writes to

---

[54] Peerage Act 1963, s. 3(2).

[55] He became a life peer as Lord Hailsham of St Marylebone in 1970 on his appointment as Lord Chancellor.

[56] Act of Settlement 1701, s. 3. Commonwealth citizens and citizens of the Republic of Ireland are not aliens for this purpose: British Nationality Act 1981, s. 50(1).

[57] Insolvency Act 1986, s. 427(1).

[58] Forfeiture Act 1870, s. 2. The Lord Chancellor informs the House when a peer is sentenced to imprisonment for any offence. For recent examples see 550 H.L. Deb. 1113 (13 December 1993) (Marquess of Bristol), 569 H.L. Deb. 495 (13 February 1996) (Lord Brocket), 574 H. L. Deb. 1371 (24 July 1996) (Duke of Manchester).

[59] S.O. No. 2.

[60] See Chapter 10. Mental illness, for example, does not disqualify a peer, and compulsory detention under the Mental Health Act 1983, Part II, probably raises no issue of privilege: see Report by the Committee for Privileges on Parliamentary Privilege and the Mental Health Legislation, H.L. 254 (1983–4), especially para. 4; agreed to by the House at 455 H.L. Deb. 13–14 (23 July 1984). The Parliament (No. 2.) Bill, cl. 7, would have provided that such compulsory detention would disqualify a peer from sitting or voting or receiving a writ of summons during such detention.

[61] S.O. No. 20. For the background see Report from the Select Committee on Leave of Absence, H.L. 60 (1957–8); and see 494 H.L. Deb. 430 (7 March 1988).

all those peers already with leave of absence asking if they wish to have leave of absence for the new Parliament. Leave of absence is only granted to peers who apply for it. A peer with leave is expected not to attend, although he may cancel his leave by giving one month's notice; and if a peer sits and votes despite leave the House can do nothing about it.[62] Usually some 130 to 150 peers have leave; in the 1997–98 session the number was 67.[63] A new peer need never take his seat,[64] or having done so need never be seen in the House again: attendance is not compulsory and there are of course no constituents who might object.

Organization in the House

Leaving out of account peers with leave of absence and those who are dis- qualified there is a House of about 1,200 potential members, of whom some two-thirds are hereditary peers. But a visitor to the public gallery on an average day would see a very different picture. The usual daily atten- dance is about 300, of whom life peers and hereditary peers of first creation will normally be in a small majority.[65] That same visitor might assume that the Conservative Party is always firmly in control of the House, but that assumption is not entirely correct. Once more leaving aside peers with leave of absence, in 1998 the Conservatives had 480 supporters in the Lords, Labour had 173 adherents, the Liberal Democrats 70, and the cross- bench, or independent, peers and peers with no allegiance totalled 440.[66] What is true is that the Conservative Party is the largest single group in the House on an average day, but even that (as will be seen later) does not make the House a supine body ready to do the bidding of a Conservative gov- ernment in an unquestioning way.

Each year the House of Lords sits on about 150 days (compared with the Commons' average of some 175 days).[67] It only sits on Fridays at all

---

[62] Report by the Select Committee on the Powers of the House in Relation to the Attendance of its Members, H.L. (7), (66-I), (67)(1955–6), especially paras. 29–39.

[63] Peers with leave of absence may still use the House of Lords Library, dining room, and guest room, thus continuing to enjoy what may be termed the club facilities of the House.

[64] Rather like Gerry Adams and Martin McGuinness in the other House, who were elected as Sinn Fein MPs but have not taken their seats.

[65] In the 1996–97 session the average daily attendance was 381. The lowest average daily attendance in the last decade was 284 in 1981–82: information from the House of Lords Jour- nal and Information Office. (Unless otherwise stated in this chapter statistics for sessions which were interrupted by dissolutions are omitted.)

[66] Information from the House of Lords Information Office.

[67] The 1985–86 session was a heavy one, the Lords sitting on 165 days; the lowest annual

regularly in the late spring and in summer when the volume of Bills sent to the Lords having passed the Commons increases sharply. General precedence is given in the Lords to legislation, but the actual business is arranged each day by the Leader of the House of Lords and the Government Chief Whip, in consultation with the other parties. The House as a whole regulates its proceedings and maintains the rules of order, in the light of which the Lord Chancellor's title of Speaker of the House of Lords is something of a misnomer, especially as it is the Leader of the House who advises peers on matters of procedure and who acts as the principal voice of the House in maintaining order.[68] The House of Lords is a quiet and indeed rather relaxed legislative chamber, quite unlike the other House. If 'heat is engendered in debate' any peer may move that the Standing Order on Asperity of Speech be read by the Clerk, but it has only been read three times in this century.[69] If a peer's speech is thought to be seriously transgressing the accepted practice of the House it is open to another peer to move that he be no longer heard, but that, too, is resorted to only exceptionally in a House which rightly prides itself on its civilized manner of conducting its affairs.[70]

Members of the House of Lords in general receive no salaries. All peers are, however, entitled to certain allowances and expenses in connection with their parliamentary work. They may claim up to £33.50 a day as general office, secretarial, and research allowance. A subsistence allowance of up to £34.50 a day (or £78 if an overnight stay in London is involved) is also recoverable.[71] And travel expenses within the United Kingdom on parliamentary business are reimbursed. A few peers are salaried: the Leader of the Opposition in the Lords receives £43,600 a year and the Opposition Chief Whip £39,600; as in the Commons, other party Leaders, including the Convenor of the Cross-bench Peers, receive no salary. The Lord Chancellor receives 14 per cent of his £151,000 annual salary as Speaker of the House. The Lord Chairman of Committees and the Principal Deputy Chairman of Committees are paid £53,250 and £50,000 respectively as

total of sitting days in the last decade was 143 in 1980–81: information from the House of Lords Information Office.

[68] The House confirmed in 1988 that the system of self-regulation should continue and that a Speaker with disciplinary powers was undesirable: see 493 H.L. Deb. 937 (22 February 1988).

[69] See the Lord Privy Seal at 587 H.L. Deb. 216 (11 March 1998).

[70] The motion 'that the noble Lord be no longer heard' was, however, carried in 1985 against Lord Hatch of Lusby: see 459 H. L. Deb. 560–1 (29 January 1985), and three years later against Lord Sefton: see 496 H.L. Deb. 428 (3 May 1988).

[71] These rates are increased regularly.

recompense for their heavy load in presiding over committees and in the Committee of the Whole House. Lords of Appeal in Ordinary each receive £139,000 as judicial salary. Ministers and Whips in the Lords, of whom there were over 20 in 1998, receive a ministerial salary. It had been envisaged in the 1968 White Paper 'House of Lords Reform' that in the planned new House life peers and hereditary peers of first creation would become voting peers and as such receive a salary:[72] £2,000 a year was mooted. That proposal was, however, so heavily criticized as an indefensible gilding on prime ministerial patronage (for the Prime Minister would have been able to distribute peerages *and* £2,000 a year!) that it was dropped.[73]

Peers are bound to act always on their personal honour and should never accept any financial inducement as an incentive or reward for exercising parliamentary influence. They must not speak or vote at all on legislation in relation to which they have been acting for payment or reward.[74] A register of peers' interests was set up for the first time in 1995.[75]

The work of the Lords

No official and systematic statement of the actual or ideal functions of the House of Commons has ever been written, which is odd because that is easily the more important House, yet it is understandable because no government-sponsored attempt has been made for well over a century to reform it. The functions of the House of Lords, on the other hand, have been considered since 1900 to a greater or lesser extent by four official bodies.[76] So, for example, it was concluded in the 1968 White Paper 'House of Lords Reform' that the House has seven main functions: (a) to be the supreme court of appeal; (b) to provide a forum for debates on matters of public interest; (c) to revise public Bills passed by the House of Commons;

---

[72] Cmnd. 3799 (1968), para. 52.

[73] The Prime Minister's reasons for abandoning the proposal were given in the second reading on the Parliament (No. 2) Bill at 777 H.C. Deb. 54 (3 February 1969).

[74] 566 H.L. Deb. 1630–40 (7 November 1995).

[75] 566 H.L. Deb. 1641 (7 November 1995). It has three categories, embracing consultancies, financial interests in businesses involved in parliamentary lobbying, and any other particulars which peers wish to register which might affect the public perception of how they discharge their parliamentary duties.

[76] See Report of the Conference on the Reform of the Second Chamber, Cd. 9038 (1918)—the Bryce Report; *Agreed Statement on the Conclusion of the Conference on the Parliament Bill 1947*, Cmnd. 7380 (1948); 'House of Lords Reform', Cmnd. 3799 (1968); and Report of the Royal Commission on the Constitution, Cmnd. 5460 (1973), vol. i, para. 1073.

(d) to initiate less controversial public legislation and private peers' Bills; (e) to consider subordinate legislation; (f) to scrutinize the activities of the executive; and (g) to consider private legislation.[77] That order of functions does not reflect their order of importance, and here the work of the modern House will be examined in relation to the consideration given to public Bills; general debates; scrutiny of the government through questions; and its scrutiny of the government and other work conducted through committees of the House of Lords.

The examination and amendment of Bills sent up by the Commons is easily the most important work of the House of Lords and takes up over half its time.[78] The Lords made over 2,500 amendments to public Bills brought from the Commons in the 1985–86 session: this was an exceptionally high total,[79] but even so about 1,500 are made in an average session.[80] This is work well done as most Lords' amendments are accepted by the government and the other House, but it is important to put the Lords' revising work into context. Of the hundreds of amendments which are made to government Bills from the Commons, most are proposed by Ministers who are prompted to do so by changes of mind during the passage of those Bills, or by ministerial promises to either House to reconsider particular matters, or sometimes as concessions to pressures in one or other House or from outside Parliament; the largest single category of Lords' amendments accepted by the government comprises those of a technical nature which improve drafting and which do not affect the policy underlying the legislation

---

[77] Since then the House has set up machinery to scrutinize European Community legislation, which will be considered below. Functions (a), (e), and (f) will not be considered further here.

[78] It spends nearly 48 per cent of its time on such Bills in the average session. For ease of comparison, the approximate division of time may be set out thus:

Topic	Time (%)
Public Bills from Commons	48
General debates	20
Unstarred questions (i.e. leading to debate)	7
Other questions	7
Ministerial statements	3
Subordinate legislation	4
European Communities Committee reports	4
Private Bills	1
Other	6
	100

[79] The Financial Services Bill 1985–86 alone accounted for 784 amendments.

[80] Information from the Public Bill Office of the House of Lords.

in any way. Such drafting help is naturally welcome and this is reflected in the government's (and therefore the Commons') acceptance of so many Lords' amendments. Amendments which are unacceptable to the government may be voted down in the House of Commons.[81] The House of Lords gives a fair wind to Private MPs' Bills which have passed the Commons. They are usually approved so as to allow them to pass into law.[82]

Quite unlike the other House, the House of Lords usually takes the committee stage of public Bills in Committee of the Whole House.[83] Any peer may speak in committee and put down amendments, so that the opportunities for back-bench peers to influence the form of legislation are accordingly much better than those of their counterparts in the other House. Experiments in which Public Bill Committees[84] have taken the committee stage in order to save time in the chamber were very limited: only six public Bills were dealt with in that way between 1968 and 1978, none was sent to a committee between 1978 and 1985, one in the 1986–87 session, and one in the 1991–92 session. A Special Public Bill Committee procedure was introduced in 1994. The committee may take written and oral evidence, after which it proceeds by examining the Bill closely, amending it if necessary. The Bills which became the Law of Property (Miscellaneous Provisions) Act 1994 and the Private International Law (Miscellaneous Provisions) Act 1995 went through this procedure.

A factor in the ability of the House fully to consider and revise Bills is, obviously, the time available to the House to do so, which in turn is affected by the House in which Bills are first introduced. Most government Bills are introduced into Parliament in the House of Commons because they will be politically controversial and the elected House is where such controversies are fully argued; the Ministers responsible for the Bills will be in the Commons in most cases, and many Bills have a financial content over which MPs consider themselves supreme. So government business managers have to decide before and at the start of each session which public Bills may, within those constraints, safely be started in the House of Lords, and

---

[81] Occasions on which the government has had to defer to the Lords over legislation are considered later.

[82] All such Bills have been passed by the Lords in the last few years.

[83] S.O. No. 45. Since 1995 a Grand Committee has been able to take the committee stage of such Bills. It sits in the Moses Room; amendments are tabled and considered as in a Committee of the Whole House; all peers are free to attend and participate, but no divisions may take place.

[84] See generally 3rd Report from the Select Committee on Procedure, H.L. 131 (1970–71), para. 6. See also 1st Report from the Select Committee on Procedure, H.L. 20 (1996–7), approved at 577 H.L. Deb. 554 (21 January 1997).

they manage to compile a list of about a dozen from a total of some 50 or so government Bills which are introduced into Parliament each year.[85] Law reform and revision Bills are invariably introduced into the House of Lords first.[86] Given the preponderance of government Bills started each October or November in the Commons,[87] the Lords will have less legislative work to do in the first half of the session but its workload will increase dramatically each spring and summer as Bills emerge from the Commons. (Peers complain every year about this uneven level of work, and every year the Leader of the House of Lords hopes that things will be better ordered in the following session.) Government business managers in the Lords see prorogation as a deadline to be achieved if the government's legislation is to reach royal assent—and they must, of course, allow time for the Commons to consider any Lords' amendments, and for the Lords to react to the Commons' treatment of those amendments. Government Bills do normally pass in time, despite the complete absence of a legislative guillotine in the House of Lords, or of any power to allow the Lord Chairman of Committees to select only certain amendments for debate, and the rarity with which the closure is moved.[88]

Any back-bench peer may introduce his own Bill without giving notice, without going through any ballot, and without needing the leave of the House. He has much more freedom in that respect than his Commons

---

[85] Some significant Bills which have started in the Lords recently have included the Shops Bill in 1985–86 (which came to grief in the Commons: see Chapter 10), the Criminal Justice Bill in 1987–88, and the Human Rights Bill in 1997–98.

[86] These are (a) consolidation Bills; (b) Bills presented under the Consolidation of Enactments (Procedure) Act 1949; (c) Bills to consolidate with amendments to give effect to Law Commission recommendations; (d) Law Commission Statute Law (Repeals) Bills to repeal enactments no longer of practical utility; (e) statute law revision Bills (which have largely been replaced by type (d)); and (f) statutory instruments to consolidate or revise Northern Ireland statute law. After second reading all such measures are referred to the Joint Select Committee on Consolidation Bills, which has 12 members from each House. After taking evidence from Parliamentary Counsel and sometimes from departmental sources the Bills are reported to the House with any suggested amendments. A Committee of the Whole House then considers them very briefly before passing them.

[87] Or in whichever month Parliament resumes after a dissolution.

[88] If it is moved, the Lord Chancellor or Lord Chairman of Committees is bound by standing order to read out—'slowly'—that the closure is a most exceptional procedure and that the House will not accept it save in circumstances where it is felt to be the only means of ensuring the proper conduct of business: see 1st Report from the Select Committee on Procedure, H.L. 129 (1960–1), para. 6; 6th Report from the Select Committee on Procedure, H.L. 169 (1970–1), para. 2. The closure motion 'that the question be now put' was first moved, amid considerable controversy, in 1926, and not again until 1961. The last attempt to move that motion was in 1985, when the Deputy Chairman declined to put it: see 464 H.L. Deb. 718–9 (4 June 1985).

counterpart. Given that the House of Lords has more time at its disposal, particularly in the first half of the session, and that there is no guarantee that any MP will take up a private peer's Bill, or that (even if one does) the Commons will pass it, the government does not oppose any such Bills which it finds uncongenial by forcing a division against them in the House of Lords.[89] Between one and two dozen back-bench peers' Bills are introduced each session but no more than six of them usually pass into law, the high failure rate resulting from lack of opportunity to introduce them into the other House, or from opposition to them there.[90] The House of Lords spends about 5 per cent of its time on such Bills each session, and even those which get no further than that House allow public discussion of the ideas in them. Some controversial statutes have begun in this way, such as the Sexual Offences Act 1967 which made consenting male homosexual conduct in private no longer criminal.

Some 20 per cent of the time of the House of Lords is devoted to general debates. One day each week, usually Wednesday, is given over to debating a topic on a neutral motion calling for papers or on a motion to take note. Subjects for debate are agreed through the usual channels. Additionally one day a month, again usually a Wednesday, up to the Whitsun recess is used for short debates, each up to a maximum length of two-and-a-half hours.[91] The right to select matters for short debates is entirely reserved to back-bench and cross-bench peers, the actual choice being made by ballot a few weeks before the day of the scheduled debate. It is common ground that the quality of general debate can be high, as it should be, given the diversity of the backgrounds of the life peers in particular, and the lack of any overwhelming desire (so common among MPs) to score party political points across the chamber. It was partly as a recognition of this quality that Professor Stanley de Smith stated his considered view that the House 'is the best second chamber in the Commonwealth and one which stands comparison with its counterparts in almost any developed country in the world'.[92]

---

[89] Very rarely peers on a free vote decline to give a second reading to a back-bench Bill. This happened when the Hereditary Peerages Bill was denied a second reading: see 540 H.L. Deb. 1165–6 (26 November 1992); and similarly with the Blasphemy (Abolition) Bill: see 561 H.L. Deb. 1215–44 (22 February 1995).

[90] Twenty-one such Bills were introduced in the 1996–97 session.

[91] S.O. No. 35. By Whitsun the rate of Bills coming from the Commons increases dramatically, and so short debates are abandoned from then.

[92] S. A. de Smith, *Constitutional and Administrative Law* (5th edn., 1985 by H. Street and R. Brazier), p. 310.

Questions in the House of Lords are organized on a different, and in some respects more logical, basis than in the Commons. There are four different types of question. First, if a peer wishes to elicit factual information he may put down a starred question upon which no debate is permitted.[93] Such questions may be tabled on any day, although 24 hours' notice is required[94] and not more than four starred questions may appear on the order paper on any day. Supplementary questions may be asked, and some debating points do creep in. Up to 20 minutes a day are spent on starred questions as the first item of substantive business. Some 600 starred questions are dealt with in an average session, consuming about 6 per cent of the House's time. Should a peer not wish to put a supplementary at all he will table a different type of question, one for written answer,[95] and he will receive a reply in under two weeks. This is easily the largest category of Lords' questions, some 1,100 being tabled in an average session.[96] The third type is the unstarred question, which is designed to be the basis for debate. Such a question may be put down by any peer, but only one on each day,[97] and it is customary for the government Whips' Office to be consulted about a suitable date. It is taken as the final item of daily business; at the end of the debate a Minister or Whip will reply. Some 40 unstarred questions are tabled each session, accounting for about 5 per cent of the time of the House. Finally, a peer may seek to put down a private notice question.[98] To do so he must try to convince the Leader of the House privately that it is a matter of urgency justifying an immediate reply: he will rarely succeed.[99] These procedures are superior to those of the Commons in two respects. There is no constraint of a ministerial rota for answering questions, as questions in the Lords are tabled to the government, not usually to a particular Minister,[100] and so peers may be able to raise a given issue through questions more quickly than may back-bench MPs. Moreover, the only distinction between questions in the Commons is between those for oral or

---

[93] S.O. No. 32.

[94] As against the 48 hours' notice required for Commons questions.

[95] S.O. No. 42.

[96] It is, however, way below the Commons total which receive a written answer.

[97] A second unstarred question may be put down if the day's business is exceptionally light. Debate on an unstarred question cannot exceed two hours, and no such debate is held on Fridays.

[98] S.O. No. 33.

[99] Fewer private notice questions are allowed in the Lords than in the Commons. An example was the one which was allowed to be put to the Lord Advocate on the Special Branch raid on BBC headquarters in Glasgow over the planned 'Project Zircon' programme: see 484 H.L. Deb. 199 (4 February 1987).

[100] Questions may, however, be addressed to the Leader of the House on procedural and business matters.

written answer, both of which have the notional purpose of seeking factual information, although in the former debating points are scored in supplementary questions. The Lords' arrangements go beyond that rather crude distinction by recognizing that the purpose of some questions is to elicit facts (through Lords' starred questions and questions for written answer), and that of others is to spark off debate (Lords' unstarred questions).

Up to 1974 the committee work of the House of Lords was restricted to the procedure and administration of the House itself, together with the committee stage of Bills taken in Committee of the Whole House (which is a committee only in name). Since 1974, however, the use of committees has increased, although the House has not sought to set up committees to oversee the work of government departments. In a major review of the committee work of the Lords, the Select Committee on the Committee Work of the House reported in 1992 and recommended that the system of committees should continue to complement, not duplicate, that of the Commons.[101] The committee noted that no significant increase in committee work would be possible, because the number of peers who were prepared to serve was limited. It also recommended that Bills should continue to be taken in Committee of the Whole House, although the committee stage of one or two Bills each session should be taken off the floor of the House. The establishment of more *ad hoc* select committees was recommended, as was the setting up of a liaison committee to oversee all Lords committees.[102] These suggestions were all accepted by the House.

With very few exceptions (the most significant being the Committee of the Whole House) all Lords' committees are select committees.[103] Such committees can be appointed by the House to examine anything which in its view requires investigation. Once the House has agreed to establish a select committee the Committee of Selection[104] reports to the House the names of peers to form it, after consultations through the usual channels. There is no understanding as exists in the Commons that the government will have a majority of members. The select committee's scope of inquiry

[101] Report of the Select Committee on the Committee Work of the House, H.L. 35 (1991–2), debated at 537 H.L. Deb. 899–1017 (3 June 1992).

[102] Following the 1st Report from the Liaison Committee, H.L. 40 (1992–3), a Delegated Powers Scrutiny Committee was set up to scrutinize Bills and to report to the House whether the provisions of any Bill would inappropriately delegate legislative power. See also 543 H.L. Deb. 1225–8 (15 March 1993). See C. M. G. Himsworth, 'The Delegated Powers Committee' [1995] *Public Law* 34.

[103] S.O. Nos. 61, 63–5.

[104] S.O. No. 61. The Committee consists of 11 peers from all parties and a representative of the cross-bench peers, with the Leader of the House as chairman.

will be defined in its order of reference. Again unlike select committees in the Commons, any peer (whether or not a member of a given select committee) may attend and speak at its meetings, other than those at which a committee considers its findings. A select committee may call any witness it needs; ordinarily witnesses attend and documents are produced voluntarily, but if necessary the House itself could order witnesses to attend or papers to be delivered, and refusal or failure would be a contempt of the House.[105] Select committees report if necessary by a majority vote; as with the Commons' equivalents minority reports are not in order, but such reports may be moved and voted on. *Ad hoc* select committees have become influential since the 1970s, having been set up either to consider the merits of possible legislation or to investigate a particular matter which the House has thought needed detailed study. Some examples have included the Select Committees on a Bill of Rights, on Unemployment, and on Overseas Trade.[106] Advantages of investigations into particular topics lie in the expertise which can be brought to bear and in that there is no guarantee that a select committee will necessarily tell a government what it wishes to hear (thus echoing, as was seen in the last chapter, some of the Commons' departmental select committees). A good example of the latter point can be seen in the 1982 Report of the Select Committee on Unemployment,[107] which called for major changes in the government's policies towards unemployment, including significantly increased government spending to try to increase the number of people in work. Sessional select committees[108] are greater in number and always include two Appellate Committees,[109] the Joint Select Committee on Consolidation Bills,[110] the Joint Select Committee on Statutory Instruments,[111] the Committee for

---

[105] Erskine May, n. 11 above, ch. 9.

[106] For their reports, see respectively H.L. 176 (1977–8), H.L. 142 (1981–2), H.L. 238 (1984–5).

[107] H.L. 142 (1981–2), debated at 436 H.L. Deb. 425–513 (16 November 1982). A report critical of the government's civil research and development policy, 1st Report from the Science and Technology Committee, H.L. 20 (1986–7) was agreed to by the House at 484 H.L. Deb. 1251–332 (19 February 1987); the government accepted several of the Committee's findings, including the need for a new central structure for such work, in a White Paper, Cm. 185 (1987). There are several other examples of Lords select committees reporting adversely on government policies.

[108] That is, select committees regularly set up for the duration of each session.

[109] S.O. No. 82.   [110] S.O. No. 49; see n. 86 above.

[111] Statutory instruments are subject to scrutiny by the Joint Select Committee on Statutory Instruments of seven peers and seven MPs which may draw any instrument to the attention of both Houses on any ground which does not impinge on its merits or on the policy behind it.

Privileges,[112] the Procedure Committee, the Science and Technology Committee, and the European Communities Committee. The work of the last two is worth amplification.

The Science and Technology Committee was first set up in 1980 as a direct result of the House of Commons' decision not to appoint a successor to its Select Committee on Science and Technology when the departmental select committees were established. The Committee has about 14 members who work through a general purposes subcommittee and two other subcommittees. Its terms of reference are simply 'to consider science and technology': subjects are chosen which concern areas where Parliament can stimulate the advancement and application of science and technology or in which the government is involved, or which involve issues over which there is public concern. The Committee appoints specialist advisers. On average the Committee produces two major reports a year: investigations have included ones on occupational health and hygiene services, education and training for new technologies, marine science and technology, civil research and development, innovation in surface transport, space policy, priorities in medical research, and cuts in government spending on science. The European Communities Committee was first established in 1974.[113] It has 25 members, but an additional 80 peers are usually co-opted and any other peer may attend. Its purpose is to consider European Union proposals (whether in draft or otherwise), to obtain all necessary information about them, and to report on those which in its opinion raise important policy questions or matters of principle or which for any other reason should be drawn to the attention of the House. The Committee may appoint subcommittees: at present there are seven.[114] The chairman refers European Union proposals to the subcommittees, distinguishing between 'A-type' (which do not require parliamentary attention— usually some two-thirds of the total) and 'B-type' (which he thinks will require parliamentary scrutiny). The volume of paper which faces the Committee is daunting: some 66 documents, on average, are deposited each month. The Committee appoints specialist advisers, and has a legal adviser. It may confer with the Commons Select Committee on European Legislation.

---

[112] S.O. Nos. 73–7.

[113] See the Report of the Select Committee on Procedure for Scrutiny of Proposals for European Instruments, H.L. 194 (1972–3); H.L. 62 and 139 (1973–4).

[114] Subcommittee A (on finance, economics, and regional policy); B (on external relations, trade, and industry); C (on education, employment, and social affairs); D (on agriculture, food, and consumer affairs); E (on legal implications of European Community legislation); F (on energy, transport, technology, and research), and G (on environmental matters).

All reports which are recommended by the Committee for debate on the floor of the House are debated there, a total of a dozen or so every session.[115] This is laborious and undramatic work which enhances the House's understanding of developments in the European Union, and so indirectly the comprehension of interested individuals and groups outside Parliament.

Because the House of Lords has more time available than has the House of Commons, the Lords can and does debate all the reports from its committees—something which has proved impossible so far in the Commons, an inability which has detracted from the usefulness of Commons select committees. The efforts of both the Science and Technology Committee and the European Communities Committee have proved entirely worthwhile and, especially in the case of the former Committee, have allowed parliamentary work to be accomplished which otherwise would not have been undertaken. The types of inquiry into subjects conducted by *ad hoc* select committees, too, in no sense duplicate any efforts of the House of Commons. The decision not to set up departmental select committees has avoided pointless duplication and what would have been an intolerable burden on Ministers and civil servants. I suggest that a valuable development of the committee work of the House would be the creation of a sessional Select Committee on Law Reform, made up of a Lord of Appeal in Ordinary (if he could be spared) together with other Law Lords and peers with expertise or interest in legal affairs and the subject-matter of particular reform proposals. Such a committee could automatically consider the law reform reports as published of the Law Commission,[116] the Criminal Law Revision Committee, and the Law Reform Committee without waiting for any reference to it by the government. Its primary purpose would be to act as a pre-legislative stage on the draft Bills which are usually appended to such reports. Such detailed and expert committee work ought to reduce the amount of parliamentary time which would otherwise be needed for such proposals, and so might encourage governments to introduce more of them into Parliament.

Lords and government in conflict

The routine work of the House of Lords may now be left aside so as to consider conflicts which have arisen between that House and the government

---

[115] Occasionally an unstarred question is also used to debate a Committee report.
[116] Apart from those currently considered by the Joint Select Committee on Consolidation Bills.

over legislation. The powers of the House over legislation were of course reduced by the Parliament Acts of 1911 and 1949 but were otherwise confirmed by those statutes. It is therefore possible to view the infrequent but sometimes dramatic conflicts between the Lords and the government as the exercise of authority expressly conferred by law on that House. The House's powers under the Parliament Acts may conveniently be considered in three groups: veto powers, Money Bill powers, and delaying powers.

The first of those groups, veto powers, is a ragbag in which are retained the pre-1911 prerogatives of the House of Lords over four disparate types of legislation. Thus the consent of the Lords remains necessary before royal assent may be given to a Bill to extend the maximum life of Parliament beyond five years,[117] or to a provisional order confirmation Bill,[118] or to a private Bill; and the Lords' veto over subordinate legislation remains as well.[119] The ability to ensure that general elections take place at least every five years is of great theoretical importance but of course no occasion has arisen on which the House of Lords has even had to consider using it. There would be nothing to prevent[120] a government removing any or all of these veto powers by causing a Bill to be passed under the Parliament Act procedure (that is, subject to a maximum Lords' delay of just over 12 months) to delete those powers and to substitute some (or no) delaying power. The second group of Parliament Act powers concerns Money Bills. In essence, the House of Lords may delay a Money Bill sent up to them by the Commons for up to one month (provided it reaches the Lords at least one month before the end of a session). If after that time the Lords have not passed it unamended the Bill may receive royal assent despite the absence

---

[117] Parliament Act 1911, s. 2(1).

[118] Ibid., s. 5. Both those veto powers would have remained under the 1968 proposals, the first because the reason for its existence was taken to be self-evident (see Cmnd. 3977, para. 56), the second on the ground that it was never likely to cause conflict between the government and the Lords (para. 55).

[119] The Parliament Act 1911, ss. 2 and 5 refer to 'Public Bills': private Bills and subordinate legislation are therefore not embraced. The last (and probably the first) Lords' veto of subordinate legislation was in 1968, when the House voted down the Southern Rhodesia (United Nations Sanctions) Order, largely on the ground that the economic sanctions which had been imposed against the regime which had made an unlawful declaration of independence in Rhodesia in 1965 had had little effect, and that mandatory UN sanctions would be no more effective: see 293 H.L. Deb. 515–98 (18 June 1968). The House passed a similar Order at the second time of asking in deference to the House of Commons: see 295 H.L. Deb. 447–504 (18 July 1968). The government retaliated against this veto by abandoning all-party talks on reform; see also n. 144 below. Such a veto would have been removed by the Parliament (No. 2) Bill.

[120] Subject, perhaps, to what was said in Chapter 9 about the Queen's reserve powers.

of Lords' assent.[121] A Money Bill is one which, in the Speaker's opinion, has provisions which relate *only* to central government taxation, expenditure, or loans.[122] The definition of a Money Bill is narrow: indeed, most annual Finance Bills based on the Budget have not been certified as Money Bills.[123] To be valid the Speaker's certificate must be endorsed on a Money Bill before it leaves the Commons and is conclusive for all purposes.[124] The final group of powers—and in practice easily the most important—are the delaying powers of the House of Lords. These permit the Lords to hold up the passage of all other types of legislation for somewhat over one year, after which the will of the Commons prevails. There are five basic rules.[125] (a) If the House of Commons passes a public Bill[126] in two successive sessions (whether or not in the same Parliament) and the Lords reject it in both of them, then on that second rejection the Bill may receive royal assent. (b) The Bill must be sent up to the Lords at least one month before the end of both sessions. (c) One year must elapse between the initial occasion on which the Bill had a second reading in the Commons and the second occasion on which it passed that House. (d) The Bills rejected on both occasions must be the same: they must either be identical, or contain such alterations as are certified by the Speaker as being necessary through lapse of time.[127] Any Lords' amendments agreed to by the Commons do not, however, offend against this rule. (e) The Speaker must certify any Bill passing under the Parliament Acts as having complied with all these rules; such a certificate is conclusive for all purposes. Now the fact that the House of Commons can in the last resort overcome the opposition of the Lords to legislation through this procedure is *numerically* not very important—after all, it has only been used four times.[128] Of much greater significance are

[121] Parliament Act 1911, s. 1(1). The House of Lords has occasionally made minor amendments to Money Bills which the House of Commons has accepted.
[122] The Parliament Act 1911, s. 1(2) (as amended by the National Loans Act 1968, s. 1(5)) elaborates this as a public Bill containing only provisions dealing with the imposition, repeal, remission, alteration, or regulation of taxation; the imposition of charges on the Consolidated Fund or the National Loans Fund or on money provided by Parliament; the appropriation, receipt, custody, issue, or audit of accounts of public money; and the raising or guarantee of any loan or repayment of it—none of which includes taxes, money, or loans raised by local authorities or bodies for local purposes.
[123] Erskine May, n. 11 above, pp. 751–3.
[124] Parliament Act 1911, s. 3. See generally R. Brazier, 'The Financial Powers of the House of Lords' (1988) 17 *Anglo-American Law Review* 131.
[125] Parliament Act 1911, s. 2 (as amended by the Parliament Act 1949, s. 1).
[126] Other than a Money Bill or one to extend the life of Parliament beyond five years.
[127] For example, to change the year in the short title.
[128] To secure the passage of the Welsh Church Act 1914, the Government of Ireland Act 1914, the Parliament Act 1949, and the War Crimes Act 1991. The 1991 Act was notable for

both the sort of adverse amendments which the House of Lords makes to the legislation of both Labour and Conservative governments (and which those governments decide cannot be resisted), and the delay which is thereby caused—all without the Parliament Act procedure being invoked at all. That aspect will be considered now.

It has been traditionally assumed that Labour governments are more susceptible than Conservative governments to legislative defeat in the House of Lords. Mr Wilson's government up to 1970[129] suffered 116 defeats at the hands of the Lords,[130] of which the most notable were the effective killing of the House of Commons (Redistribution of Seats) Bill in 1969 (the Lords insisting on wrecking amendments which the government refused to accept, and the Bill lapsing on prorogation)[131] and the rejection of the Southern Rhodesia (United Nations Sanctions) Order in 1968 (which had the immediate effect of ending the all-party talks on House of Lords reform).[132] The minority, or small majority, Labour governments of 1974 to 1979 received 355 legislative setbacks in the House of Lords.[133] The House used its delaying power to the full over the Trade Union and Labour Relations (Amendment) Bill in the 1975–76 session, holding it up for slightly under one year. Peers attacked the Bill on the ground that it would pose a major threat to press freedom, and only when the government decided that if necessary the Bill would be forced through under the Parliament Acts did the House of Lords allow it to pass. A longer delay was imposed over the Aircraft and Shipbuilding Industries Bill in the same session: the Lords attached amendments to exclude the ship-repairing industry from its provisions and insisted on those amendments, so that the Bill was lost on prorogation. On its reintroduction in the following session the government withdrew the clauses relating to the ship-repairing industry so as to get the Bill enacted with a minimum of further delay; the Bill passed into law in 1977. For that government the unhappy combination of a

---

being the only one of the four to be insisted upon by a Conservative government contrary to the wishes of the House of Lords. That House had rejected the measure by large majorities. See 519 H.L. Deb. 1080–1208 (4 June 1990); 528 H.L. Deb. 619–742 (30 April 1991). Of course, the existence of the Parliament Acts must have persuaded the Lords not to persist in resisting certain Bills.

[129] On which see Janet Morgan, *The House of Lords and the Labour Government 1964 to 1970* (1975).

[130] See Brigid Hadfield, 'Whether or Whither the House of Lords?' (1984) 35 *Northern Ireland Legal Quarterly* 313.

[131] For the details, see S. A. de Smith and R. Brazier, *Constitutional and Administrative Law* (8th edn., 1998), pp. 241–3.

[132] See n. 119 above.   [133] Hadfield, n. 130 above.

House of Lords prepared to resist certain legislation and the lack of homogeneity among its own back-benchers in the Commons resulted in the Dock Work Regulation Act 1976 being passed without the government's original and main proposal. In relation to all these measures the majority in the House of Lords could claim with some justice that it had forced the government to take time to think again and further justify its plans, through the proper exercise of the peers' powers enshrined in the Parliament Acts.[134]

It has, however, become apparent over the last 30 years (and especially during the life of the late Conservative government) that the House of Lords has acted in a more even-handed manner towards both Labour and Conservative legislation to which it objects. Mr Heath's government suffered 26 (not very significant) adverse votes in the House of Lords.[135] The late Conservative administration sustained its two hundredth legislative reverse in the Lords in June 1992, roughly at the same rate as was inflicted on the 1964 Labour government, and suffered a total of 231 defeats by 1997; several of those defeats were quite major. A few instances may be cited by way of example. The Education (Corporal Punishment) Bill had to be withdrawn by the then government in 1985 after the Lords had inserted a wrecking amendment to abolish all corporal punishment in schools, whereas the Bill had been designed to give parents the right to opt their children out of such punishment.[136] Following the insertion of an Opposition clause into the Telecommunications Bill in 1984 to regulate telephone tapping, the then government was forced to promise its own legislation on that topic—legislation which it almost certainly would not have volunteered—in order to persuade the House of Lords to drop the Opposition clause.[137] Clauses were struck out of other Conservative Bills

---

[134] Under the Salisbury doctrine (so named after Lord Salisbury who developed it during the Attlee government), a Conservative Opposition in the Lords does not, in general, seek to reject Labour governments' Bills which had been foreshadowed in a general election manifesto. The doctrine has not been applied wholly consistently. It was debated at 545 H.L. Deb. 1780–1813 (19 May 1993); see also R. Brazier, 'Defending the Hereditaries: the Salisbury Convention' [1998] *Public Law* 371.

[135] Information from the House of Lords Journal and Information Office.

[136] For the defeat see 465 H.L. Deb. 1314–33 (4 July 1985). The government subsequently conceded that its original proposals had no chance of passing the Lords and so caused Parliament to confirm the House's 1985 decision by abolishing corporal punishment in all state schools: see the Education (No. 2) Act 1986, s. 47. The government had also decided to abandon the Protection of Official Information Bill 1979–80 because, although it had been given a second reading in the Lords, its ultimate chances of survival were slim: for the second reading debate see 402 H.L. Deb. 608–80 (15 November 1979).

[137] See 448 H.L. Deb. 632–44 (21 February 1984); 449 H.L. Deb. 1032–6 (19 March 1984).

by the peers, and the then government decided not to try to restore them: an outstanding example was the clause in the Prosecution of Offences Bill of 1985 which would have enabled the Attorney-General to refer 'lenient' sentences to the Court of Appeal for its opinion: the House disliked and rejected the idea.[138] Perhaps the most publicized and dramatic clash took place over the then government's plan to abolish the 1984 elections to the Greater London Council and to the metropolitan county councils, and to put in government-nominated boards to run their affairs, pending the statutory abolition of those authorities. The House passed a wrecking amendment to the Local Government (Interim Provisions) Bill by a majority of 48: the abolition of elections was something to which peers took great exception, and the number of Conservative defections was so high that the then government had to cause the Bill to be further amended, with the Lords' consent, so as to extend the life of the authorities to 1986 without elections in 1984, and to dispense with the expedient of nominated boards.[139]

It is impossible by considering the kinds of defeats inflicted on government legislation over the past few decades to discern any understanding— still less any consistent practice—on the part of the House of Lords as to what makes any given legislation in its view properly susceptible to defeat and delay there. Delay seems to be imposed on an *ad hoc* basis for the simple reason that the House disagrees with some policy aspect underlying the legislation in question.

In the light of the peers' record over Conservative legislation from 1979 to 1997 any left-wing rhetoric about the uniquely anti-left nature of the modern House of Lords will have a rather old-fashioned ring about it. Criticism from either the Labour or Conservative Parties that the House of Lords has thwarted the will of the Commons invites the retort that there is little point in retaining the co-ordinate legislative powers of the House of Lords unless it uses them from time to time. That, in its turn, invites a discussion of possible reform.

---

[138] See 459 H.L. Deb. 386–406 (24 January 1985). The Prosecution of Offences Act 1985 was passed without that provision; the government tried again in the Criminal Justice Bill 1986–87 (but that and other clauses of the Bill were dropped so that a much shorter Criminal Justice Act 1987 could pass before the 1987 dissolution). The government achieved its aim, at last, in the Criminal Justice Act 1988, ss. 35, 36.

[139] For the defeat see 453 H.L. Deb. 1033–70 (28 June 1984), and for the compromise provision see the Local Government (Interim Provisions) Act 1984, s. 2. Details of legislative defeats inflicted on governments from 1974 to 1991 are given at 512 H.L. Deb. 534–6 (written answers 6 November 1989), and 532 H.L. Deb. 62–4 (written answers 19 November 1991).

Assessment—and reform?

The House of Lords as presently constituted and as it currently works demonstrates a number of strengths. It has adequate time to fulfil its functions so that it may do so thoroughly and in a manner which allows backbenchers to take a full part in all aspects of the House's work. That partly accounts for the usefulness of the House of Lords as a worthwhile legislative chamber: uncontroversial government Bills are introduced there (so reducing the pressure on time in the Commons); helpful amendments to Commons' Bills are made; back-bench peers may introduce Bills without let or hindrance (and a few become law each year); and the House is showing a certain impartial rigour towards the legislation of both parties. It is also a useful deliberative chamber, as it should be, given the expertise available in it. And undramatic but necessary committee work is done there as a complement to that achieved in the Commons. The House of Lords also paved the way for the televising of both Houses. Yet it could be argued that the House is weakened in three fundamental respects: it is anomalous, unrepresentative, and on an average day Conservative-led. No modern state seeking to create a new legislature would devise anything remotely resembling a House most of whose members may sit on the basis of heredity while the rest of its members exist on the unrestricted patronage of the head of government. Heredity does occasionally provide young peers, and once even a Communist baron but such events are rather exceptional. The House is unrepresentative (or representative of only certain sections of society); former Ministers and ex-MPs make up a sizeable proportion of the working House. And it cannot be right in principle that one party is permanently in a stronger position in the House of Lords than any other— even if that does not guarantee the sacrosanctity of all Conservative legislation in that House.

There is, however, no political consensus over possible reform. The late Conservative government had no plans to alter the House of Lords in any way.[140] Since its defeat at the 1997 general election and the election of Mr William Hague as Conservative Leader, however, the Conservative Party seems to have abandoned its former committed defence of hereditary

---

[140] A party committee under Lord Home recommended in 1978 reform based on 268 members elected by proportional representation and 134 members nominated by the Sovereign on the Prime Minister's advice tendered after consulting all the party Leaders, but no Leader of the Conservative Party has not accepted that plan: see 'The House of Lords: The Report of the Conservative Review Committee' (1978).

peers. The party seems to be moving towards advocating a partly-elected second chamber. From the late 1970s to the late 1980s the Labour Party was committed to the abolition of the House of Lords and to the transfer of necessary functions to the House of Commons.[141] That flirtation with uni-cameralism was, however, overcome by 1989 when the party decided to advocate the replacement of the Lords by a second chamber, directly elected by proportional representation.[142] Subsequently the Labour Party adopted a two-stage plan for reform, for which it obtained a mandate at the 1997 general election. First, a Bill would be enacted to exclude hereditary peers from membership, and indeed a Bill has been introduced into Parliament for that purpose. If necessary, the Labour government will use the Parliament Acts to procure its passage. Secondly, consultations would take place to devise a plan for a more democratic and accountable second chamber. The Liberal Democrats want the House of Lords to be replaced by a Senate of about one hundred members, elected by proportional representation, and with *greater* powers than the present House.[143] Over the years the parties have thus scattered away from the virtual all-party agreement on reform which had been achieved in 1968.[144] That might well have been the last opportunity for reform based on consensus;[145] with the benefit of

---

[141] The 1977 Labour Party conference adopted that position by an overwhelming vote; Mr Callaghan managed to exclude it from the party's 1979 general election manifesto, but it was in the 1983 (though not in the 1987) manifesto.

[142] See *Meet the Challenge: Make the Change* (Labour Party, 1989), pp. 55–6.

[143] See *Here We Stand: Proposals for Modernizing Britain's Democracy* (Liberal Democrat Federal White Paper No. 6), pp. 23–4. On House of Lords reform generally, see Constitution Unit, *Reform of the House of Lords* (1996). See generally R. Brazier, *Constitutional Reform* (2nd edn., 1998), ch. 5.

[144] The Labour government's proposals followed very closely those already agreed at the all-party talks: see Harold Wilson, *The Labour Government 1964–1970: A Personal Record* (1971), p. 608. Briefly, the White Paper 'House of Lords Reform', Cmnd. 3799 (1968) envisaged a two-tier House of voting and non-voting peers. Voting peers (numbering about 250) would have been those life peers and hereditary peers of first creation who were prepared to attend at least 30 per cent of all sittings; all other peers would (unless some of them received life peerages, as was planned) have become non-voting peers who could, however, speak in the House. Succession to a peerage in future would no longer have led to membership at all. The Lords Spiritual would have been progressively reduced to 16; Lords of Appeal in Ordinary would have continued as before. After each general election at which the government changed enough new life peers would have been created to give the new government a 10 per cent majority over the opposition peers (but not over the opposition and cross-bench peers together). The delaying power would have been halved to six months; the veto over subordinate legislation would have become a delaying power.

[145] The 1968 White Paper was approved in both Houses by large, cross-party majorities and the Parliament (No. 2) Bill received its second reading in the Commons by 285 to 135: see 773 H.C. Deb. 1305–434 (20 November 1968); 297 H.L. Deb. 641–1094 (21 November 1968); 777 H.C. Deb. 43–172 (3 February 1969). Back-benchers on both sides opposed the

hindsight it might have been better had the Labour government been rather less punctilious in refusing to introduce a guillotine to ease the passing of the Parliament (No. 2) Bill on the ground that major constitutional Bills should not be guillotined.[146] Another major brake on any movement towards reform is the attitude of the House of Commons as a whole, ever jealous of its position at the centre of the political and legislative process and so never naturally enthusiastic about proposals which might transform the other House into a true rival.

Three matters should be kept in mind when House of Lords reform is being considered. First, the importance of the House of Lords must not be exaggerated. It is much the less powerful and the less significant House: it accomplishes sound work, but the formation and continuance of governments do not turn on it in any way—any vote of no confidence carried there is ignored:[147] it is just not in the same rank of importance in the constitution as the Commons. Secondly, the legitimate complaint that the House of Lords caused trouble for Liberal, and later for Labour, legislation, but resembled a rubber-stamp for Conservative measures, has to an extent been rectified. Experience since 1970 has been that the Lords has used its statutory powers over legislation regardless of which party has been in office, use which is objectionable only to those who believe in a unicameral legislature. And the possible efficiency of a unicameral Parliament based on the Commons may be strongly doubted: that House has shown itself to be slow in reforming its procedures so as to be either efficient or a real check on the government; it would be hard to see how a single chamber could adequately scrutinize legislation, particularly when it had to be guillotined, and no other parliamentary democracy which has to legislate for a large population has opted for a single chamber. Thirdly, the worst incidents of the unreformed House of Lords have already been removed by

---

Bill and talked at inordinate length, and the government subsequently withdrew the Bill so as to make time for urgent industrial relations legislation (which, ironically, was never introduced). The text of the Parliament (No. 2) Bill is given in Rodney Brazier, *Constitutional Texts* (1990), pp. 529–40.

[146] However, James Callaghan, who, as Home Secretary, was in charge of the Bill, has written in his memoirs that 'Our own Labour Members were unenthusiastic [about the Bill] and this may explain the Prime Minister's reluctance to agree to a guillotine motion': *Time and Chance* (1987), p. 503. The Labour Party had changed its attitude towards guillotining constitutional measures by the time of the Scottish and Welsh devolution Bills in the 1970s, and there is now no convention that constitutional Bills will not be guillotined. Indeed, the Scotland Act 1998 and the Government of Wales Act 1998 were guillotined.

[147] For example, the House of Lords passed a vote of no confidence in the Labour government's defence policy in 1967, of which the government took no notice: 285 H.L. Deb. 692–830 (25 July 1967).

statute. Thus the House of Commons is the dominant House generally in relation to legislation, and is omnipotent over financial legislation; heredity has not been the sole basis for membership of the House of Lords since 1958, and indeed a life peerage has been practically the only route into the House for new peers since 1964; peers succeeding to hereditary peerages may disclaim them; hereditary peeresses and Scottish peers have not been discriminated against since 1963. Accordingly, the only small change which is mooted here is based on the only existing all-party practice. All the party Leaders put names to the Prime Minister of people who will serve as working peers, and that process in my view could usefully be formalized and extended. The party Leaders could (perhaps privately) acknowledge that all the parties represented in the Commons have a legitimate expectation of representation in the House of Lords;[148] that active party strengths in the House of Lords, and votes and seats won at the previous general election, should be taken into consideration in drawing up lists of working peers; that all the nations and regions of the United Kingdom should be fully represented, and that as many more women as possible should be nominated. The party Leaders could meet together on Privy Counsellor terms to discuss the annual working peer lists, although the responsibility of recommending peerages to the Sovereign would formally remain with the Prime Minister.[149]

[148] Perhaps subject to some minimum number of MPs to qualify.
[149] For a fuller discussion, see Brazier, n. 143 above.

12

THE CONSTITUTIONAL
POSITION OF THE JUDGES

In this chapter the constitutional position of all ranks of the judiciary will be explained. The rights and powers of judges, Ministers, and Parliament in relation to each other are not ideal. The extensive powers of two Ministers over the judiciary are not entirely desirable: in particular, the personal role of the Lord Chancellor is crucial in the appointment, promotion, and removal of judges. Governments place judges firmly into political questions by using them in extra-judicial inquiries more than is really necessary; conversely, governments have acquiesced in over-restrictive parliamentary rules which prevent MPs from adequately discussing the administration of justice and other judicial matters. Behind most of these issues is the question whether there should be reform of the office of Lord Chancellor, possibly involving the creation of a new Department of Law.

The formal statutory framework within which members of the judiciary are appointed will be considered first, progressing from the bottom of the judicial hierarchy (lay magistrates) to the top (Lords of Appeal in Ordinary). To do this requires the presentation of a far from exciting catalogue, but this is unavoidable. Then the Lord Chancellor's appointment policies and practices will be examined: these are clearer since the publication of his pamphlet *Judicial Appointments*.[1]

---

[1] Lord Chancellor's Department (3rd edn., 1995); it was first published in 1986. Some of the matters in this chapter which refer to the lower judiciary are considered more fully in my 'The Appointment and Removal of the Lower Judiciary' (1986) 15 *Anglo-American Law Review* 173. I am grateful to the Lord Chancellor's Department for some of the statistical information in this chapter.

Appointment, pay, and promotion

Lay magistrates[2] are appointed by the Lord Chancellor[3] by instrument on behalf and in the name of the Queen.[4] In considering appointments the Lord Chancellor may act on the recommendation of the crucially important local advisory committees,[5] of which there are about a hundred. Their membership is invariably made up of serving magistrates, and the membership is published[6] so that either candidates can be recommended or individuals may nominate themselves. The Lord Chancellor requires that candidates 'should be personally suitable in character, integrity and understanding . . . and . . . should be generally recognized as such by those among whom they live and work'.[7] Candidates' political views are officially neither a qualification nor a disqualification, but at least since the term of office of Lord Gardiner LC (1964–70) the Lord Chancellor has wanted to know candidates' political affiliations so as to seek to avoid any bench becoming overweighted in favour of any one party.[8] There are over 30,000 lay magistrates currently on the active list. By disposing of some 97 per cent of all criminal cases they obviously make an outstanding numerical contribution to the administration of criminal justice.

Following a major change in the law, eligibility for all other judicial appointments no longer turns on whether candidates are barristers or solicitors (or, in Scotland, advocates). Instead, eligibility turns on possession of an advocacy qualification for a minimum specified period, usually for 10 years. That qualification enables the holder to appear in proceedings in particular courts: thus, for example, a High Court qualification entitles the holder to appear as an advocate in all proceedings in the High Court, and appointment as a High Court judge requires a candidate to have possessed such a qualification for at least 10 years.[9]

    [2] See generally Sir Thomas Skryme, *The Changing Image of the Magistracy* (2nd edn., 1983); E. Burney, *J.P.: Magistrate, Court and Community* (1979).

    [3] Lay magistrates are appointed to commissions in Greater Manchester, Merseyside, and Lancashire by the Chancellor of the Duchy of Lancaster: Justices of the Peace Act 1997, s. 26 (hereafter the '1997 Act').

    [4] Ibid., s. 6(1).   [5] On which see B. Cooke (1984) *Magistrate* 69.

    [6] The Lord Chancellor insisted in 1988 that the previous secrecy about membership be removed.

    [7] *The Appointment and Duties of Justices of the Peace in England and Wales* (Lord Chancellor's Department).

    [8] See P. F. Smith and S. H. Bailey, *The Modern English Legal System* (3rd edn., 1996), pp. 196–8.

    [9] See the Courts and Legal Services Act 1990, s. 71 and Schedule 10 (hereafter 'the 1990 Act').

Acting stipendiary magistrates are appointed by the Lord Chancellor when it appears to him that it is necessary to do so to avoid delays in the administration of justice in any area where a full-time stipendiary magistrate could be appointed.[10] Appointments are made for a period which the Lord Chancellor thinks fit, up to three months at a time.[11] The minimum qualification is to have held a general advocacy qualification for at least seven years.[12] Anyone wishing to be considered for appointment must apply to the Lord Chancellor's Department. After training, an acting stipendiary will be called on to sit regularly. There are at present 40 acting metropolitan stipendiaries and 50 acting provincial stipendiaries. Next, Assistant Recorders are appointed by the Lord Chancellor when it appears to him that it is expedient as a temporary measure to facilitate business in the Crown Court or a county court.[13] In practice Assistant Recorders are always in office in main centres and, as will be seen, are regarded as apprentices for Recorderships and Circuit judgeships: the 'temporary' nature of the office has been overtaken by the exigencies of crime and the Lord Chancellor's appointment policy. The appointment, from those who have held a general advocacy qualification for at least 10 years, is made during such a period or on such occasions as the Lord Chancellor thinks fit. Anyone who wishes to be considered for appointment must apply to the Lord Chancellor's Department.[14] There are at any one time some 500 Assistant Recorders in office. On the next rung up are Recorders, who are part-time judges of the Crown Court, appointed by the Queen on the Lord Chancellor's recommendation, with the same minimum qualification as Assistant Recorders.[15] Appointment is for a stated term and the frequency and duration of the occasions on which they will be expected to sit will be specified in each appointment.[16] The term is usually for three years, and is renewable; the commitment is to sit for at least 20 days a year with one continual period of 10 days.[17] Some 760 Recorders are currently in post.[18] The Lord Chancellor's policy since 1981 has been to appoint to a Recordership only someone who has first proved himself as an Assistant Recorder.[19]

---

[10] 1997 Act, ss. 13 (provincial), 19 (metropolitan).
[11] Ibid., ss. 13(1)(a), 19(1).   [12] 1990 Act, s. 71 and Schedule 10.
[13] Courts Act 1971, s. 24, as replaced by the Supreme Court Act 1981, s. 146.
[14] *Judicial Appointments*, n. 1 above, p. 6.   [15] 1990 Act, s. 71 and Schedule 10.
[16] Courts Act 1971, s. 21(3).
[17] *Judicial Appointments*, n. 1 above, p. 9; Lord Chancellor's statement on the terms and conditions of service of Recorders (1971) 68 *Law Society Gazette* 303.
[18] Of whom an increasing proportion are solicitors.
[19] *Judicial Appointments*, n. 1 above, p. 9.

Circuit judges are appointed from the ranks of Recorders who have held office for at least three years.[20] They are appointed by the Queen on the Lord Chancellor's recommendation.[21] There are at present some 500 Circuit judges. The Lord Chancellor will, again, only recommend those who have first proved themselves as Assistant Recorders and Recorders. Candidates are expected to apply, and vacancies are advertised. Candidates are interviewed in the Lord Chancellor's Department and by the Circuit Administrator of the Circuit on which they would like to sit. The last junior judicial officers to be mentioned, stipendiary magistrates, are appointed from those who have held a general advocacy qualification for at least seven years.[22] Up to 40 stipendiaries may be appointed outside London, and up to 60 in Inner London and the City at any one time;[23] there are 14 provincial stipendiaries and 49 metropolitan stipendiaries in post. A stipendiary may do anything which two lay justices may lawfully do.[24] The Lord Chancellor will only make recommendations from those who have served satisfactorily as acting stipendiary magistrates over at least two or three years.[25] In London, the Chief Metropolitan Magistrate[26] prepares a short list from acting metropolitan stipendiaries, and candidates are interviewed by a board which includes the Chief Metropolitan Magistrate; the board advises the Lord Chancellor. In the provinces the selection procedure is similar (although there is no equivalent of Chief Magistrate). Stipendiaries may serve as Recorders, and some have gone on to become Circuit judges. In 1993 the Lord Chancellor announced that vacancies for appointments up to the level of Circuit judge would be advertised. He rejected any more radical change to the system of appointments.

For the most part High Court judges are appointed from the ranks of leading Queen's Counsel.[27] It is therefore worth noting the arrangements which govern how barristers (and now solicitors) take silk. The Lord Chancellor recommends to the Queen the names of practising barristers[28]

[20] 1990 Act, s. 71 and Schedule 10.   [21] Ibid.   [22] Ibid.
[23] Justices of the Peace Act 1997, ss. 11(4), 16(1). A larger number may be specified by Order in Council: none has been.
[24] Ibid., ss. 14(3), (4), 18.   [25] Judicial Appointments, n. 1 above, pp. 18–19.
[26] One of the metropolitan stipendiaries is designated Chief Metropolitan Magistrate by the Lord Chancellor: 1997 Act, s. 16(3).
[27] See generally Judicial Appointments, n. 1 above, pp. 24–6; Report of the Royal Commission on Legal Services, Cmnd. 7648 (1979), i. 465–71. Treasury Counsel, who are normally elevated to the High Court bench after so serving, do not usually take silk. See also 211 H.C. Deb. 3 (written answers 6 July 1992).
[28] Employed barristers who have made a significant contribution to the public life of the profession are also considered, and honorary silk is also granted to barristers who have given distinguished service to the law through public service or in the academic world.

or solicitors of sufficient standing (which is usually 10 years or more) whom the Lord Chancellor is satisfied have reached an appropriate level of professional distinction. Candidates must apply for consideration, according to a fixed annual timetable. The Lord Chancellor's Department consults the Leaders of Circuits, Presiding Judges,[29] and other judges about applicants; the Lord Chancellor consults the Law Officers and the four heads of divisions—that is, the Lord Chief Justice, the Master of the Rolls, the President of the Family Division, and the Vice-Chancellor—before finally deciding. Only between 20 and 30 per cent of applicants are successful. The Lord Chancellor considers that silk should represent a working rank, and he accordingly expects QCs to practise for at least two years before he will consider them for full-time judicial appointment (which is hardly an intolerable delay for the ambitious). There are currently over 750 QCs in private practice. High Court judges are appointed by the Queen on the Lord Chancellor's advice from those who have held a High Court qualification for at least 10 years, or from those who have been Circuit judges for at least two years,[30] up to a current maximum of 98.[31] Lords Justice of Appeal are appointed by the Queen on the Prime Minister's recommendation from those who have held a High Court qualification for 10 years, or from the High Court bench.[32] At present up to 35 Lords Justices may hold office.[33] The four heads of divisions may be appointed on the Prime Minister's advice from the judges of the Court of Appeal or the High Court.[34] All these members of the High Court and of the Court of Appeal are conveniently referred to collectively as judges of the Supreme Court.[35]

Lords of Appeal in Ordinary (who do not form part of the Supreme

[29] Two High Court judges are appointed by the Lord Chancellor as Presiding Judges in each Circuit (there are three in the South Eastern Circuit). They perform a judicial role parallel to the administrative role assigned to the Circuit Administrators, acting with them to see that cases are assigned efficiently according to the expertise available. For details, see E. C. Friesen and I. R. Scott, *English Criminal Justice* (1977), p. 124.

[30] 1990 Act, s. 71 and Schedule 10.

[31] Supreme Court Act 1981, s. 4(1)(e), 4(4), (5). Maximum Number of Judges (No. 2) Order 1993, S.I. 1993 No. 1255.

[32] 1990 Act, s. 71 and Schedule 10.

[33] Supreme Court Act 1981, s. 2(1), (4), (5). That maximum was set by the Maximum Number of Judges Order 1996, S.I. 1996 No. 1142.

[34] 1990 Act, s. 71 and Schedule 10.

[35] The Supreme Court Act 1981, s. 1(1) provides that 'The Supreme Court of England and Wales shall consist of the Court of Appeal, the High Court and the Crown Court'. Although Circuit judges, Assistant Recorders, and Recorders sit in the Crown Court, they are not judges of the Supreme Court: ibid., ss. 10 to 13.

Court[36]) are appointed on the Prime Minister's advice by the Queen from those who have held for at least two years high judicial office as Lord Chancellor, judge of the Supreme Court or the Court of Session or of the Supreme Court of Judicature of Northern Ireland, or from those with a Supreme Court qualification.[37] Up to 12 may hold office at any time.[38]

It is striking from this survey that the entire judiciary owes its appointment to one, and occasionally two, politicians, with the danger to judicial integrity which that dependency could entail. Anyone wishing to become a judge—however low and however high—must receive the approval of the Lord Chancellor. Even those aspiring to the highest judicial offices, to which appointment is made on the advice of the Prime Minister rather than the Lord Chancellor, must in practice win the Lord Chancellor's support, because he is always consulted by the Prime Minister about these appointments;[39] and it would be inconceivable nowadays that the Prime Minister would make a recommendation if the Lord Chancellor were opposed to it. There have, it is true, been three recorded cases this century in which Prime Ministers have been prepared to stand by the letter of their conventional authority to recommend a judicial appointment. In 1923 Baldwin insisted that a former Law Officer, Sir Ernest Pollock, be made Master of the Rolls rather than Bankes LJ whom Lord Cave LC preferred;[40] and in 1951 Churchill assured Walter Monckton that, if he would agree to become Minister of Labour, Churchill would appoint him Lord Chief Justice on the next vacancy: Monckton joined the Cabinet, but never became Lord Chief Justice.[41] And Mrs Thatcher decided on one occasion

---

[36] The judicial House of Lords is not within the definition of the Supreme Court given in the 1981 Act. The Liberal government's Supreme Court of Judicature Act 1873 would have abolished the judicial functions of the House of Lords, but Gladstone's government fell and the new Conservative government procured fresh legislation (ultimately the Appellate Jurisdiction Act 1876) to preserve that jurisdiction. Perhaps by an oversight, however, the House of Lords was not incorporated into the Supreme Court. Neither the consolidating legislation of 1925 nor the 1981 Act sought to correct the anomaly.

[37] Appellate Jurisdiction Act 1876, ss. 6, 25; 1990 Act, s. 71 and Schedule 10.

[38] Administration of Justice Act 1968, s. 1. Only 10 held office for many years; 12 are now in office; the statutory maximum may be increased by Order in Council (and was last so raised in 1994): ibid. For other peers who may sit as Law Lords, see Chapter 11.

[39] Lord Hailsham of St Marylebone LC wrote in his autobiography that 'in practice the Lord Chancellor greatly influences [the Prime Minister's] decision': *The Door Wherein I Went* (1975), p. 254. Lord Mackay of Clashfern LC confirmed that the Lord Chancellor advises the Prime Minister on these appointments in the first instance: see 'The Lord Chancellor in the 1990s' [1991] *Current Legal Problems* 241 at 243, and 263 H.L. Deb. 391 (written answers 10 July 1995).

[40] See R. F. V. Heuston, *Lives of the Lord Chancellors 1885 to 1940* (1964), p. 428.

[41] Lord Simon of Glaisdale, book review (1965) 81 *Law Quarterly Review* 289 at 295. The incumbent, Lord Goddard, outlasted Churchill in office by three years.

not to recommend the first name on one of Lord Hailsham LC's lists for a judicial appointment, but opted instead for his second choice: according to Lord Hailsham the Prime Minister's selection turned out to be an outstanding success.[42] These are very isolated examples, and today even a Prime Minister who happened to be a qualified lawyer would rarely do other than endorse the Lord Chancellor's knowledgeable view, save in a most unusual case.

Obviously, the longer a Prime Minister and Lord Chancellor hold office the more judicial vacancies will occur and the more appointments will have to be made to fill them. So, for example, Mrs Thatcher and her first Lord Chancellor Lord Hailsham of St Marylebone between them effectively appointed all the current Lords of Appeal in Ordinary save one,[43] all the Lords Justices of Appeal, and well over half the High Court judges. Such ministerial patronage causes legitimate concern over the precise role of politicians in the appointing process, and in order to remove unnecessary secrecy surrounding the appointment of judges Lord Hailsham LC arranged the publication of *Judicial Appointments* in 1986. Although it is very informative about the machinery of junior appointments it is not at all detailed in its exposition concerning senior appointments. According to that publication the Lord Chancellor's policy is to appoint to every judicial post the person who appears to him to be best qualified to fill it, regardless of party, sex, religion, or ethnic orgin. Professional ability, experience, standing, and integrity are the criteria, together with good health and the absence of any personal unsuitability.[44] The Lord Chancellor is assisted within his Department by a Judicial Appointments Group, headed by a Deputy Secretary. Potential candidates are welcome to contact the Deputy Secretary for 'career advice'.[45] In considering appointments the Lord Chancellor follows two guiding principles.[46] First, no one person's view of a candidate (whether positive or negative) is to be regarded as decisive in itself, however authoritative or eminent the person giving it. Rather, the Lord Chancellor's officials seek an independent view from a spread of observers and colleagues in a position to assess a candidate's work and personality, and great weight is attached to that view. Secondly, as far as possible candidates will only be appointed to permanent, full-time, judicial posts after they have proved themselves in an associated, part-time capacity. This principle has been applied since 1981 to all appointments up to

---

[42] Lord Hailsham, *A Sparrow's Flight* (1990), p. 427.
[43] Lord Keith of Kinkel, appointed in 1977.
[44] *Judicial Appointments*, n. 1 above, p. 5.   [45] Ibid., p. 6.   [46] Ibid., p. 5.

that of Circuit judge; the Lord Chancellor is extending it progressively to all other appointments made on his recommendation, including High Court judgeships; it will eventually therefore (as will be seen later) apply to all senior appointments, because in practice all appointments to the Court of Appeal and to the judicial House of Lords are made from the ranks of senior judges. There is accordingly a developing career progression for successful candidates, from acting stipendiary magistrate to stipendiary magistrate, and from Assistant Recorder to Recorder to Circuit judge or deputy High Court judge, and then to High Court judge and above. To apply these principles the Deputy Secretary undertakes continuous consultations with judges and senior members of the profession. He reviews annually appointments on the six Circuits, discussing matters with the Presiding Judges.

All that *Judicial Appointments* says about High Court judgeships[47] is to set out the statutory qualification for appointment. Since 1997 vacancies for High Court judgeships have been advertised, and the Lord Chancellor consults the heads of division about potential appointments.[48] It was suggested—before the passing of the Courts and Legal Services Act 1990—that the Lord Chancellor has only a very small group to choose from, namely experienced silks aged between 45 and 60, so that each short list could be as small as six.[49] The effect of the 1990 Act, at least in time, should be to increase the size of that group.

It is generally accepted that, although the appointment process depends on politicians' choices, party political considerations have not affected senior judicial appointments since at least 1945.[50] That proposition must be qualified, first because in a marginal case any known political views of rival candidates might just tip the choice, and secondly because very occasionally an appointment not wholly devoid of political considerations may still

[47]   Ibid., p. 15. There is no information in it about appointments to the Court of Appeal or to the House of Lords.

[48]   For personal factors which might prevent appointment as a High Court judge, see Shimon Shetreet, *Judges on Trial* (1976), pp. 61–79. He lists as bars to preferment (among other things) 'disgraceful' conduct in the background to divorce; conviction of a crime involving moral turpitude; serious breach of professional etiquette; bankruptcy; and inappropriate personal behaviour such as adultery. Some of those bars may, perhaps, be more insuperable than others.

[49]   See J. A. G. Griffith, *The Politics of the Judiciary* (5th edn., 1997), p. 17—an excellent work.

[50]   Politics still count in the appointment of many lay magistrates, both because of the need to try to achieve politically balanced benches and because in some areas the parties put up slates of candidates.

be made, such as the promotion of Sir John Donaldson to be Master of the Rolls in 1982, a step understood to have been warmly recommended by Mrs Thatcher.[51] Certainly past political activity even of an extremist kind is not necessarily a bar to preferment: Frederick Lawton, for example, had been a candidate for the British Fascist Party in 1936 but he was later appointed to the High Court and subsequently to the Court of Appeal. A slightly different question is the extent to which politicians appoint active politicians to be judges. From 1873 to 1945 only four Attorneys-General from a total of 23 holders of that office failed to go on to hold high judicial office, and in the same period over half the Solicitors-General were similarly promoted.[52] But since 1945 the picture has been very different. Only two Solicitors-General out of 16 have been promoted to the High Court;[53] only four Attorneys-General, from a total of 11, have received judicial appointments—all four as Lord Chancellor; and a former Lord Advocate, who subsequently served as a Lord of Appeal in Ordinary, became Lord Chancellor in 1987—Lord Mackay of Clashfern.[54] Writing in 1972, Henry Cecil recorded that of 117 judges then in office, only 10 had been MPs and only a further five had been parliamentary candidates.[55] There is, of course, no reason why a Law Officer or a lawyer-MP should not become a judge— Lord Hailsham regretted that he was unable to appoint any[56]—provided obviously that that is not done as a reward for political services rendered; it

[51] He had been a Conservative councillor for a time and President of the controversial National Industrial Relations Court throughout its 2½ year life. He remained in the High Court under the 1974–79 Labour government, even though promotion was generally thought to be due. Lord Elwyn-Jones LC thought that promotion would cause a bitter reaction among Labour MPs. Donaldson was appointed to the Court of Appeal in 1979 on Mrs Thatcher's recommendation.

[52] See Smith and Bailey, n. 8 above, pp. 229–30.

[53] Sir Lynn Ungoed-Thomas (Solicitor-General 1951; High Court judge 1962–72); Sir Jocelyn Simon (Solicitor-General 1959–62; President, Probate, Divorce and Admiralty Division 1962–72; Lord of Appeal in Ordinary 1971–77).

[54] Sir William Jowitt (Attorney-General from 1929–32; Lord Chancellor 1945–51); Sir David Maxwell-Fyfe (Attorney-General 1945; Lord Chancellor 1954–62 as Lord Kilmuir); Sir Reginald Manningham-Buller (Attorney-General 1954–62; Lord Chancellor 1962–64 as Lord Dilhorne); Sir Michael Havers (Attorney-General 1979–87; Lord Chancellor 1987). The Lord Chancellor is head of the judiciary as President of the Supreme Court (Supreme Court Act 1981, s. 1(2)), *ex officio* member of the Appellate Committee (Appellate Jurisdiction Act 1876, s. 5(1)), of the Court of Appeal (1981 Act, s. 2(2)(a)), and of the High Court (1981 Act, s. 4(1)(a)).

[55] *The English Judge* (2nd edn., 1972), p. 19.

[56] *The Door Wherein I Went* (1975), p. 256. Lord Hailsham had himself been a career politician (and never a Law Officer), and had contested the Conservative Party Leadership in 1963 before becoming Lord Chancellor for the first time in 1970.

is natural, too, that the Lord Chancellor should previously have been a Law Officer, although, of course, this is not essential.

Whether any changes should be made in the system of judicial appointments will be considered at the end of this chapter.

The salaries paid to full-time judges reflect a number of desirable precepts. They are sufficiently high that potential judges would not face an unacceptable cut in income if they were to accept appointment; the rates of salaries enhance the dignity of judicial offices, and reflect the promotional stages between various ranks; judicial salaries are not at even a theoretical risk of regular review by Parliament, and the amounts paid are increased periodically so as to keep pace with other professional incomes and with inflation. Judicial salaries are now substantial.[57] Thus, for instance, a Circuit judge receives £88,000 a year, a High Court judge £118,000, and a Lord of Appeal in Ordinary £139,000. While top silks earn considerably more than a High Court judge's salary, appointment to the bench brings other advantages which may compensate for an immediate drop in income, such as somewhat less arduous work, an agreeable life in judge's lodgings on circuit, and a pension; and, as a judge is promoted, so his salary rises. Judicial salaries are determined by the Lord Chancellor with the consent of the Minister for the Civil Service; they may be increased, but not reduced, in the same way;[58] Parliament has no say in the matter. The rates are recommended by the Senior Salaries Review Body, which takes into account professional earnings as well as salaries payable to Permanent Under-Secretaries of State as relevant, though not determinant, factors. The government may or may not accept proposed increases, but the existence of the Body is a useful source of independent evidence about

---

[57] The following are the salaries currently payable.

Office	Annual salary
Lord of Appeal in Ordinary	139,000
Lord Justice of Appeal	132,000
Lord Chief Justice	148,000
Master of the Rolls	139,000
President, Family Division	132,000
Vice-Chancellor	132,000
High Court judge	118,000
Circuit judge	88,000
Stipendiary magistrate	70,000

[58] Administration of Justice Act 1973, s. (9)(1)(a); Supreme Court Act 1981, s. 12(1), (3); Courts Act 1971, ss. 21(7), 24, as replaced by the Supreme Court Act 1981, s. 146.

appropriate salaries. Salaries of Circuit judges, of judges of the Supreme Court, and of Lords of Appeal in Ordinary form part of Consolidated Fund Services,[59] and as such are paid without annual authorization; Parliament is accordingly denied any regular opportunity to debate either the judiciary or the administration of justice, the later inability being less obviously desirable. Whether these provisions are themselves a barrier to corruption may be strongly doubted. No evidence of attempts to corrupt judges has existed for a very long time, and judges would be immune to any such attempts for professional and personal reasons, not because they are well paid. If a person were susceptible to corruption would he not be so almost regardless of his income?

As is plain from the Lord Chancellor's appointment policy, there is a clear judicial promotion system, at the lower end from Assistant Recorder to Recorder to Circuit judge, and from Recorder or Circuit judge or deputy High Court judge to High Court judge and beyond. Even before 1981 promotions straight from the Bar to the Court of Appeal,[60] or from the Bar to the House of Lords,[61] or from the High Court to the Lords[62] were most infrequent: an orderly progression up the senior hierarchy was and remains the norm, and the Lord Chancellor's formally declared policy merely reflects that. Promotion carries numerous although not equally important advantages—an enhanced personal status; an increased salary; a knighthood for High Court judges; a Privy Counsellorship for Lords Justices;[63] a life peerage for Lords of Appeal; and an end to travelling on circuit for those promoted to the Court of Appeal and to the House of Lords. Now such a promotions system in theory incorporates two risks: that judges might try where possible to frame their judgments so as to please the Lord Chancellor and Prime Minister who might in time promote them, and that those Ministers might promote to high office those whose judicial philosophy seems closest to their own politics. Neither risk is very real, for Prime Ministers and Lord Chancellors come and go[64] and a sudden change

---

[59] Supreme Court Act 1981, s. 12(5); Administration of Justice Act 1973, s. 9(5).

[60] The only such promotions this century have been Lord Justices Slessor (1929), Scott (1935), Somervell (1946)—all of whom had been Law Officers—Duke (1918), and Greene (1935).

[61] There have been only two examples in the last 40 years: Lords Reid (1948) and Radcliffe (1949).

[62] Only Lords Uthwatt (1946) and Wilberforce (1964) in the last 40 years.

[63] This convention was created at the formation of the new Supreme Court of Judicature in 1873, the new Lords Justices opting for that honour rather than to receive a salary higher than that of High Court judges.

[64] Lord Chancellors tend to hold office longer than other Ministers, and indeed there has only been about the same number of Lord Chancellors as there has been Prime Ministers since 1900.

of party at a general election could make judicial trimming worthless if the trimmer had backed the wrong horse; there is also in any case little incentive for a Prime Minister or Lord Chancellor to promote (or indeed to appoint) 'loyal' judges, for there would be no guarantee that, once promoted (or appointed) they would deliver the goods,[65] and (as will be shown later) there is no way in practice of getting rid of them.

Judges and Parliament

In the last 25 years or so Members of Parliament have been prepared to criticize particular judges and particular verdicts and sentences much more than was previously the case. Such criticism heightens the need for clear principles and rules to govern the relationship between the judiciary and Parliament. That relationship ought to entail that, as a matter of comity, each respects the other as a vital branch of the constitution; that judges should be slow to attack the motives of Parliament in the way in which it has legislated; that MPs and peers[66] should not interfere in trials or litigation, and should be reluctant to attack individual judges (partly because there is no acceptable way in which they can defend themselves); and that senior judges who are in Parliament (the Lord Chancellor and the Lords of Appeal in Ordinary and some others such as the Lord Chief Justice and the Master of the Rolls) must remain keenly aware of their awkward constitutional position. With some exceptions, those are the characteristics of the relationship today.

In the course of conducting cases judges may criticize not only the technical form of legislation but also the policy behind it, provided that this is done in a measured and responsible way. Melford Stevenson J's description in 1978 of the Sexual Offences Act 1967 as a 'buggers' charter' was disparaging and verging on vulgar abuse, and as such was clearly outside what is appropriate.[67] Judges may also be forthright in their criticism of ministerial conduct, but they must be careful to avoid taking sides in politically controversial issues and certainly must not be seen to favour one political party. In the main judges stay within these precepts.

Parliamentary criticism of the judiciary is potentially a greater problem.

---

[65] As many Presidents of the USA could testify in relation to their nominees to the Supreme Court.

[66] Peers have been traditionally much more restrained than MPs in criticizing the judiciary.

[67] See *The Times*, 6 July 1978. The Lord Chancellor 'strongly deprecated' his remarks.

The administration of justice is a proper topic for parliamentary discussion, for it underpins the democratic society to which Parliament is wholly committed; it also requires the annual disbursement of large amounts of taxpayers' money. Equally, judges are entitled to do their daily duty free from improper interference from MPs and peers. In order to reconcile these conflicting rights three rules have been developed in Parliament, concerning the permissible limits of ministerial comment and criticism, the manner in which MPs and peers may discuss the judiciary, and imposing restraints on parliamentary discussion of cases before the courts.[68]

Ministers are by convention expected to show due inhibition when commenting in Parliament[69] on judicial words and deeds: indeed, in practice they would probably voice little comment at all were it not for the temptation of parliamentary questions. So, when Lord Hewart LCJ published a number of politically controversial and highly paid articles in the *News of the World* his brethren and others objected both to the subject-matter and to the vehicle which he had chosen to propagate his views; the Prime Minister was asked in the Commons about the propriety of what Hewart had done. Baldwin replied pithily and magisterially that 'it was obviously undesirable that His Majesty's judges should write for publication on matters of political controversy'.[70] Again, after Lord Kilmuir had been required to resign as Lord Chancellor in Macmillan's Cabinet purge in 1962 he immediately took up a business appointment; Macmillan was asked whether this was proper. The Prime Minister defended Kilmuir's decision, pointing out that he was not drawing his pension during that appointment.[71] More recently, Mrs Thatcher was forthright in giving her views at Question Time on judicial decisions with which she disagreed. In 1982, for instance, she categorized as 'incomprehensible' a suspended sentence of imprisonment which had been passed for the rape of a very young girl, and informed the House of action which the Lord Chancellor had taken to ensure that in future only those judges who were authorized to take murder trials would be able to try rape cases.[72] On the other hand,

---

[68] See generally Erskine May, *Parliamentary Practice* (21st edn., 1989), pp. 379–80.

[69] It would never be proper for Ministers to criticize the judiciary outside Parliament. Although Mr Michael Foot when Lord President of the Council in 1977 criticized, at a trade union rally, the historical role of the judges, that was a wholly isolated incident.

[70] 303 H.C. Deb. 799 (24 June 1935). Hewart's lame defence was that he had been writing not as Lord Chief Justice but as a peer, besides which (as he put it), 'I need the money': see Robert Jackson, *The Chief: The Biography of Gordon Hewart* (1959), pp. 327–8.

[71] 667 H.C. Deb. 999–1003 (20 November 1962).

[72] 34 H.C. Deb. 123–6 (14 December 1982), and, for the Speaker's later ruling that the Prime Minister had been in order, see 34 H.C. Deb. 285–6 (15 December 1982).

when she was asked in 1987 whether a fine of £25,000 and a suspended sentence of imprisonment adequately fitted the crime of insider dealing her reply was much more circumspect, setting out the legal background of the offence but adding that she was 'not able to comment on any particular sentence'.[73] On a later point of order the Speaker explained that the Prime Minister could have so commented, adding that such questions were not unusual and that it was 'perfectly in order to criticize or to question a sentence; but it is not in order to criticize a judge. That has to be done by motion'.[74] Informed and responsible parliamentary comment on sentencing and other judgments and Ministers' reactions to it is, it is suggested, entirely desirable so that as in any other area Ministers and MPs can decide whether legislative or other changes should be made.

Back-bench MPs have more scope than Ministers to comment on judicial conduct. The general rule is that no reflection may be cast on a judge's conduct, or on judges generally, unless it is done during a debate based on a relevant substantive motion on which a vote could be taken.[75] The scope of that rule was explored and slightly relaxed in 1973 against the background of the short-lived National Industrial Relations Court. The President of that Court, Sir John Donaldson,[76] defended one of its controversial decisions during (of all things) an after-dinner speech. Over 180 Labour MPs signed an early-day motion which called for his dismissal; the Shadow Cabinet, however, did not support it and the motion was never debated. But the House did subsequently debate an Opposition motion demanding the abolition of the National Industrial Relations Court, and in the course of it Opposition MPs wished to criticize its President. The Speaker ruled that MPs could argue, with reasons, during debate that a judge's decision was wrong, but that no reflection could be made on his character or his motives save on a motion which called for his dismissal.[77] As far as back-bench MPs are concerned, therefore, the situation now is that (a) they need not show the same restraint in relation to the judiciary as is expected of Ministers, and (b) they may criticize a particular decision or sentence during debate although (c) they may only attack a judge's character or motives during a debate on a substantive motion calling for his dismissal. Now rule (d) blocks off almost any opportunity for sustained criticism and argument,

---

[73] 118 H.C. Deb. 622 (2 July 1987).   [74] 118 H.C. Deb. 641 (2 July 1987).
[75] Erskine May, n. 68 above, pp. 379–80.
[76] He was seconded from the High Court for the duration of the appointment.
[77] 865 H.C. Deb. 1092 (4 December 1973). Should a judge write to an MP, however, he can be criticized for the contents of the letter: for an example, see 128 H.C. Deb. 166 (23 February 1988).

because governments do not put down or find time for such motions (no doubt because they see no reason to do so), and Oppositions do not generally table, or provide their own time to debate, such motions either (perhaps attempting to be statesmanlike). Back-benchers must therefore use their ingenuity in two Commons' procedures to express their criticisms of judges. First, any MP may put down an early-day motion[78] which can set out in some detail his concerns about judicial conduct. In 1975, for example, one was tabled demanding the resignation of Judge Christmas Humphreys after he had imposed a suspended sentence of imprisonment in a rape case.[79] The government will not, of course, provide time for any such motion to be debated, and the Shadow Cabinet will not normally devote any part of an Opposition day to take it either.[80] But every Thursday the Leader of the House is asked by his shadow counterpart to state the business for the following week; the answer will already have been conveyed through the usual channels, but the answer given in the House of Commons allows the Shadow Leader of the House to complain about the government's arrangement of business—and allows those back-benchers who catch the Speaker's eye to do likewise. So an MP may ask whether the Leader of the House is aware of the strength of support for his early-day motion asking for the removal of Mr Justice X or Judge Y, and why time cannot be found for it to be debated; in the course of his question he may put as many debating points as he can before the Speaker calls him to order.[81] In that way his criticism will have been made; Ministers and MPs will have heard it; everyone can read about it; no judge could be wholly impervious to it, particularly if a substantial number of MPs have signed the motion. Secondly, although the Table Office will not accept a question which reflects on a judge's character,[82] an MP may be able to make his point during a supplementary question. So a question which asks the Attorney-General when he next expects to meet the Lord Chief Justice may be followed by a supplementary during which criticisms can be slipped in before the Speaker calls the questioner to order. In that way the MP will

---

[78] On which see Chapter 10.   [79] *The Times*, 23 June 1975.

[80] The motion demanding the abolition of the National Industrial Relations Court in 1973 was exceptional. In 1925 the Labour Opposition moved a motion of censure on the government for 'initiating' a prosecution, for conspiracy to incite mutiny, against 12 Communist Party members, claiming that it was a violation of free speech. During the debate the trial judge, Swift J, was criticized by the Opposition for his offer of clemency if those accused without previous convictions would forswear the Communist Party: none did so, and each received six months' imprisonment. See 188 H.C. Deb. 2075–189 (1 December 1925).

[81] For an example of such a process, see 120 H.C. Deb. 494 (23 July 1987).

[82] Erskine May, n. 68 above, p. 287–8.

have been able (albeit briefly) to make his complaint about judicial conduct.[83]

The final restraint which limits the freedom of all MPs during any business of the House in relation to the courts is the *sub judice* rule.[84] In essence, this requires that matters awaiting the adjudication of a court may not be commented on in parliamentary proceedings, the justification being that Parliament should not seek to influence judicial decisions. More fully, the *sub judice* rule bars references to matters awaiting or under adjudication (a) in all criminal courts from the moment a person is charged to the time of verdict and any sentence or to the time any appeal is decided, and (b) in civil courts from the time the case is set down for trial until it is finally disposed of. In 1972 the House slackened the rigidity of the rule in civil matters so that (subject to the Speaker's discretion) reference may be made to active civil cases if they relate to a ministerial decision which can only be challenged in court on the grounds of misdirection or bad faith, or if they concern issues of national importance (such as the economy, public order or the essentials of life). In exercising his discretion the Speaker will disallow references if he thinks that there is a real and substantial danger of prejudice to the proceedings.[85] Under this relaxation the thalidomide tragedy was debated even though proceedings had been started.[86] As the furore over Mr Peter Wright's memoirs *Spycatcher* showed, the *sub judice* rule does not prevent the House from debating matters which are under adjudication in courts outside the United Kingdom.[87] Nor does it preclude Parliament from legislating on the subject-matter of current litigation, as was demonstrated by the passage of the War Damage Act 1965 during the Burmah Oil litigation.[88]

These arrangements in general represent a sensible balance between judicial freedom from wrongful parliamentary pressure and Parliament's

---

[83] So, for example, in 1980 a supplementary question of that type ran: 'Many people . . . fear that [Lord Denning's recent judgment] will provide more explosive material in an already dangerous minefield. Lord Denning has made the law even more uncertain, and he is bringing the law, and the rule of law, into disrepute. Will the Solicitor-General advise [him] that, although hon. Members have respected Lord Denning in the past, the time has now come for him to retire?' The Speaker then intervened to call the questioner to order. See 977 H.C. Deb. 930 (28 January 1980).

[84] On which see Erskine May, n. 68 above, pp. 377–9; 916 H.C. Deb. 882–4 (29 July 1976); 560 H.L. Deb. 88–9 (10 January 1995).

[85] The House agreed to that relaxation at 839 H.C. Deb. 1589–627 (28 June 1972).

[86] For the debate, see 847 H.C. Deb. 432–510 (29 November 1972). For other examples, see 160 H.C. Deb. 151–8 (13 November 1989); 200 H.C. Deb. 30–34 (2 December 1991).

[87] See Speaker's ruling at 119 H.C. Deb. 704–5 (13 July 1987).

[88] *Burmah Oil Co.* v. *Lord Advocate* [1965] A.C. 75.

rights in relation to the administration of justice.[89] The *sub judice* rule in relation to civil litigation and criminal appeals, however, could and should be further weakened or even abolished, for judges in such jury-less proceedings are unlikely to be improperly influenced in their duty by parliamentary remarks.[90] While it was also highly regrettable that the House of Commons did not establish a select committee on the Lord Chancellor's Department or on the Law Officers' Department in 1979, that deficiency has been made good.[91]

The Lord Chancellor and the Lords of Appeal in Ordinary are both judges and legislators. The office of Lord Chancellor is a complete denial of the doctrine of the separation of powers: because the incumbent has to speak as a Minister and act as Speaker of the House of Lords there is potential for difficulty when he sits in the Appellate Committee or in the Judicial Committee of the Privy Council,[92] and when he speaks as head of the judiciary. This calls at the least for considerable tact and political sensitivity. The Lords of Appeal, too, must be careful when taking part in the parliamentary functions of the House: it has been said that their interventions have mainly been restricted to acting as resident legal experts helping with technical points, but they have also spoken on a wide range of politically controversial topics, very occasionally using strong political argument.[93] Indeed, six Lords of Appeal roundly condemned the Lord Chancellor's proposals to reform the legal profession (which were subsequently embodied in the Courts and Legal Services Act 1990). They were joined in the House of Lords by the Lord Chief Justice, the Master of the Rolls and (less controversially) by three former Lord Chancellors.[94] In a better ordered system the office of Lord Chancellor would be reformed (and suggestions about that will be offered at the end of this chapter), and the judicial House of Lords would be constituted as a court quite separate from Parliament.

[89] The restraints which protect judges from criticism inside Parliament are reflected outside it in the rule that scurrilous abuse of a judge may be punished as contempt of court as scandalizing the court; but '[n]o criticism of a judge, however vigorous, can amount to contempt of court, provided it keeps within the limits of reasonable courtesy and good faith': per Salmon LJ in *R. v. Metropolitan Police Commissioner, ex p. Blackburn (No. 2)* [1968] 2 Q.B. 150 at 155. See generally Clive Walker, 'Scandalizing in the Eighties' (1985) 101 *Law Quarterly Review* 359.

[90] The rule would have to remain in those civil actions which may still be tried by a jury, such as defamation.

[91] See Chapter 10.

[92] In recent years the Lord Chancellor has sat judicially on as many as 20 days a year: see 539 H.L. Deb. 82–3 (written answers 20 October 1992).

[93] For examples, see J. A. G. Griffith, n. 49 above, pp. 42–5.

[94] For the details, see J. A. G. Griffith, n. 49 above, pp. 51–7; and 505 H.L. Deb. 1307–1480 (7 April 1989). During the 1990s senior judges in the House of Lords were very

Extra-judicial activities

Judges must know what is permissible in their out-of-court activities,[95] and the government must appreciate what it may properly ask judges to do in addition to their ordinary work. It is those questions which will be addressed now.

Just as it has been made difficult for MPs to develop critical arguments about the judiciary, so a cordon sanitaire has been constructed to keep the more senior judiciary from entering active party politics. Thus judges of the Supreme Court, Circuit judges, stipendiary magistrates, judges of the Court of Session, and sheriffs, and judges of the High Court and Court of Appeal in Northern Ireland, are disqualified from membership of the House of Commons.[96] On the other hand, part-time judges such as Assistant Recorders, Recorders, and lay magistrates may be MPs, and indeed there are usually several Recorders in the House. Moreover, the superior judiciary are required by custom to avoid partisan controversy: party political activity is unacceptable. So, Baldwin was of the view in 1929 that Hewart's membership of Lord Ullswater's Committee on Electoral Reform was inconsistent with his office of Lord Chief Justice, and Hewart resigned from the Committee.[97] Again, in 1968 Lord Avonside, a judge of the Court of Session, was nominated by the Lord President of the Court of Session at the request of the Leader of the Opposition, Mr Edward Heath, to membership of a Conservative Party committee to investigate possible changes in the government of Scotland. The Lord Advocate (a member of the then Labour government) objected that this appointment broke the convention that judges should not involve themselves in party political matters; Lord Avonside resigned from the committee.[98] Such limitations do not affect the lower judiciary, and lay magistrates in particular are frequently active in local politics.

Obviously full-time judges may not continue to practise law. A largely

---

critical of a number of Criminal Justice Bills promoted by the Conservative government. By way of example, see the attack on what became the Crime (Sentences) Act 1997 by Lord Bingham of Cornhill LCJ at 577 H.L. Deb. 983–90 (27 January 1997).

[95] For a full analysis of the personal behaviour required of judges, see Shetreet, n. 48 above, ch. 15.

[96] House of Commons Disqualification Act 1975, s. 1(1) and Schedule 1, Part I.

[97] Robert Jackson, n. 70 above, pp. 216–17.

[98] *The Times*, 26 July–6 August 1968. The Lord President perhaps acknowledged that he had made a mistake in the matter when, during this episode, he refused the request of the Scottish National Party to nominate any Scottish judge to serve on one of its committees.

conventional rule to that effect was made statutory in 1990.[99] Solicitors and barristers who are Recorders must comply with a number of rules designed to avoid professional embarrassment which could arise by appearing as advocates in courts in which they sit;[100] barristers who sit as deputy High Court or deputy Circuit judges[101] must also avoid professional embarrassment. A practising barrister who is in addition a lay magistrate must avoid any clash between those roles; a practising solicitor-magistrate may not act in any case in an area where he sits judicially.[102]

Although there is no requirement of regular financial disclosures by full-time judges, they are expected not to hold directorships in, or to be trustees or advisers of, any public company, nor to carry on a business. Personal investment is entirely permissible,[103] subject of course to the usual rules of natural justice to prevent any clash of interest. Nor is there any requirement that, after leaving the bench, judges should seek permission before taking up other employment; such a rule is unnecessary because judges do not usually resign prematurely (rather than leaving the bench at retirement age). Fisher J attracted criticism in 1970 when he resigned after only two years or so as a judge in order to join a merchant bank, and clearly there must never be any suggestion (as there was not in Sir Henry Fisher's case) that a senior judge might be considering what effects his judgments might have on his later employment prospects.[104] Giving public lectures and publishing books have not, in the main, caused any conflict of interest for serving judges, and there is no reason why fees and royalties should not be paid as long as the judge is not put under any obligation outside his contract to the payer. Scarman LJ's controversial Hamlyn Lectures in 1974[105] did not represent the first public voicing of legal opinions off the bench,[106] but

---

[99]   Courts and Legal Services Act 1990, s. 75 and Schedule 11.

[100]   See Lord Chancellor's statement on the terms and conditions of service of Recorders (1971) 68 *Law Society's Gazette* 303 (as amended by Lord Chancellor's Department Circular of 29 November 1971).

[101]   See Courts Act 1971, s. 24, as replaced by Supreme Court Act 1981, s. 146.

[102]   Solicitors Act 1974, s. 38.

[103]   Although if a judge were to go bankrupt he would have to resign.

[104]   Lord Hailsham LC said after Sir Henry Fisher's resignation that, when interviewing potential judges, he would tell them that they should treat a judicial career as a permanent one: see 312 H.L. Deb. 1314 (19 November 1970).

[105]   Published as *English Law: The New Dimension* (1974).

[106]   Lord Parker LCJ had doubted in 1967 whether judges could ever publicly discuss policy or possible legislation, orally or in writing, rather than speaking privately to the Lord Chief Justice who would convey those views to the government; but subsequently McKenna J, Lord Widgery LCJ, Sir Jocelyn Simon P, and Danckwerts LJ spoke in lectures or at dinners or gave press interviews about various legal issues before Scarman LJ's Hamlyn Lectures in 1974. Since 1974 judges have continued to lecture and publish.

since then no one could challenge the propriety of a judge offering his considered views on the law through a public lecture or book, within the bounds of discretion. Nor can there be any objection to a judge writing or editing practitioners' works: after all, two Lord Chancellors have done so.[107] Lord Hewart's *The New Despotism* (published in 1929) was, however, a vehement polemic unworthy of a judge; Judge James Pickles's *Straight from the Bench* (published in 1987) was the latest episode in a fraught relationship with the Lord Chancellor's Department, although it is difficult to argue that he was wrong to publish it. Whether a judge of the Supreme Court or a Lord of Appeal may properly publish articles or give press interviews or take part in television or radio programmes is entirely a matter for his or her personal discretion. They have taken part in broadcasts, such as BBC Radio 4's *Law in Action* programme; Lord Denning MR gave the BBC television Dimbleby Lecture in 1980; the then Lord Chief Justice, Lord Taylor, appeared on the *Any Questions* television programme in 1993; and some senior judges have given press interviews. Lord Taylor LCJ in particular did much to publicize the work of and the constraints on the judiciary, and he publicly criticized some government policies. Lord Bingham of Cornhill LCJ has continued the policy of openness begun by his predecessor, for example by giving occasional press conferences. The lower judiciary, however, have not been so free in such matters, partly because of the so-called Kilmuir Rules[108] and partly because the Lord Chancellor has been able to support those rules with disciplinary sanctions. In 1955 the Director-General of the BBC wrote to Lord Kilmuir as Lord Chancellor with what now seems a wholly anodyne proposal that a judge (or judges) might appear in a planned series of radio talks about great judges of the past. Having consulted the heads of divisions the Lord Chancellor replied (in a letter immortalized as embodying the Kilmuir Rules) refusing permission. It was considered 'undesirable for members of the Judiciary to broadcast on the wireless or appear on television'—although as the Lord Chancellor acknowledged he had no disciplinary jurisdiction over senior judges. So, while the Lord Chancellor's Department may advise senior judges about these issues, it is for them to decide what to do in the end; but members of the lower judiciary gave interviews or wrote in the press or appeared on the broadcasting media at their peril. Now appearing on

---

[107] The 1st Viscount Hailsham LC and Lord Hailsham of St Marylebone LC edited the second and fourth editions of *Halsbury's Laws of England*; a retired Lord Chancellor, the Earl of Halsbury, received 10,000 guineas for editing the first edition: see R. F. V. Heuston, n. 40 above, p. 487. Megarry J continued to co-produce editions of *The Law of Real Property* after his elevation.

[108] On which see A. W. Bradley [1986] *Public Law* 383–6.

television or radio can be a risky business for a judge, but common sense would no doubt steer him clear of a chat show and towards a serious programme; in any case, judges are very busy people who may not be tempted to write or broadcast, and the need for formal restrictions on them may be exaggerated. Lord Mackay of Clashfern LC, in effect though not in form, suspended the Kilmuir Rules. At a press conference soon after succeeding to his office in 1987 he said that judges should observe the spirit of the Rules, but that they should be trusted to decide for themselves whether to talk to the media—although they had to be careful not to say anything which might damage their authority or prejudice the performance of their judicial work.

After retirement a judge is not expected to return to the Bar, presumably because it might give him an unfair advantage over other practitioners;[109] there does not yet seem to be an established understanding in relation to retired solicitor-judges. Retired senior judges could go into politics, but only rarely do so;[110] they continue to be free to publish or broadcast as they see fit.[111] No retired Lord Chancellor has returned to the Bar; former occupants of the Woolsack are under a moral obligation to serve as a Law Lord if asked,[112] and can (not without controversy) go into business (as did Lords Birkenhead and Kilmuir), provided that they do not draw their judicial pension.[113]

---

[109] 'Several' High Court judges sought permission to return to the Bar in the early 1950s according to Winston Churchill, moving the second reading of the Judges' Remuneration Bill, 525 H.C. Deb. 1063 (23 March 1954). None did so.

[110] Lord Reading (Lord Chief Justice 1913–21) became Viceroy of India 1921–25 and Foreign Secretary briefly in 1931—a wholly exceptional case.

[111] Lord Denning was a frequent visitor to broadcasting studios after his retirement as Master of the Rolls.

[112] Lord Dilhorne (Lord Chancellor 1962–64) insisted on being appointed a Lord of Appeal in Ordinary after his retirement (and on receiving the appropriate salary) before sitting regularly in the Appellate Committee; he did not draw his pension while a Lord of Appeal.

[113] See R. F. V. Heuston, n. 40 above, p. 398. The maximum annual judicial pension is the equivalent of one-half of a judge's last annual salary, index-linked. Some examples of the conditions on which such pensions become payable are set out below, derived from the Judicial Pensions and Retirement Act 1993; a lower rate of pension is payable after shorter periods of service.

Judge		Conditions
Lord of Appeal in Ordinary/		(a) at age 70
Judge of Supreme Court	or	(b) after 15 years' service
	or	(c) on permanent disablement
		(a) at age 65
Circuit judge	or	(b) after 15 years' service
	or	(c) on permanent disablement
		(a) at age 65
Stipendiary magistrate	or	(b) after 20 years' service
	or	(c) on permanent disablement

All governments ask senior judges to preside over some Royal Commissions, departmental committees, and committees of inquiry.[114] This is done for fairly obvious reasons. Judges are trained to ascertain facts in complex issues, to preside over inquiries, and are seen as impartial; setting up an inquiry may also delay the need for the government to take an awkward decision, and the judge as chairman may helpfully take the responsibility for an inconvenient result. The remits entrusted to the judiciary, and which they take to be part of their public duty to accept, have been extremely varied, from matters of social concern (such as the working of the Abortion Act 1967),[115] to issues involving entirely political choices (like the proper levels of police pay),[116] and to highly controversial matters (including the legal procedures to deal with terrorists[117] and the events of 'Bloody Sunday' in Northern Ireland).[118] The 1979 Conservative government called in aid two senior judges to help with highly sensitive political issues. Sir Richard Scott, the Vice-Chancellor, headed an inquiry into whether defence equipment had been exported to Iraq in breach of the government's own guidelines; and Lord Nolan (a Lord of Appeal in Ordinary) became the first Chairman of the Committee on Standards in Public Life (which has become a standing committee).[119] There are two clear drawbacks in using judges in these ways. First, in a controversial inquiry the judge may be criticized by the losing side for producing a whitewash or a wrongheaded report, the result of which is to drag him into further disputes. In any inquiry with political, and to an extent social, implications that result is likely—and even the government which commissioned the report may reject it. The second danger arises in the use of judges in those standing bodies in which political considerations must necessarily be present. The National Industrial Relations Court was fatally flawed from the start

---

[114] On which see D. G. T. Williams, *Not in the Public Interest* (1965), pp. 188–91; G. Zellick [1971] *Public Law* 1; T. J. Cartwright, *Royal Commissions and Departmental Committees in Britain* (1975); G. Rhodes, *Committees of Inquiry* (1975); J. A. G. Griffith, n. 49 above, ch. 2. For a list of such investigations since 1900 in which judicial chairmen can be noted, see David Butler and Gareth Butler, *British Political Facts 1900–1985* (6th edn., 1986), ch. 7. It has been estimated that the time of three High Court judges is taken up in extra-judicial work at any one time: Report of the Committee on the Deployment of the High Court Bench (Lord Chancellor's Department, 1988).

[115] Chairman: Lane J; Cmnd. 5579 (1974).

[116] Chairman: Lord Edmund-Davies; Cmnd. 7283 (1978).

[117] Chairman: Lord Diplock; Cmnd. 5185 (1972).

[118] Chairman: Lord Widgery; H.C. 220 (1971–2).

[119] For the Scott Report see H.C. 115 (1995–96); for the First Report of the Nolan Committee see Cm. 2850 (1995). Lord Nolan has been succeeded by Lord Neill, who was not a judge.

because trade unionists saw it as an enforcement arm of the government's industrial relations policy. The Security Commission, of which a senior judge is Chairman, has to carry out investigations and to supervise matters which arguably could more appropriately and effectively be discharged through parliamentary machinery. On the other hand, the deployment of judges on standing official law reform bodies like the Law Commissions, the Criminal Law Revision Committee, and the Law Reform Committee is unexceptionable, because although they have to grapple with social issues their work will only infrequently be controversial in the eyes of politicians and the public.

So what in the result may be suggested as the proper use of judges by the government in extra-judicial tasks? I suggest that all governments, in order to save judges from the unfortunate results just mentioned, should bind themselves by self-denying ordinance to leave judges in the courts to the greatest possible extent. To that end, if a subject which fell for investigation would ultimately involve political decisions by Ministers, a committee chaired by a junior Minister, perhaps with outside advisers, would be preferable to any judicial inquiry carrying with it the unpleasant sight of Ministers trying to hide behind judges' robes. If an inquiry could just as well be chaired by any of the great and the good,[120] then no judge should be used.[121] And some matters would be better undertaken by senior Privy Counsellors on behalf of Parliament.[122] If governments were to follow such suggestions the judiciary would be more independent of government decision-making than heretofore, but they are put forward with, alas, no confidence that they will be accepted.

Tenure, discipline, and removal

In October 1940 Lord Hewart, who had been Lord Chief Justice for 18 years (and the worst since the seventeenth century)[123] received a telephone call from Number 10 Downing Street to inform an astounded Hewart that his resignation would be announced the following day, which it

---

[120] A list of people who could serve on Royal Commissions and departmental inquiries—the great and the good—is maintained by the Public Appointments Unit within the Cabinet Office.

[121] An example would be Lord Radcliffe's Committee of Privy Councillors on Ministerial Memoirs, Cmnd. 6386 (1976), which is referred to in Chapter 6.

[122] For example, some (or all) of the functions of the Security Commission.

[123] R. F. V. Heuston, n. 40 above, pp. 603–4, a view from which there is no dissent.

was.[124] Now even though Hewart had been very ill for some time and had told the Prime Minister that he intended to resign fairly soon, this was an extraordinary prime ministerial removal of a very senior judge.[125] Because of its special facts, however, it does not represent the security of tenure enjoyed by senior judges, which is still based on the arrangements made in the Act of Settlement 1701. Under the Supreme Court Act 1981[126] Lords Justices and High Court judges hold office 'during good behaviour, subject to a power of removal by Her Majesty on an address presented to Her by both Houses of Parliament', and by the Appellate Jurisdiction Act 1876[127] a Lord of Appeal 'shall hold his office during good behaviour, . . . but he may be removed from such office on the address of both Houses of Parliament'. They will all hold office (unless removed) until the retiring age of 70.[128] In practice the address procedure would be the only method of removing an errant senior judge: as a consequence, their tenure is very secure. The tenure enjoyed by the different ranks of the lower judiciary, however, is varied and insecure. Curiously, the most junior of the lower judiciary, the lay magistrate, is in a sense in a rather securer position than acting stipendiaries, Assistant Recorders, and even Recorders, who are all in terms of status and powers hierarchically superior to him. Lay magistrates are appointed until the age of 70,[129] although they may be removed by the Lord Chancellor at any time.[130] A lay magistrate will therefore remain in office until that age unless he so falls into error that the Lord Chancellor dismisses him: there is no machinery for regular review of a lay magistrate's performance. On the other hand, the other part-time judges have no such long, unreviewed run. Acting stipendiaries will normally be considered for promotion to stipendiary after two years. Assistant Recorders, after three to

[124] Jackson, n. 70 above, p. 335.

[125] There was a certain irony in it in that Hewart's immediate predecessor Lord Trevethin had himself been churlishly treated in Hewart's interest. When the office of Lord Chief Justice had become vacant in 1921 Hewart, as Attorney-General, had a claim to it under the then practice, but Lloyd George could not spare him. A. T. Lawrence J, aged 77, was appointed Lord Chief Justice as Lord Trevethin on the understanding that he would retire whenever Lloyd George wished, and indeed Lawrence signed an undated resignation letter. In the following year Trevethin read of his resignation as Lord Chief Justice in *The Times*. Lord Birkenhead LC objected strongly to this disgraceful arrangement, but oddly the normally punctilious George V apparently saw nothing objectionable in it. See Shetreet, n. 48 above, pp. 69–70; 97–8; Jackson, n. 70 above, ch. 7.   [126] See s. 11(3).   [127] See s. 6.

[128] Or 75 if appointed before the coming into force of the Judicial Pensions and Retirement Act 1993; and see Supreme Court Act 1981, s. 11(2). Lord Irvine of Lairg LC gave his definition of judicial independence at 576 H.L. Deb. 106 (written answers 16 December 1996).

[129] Justices of the Peace Act 1997, s. 7(2).   [130] Ibid., s. 5.

five years of sitting,[131] will be considered for a Recordership: if the Lord Chancellor's Department is not satisfied by an Assistant Recorder's performance 'he will be thanked for his services and stood down from further sitting'.[132] Recorders are appointed normally for renewable three-year periods up to age 70,[133] and their performance will thus be reviewed every three years. The two full-time judgeships, Circuit judges and stipendiary magistrates, are appointed (subject to the power of removal) until retirement age, 70.[134] A metropolitan stipendiary magistrate[135] may be removed for inability or misbehaviour,[136] and a Circuit judge and Recorder for incapacity or misbehaviour.[137]

Judges rightly conduct cases in public and under the watch of the media. A slip is easily made; a remark said cannot be unsaid; and a judge should no more be condemned for an isolated error than anyone else. Disciplinary machinery is in place to seek to correct those errors which, however, cannot be overlooked. All judges will have decisions upset on appeal, and the appellate courts may be viewed as part of that disciplinary machinery, particularly when a complaint is based on unjudicial behaviour.[138] No judge will be impervious to criticism from his senior colleagues, and it could well affect his future conduct. The consequences can range from a simple reversal or an acquittal on appeal, to an appellate rebuke, to an intervention by the Lord Chancellor. So appellate courts have criticized judges for improper behaviour such as falling asleep and thus missing something of significance,[139] for making impatient gestures and noises,[140] for interrupting excessively,[141] for incompetence,[142] for commenting in the press about a case he was still trying,[143] and—an outrageous case—for threatening a jury

---

[131]   One or two years in the case of QCs: *Judicial Appointments*, n. 1 above, p. 9.

[132]   Ibid.   [133]   Courts Act 1971, s. 21(5).

[134]   Judicial Pensions and Retirement Act 1993, s. 26 and Schedule 5.

[135]   A provincial stipendiary magistrate may merely be removed 'on the Lord Chancellor's recommendation': 1997 Act, s. 11(2), (3).   [136]   Ibid., s. 16(4).

[137]   Courts Act 1971, ss. 17(4) (Circuit judge), 21(6) (Recorder).

[138]   See Smith and Bailey, n. 8 above, p. 237; Alec Samuels, 'Judicial Misconduct in the Criminal Trial' [1982] *Criminal Law Review* 221.

[139]   *R.* v. *Edworthy* [1961] Criminal Law Review 325; *R.* v. *Langham* [1972] Criminal Law Review 457.

[140]   *R.* v. *Hircock* [1970] 1 Q.B. 67.

[141]   *Jones* v. *National Coal Board* [1957] 2 Q.B. 55: the Lord Chancellor subsequently saw the trial judge, Hallett J, who later resigned. In *Bunting* v. *Thorne Rural District Council, The Times,* 26 March 1957, after a witness had declined to take the oath because he was an atheist, Hallett J had added, 'And no morals either'.

[142]   *Taylor* v. *Taylor* [1970] 2 All E.R. 609.

[143]   *R.* v. *Earnshaw* [1990] Criminal Law Review 53.

that if it did not return a verdict within 10 minutes it would be locked up overnight.[144] Strong appellate criticism has produced the resignation of a High Court judge, Harman J: he resigned in 1998 after the Court of Appeal had heavily criticized his unconscionable delays in dealing with a case.[145] Sometimes control by an appeal court is not enough and the Lord Chancellor will have to invoke his own informal discipline (involving an interview with the judge, perhaps followed by administrative action) or a more formal procedure (involving a public rebuke). As an example of the former, in 1978 the Lord Chancellor discussed Judge McKinnon's conduct of a trial for incitement to racial hatred with him; some of the judge's remarks could have been taken as condoning the defendant's alleged behaviour. Judge McKinnon asked that no similar cases be listed before him, a request with which the Lord Chancellor complied. Similarly, in 1993 Judge Prosser asked not to try any further sexual crimes for a time after his award of a £500 compensation order in favour of a rape victim to pay for a holiday was criticized.[146] The Lord Chancellor might go further in a more serious case and suggest to a judge that he resign: that end might be desirable, but the method (pressure by one who, albeit head of the judiciary, is also a Minister) may not be. A formal and public rebuke is the Lord Chancellor's heaviest punishment short of dismissal (or, in the case of a senior judge, causing Parliament to remove the transgressor). The Lord Chancellor's reaction to Melford Stevenson J's remarks in 1978 has already been noted. In 1982 the Lord Chancellor 'repudiated' a judge's comment that a rape victim had been contributorily negligent by hitch-hiking alone.[147] A Recorder who castigated the decision of a large store to prosecute a 77-year-old woman for shoplifting received a public reprimand. And in 1987 Lord Havers LC informed the House of Lords that he had written to Judge Argyle 'severely reprimanding him for a number of unfortunate remarks' which he had made during an after-dinner speech: the judge had suggested that there were five million illegal immigrants in the United Kingdom, that judges should have the power to impose the death penalty for any crime carrying a maximum sentence of 15 years or more, and that the government's policy for fighting crime had resulted in criminals 'walking all over us'.[148] Then the Honorary Recorder of London was told by the Lord

[144] *R.* v. *McKenna* [1960] 1 Q.B. 411: the jury (not surprisingly) returned within six minutes with a verdict (of guilty) which was quashed on appeal. Stable J's conduct was the subject of an early-day motion which deplored his conduct in the case; it was signed by over 100 MPs.

[145] *Goose* v. *Wilson Sandford & Co.*, *The Times*, 13 February 1998.

[146] See *The Guardian*, 16 February 1993.   [147] *The Times*, 6 and 12 January 1982.

[148] *Observer*, 28 June 1987; 448 H.L. Deb. 1376 (written answers 21 July 1987).

Chancellor that his racially offensive remarks during an after-dinner speech in 1989 were 'totally unacceptable'.[149] In 1993 a District Judge was publicly rebuked by the Lord Chancellor for his second drink-driving offence, and was warned that any such further conviction would lead to his dismissal.[150] More serious, or repeated, such lapses might well call into question a judge's continuance in office.

A judge may leave office through resignation (perhaps as the result of private pressure), through retirement,[151] or through removal. It is to removal that attention will now be turned. The most limited (and so far unused) removal provision has been available since 1973:[152] if a judge of the Supreme Court is disabled by permanent infirmity from performing his duties and is for the time being incapacitated from resigning, the Lord Chancellor may, if satisfied by a medical certificate to that effect, declare his office to have been vacated.[153] Next, the Lord Chancellor has very wide powers to dismiss, and not to renew the part-time appointments of, the lower judiciary. If the Lord Chancellor is not satisfied with an acting stipendiary's performance, the latter may receive some guidance or, exceptionally, may be stood down. If he is dissatisfied by an Assistant Recorder's performance, he too will be stood down; if not satisfied by a Recorder's discharge of his office, or if the Recorder has broken his terms of appointment (perhaps by not being available to sit as agreed), his three-year term will not be renewed.[154] The monitoring methods used to help the Lord Chancellor to decide whether to renew or stand down, to promote or to dismiss, have become a little clearer since the publication of an article about Mr Manus Nunan.[155] According to that article Mr Nunan was made a Recorder in 1978.[156] His appointment was renewed in 1981 and was due for renewal in 1984, but after an interview at the Lord Chancellor's Department in September 1984 he was informed by letter that the Lord Chancellor had decided not to reappoint him in the light of further extensive consultations after his interview. The reason for the non-renewal

---

[149] See *The Independent*, 2 March 1989.   [150] See *The Independent*, 2 June 1993.
[151] Or early retirement: Judge Sir Harold Cassel retired on medical grounds aged 72 after substantial public and parliamentary criticism of his remarks on sentencing a man to probation for sexual assaults on his daughter: see 143 H.C. Deb. 18 (written answers 5 December 1988).
[152] It is now contained in the Supreme Court Act 1981, s. 11(8), (9).
[153] If the stricken judge is a head of division, two other heads must concur before the vacancy may be declared; if he is a Lord Justice, the Master of the Rolls must concur; if a High Court judge, a senior judge of his division must concur: ibid., s. 11(9).
[154] *Judicial Appointments*, n. 1 above, p. 9.
[155] See *The Guardian*, 13, 14 and 16 June and 2 December 1986.
[156] The career progression outlined earlier only began to be followed in mid-1981.

remains disputed. Lord Hailsham LC explained in a published letter that he had decided not to renew after consultations with a number of Circuit judges, senior members of the profession, and the Presiding Judges of the Circuit. This, he said, was the normal procedure when considering re-appointment of Recorders, for they are appointed for limited periods and Parliament plainly considered that, in order to safeguard the public interest, their continued suitability for judicial office should be regularly reviewed: accordingly, there is no right to or guarantee of renewal. Lord Hailsham stated that Mr Nunan had been informed at the interview in Sep-tember of the defects in his judicial performance, but that neither he nor his officials could disclose details of the comments and advice received because it was always given in strict confidence. The Lord Chancellor reconsidered his decision, but upheld it in November 1986. The Attorney-General con-firmed this procedure in answer to a parliamentary question, adding that the Lord Chancellor had never declined to renew except in accordance with advice received from the sources indicated by Lord Hailsham.[157]

Numerically far more lay magistrates have been removed from office for misbehaviour than any other class of judge. About a dozen JPs are removed by the Lord Chancellor[158] each year, most having been given the opportun-ity to resign first.[159] If an allegation of misbehaviour or incapacity is made it is referred to the local advisory committee for the area in which the magis-trate sits. If the committee concludes that the magistrate should be removed it so reports to the Lord Chancellor, but if the magistrate dissents from that conclusion there is a further investigation by the Secretary of Commissions,[160] who may interview him. A conviction for a minor motoring offence will lead to a reprimand. A conviction for an offence of driving with excess alcohol in the blood will result in removal if the period of disqualification is for 12 months or more. Behaviour which cannot be tolerated and which invites removal of a lay magistrate includes conviction

---

[157] 101 H.C. Deb. 167 (written answers 9 July 1986). He has also indicated that between January 1981 and January 1987 the appointments of 27 Recorders were not renewed, the per-formance of 'at least seven' of whom had not satisfied the Lord Chancellor: see 107 H.C. Deb. 431 (written answers 16 December 1986); 108 H.C. Deb. 574 (written answers 21 January 1987).

[158] The Chancellor of the Duchy of Lancaster has no role in removing lay magistrates.

[159] Lord Hailsham, reported in *The Times*, 1 October 1985. Sir Thomas Skryme, n. 2 above, p. 15, says that about one per cent of magistrates on the active list are removed annu-ally because they are unable to do their fair share of the work and another one per cent are removed because they have left their commission area. For figures from 1984–89, see 162 H.C. Deb. 450 (written answers 1 December 1989).

[160] He is a senior civil servant in the Lord Chancellor's Department.

of an offence involving moral turpitude,[161] refusal to apply a law with which he disagrees,[162] breaking his undertakings given as a condition precedent to appointment,[163] and bringing the law into disrepute.[164] So what misbehaviour might jeopardize any judge's continuance in office?[165] Plainly moral turpitude, in the senses of corruption, partiality, perverting the course of justice, or dishonesty, would disqualify. Judge Bruce Campbell was removed in 1983 after he had been convicted on two counts of smuggling whisky and cigarettes into England from the Channel Islands, for which he had been fined £2,000—the only instance since the passage of the Courts Act 1971 of the dismissal of a Circuit judge. Such a conviction is based on dishonesty and so must disqualify any judge of any rank from office. Refusal to apply the law, bringing the law into disrepute, gross neglect of duty, severe mental disability, and gross misconduct in private life could all be additional grounds, although questions of degree could clearly be involved. Thus, for instance, a Recorder offered to resign in 1988 after details of his homosexual life were published in a popular newspaper: his offer was accepted by the Lord Chancellor. Three years later, however, the Lord Chancellor (in a change of policy) announced that homosexuality was not a bar to becoming or remaining a judge, but that 'insofar as it comes into consideration, [his] sexual orientation and behaviour is a matter of the individual circumstances'.[166] Lord Dervaid had resigned in 1989 following an official investigation into alleged homosexual conduct. Judge Angus MacArthur resigned in 1997 before being sentenced to 28 days' imprisonment for his third drink-driving offence. Not all allegations of judicial misbehaviour will, therefore, be based on criminal convictions. For example, Sheriff Thomson was warned in 1974 that he should cease to advocate the holding of a referendum on home rule for

---

[161] Lord Hailsham, n. 159 above.

[162] Skyrme, n. 2 above, pp. 156–7; Lord Hailsham (1972) 28 *Magistrate* 132–4.

[163] These include undertakings to undergo specified training, to carry out a fair share of magisterial duties and to resign if the magistrate becomes unable to carry out his duties owing to change of residence, infirmity, or any other cause.

[164] An example of this concerned a magistrate who demonstrated outside her own courthouse in support of a defendant who was on trial inside. She was dismissed, and her application for judicial review of the Lord Chancellor's decision was rejected as Mann J thought that there was inadequate evidence to justify it: *The Times*, 25 September 1985; (1985) 135 *New Law Journal* 976; Lord Hailsham (1985) 41 *Magistrate* 179.

[165] For a detailed account see Shetreet, n. 48 above, chs 13 and 14. No formal procedures are in place to monitor the full-time judiciary: see 241 H.C. Deb. 389–90 (written answers 20 November 1992).

[166] See *The Independent*, 30 October 1991. His predecessor, Lord Hailsham, claimed that he had only appointed married judges to avoid the possibility of homosexual scandal.

Scotland, but in 1977 he published a pamphlet recommending just that. On the ground that such an action amounted to the judge participating in party political activity inconsistent with his judicial office, the responsible Minister, the Secretary of State for Scotland, put in train the removal procedure under the Sheriff Courts (Scotland) Act 1971, section 12. A sheriff can only be removed through a judicial and legislative mechanism which (as will be argued later) is much preferable to the English equivalent for removing Circuit judges and metropolitan stipendiaries. The Lord President of the Court of Session and the Lord Justice-Clerk carry out a joint inquiry to establish whether a sheriff is unfit to continue in office by reason of inability, neglect of duty, or misbehaviour; if they do so conclude it is then for the Secretary of State for Scotland to lay a removal order before Parliament. Sheriff Thomson was removed by this process.[167] After a similar investigation, Sheriff Ewan Stewart was removed form office in 1992: the Secretary of State for Scotland concluded that he had been rightly criticized for his judicial performance.[168] And in the same year the Deputy Bailiff of Jersey was removed from office by the Queen on the Home Secretary's advice because of his delay in coming to judgments.[169] On the other hand, not every criminal conviction will lead to dismissal. In 1969 a Lord Justice of Appeal, and in 1975 a High Court judge, were convicted of driving with excess alcohol in the blood. No government-supported steps[170] were taken to remove them; indeed, they were later promoted to the House of Lords and the Court of Appeal respectively. In a very bad case if the judge did not first resign the Lord Chancellor would dismiss him or (as the case may be) the government would probably begin the address procedure to secure his removal: if the government decided so to act it would take either a very perverse senior judge or one sure of his innocence not to resign then and there.

Now in theory a Lord of Appeal or a judge of the Supreme Court could be removed in a number of ways, for example, by impeachment, or proceedings in the Queen's Bench Division by writ of *scire facias* for the repeal of the Letters Patent by which he had been appointed, or proceedings in

[167] See J. A. G. Griffith, n. 49 above, p. 23.

[168] See 211 H.C. Deb. 612 (written answers 14 July 1992); *The Guardian*, 15 July 1992; *Stewart v. Secretary of State for Scotland*, *The Times*, 28 January 1998. This procedure will change when the Scotland Act 1998, s. 95 is in force. It will be for the Queen to remove a judge on the recommendation of the Scottish First Minister, who will be able so to recommend only if two-thirds of the Scottish Parliament votes in favour of removal.

[169] See *The Guardian*, 13 May 1992.

[170] Without government support no attempt to remove a senior judge could succeed.

the same Division to restrain the judge from acting in an office to which he was no longer, as a result of misbehaviour, entitled.[171] But the only method which would be essayed now would be the address procedure. Although an entirely proper interpretation of the two statutory provisions on the tenure of such judges is that they could be removed *either* by the Crown for misbehaviour *or* as the result of an address passed on any ground,[172] as a matter of political reality, it is suggested, no government would want to take sole responsibility for advising the Sovereign to dismiss a senior judge. Allegations of secret ulterior motives and the possibility (however misguided) of a dispute as to whether that method was lawful would ensure that the government would only act with the authority of Parliament. The address procedure, in summary, probably requires[173] that the process begin in the Commons by a motion for an address calling for an inquiry into the judge's conduct; a select committee might then be authorized to investigate, and a precise charge or charges would have to be formulated against the judge; the committee would hear witnesses and the accused; the committee would report to the House. A similar procedure would be followed in the House of Lords,[174] after which the motion for an address would be voted on. Despite some absence of judicial authority, it is submitted that any judge of any rank is entitled to natural justice before he may be lawfully removed or dismissed from his office. In the case of those judges who may only be removed for a cause specified in statute, that protection stems from *Ridge* v. *Baldwin*:[175] there is a duty to act fairly in relation to them before they may be dismissed. In the case of those judges who hold office at pleasure, the trend of the natural justice cases tends to afford them similar protection,[176] which is as it should be because dismissal from any judicial office is a grave matter and so should be characterized by scrupulous fairness. Any lay magistrate who suffers the indignity of removal from office will endure damage to his general reputation.[177] Any other lower judge

---

[171] See S. A. de Smith and R. Brazier, *Constitutional and Administrative Law* (8th edn., 1998), p. 381.

[172] See Sir Kenneth Roberts-Wray, *Commonwealth and Colonial Law* (1996), pp. 486–90.

[173] See Shetreet, n. 48 above, pp. 129–51. See also Margaret Brazier, 'Judicial Immunity and the Independence of the Judiciary' [1976] *Public Law* 397 at 400–4.

[174] A joint select committee, it is submitted, would be a more efficient process and fairer on all parties.

[175] [1964] A.C. 40.

[176] For example, in cases like *Malloch* v. *Aberdeen Corporation* [1971] 1 W.L.R. 1578.

[177] The Lord Chancellor's Department believes that the procedure followed when lay magistrates are dismissed fully meets the requirements of natural justice: see letter from the Secretary of Commissions at (1986) 136 *New Law Journal* 1045.

who is dismissed will suffer damage to his professional reputation; he will lose the opportunity to achieve promotion to a permanent and full-time judgeship; he will lose income—and if he is able to return to full-time practice, the fact of his dismissal could damage that practice. As a matter of procedure, the duty to act fairly in relation to a judge threatened with removal requires that he have made clear the detailed charges against him, the source of complaint upon which they are formulated, enough time to prepare his defence, and an opportunity to be heard in his defence.[178] It is further submitted that exactly the same considerations apply to the non-renewal of the appointments of part-time judges. Non-renewal cannot really be distinguished from removal, for the judges ceases to hold office, his professional reputation is damaged, and so on.

The reluctance of any government to remove any senior judge other than by the long-winded address procedure; the refusal of successive governments to initiate that procedure, even when a judge has been convicted of an offence as serious as drunken driving; the government's ability to control Commons' business and thereby to prevent discussion of any early-day motion critical of the judiciary; and the government's power to vote down any Opposition motion debated in Opposition time, taken together all mean that the tenure of office of the senior judiciary is extremely secure. Conversely, the lower judiciary, even allowing for the requirements of natural justice, is at present subject to removal (or non-renewal) by a Minister, with no need, for example, for any inquiry by his peers or by Parliament.

Reform

Given the career progression in the judiciary, it is important that the system for appointing junior judges be changed. That rank is the backbone of the judicial system, having far more members than the 150 or so senior judiciary. Four main objections to the existing procedure can be adumbrated. First, however broad and deep may be the informal soundings about potential junior judges, the concentration of the power of appointment in the hands of one person, without the benefit of a structured system of advice, is objectionable. The patronage power of successive Lord

---

[178] In *Ex parte Ramshay* (1852) 18 Q.B. 173 a county court judge, dismissible for cause, was held to have the rights to notice of the charge against him and to the opportunity to be heard in his defence.

Chancellors, to put it bluntly, looks bad. Secondly, the increasing size of both branches of the legal profession means that the civil servants in the Lord Chancellor's Department cannot have adequate knowledge of all potential candidates for junior judicial office or of the particular situation in each of the six Circuit areas. Despite the soundings taken from the Department, the appointments system is too centralized. Thirdly, it has been suggested that lawyers who are not appointed to judgeships will never know the reason. It is possible to detect a continuing preference for non-disclosure in such an ancient and traditional department of state as the Lord Chancellor's Department. Lastly, it is notorious that the present system does not produce many black or women judges. Relatively few of the professional judges are black or of Asian origin, and few are women.[179] There may, of course, be reasons why this is not entirely the fault of the appointments system: for example, if there is prejudice in the professions against blacks, fewer will be able to enter or stay in them and the pool of potential candidates will be smaller. But, again, a new system of advising on appointments could bring greater enthusiasm for seeking out and recommending adequately qualified people from groups which are at present absurdly under-represented on the bench. One scarcely radical change would be to establish an advisory Circuit Judicial Committee in each of the six Circuits to advise the Lord Chancellor on the appointment of acting stipendiary and stipendiary magistrates, Assistant Recorders, Recorders, and Circuit judges. The composition of each might include the Presiding Judges, a Circuit judge or judges, the Circuit Administrator, the Leader of the Circuit, a local Law Society representative, and perhaps one representative of the junior Bar and of junior solicitors, together with a civil servant from the Lord Chancellor's Department. All candidates for judgeships could be instructed to apply for consideration. Candidates for office would be interviewed by the Committee and so far as possible they would be given reasons for any adverse recommendation. Such a system would have the advantage that advice to the Lord Chancellor would be formalized and identified; decisions to appoint would be influenced by a number of people representative of legitimate interests, acting locally, and the Lord Chancellor would retain the final power to appoint and would remain responsible for it.

All judges must be able to carry out their duties free from the threat of improper influence from Ministers and Parliament. At the same time there must be a system which, consistently with fairness, can efficiently remove

---

[179] See 246 H.C. Deb. 483–4 (written answers 12 July 1994).

from office any judge whose behaviour has disqualified him from holding it. The tenure of the lower judiciary and the Lord Chancellor's powers to remove and not to renew members of it cannot be said to further the first of these propositions. The Lord Chancellor's power to remove[180] a lower judge is, subject to his duty to act fairly, virtually unlimited and is a disturbing accretion of power in the hands of a Minister in relation to the judiciary. Even Lord Hailsham LC acknowledged that this was undesirable and gave his approval in principle for a judicial complaints board.[181] Now it is true that, in the exercise of this power, the Lord Chancellor is responsible to Parliament. This has, however, proved to be an empty phrase. Since the enactment of the Courts Act 1971 no member of the House of Lords has chosen to test that responsibility. There has been no debate in the House of Lords about judicial appointments or removals, even though there has been ample opportunity during, for example, the passage of relevant legislation. No questions were tabled to the Lord Chancellor about the removal of Judge Campbell in 1983 or about the Lord Chancellor's long-running difficulties over Judge Pickles. There is oversight now of the Lord Chancellor's Department and the Law Officer's Department by the Home Affairs Select Committee; and there is now a Parliamentary Secretary, Lord Chancellor's Department, in the House of Commons. Both developments are welcome. But what is really needed is a new statutory procedure to investigate complaints which would be fair to all parties. This could be achieved, I suggest, by using the proposed Circuit Judicial Committees. The Lord Chancellor could refer any complaint about a judge to the Committee for his area, which could cause it to be investigated. The judge would, of course, be entitled to a hearing. The Committee would in due course make a recommendation to the Lord Chancellor. If the recommendation were that a Circuit judge or stipendiary magistrate should be removed from office, the essence of the much preferable Scottish system could be incorporated so that the Lord Chancellor would lay an order before Parliament to effect the removal. Such a procedure would ensure that a due mechanism of checks and balances between the judiciary (the Circuit Judicial Committee), the executive (the Lord Chancellor), and the legislature should ensure that any removal was demonstrably right. It is also suggested that the Circuit Judicial Committees should make recommendations to the Lord Chancellor on the renewal of Assistant Recorderships and

---

[180]   And not to renew temporary appointments.

[181]   His remarks were made on the publication of *Judicial Appointments*, n. 1 above: see *The Times*, *The Guardian*, 30 May 1986.

Recorderships, for again it is within his or her Circuit that a part-time judge is known best.

The tenure of judges of the Supreme Court and of Lords of Appeal in Ordinary is rightly very secure. It would, perhaps, be desirable for any serious complaint about their conduct to be considered formally by a group of their peers. If such a judge were condemned by his peers he would be much more likely to attach considerable weight to that—and certainly more than to most of the early-day motions which have been laid in the past—so that resignation would probably follow. The address procedure, preferably streamlined, could remain for disputed cases.

In Opposition the Labour Party committed itself to establishing a Judicial Appointments and Training Commission (a policy also favoured by the Liberal Democrats). No such proposal appeared, however, in the party's 1997 election manifesto. The Home Affairs Select Committee had reported against such an idea, and generally in favour of the existing judicial appointments system—but by a majority vote of Conservative MPs on the committee.[182] The new Labour Lord Chancellor began consultations about a new appointments commission, but he suspended work on it in view of the other heavy demands on his department.

A larger question still remains behind the present constitutional position of the judiciary, namely whether there ought to be a Ministry of Justice—or in more modern parlance a Department of Justice, or a Department of Law. At the lowest there is a sensible case in terms of efficiency and greater parliamentary accountability for a reallocation of ministerial responsibility between the Home Office and the Lord Chancellor's Department.[183] If, further, it is considered that the Lord Chancellor's three roles are not efficiently discharged by one person (or that, even after so long, such a breach of the doctrine of the separation of powers is unacceptable), then there is no reason why he should continue to sit as Speaker of the House of Lords or as a judge. If those two latter tasks were shed it would be even clearer that the Lord Chancellor is, after all, as much a Minister as any other member of the Cabinet. A more fundamental question is whether a Minister should have effective responsibility for the appointment of the entire judiciary. If that question were answered negatively, a Judicial Service Commission largely made up of senior judges could assume that duty, and the Circuit Judicial Committees already described could report directly to it. A new

---

[182] See 3rd Report from the Home Affairs Committee, *Judicial Appointments Procedures*, H.C. 52 (1995–6).

[183] A small reorganization in 1991 transferred responsibility for magistrates' courts to the Lord Chancellor's Department from the Home Office.

Department of Law, taking most of the functions of the Lord Chancellor's Department (but not those of appointing, promoting, and removing judges), all the administration of justice functions from the Home Office, and practically all responsibility for the state of the law and law reform, might be the logical conclusion of such a reform process.[184] And—who knows?—perhaps the Secretary of State might not even be a lawyer.

---

[184] For a fuller consideration of some of these matters, see R. Brazier, 'Government and the Law: Ministerial Responsibility for Legal Affairs' [1989] *Public Law* 64, and *Constitutional Reform* 2nd edn., (1998), ch. 9; G. Drewry, 'The Debate About a Ministry of Justice' [1987] *Public Law* 502; JUSTICE, *The Judiciary in England and Wales* (1992). The then Prime Minister was asked in the House of Commons whether he would abolish the office of Lord Chancellor, and establish a Department of Law: he replied 'No': see 201 H.C. Deb. 232 (written answers 20 December 1991).

Appendix A

SENIOR MINISTERS SINCE 1945

Date	Prime Minister	Deputy	Chancellor of the Exchequer
May–July 1945	Winston Churchill	A. Eden	Sir J. Anderson
July 1945–October 1951	Clement Attlee	H. Morrison (Lord President)	H. Dalton Sir S. Cripps H. Gaitskell
October 1951–April 1955	Winston Churchill	A. Eden	R. A. Butler
April 1955–January 1957	Sir A. Eden	R. A. Butler	R. A. Butler H. Macmillan
January 1957–October 1963	H. Macmillan	R. A. Butler	P. Thorneycroft D. Heathcoat-Amory S. Lloyd R. Maudling
October 1963–October 1964	Sir A. Douglas-Home	R. A. Butler	R. Maudling
October 1964–June 1970	H. Wilson	G. Brown M. Stewart	J. Callaghan R. Jenkins
June 1970–March 1974	E. Heath	R. Maudling (none after 1972)	I. Macleod A. Barber
March 1974–April 1976	H. Wilson	E. Short (Lord President)	D. Healey
April 1976–May 1979	J. Callaghan	M. Foot (Lord President)	D. Healey
May 1979–November 1990	M. Thatcher	W. (late Lord) Whitelaw Sir G. Howe (Lord President)	Sir G. Howe N. Lawson J. Major
November 1990–May 1997	J. Major	(None until 1995) M. Heseltine	N. Lamont K. Clarke
May 1997–	T. Blair	J. Prescott	G. Brown

Foreign Secretary	Home Secretary	Reason for resignation of PM or of government
A. Eden	Sir D. Somervell	Loss of 1945 election
E. Bevin H. Morrison	C. Ede	Loss of 1951 election
A. Eden	Sir D. Maxwell-Fyfe G. Lloyd-George	Retirement of Churchill
H. Macmillan	G. Lloyd-George	Resignation of Eden
S. Lloyd Earl of Home	R. A. Butler H. Brooke	Resignation of Macmillan
R. A. Butler	H. Brooke	Loss of 1964 election
P. Gordon Walker M. Stewart G. Brown M. Stewart	Sir F. Soskice R. Jenkins J. Callaghan	Loss of 1970 election
Sir A. Douglas-Home	R. Maudling R. Carr	Loss of February 1974 election
J. Callaghan	R. Jenkins	Retirement of Wilson
A. Crosland D. Owen	R. Jenkins M. Rees	Loss of 1979 election
Lord Carrington F. Pym Sir G. Howe J. Major D. Hurd	W. Whitelaw L. Brittan D. Hurd D. Waddington	Loss of 1990 Leadership ballot
D. Hurd M. Rifkind	K. Baker K. Clarke M. Howard	Loss of 1997 election
R. Cook	J. Straw	

Appendix B

THE PARTY LEADERSHIP
ELECTION RULES

The Conservative Party

Rules for the Election of the Leader

1   The Leader shall be elected by the Party Members and Scottish Party Members.
2   A Party Member or Scottish Party Member shall not be entitled to vote in a Leadership election unless the member has been a Party Member or a Scottish Party Member for at least three months immediately prior to the initiation of an election for Leader.
3   Upon the initiation of an election for the Leader, it shall be the duty of the 1922 Committee to present to the Party, as soon as reasonably practicable, a choice of Candidate for election as Leader.
4   For the avoidance of doubt, the rules for deciding the procedure by which the 1922 Committee selects Candidates for submission for election shall be as determined by the Executive Committee of the 1922 Committee after consultation with the Board.
5   Subject to the provisions of this Constitution, the rules for the conduct of the ballot or ballots of Party Members and Scottish Party Members shall be agreed by the Board and the Executive Committee of the 1922 Committee.
6   The Chairman of the 1922 Committee, acting on behalf of the Party, shall act as Chief Returning Officer for all stages of the election.
7   The election shall take place by postal ballot, and it shall be a ballot of Party Members and Scottish Party Members on the basis of one member, one vote.
8   A Candidate with more than 50% of votes cast in his favour shall be declared Leader of the Party provided that if there is only one Candidate, he shall be declared Leader of the Party.

The Labour Party

Constitution, clause VII

(1) There shall be a leader and a deputy leader of the party who shall be *ex-officio* leader and deputy leader of the Parliamentary Labour Party.

(2) The leader and deputy leader of the party shall be elected or re-elected from amongst the Commons members of the Parliamentary Labour Party in accordance with conference procedural rule 5 [see below], at a party conference convened in accordance with clause VI of these rules. In respect to the election of the leader and deputy leader, the standing orders of the Parliamentary Labour Party shall always automatically be brought into line with these rules.

Rule 5—Election of leader and deputy leader

5.1 The leader and deputy leader shall be elected separately in accordance with rule 5.3 below, unless 5.5 applies.

5.2 Nomination:

(a) In the case of a vacancy for leader or deputy leader, each nomination must be supported by 12.5 per cent of the commons members of the PLP. Nominations not attaining this threshold shall be null and void.

(b) Where there is no vacancy, nominations shall be sought each year prior to the annual session of party conference. In this case any nomination must be supported by 20 per cent of the Commons members of the PLP. Nominations not attaining this threshold shall be null and void.

(c) Affiliated organisations, constituency parties and Labour Members of the European Parliament may also nominate for each of the offices of leader and deputy leader. All nominees must be Commons members of the PLP.

(d) Nominees shall inform the general secretary of the acceptance or otherwise of their nomination at least two clear weeks before the commencement of the procedures for voting laid out in 5.3. Unless consent to nomination is received, nominations shall be rendered null and void.

(e) Valid nominations shall be printed in the final agenda for Conference, together with the names of the nominating organisations and Commons members of the PLP supporting the nominations. In the case of a vacancy under 5.5 this information shall be included with the documentation circulated with any ballot.

(f) Nominees who do not attend the relevant party conference shall be deemed to have withdrawn their nominations, unless they send to the secretary—on or before the day on which the conference opens—an explanation in writing of their absence satisfactory to the CAC.

5.3 Voting:

(a) Voting in the election of leader and deputy leader shall take place so that the results are declared at an annual session of party conference; except in the case of a vacancy occurring under 5.5 of this rule when the timetable for the ballot shall be as determined by the NEC.

(b) Voting shall take place consecutively in three sections as follows:
Section 1 shall consist of Commons members of the PLP and members of the European PLP. Each such member shall be entitled to one vote in each ballot held under this section of the rules.
Section 2 shall consist of a vote of all eligible individual members of the party on the basis of one member one vote. This ballot shall take place on a national basis and shall be counted and recorded as an aggregate vote broken down by constituency party. Eligible members shall be those currently on the national membership list who are endorsed and have not lapsed from membership.
Section 3 shall consist of those members of affiliated organisations who have indicated their support for the Labour Party and that they are not members or supporters of any other party or otherwise ineligible to be members of the Labour Party. Voting shall take place under the procedures of each affiliated organisation, but on a one person one vote basis recorded by affiliated organisations and aggregated for a national total. The ballot paper shall provide for the declaration of support and eligibility required under this rule if no prior declaration has been made.

(c) The votes of each nominee in each section shall be calculated as a percentage of the total votes cast in that section and shall then be apportioned as follows:
Section 1 (Members of the Commons and European PLPs)—one third
Section 2 (Individual members of the Labour Party)—one third.
Section 3 (Members of affiliated organisations)—one third.

(d) The votes apportioned as provided in 5.3(c) above, shall be totalled and the candidate receiving more than half of the votes so apportioned shall be declared elected. If no candidate reaches this total on the first ballot, further ballots shall be held on an elimination basis. The redistribution of votes shall be according to preferences indicated on the ballot paper.

(e) The votes cast for each nominee in each section shall be recorded and published in a form to be determined by the NEC as soon as possible following any election.

5.4 Timing of an election:

(a) When the PLP is in opposition in the House of Commons, the election of the leader and deputy leader shall take place at each annual session of party conference.

(b) When the PLP is in government and the leader and/or deputy leader are prime minister and/or in Cabinet, an election shall proceed only if requested by a majority of party conference on a card vote.

(c) In any other circumstances an election shall only be held when a vacancy occurs, subject to 5.5 below.

5.5 Procedure in a vacancy:

(a) When the party is in government and the party leader is prime minister and the party leader, for whatever reason, becomes permanently unavailable, the Cabinet shall, in consultation with the NEC, appoint one of its members to serve as party leader until a ballot under these rules can be carried out.

(b) When the party is in government and the deputy leader becomes party leader under (a) of this rule, the Cabinet may, in consultation with the NEC, appoint one of its members to serve as deputy leader until the next party conference. The Cabinet may alternatively, in consultation with the NEC, leave the post vacant until the next party conference.

(c) When the party is in government and the deputy leader, for whatever reason, becomes permanently unavailable, the Cabinet may, in consultation with the NEC, appoint one of its members to serve as deputy leader until the next party conference. The Cabinet may alternatively, in consultation with the NEC, leave the post vacant until the next party conference.

(d) When the party is in opposition and the party leader, for whatever reason, becomes permanently unavailable, the deputy leader shall automatically become party leader on a pro-tem basis. The NEC shall decide whether to hold an immediate ballot as provided under 5.3 above or to elect a new leader at the next annual session of party conference.

(e) When the party is in opposition and the leader and deputy leader, for whatever reason, both become permanently unavailable, the NEC shall order a postal ballot as provided under 5.3 above. In consultation with the Parliamentary Committee (Shadow Cabinet) they may choose to appoint a member of the Parliamentary Committee to serve as party leader until the outcome of that ballot.

The Liberal Democrats

Constitution, articles 8 and 10

8.4 The Federal Executive shall have power, after appropriate consultations and subject to ratification by the Federal Conference, to make and from time to time vary rules as to membership, elections and such other matters as it may consider necessary or desirable to give effect to or supplement the provisions of this Constitution. Any election rules must provide for elections to be by STV and secret ballot.

10.1 The Leader of the Party shall be elected by the members of the Party in accordance with election rules made pursuant to Article 8.4.
10.2 An election for the Leader shall be called upon:

(a)   the Leader asking for an election;
(b)   the death or incapacity of the Leader;
(c)   the Leader ceasing to be a Member of the House of Commons (other than a temporary cessation by reason of a dissolution);
(d)   the receipt by the President of the resignation of the Leader or of a declaration of intent to resign upon the election of a new Leader;
(e)   a vote of no confidence in the Leader being passed by a majority of all Members of the Parliamentary Party in the House of Commons;
(f)   the receipt by the President of a requisition submitted by at least 75 Local Parties (including for this purpose the specified associated organisation or organisations representing youth and/or students) following the decision of a quorate general meeting; or
(g)   the first anniversary of the preceding general election being reached without an election being called under any of paragraphs (a) through (f), provided that:
   (i)   the Federal Executive may postpone such an election for no more than one year by a two-thirds majority of those present and voting; and

(ii) this paragraph (g) shall not apply if the Leader is a member of the Government.

10.3 Upon election, the Leader shall hold office until death, incapacity or resignation or the completion of an election called under this Article.

10.4 Upon the calling of an election, the Federal Executive shall publish a timetable for nominations, withdrawals, despatch, and receipt of ballot papers and the holding of ballots and shall appoint a disinterested person or body to receive and count the ballot papers.

10.5 Nominations must be of a Member of the Parliamentary Party in the House of Commons, who must be proposed and seconded by other such Members and supported by 200 members in aggregate in not less than 20 Local Parties (including, for this purpose, the Specified Associated organisations representing youth and students as provided by Article 13.8) and must indicate acceptance of nomination.

Appendix C

THE FORMAL RESIGNATION AND APPOINTMENT OF MINISTERS: A MEMORANDUM BY THE CLERK OF THE PRIVY COUNCIL

Privy Council Office
Whitehall, London SW1A 2AT
10 September 1987

1. It is perhaps simplest to begin with the relinquishment of appointments. There is very little in the way of formalities connected with the giving up of Ministerial posts. Broadly speaking, the relinquishment is effected by a resignation, express or implied. The resignation of a Prime Minister—other than in his personal capacity—normally carries with it the resignation of the whole of his administration. A reshuffle may be prompted by a Ministerial resignation or resignations. When the initiative comes from the Prime Minister it is normally formalized by subsequent letters of resignation from those leaving office. In the case of a Minister leaving one office for another his resignation of the former is implicit. In the case of appointments for which the mechanics include Letters Patent or formal warrants the normal practice is for these instruments to include an express revocation of the previous appointment. The Lord Chancellor and the Chancellor of the Duchy of Lancaster have the privilege of claiming a private audience with The Queen for the purpose of delivering up their seals. Formerly it was the practice for other Ministers who had seals to deliver up to do so at a private audience with the Sovereign. More recently, that practice has been discontinued. The Royal Household normally arrange individual private audiences with The Queen for outgoing Ministers. These audiences, however, are entirely a matter of courtesy and form no part of the machinery of relinquishing office. The seals of outgoing Ministers, other than the Great Seal and that of the Duchy of Lancaster, are now

simply collected by this office in preparation for their delivery to their new holders.

2. The position with regard to appointments is much more complicated. Although taking the oath of office is properly a consequence of an appointment and not the appointment itself, it is helpful to deal first with the Promissory Oaths Act 1868. This prescribes, in section 3, the terms of the oath of office and section 5 requires that oath shall be tendered to and taken by each of the officers named in the first part of the Schedule of the Act as soon as may be after his acceptance of office. The Schedule directs that the oath to be taken by officers listed in the first part is to be tendered by the Clerk of the Council and taken in the presence of Her Majesty in Council or otherwise as Her Majesty shall direct. The power to direct otherwise has been exercised twice. First by the Order in Council, directing the manner in which the oath of allegiance and the official oath as to England shall be tendered and taken by certain officers, dated 9 August 1872; secondly by the Promissory Oaths Order S.I. 1939/916. The 1872 Order is now applicable only in relation to the Chancellor of the Duchy of Lancaster. For all other purposes the 1939 Order is now effective, its effect being to require the oath of office to be taken by members of the Cabinet before The Queen in Council and by those Ministers included in Part I of the 1868 Act Schedule but not in the Cabinet before another senior Minister, usually the Lord President. To take the oath in Council, the person concerned must be a member of the Council. Accordingly, on becoming a member of the Cabinet a Minister, if he is not one already, is made a Privy Counsellor. It would, in any case, be the normal practice for all members of the Cabinet to be made Privy Counsellors. The provisions of the 1868 Act make this invariable.

3. It is for this reason that, in rehearsing the provisions of section 5 of the 1868 Act above, I omitted any reference to the oath of allegiance. This oath is one of the two oaths taken when a person is sworn into the Council. The swearing in of new Counsellors is the first item of business at any Council. A person who becomes a Cabinet Minister who was not previously a Privy Counsellor accordingly takes the oath of allegiance separately from and before taking the oath of office. The oath of allegiance, however, is taken only once. On appointment to a Cabinet post, therefore, unless the appointee is not already a Privy Counsellor, it will be unnecessary for him to take the oath of allegiance in addition to the appropriate oath of office. It is unusual, except on a change of Government, for those appointed to Cabinet posts not to be already members of the Council.

4. I have referred throughout above to swearing and the taking of oaths. There is, of course, provision for affirmation to be made by non-believers.

5. Before leaving the taking of oaths, I should mention kissing hands. This is a courtesy which follows the oath when that is taken before The Queen in Council. It is a practice which is invariably observed. It is not, however, a formality on which the appointment in any way depends.

6. Returning now to the actual mechanics of appointments, I have attached a summary at the end of this memorandum which sets out the details in tabular form.

7. The Prime Minister accepts office by attending The Queen in private audience. The appointment—and as First Lord of the Treasury—takes effect from that moment. At the audience the new Prime Minister kisses hands. There are no other formalities.

8. As regards other appointments, the general rule is that these take effect, in the absence of any other factor to the contrary, from the moment of The Queen's approval of the Prime Minister's list or lists of recommendations. Thus, although the Minister of Agriculture, Fisheries and Food, when in the Cabinet, is required to take the oath of office in Council, his appointment dates from the moment The Queen approves it and not from the Council at which he takes the oath and kisses hands. The same—that is that appointment dates from The Queen's approval—applies with nearly all other middle and junior rank Ministers.

9. The general rule is, however, displaced in various ways. The Lord President is so declared by The Queen in Council and his appointment is effected by, and from the moment of, that declaration. In the case of all offices which have seals of office the appointment is effected by the delivery of those seals by the Sovereign to the holder of the office. This takes place, with one exception, in the Council at which the oath of office is taken and the appointee kisses hands. The exception is the Chancellor of the Duchy of Lancaster who, because of the personal character of the appointment, receives the seals in private audience, usually immediately after the Council at which the other appointments are made, and takes the oath and kisses hands in that audience.

10. It should be noted that, whilst the Prime Minister does not take an oath of office as such, he or she is required to take the oath of office in his or her capacity as First Lord of the Treasury. This oath is taken with the others in Council. There is, however, no seal associated with this office. As indicated above, therefore, the appointment as First Lord takes effect at the same moment as the appointment as Prime Minister.

11. The mechanics for some appointments include formal documents. Section 4 of the Paymaster General Act 1835 prescribes a warrant under the Royal Sign Manual as the method of appointment for this office. It is, accordingly, the warrant which is effective in making this appointment which dates from the date of the warrant and not from The Queen's approval of the Prime Minister's recommendation for the appointment.

12. In a number of other appointments Letters Patent are included as part of the machinery. This is the case with both the Lord Privy Seal and the Chancellor of the Exchequer. In these cases, however, the appointment dates from the delivery of the seal and not from that of the Letters Patent. It should also be noted that the Letters Patent involved in connection with the appointment of the Chancellor of the Exchequer are distinct from the Letters Patent appointing the Commissioners of the Treasury, of which the Chancellor is one, referred to in the following paragraph.

13. The position with the Commissioners of the Treasury is different again. Their appointment is by Letters Patent and is regulated by section 2 of the Consolidated Fund Act 1816. The appointments as Commissioners of the Treasury take effect from the date of these Letters Patent. Thus, the appointment of the Prime Minister as First Lord of the Treasury and of the Chancellor of the Exchequer will normally take effect before they are formally appointed Commissioners of the Treasury. The Treasury Commission includes, of course, all the junior Treasury offices. In practice, it is not unusual for successive commissions to be issued so that the principal appointments are not held up by any delay in completing the list of junior appointments.

14. The offices of Attorney-General and Solicitor-General, which are not included in the Schedule of the 1868 Act, follow the general rule for Ministerial appointments. These two appointments are, however, confirmed by Letters Patent like the offices of Lord Privy Seal and Chancellor of the Exchequer.

15. There remain a number of 'phantom' appointments. Certain offices need to remain in being, usually because, for example, property is statutorily vested in the holder of that office. They are not held separately but are held by the occupant of another substantive office. Because of changes in allocation of Ministerial responsibilities, the identity of these offices varies from time to time and, as a result, it is impossible to give any exhaustive account of such appointments. Broadly, formalities in relation to these 'phantom' appointments are kept to a minimum. As regards appointment

proper, the Presidency of the Board of Trade is the only one calling for particular mention. This office is held in conjunction with the Secretary-ship of Trade and Industry (or of Trade when these two responsibilities are separately held). The Board of Trade is still, technically, a Committee of the Privy Council and its President is appointed by an Order in Council approved at the same time as the holder of the substantive office receives the seal and takes the oath of office. Some of these 'phantom' offices are included in the First Schedule, as amended, of the Promissory Oaths Act. This means that the holder of the substantive office with which they are held in conjunction, must also take the oath in respect of the 'phantom' office in accordance with the requirements of the Act and the Orders made under it.

16. The political appointments in the Royal Household follow the same rules as above. That is to say, they are all middle or junior Ministerial appointments and take effect when The Queen approves the Prime Minister's recommendations. The non-political appointments to the Royal Household proper are entirely a matter for The Queen. One or two of these appointments, however, are still included in the first part of the Schedule of the 1868 Act, e.g. the Lord Chamberlain, and on his appoint-ment he takes the oath of office before the Lord President.

Ministerial appointments

Office	Procedure	Documents (if any)
Prime Minister	Received in private Audience and kisses hands.	
First Lord of the Treasury	Takes oath of office, in Council, as First Lord of the Treasury and kisses hands.	Treasury Commission—as member of Treasury Board—by Letters Patent
Lord President	Declared in Council, and thereupon takes oath of office and kisses hands.	
Lord Chancellor	Takes oath of office in Council, kisses hands and receives the Great Seal.	
Lord Privy Seal	Takes oath of office in Council, kisses hands and receives the Privy Seal.	Letters Patent

Secretaries of State	Take oath of office in Council, kiss hands and receive Seals.	
Chancellor of the Exchequer	Takes oath of office in Council, kisses hands and receives Seal of Office.	Letters Patent Treasury Commission—as member of the Treasury Board—by Letters Patent (distinct from above).
Chancellor of the Duchy of Lancaster	Takes oath of office *in private Audience* (usually after the Council), kisses hands and receives the Seal of Office.	Warrant under the Sign Manual.
Minister of Agriculture/ Paymaster General	If in Cabinet, takes oath of office in Council and kisses hands, otherwise sworn before Lord Chancellor or a Secretary of State.	Warrant under the Sign Manual.
Law Officers		Letters Patent.
Other Treasury Ministers and Lords of the Treasury		Treasury Commission—as members of the Treasury Board— by Letters Patent.
'Phantom' Offices		
President of the Board of Trade	Appointee to substantive office, with which this is held, takes oath in respect of both offices.	Order in Council approved at time oath of office is taken.
Others	Oath of office is taken by holder of substantive office if required by Promissory Oaths Act and in accordance with procedure stipulated.	

No special procedure or documentation applies in the case of remaining Ministers, whose appointments take effect from the moment The Sovereign approves the relevant submission from the Prime Minister.

INDEX

abdication 204
Agriculture/Agriculture, Fisheries and
    Food, Ministry of 139, 143, 145, 311,
    314
Aircraft Production, Ministry of 69, 135
Aird, John Black 49
Anderson, Sir John 301
Andrew, Prince 204, 236, 240
appeasement 185
Armstrong, Sir Robert 107
Armstrong, Sir William 118
Ashdown, Paddy 167
Asquith, Herbert
    coalition and 54, 67
    in power 21, 34, 56, 164, 216
        and Ministers and Departments 56,
            67, 83, 108
        and monarch 184–5, 191
    resignation 52, 103
assent to legislation, Monarch's power to
    refuse 193–4
Assistant Recorders 267, 289, 298–9
Atkins, Humphrey 152
Attlee, Clement: in power 56, 69, 91, 178,
    185–6, 240, 301
    and Ministers and Departments 56, 67,
        70, 79–80, 83, 87, 117, 144
    as opposition leader 164, 174–5
Attorney-General 68, 109–10, 125, 134–5,
    260, 273, 279, 292
Australia 47
Avonside, Lord 282

back-bench
    MPs 176, 206–7, 211, 221–2, 226
    peers 249, 261
Bagehot, Walter 82
Baker, Kenneth 302
Baldwin, Stanley 67, 114, 161
    in power 21, 33, 34, 56, 96, 164
        judges and 270, 277, 282
        and Ministers and Departments 56, 67,
            109, 155–6

and monarch 183, 186
    as opposition leader 165
    resignation 19, 34–5
Balfour, Arthur 55, 165
Barber, Anthony 301
BBC 93, 210, 284
Beatrice, Princess 204
Beaverbrook, Lord 69, 135
Beckett, Margaret 25
Bell, Martin 215
Belstead, Lord 66
Benn, Tony 19, 146, 242
Bevin, Ernest 69, 302
Birkenhead, Lord 285
Blair, Tony 14, 25, 28, 119, 301
    Cabinet, and 178
    ministers, and 71, 136, 142
    opposition, and 167
    in power 61
    Shadow Cabinet 65
    style 74
Blake, Lord 212
Board of Trade 117, 145, 157, 313, 314
Bogdanor, Vernon 40
Bonar Law, Andrew 33, 67, 99, 105, 164
    resignation 14, 33, 183
Bowe, Colette 153
Boyle, Sir Edward 86
Brittain, Leon 77, 149, 153, 302
Brooke, Henry 155, 302
Brown, George 77, 79, 81, 87, 301
Brown, Gordon 71, 301
budget 111–12
Butler, David 39–40
Butler, R. A. 80, 82, 180, 301
by-elections 58, 213

Cabinet 105–31, 172, 175, 177–82
    business 105–13
    committees 113–24, 131
    meetings 113–24, 124–31
    members of see Ministers
    Office 62, 97, 106–7, 126, 133

Cabinet (*cont.*):
  secrecy 121, 124–30
  Secretary to 62, 97, 106–7, 115, 122,
    125, 127, 130, 231
Callaghan, James 30, 70, 148
  fall of government 44
  in power 15, 53, 66, 74, 76, 92, 98, 100,
    103, 186, 241, 301
  and Ministers and Departments 66, 107,
    116, 122, 141, 146, 148
Campbell, Alistair 92
Campbell, Bruce, Judge 293, 298
Campbell-Bannerman, Sir Henry 14
Canada 47, 49–50, 69, 222
caretaker government 44–5, 52, 53
Carr, Robert 302
Carrington, Lord 60, 152, 302
Casement, Sir Roger 108
Castle, Barbara 66, 101
Cecil, Henry 273
Central Policy Review Staff 61
Chalker, Lynda 58
Chamberlain, Neville 154
  in power 36, 91, 165, 185
    and Ministers and Departments 76–7,
      97, 114
  resignation 36, 103, 184
Chancellor of Duchy of Lancaster 54, 59,
  63–4, 132, 141, 311, 314
Chancellor of Exchequer 56, 69, 86, 87,
  133, 159, 314
  Budget, and 111–13
Charles, Prince 203–4, 235
Cherwell, Lord 142
Chief Whips 65, 245
choice of Prime Minister *see under* Prime
  Minister
Churchill, Sir Winston 65, 78, 142, 164,
  172, 180
  in power 21, 36, 44, 56, 69, 74, 78, 91,
    100, 216, 301
  and judges 270
  and Ministers and Departments 56,
    69–70, 78–9, 88, 117, 121, 142–3
  and monarch 69, 185, 187
  as opposition leader 172, 180
  resignation 52–3
  retirement 15, 52, 103, 302
Circuit judges 268, 272, 274, 283, 289,
  297–8
Civil Aviation, Ministry 143
Civil Contingencies Unit 116
Civil Service 62, 107, 116, 118, 231, 274

  Minister for 56
Clark, David 181
Clarke, Mr Kenneth 59, 113, 301–2
Clarke, Tom 178
coalition governments 13, 67
  emergency 20–3, 29
  hung parliament 30, 32–4, 35–6, 44,
    47–8
  transfer of power 52, 53, 67
  see also under war
Cockfield, Lord 157
collective responsibility 144–8
  of Ministers 150–8
Colonial Office 138
Commission for Local Administration 213
Committee of Selection 230
committees
  Cabinet 113–24, 131
  in House of Commons 165, 226–32
  in House of Lords 252–6
Comptroller and Auditor-General 93, 229
conduct
  of judges 289–91, 291–6
  of Ministers 143–58
conferences, party 25, 27–8, 214
confidence, motion of no 217–19
Conservative Party 141–2, 176
  conferences 214
  government 65, 100, 142, 149, 184
    caretaker 44
    coalition 20, 22, 48
    and monarch 184, 185
    see also transfer *below*
  in House of Commons 211, 213–4
  and House of Lords 241, 244, 258–63
  and hung parliament 32–5, 41–2, 44,
    47–8, 50–1
  and judges 278–282
  leadership 63, 65, 80
    elections 16–17, 24, 27–8, 78, 146,
      303
    and transfer of power 63, 65
  loss of 1997 general election 101
  Shadow Cabinet 172, 176
  see also hung parliament *above and* names
    of individual leaders
Conservative Research Department 172
Consolidated Fund Services 275
constituency parties and associations 25–6,
  213–14
constitutional monarchy 183–204
  continuity and succession 202–204
  and hung parliament 34–5, 45–6

reserve powers 189–97
Scottish Parliament, and 197–202
and transfer of power 67–8, 161–2
usual powers 184–9
see also George V; George VI; Queen
constitutional practice *see* Cabinet;
Conservative; constitutional
monarchy; House of Commons
House of Lords; hung parliament;
judges; Labour; Liberal; Ministers;
Prime Minister; transfer of power
continuity of monarchy 202–4
Cook, Robin 71, 302
Court of Appeal 269, 271, 272, 294
see also Lords of Appeal
Court of Session 282
Cousins, Frank 58
Crichel Down affair 153–4
Cripps, Sir Stafford 301
Crosland, Anthony 302
Crossman, Richard 66, 82
Crown Court 267
Crown Prosecution Service 109, 135
Cunningham, Dr Jack 173, 181
Curry, David 171
Cyprus problems 109

Dalton, Hugh 69, 301
Davies, Clement 180
Davis, William 49–50
de Ferranti, Basil 157
de Smith, Stanley 250
death sentence 108–9
Defence, Ministry of 60, 76, 85, 121, 132,
143, 149, 151
Defence and Overseas Policy Committee of
Cabinet 115, 118, 121
Defence Select Committee 231
Denning, Lord 284
Departments 138–41
see also Ministers
deputy leaders 25, 78–9, 102
Dervaid, Lord 293
devaluation 87, 100
devining the constitution 1–10
devolution 5–9
Dewar, Donald 181
differ, agreement to 148
Director of Public Prosecutions 109, 110
discipline of judges 289–90, 292–6
dismissal
of government, Monarch's right to insist
on 197

see also resignation
disqualification of peers 244
dissolution of parliament 205
Honours List 239
of hung parliament 33–4, 45–50
and monarchy 205
right to insist on 191, 192
and Prime Minister's power 94–6
Dobson, Frank 181
Donaldson, Sir John 273, 278
Douglas-Home, Sir Alec 60, 65, 243,
301–2
in power 74–5, 82, 99, 240
and Ministers and Departments 81, 86
as opposition leader 180
Duchy of Lancaster, Chancellor of 54, 59,
63, 132, 142, 311, 314
Dugdale, Sir Thomas 153

Economic Affairs, Department of 56,
77, 84
Economic Strategy Committee of Cabinet
121
Ede, Chuter 302
Eden, Anthony 76, 78, 180, 301
in power 66, 76, 100, 301
and Ministers and Departments 97
resignation 15, 16, 52, 302
Edinburgh, Duke of 203, 236
Education/Education and Science,
Ministry/Department of 139, 181
Edward, Prince 204, 236
Edward VII, King 183, 191
Edward VIII, King 114, 164, 183
elections
by-elections 58, 213
electoral systems 22–3
see also general elections *and under*
leadership
electoral college of Labour Party 25–6, 28,
103
Elizabeth II *see* Queen
emergency coalition governments
20–3, 29
Employment, Ministry/Department of 59,
63, 142
Employment Select Committee 232
Energy, Department of 61, 139, 146
Environment, Department of the 136, 139,
146
Eugenie, Princess 204
European Communities Committee of
House of Lords 254

European Economic Community 97, 100,
    117, 142, 145, 148, 232

Fairbairn, Nicholas 152
Falklands conflict 110, 152
Family Division, President of 93, 274
Federal Policy Committee 214
financial affairs
    of judges 283–4
    of Members of Parliament 157, 206–8
    of peers 245–6
Finer, S. E. 156
first-past-the-door electoral system 22
First lord of the Treasury 55
Fisher, Sir Henry 283
Foot, Michael 25, 79, 301
Foreign Affairs Select Committee 231
Foreign and Commonwealth Office 38,
    70–1, 97, 139, 142, 152, 155, 186
Foreign Office/Secretary 59–60, 69, 77–8,
    84, 97, 133, 135, 155, 165, 180
Foreign Policy Committee of Cabinet 114
Franks Report on Official Secrets Act
    (1972) 126
Fraser, Peter 59
free-trade question 33, 148

Gaitskell, Hugh 112, 166, 301
Gardiner, Lord 266
general elections 12–14
    and House of Commons 205, 209–10
    and monarch 190–1
    request for 47, 48
    and transfer of power 52, 53
George V, King 46
    and Asquith 184, 191
    and Lloyd George 68
    and MacDonald 20–1, 34–5, 67, 186
George VI, King 21, 69, 79, 185, 187
Gordon Walker, Patrick 58, 122, 302
government see caretaker; coalition;
    dissolution; House of Commons;
    hung parliament; and under
    Conservative; Labour
Government Communications
    Headquarters (Cheltenham) 232
Government Whips 134, 137, 144, 228,
    245, 251
Governors-General 46
Gray, Hamish 58
grievances see Question Time

Hague, William 15, 24–5, 261

Shadow Cabinet, and 171, 175
Hailsham, Lord 141, 214, 243, 271, 273,
    292, 298
Haldane Committee on Machinery of
    Government (1918) 106, 107
Halifax, Lord 60, 114, 184
Hamilton, Neil 215
Hankey, Colonel Maurice 106
Hartington, Lord 106
Hastings, Sir Patrick 110
Hattersley, Roy 25
Havers, Lord 290
Healey, Denis 301
Health Service Commissioners 213
Health/Health and Social Security
    Ministry/Department of 132, 136, 139,
    143, 180
Heath, Edward 48, 65–6
    and House of Lords 259
    in power 35, 48, 61, 75, 92, 100, 162,
        180, 301
    and judges 282
    and Ministers and Departments 61,
        116, 118, 141
    resignation 35
Heffer, Eric 85
Henderson, Arthur 113
Hennessy, Peter 119
hereditary peers 235–6, 242–3, 261, 264
    peerage disclaimed 11, 242–3
Heseltine, Michael 24, 66, 81, 89, 90, 119,
    301
Heseltine, Sir William 188–9
Hewart, Lord 110, 277, 282, 288
High Court judges 269, 271–6, 282–3,
    288, 294
Hill, Charles 141
Hoare, Sir Samuel 76, 114, 155
Hogg, Quintin 66, 181
Home, Earl of 60, 65–6, 302
    see also Douglas-Home, Sir Alec
Home Affairs Select Committee 231
Home Office/Secretary 77–8, 84, 108,
    110, 115, 133, 136, 146, 154
Home and Social Affairs Committee of
    Cabinet 121
honours 92–3, 165
    and monarch 240, 241
    power to refuse excessive 191–2
    see also House of Lords; life peers
House of Commons 205–234
    elections, members and parties 205–11
    government, and 212–20

members' influence on 220–34
and House of Lords 247–8, 255–60
judges and 276–81, 282, 294–5
Ministers in 58–9
Opposition in 168, 176–7, 182
Prime Minister's questions 90–1, 210, 212, 221–2, 234
reform of 232–4
see also back-bench MPs, legislative functions
House of Lords 235–64
acquiring and losing membership 235–44
and House of Commons 255–60
assessment and possibility of reform 261–4
government, and 255–60
judges and 272, 275, 281, 295, 298
Ministers in 58
Opposition and 165, 176–7
organization in 244–6
reform of 261–4
work of 246–55
Housing and Local Government, Ministry of 181
Housing and Planning, Ministry of 136, 180
Howard, Michael 155, 302
Howe, Sir Geoffrey 23–4, 64, 80, 112, 118, 155, 301–2
human rights 9–10
hung parliament 2, 30–51, 103
government formation from 30–51
caretaker government 44–5
political negotiations and 32–7
Queen and 37–44, 46–8
second dissolution 45–50
Hunt of Tamworth, Lord 117, 130
Hurd, Douglas 24, 82, 158, 302

illness, resignation due to 52, 81, 99
'In Place of Strife' 100
India 164
India Office
Industry, Department of 85
see also Trade and Industry
inflation 100–1
Ingham, Bernard 129
Inskip, Sir Thomas 76
Ismay, Lord 180

Janvrin, Sir Robin 38
Jay, Douglas 117
Jellicoe, Earl 151
Jenkins, Roy 70, 301–2

Jennings, Sir Ivor 3–4, 85, 105, 122, 148
Joseph, Sir Keith 64
Joynson-Hicks, Sir William 147
judges/judicial system 265–300
appointment, pay and promotion 266–76
and Cabinet 108–9
extra-judicial activities 282–7
parliament and 276–81
reform 296–300
tenure, discipline and removal 287–96
Junior Ministers 70, 134, 287
see also Ministers of State
Justice, Minister of 60

Keeler, Christine 150–1
Kilmuir, Lord 277, 284, 285
Rules 284–5
Kinnock, Neil 25, 163, 170, 173
Knollys, Lord 191

Labour Party
conferences 25, 28, 214
and constitutional monarchy 184, 185–6
governments 20, 61–2, 66, 162, 177, 185–6, 217–18
Cabinet and 114, 117, 177
caretaker 44
coalition 20, 22–3, 48
devaluation and 87, 100
minority 34, 47, 51, 162
see also transfer of power *below*
in House of Commons 213–14
and House of Lords 239, 241, 258, 260
and hung parliament 30–7, 41, 44, 47–8, 50, 103
judges and 277–8
leadership
Deputy 25, 79, 102
elections 15–16, 18, 25–9, 79, 103, 304–7
reselection process 28
see also hung parliament *above, and* names of individual leaders
in opposition 171–6, 176–82
pact with Liberals 103, 174
Parliamentary Labour Party 16, 25–7, 27, 28, 65–6, 211
Shadow Cabinet 171–6, 176–82
and transfer of power 52–4, 61–3
Lambton, Lord 151
Lamont, Norman 85, 301

Land and Natural Resources, Ministry of
    140
Lascelles, Sir Alan 187
Law, Department of: suggested 265, 299
Law Lords 237–8
Law Officers 63, 130, 134, 230, 273, 281,
    298, 314
Law Reform Select Committee; House of
    Lords, suggested 255
Lawson, Nigel 301
Lawton, Frederick 273
lay magistrates 265, 266, 282, 288, 292,
    295
leadership of party
    deputy 25, 78–81, 102
    elections, 12, 15–20, 22–8, 52, 78, 103,
        303–8
    and hung parliament 30–51 *passim*
    loss of and choice of Prime Minister
        23–8
    see also names of individual leaders
leaks 124–30, 145, 153
Leathers, Lord 143
leave of absence for peers 243
legal matters and power transfer 57–63
Legislation Committee of Cabinet 121
legislative functions
    of House of Commons 212–20
    of House of Lords 246–50
Lennox-Boyd, Mr Alan 154
Letters Patent 72, 238, 294, 309–13
Liaison Committee 231, 233
Liberal Democrats 2, 36, 37, 58, 67
    in House of Commons 174, 209, 211,
        214
    and House of Lords 174, 239, 262
    and hung parliament 32, 35–6, 41–2,
        48
Liberal Party
    Alliance with SDP 209–10
    governments 48
    House of Commons 164
    House of Lords 263
    hung parliament 33–5, 36, 48, 103, 162
    leadership elections 78, 307–8
    pact with Labour 13, 174
    transfer of power 52
Liberal Party (Ontario) 49
Liberals, Samuelite 21, 22
Lieutenant-Governor of Ontario 49
life peers 236, 238–9, 240, 244
Liverpool, Lord 99
Lloyd, Selwyn 85, 112, 301

Lloyd George, David 33, 68, 302
    in power 21, 33–4, 67, 97, 103, 216
        and Ministers and Departments 67,
            68, 147
    resignation 216
Locarno Pact 96
London 8–9
Lord Advocate 58–9, 134, 273, 282
Lord Chancellor 54, 133, 135, 159, 193,
    206, 230, 237, 274, 281, 293, 297,
    309, 313
    and judges 265–300 *passim*
    and transfer of power 60, 68
Lord Chief Justice 93, 127, 239, 274, 276,
    279, 281, 284
Lord President of Council 58, 133, 141–2,
    187, 313
    and transfer of power 58, 64, 72
Lord President of Court of Session 282
Lord Privy Seal 63–4, 84, 132, 133, 141,
    313
Lords of Appeal 93, 235, 237, 255, 265,
    269–30, 271, 275, 276, 281, 288, 294,
    299
Lords Justices 93, 237, 270–1, 288
Lords Spiritual 236, 237
Luce, Richard 152

MacArthur, Judge Angus 293
MacDonald, Malcolm 58
MacDonald, Ramsay
    in power 20–1, 22, 44, 56, 58, 67, 164,
        165, 217–18
        and George V 20–1, 34–5, 67, 186–7
        and Ministers and Departments 56,
            63, 67, 97
    as opposition leader 172, 176
    resignation 14–15, 20–1, 52
MacKay of Clashfern, Lord 273, 285
McKinnon, Judge 290
Mackintosh, John 4, 87
Mackintosh, Ronald 118
Macleod, Iain 66, 86, 180, 301
Macmillan, Harold (later Earl of Stockton)
    301
    and House of Lords 242
    in power 68, 91, 92, 97, 166, 277
        and Ministers and Departments 70,
            81, 84, 97, 141, 301
    resignation 15, 16, 52, 100
McNamara, Kevin 173
Maitland, Donald 92
Major, John 301–2

in power 23, 24, 53, 62, 74, 75–6, 81,
    123–4, 131
in House of Commons 94
and House of Lords 238
and Ministers and Departments 61, 64,
    66, 85, 119, 141, 142
Marshall, Geoffrey 149
mass media
and general elections 75, 91–2
and House of Commons 162
and judges
and monarchy 188–9
and party leadership elections 25
leaks to 124–30, 145, 153
and Ministers 147, 151–2, 153
and Prime Minister 91
Master of Rolls 93, 274, 276
Maudling, Reginald 301
Maxwell-Fyfe, Sir D. 302
May, Erskine 223
Maze prison escape 154–5
Meacher, Michael 178
media see mass media
Melbourne, Lord 144
Mellor, David 151
Members of Parliament see House of
    Commons
mercy, prerogative of 108
Mills, Percy 68
miners' strike (1973–4) 100
Minister for the Civil Service 55
Minister without Portfolio 142
Minister/Ministries and Departments
    132–59
conduct 143–58
and House of Commons 222, 229
and leadership elections 17, 18–19
lists of 301–2
and monarch 37–8, 53, 67–9, 71, 177
non-departmental Ministers 141–3
pay and conditions 158–9
and Prime Minister see under Prime
    Minister
responsibilities 143–57 passim
titles 132–8
transfer of power 52–72
Cabinet chooses itself 64–7
Queen and 53, 67–8, 71
see also Cabinet; and under resignation
    and names of individual Ministers,
Ministries, Departments and Prime
    Ministers
Ministerial Committees 124

Ministers of State 135–6, 144, 159
minority governments 30–1, 33–6, 47–9,
    52, 162, 216
monarchy see constitutional monarchy
    Queen
Monckton, Walter 270
morality 151–2
Morrison, Herbert 178, 301
Munitions, Ministry of 139

National Executive Committee of Labour
    Party 173, 214
'National government' 20–1, 22–3, 67, 76,
    114, 147
National Heritage, Department of 61, 151
National Industrial Relations Court 286–7
National Labour Party 23, 148
National Liberals 148
Nationalists 215, 239
New Democrats (Ontario) 49
1922 Committee 24, 211
Northern Ireland 7–8, 164, 215, 286
    Office 139
Nunan, Manus 291
Nyasaland incident 154

oath of office 71, 310–11, 313–14
old age, resignation due to 14–18, 52
    see also retirement
O'Neill, Martin 173
Ontario 49–50
Opposition 160–82
constitutional duties 167–71
duty to Crown 166–7
in House of Commons 168–9, 176–7, 181
and House of Lords 165, 176
leader 160–7, 239, 279–80
    co-operation with Prime Minister
        163–7
    duties of 160–7
Shadow Cabinet 62, 171–6
tactics and policies 171–7
transition to power 176–82
Orders in Council 62, 71, 140–1, 158
'overlords' 143
Overseas Development, Ministry of 64, 140
Owen, David 62, 302

Parkinson, Cecil 66, 83, 151
Parliament see governments; House of
    Commons; House of Lords
Parliamentary Commissioner for
    Administration 93, 213

Parliamentary Committee of Cabinet 114, 117, 146

Parliamentary Committee of PLP 65, 173–4

Parliamentary Contributory Pension Fund 159, 209

Parliamentary Labour Party *see under* Labour Party

Parliamentary Private Secretaries 137–8, 144

Parliamentary Under-Secretaries of State/Parliamentary Secretaries 132, 134, 135, 136, 144, 151, 159, 179

patronage 76–80, 93–4, 109, 177, 238, 239–40

pay *see* salaries

Paymaster General 63, 133, 142, 314

Peel, Sir Robert 4

peerages *see* honours; House of Lords

pensions 159, 209

Permanent Under-Secretaries 93, 231

'phantom' appointments 314

Philip, Prince 203, 236

Pickles, James, Judge 284, 298

PLP (Parliamentary Labour Party) *see under* Labour Party

police 109

Police Complaints Authority 93

policy decisions by Cabinet 107–8

Policy Unit 98

political
legitimacy of House of Commons 212
matters and transfer of power 57–63
negotiation and hung parliament 32–7
philosophies of Ministers 85–6, 102
Office (at Number 10) 98
parties 205–12
see also conference; conservative; Labour; leadership; Liberal; Social Democratic; social and Liberal Democrats

Pollock, Sir Ernest 270

Ponting, Clive 110

Powell, Enoch 66, 171

power *see* transfer of power *and under* Prime Minister; Queen

Prescott, John 25, 71, 79, 301

press *see* mass media

Prices and Consumer Protection Department of 61, 139

prices and incomes policy 146

Prime Minister 73–104
choice of 11–29
emergency coalitions 20–3
general elections 12–14
loss of party leadership 23–8
see also Queen; resignation
and House of Lords 239–42
and hung parliament 30–51 *passim*
and judges 269
and Leader of Opposition 163–7
patronage 76–80, 93–4, 109, 177, 238, 239–40
power of 73–104
dissolution and 90–6
electorate's choice 75–6
high profile 90–6
over Ministers and Departments 76–90, 105, 121–2, 130
Cabinet meetings 74, 86–90
direction 96–8
patronage 90–6
reshuffles 66, 81–4, 102
question time 90, 162, 176, 210, 212, 221–2, 234
and transfer of power 52–70 *passim*
voluntary retirement 18–20
weakness 98–103
see also names of individual leaders

Prior, James 64, 83, 112, 129, 154

Private Members' Bills and motions 227–8, 250

Private Office of Prime Minister 97–8, 107

Private Secretaries
to Monarch 38–9, 41, 46, 97, 186, 191
Parliamentary 137–8, 144

Privy Council 71, 139, 163, 165, 166, 172, 176, 183, 188, 206, 275, 281, 287
memorandum on resignation and appointment of Ministers 309–314
and transfer of power 54, 71

Procedure Select Committee: House of Commons 228–9

Production, Ministry of 135

Profumo, John 100, 150–1

Progressive Conservative Party (Ontario) 49

promotion of judges 275–6

Prosser, Judge 290

Public Accounts Committee 229–30

public opinion polls 213
see also mass media

Pym, Francis 64, 84, 129, 302

Queen 92, 93, 228
and dissolution 205–6

and hung parliament 37–44, 46, 48–9
and judges 268, 269
and Ministers 53, 67–8, 309–11, 313
and peers, creation of 239, 240
powers
    reserve 189–97
    usual 184–9
and Prime Minister, choice of 11–2,
    21–2, 25, 29, 162, 177
Speech in Parliament 30, 47, 168, 183
and transfer of power 52–5
see also constitutional monarchy
Questions
in House of Commons 90, 162, 176,
    222, 234
in House of Lords 251

Radcliffe Committee on Ministerial
    Memoirs (1976) 125, 127
Recorders 267, 282, 289–94 *passim*, 297,
    298
Redwood, John 24
Rees, Merlyn 302
reform 9–10
of House of Commons 228–9
of House of Lords 235–6, 261–4
of judicial system 265, 296–300
Regency 203–4
regional development agencies 8–9
Register of Members' Interests 157–207
reshuffles, Cabinet 66, 81–2, 102
resignation
of government 52
of judges 283, 288–9, 291–6
of Members of Parliament
of Ministers 81, 84–6, 150–2, 209–13
of Prime Ministers 14–18, 25, 43–4,
    52–4, 75, 99, 160, 162, 216
responsibilities, collective, of Ministers
    144–58 *passim*
retirement
of judges 286, 291
of Prime Minister 15, 16, 20–1
Rhodesian independence 186, 258
Ridley, Nicholas 155
Rifkind, Malcolm 302
riots 119
Robertson, George 181
Robinson, Geoffrey 57
Royal Commissions 156, 165
Royal Household 63, 137, 309, 313
royalty *see* constitutional monarchy;
    queen

salaries
of judges 274–5
of Members of Parliament 206–7,
    210
of Ministers 57–8, 158–9
of peers 245–6
of Prime Ministers 55–6
Salisbury, Lord 55, 174
Samuel, Herbert 67
Samuelite Liberals 21, 22
Scarman, Lord 238
Science and Technology Committee of
    House of Lords 254
Scottish Parliament 5–7
Queen, and 197–202
Scotland 215, 298
Secretary of State for 294
Solicitor-General for 59, 134, 153
SDP *see* Social Democratic Party
secrecy 111–12, 123–4, 124–31
leaks 125–30, 145, 153
Secretaries of State 132–4, 138–40, 151,
    180, 314
for Scotland 294
Secretary to Cabinet 62, 97, 106–7, 115,
    121, 122, 127, 130, 231
Select Committees
of House of Commons 228–9
of House of Lords 252–4
seniority of Ministers 77–8
Shadow Cabinet
formalization 5
Shea, Michael 188
sheriffs 282, 293–4
Short, Edward 79, 301
Simon Commission 164
Simon of Highbury, Lord 57
Simon, Sir John 76, 114
Sinclair, Sir Archibald 164
Smith, Chris 181
Smith, F. E. 68, 110, 172
Smith, John 25
Snowdon, Earl of 236
Social Democratic Party 2, 239
Alliance with Liberals 209
Social and Liberal Democrats 307–8
Solicitor-General 134–5, 312
for Scotland 58–9, 134–152
Somervell, Sir D. 302
Soskice, Sir F. 302
South Africa 47
sovereign *see* constitutional monarchy;
    Queen

Speed, Keith 85
Stamfordham, Lord 38
Steel, David 62
Stevenson, Melford 290
Stewart, Michael 66, 77, 181, 301
Stewart, Sheriff 294
stipendiary magistrates/acting stipendiaries
 267–8, 272, 282, 298
St John-Stevas, Norman 230
Stockton, Earl of *see* Macmillan
Strang, Gavin 181
Straw, Jack 302
sub judice rule 280
succession of monarchy 202–4
Suez affair 100
supremacy *see* power
Supreme Court Judges 273–4, 282, 284,
 294, 299

Taylor, Lord 284
Technology, Ministry of 140, 146
television *see* mass media
temporary nature of Prime Minister's office
 91–2
territorial context 5–9
Thatcher, Margaret; in power 15, 53, 61,
 73–4, 80, 91, 95, 99, 101, 163, 167,
 181, 301
 and constitutional monarchy 188–9
 in House of Commons 212, 216
 and House of Lords 239
 and judges 270–1, 273, 277
 and Ministers and Departments
 as opposition leader 171, 181
 resignation 16, 23–4, 37, 103
Thomas, George 241
Thomas, J. H. 111, 114
Thomson, Sheriff 293–4
Thorneycroft, Peter 86, 301
Thorpe, Jeremy 35, 48
Trade, Board of 117, 145, 157, 313,
 314
Trade and Industry, Department of 59, 61,
 77, 136, 142, 149, 151, 154, 156, 232,
 313
trade unions 100, 213
 and leadership elections 25–6
 and Ministers 58, 82, 146
transfer of power 52–72, 161–2, 177–82
 Cabinet chooses itself 63–7
 legal, conventional and political matters
 56–63
 Ministers take office 70

Prime Minister takes office 55–6
 sovereign's influence 67–9
Transport, Ministry/Department of 64
Treasury 55, 76, 86, 118, 132, 136, 180,
 231, 312–14
Trend, Sir Burke 122

Ullswater, Lord 282
Unemployment Select Committee: House
 of Lords 253
United States, relations with 91, 97
United Ulster Unionists 35

Vehicle and General affair 154
Vice-Chancellor 93, 274
Vietnam war 146
voting 147–8
 see also elections

Waddington, David 58, 302
Wakeham, Lord 141
Wales 215, 219
Walker, Peter 83, 146
war 110, 146, 152, 185, 187, 216
 cabinet 110, 135
 coalition governments in 21, 52, 53, 67,
 114, 148
 Ministers and 64, 152
War Office 56, 133, 150
weighted voting system 24–5
Welsh Assembly 7
Welsh Office 139
Westland affair 90, 149–50, 153, 231,
 234
'wets' 102, 129
Whips 82, 134, 137, 144, 168, 175,
 210–11, 228, 245, 251
White Papers:
 'House of Lords Reform' (1968) 246
 'In Place of Strife' 100–1
 on reorganization on Ministry of
 Defence (1963) 121
Whitelaw, William (later Viscount) 24, 64,
 80, 82, 141, 154, 241, 301–2
Wilson, Harold 26
 in power 35, 45, 47–8, 56, 73, 75,
 94, 98, 100, 162, 178, 180, 218,
 301
 and House of Lords 240, 258
 and Ministers and Departments 70,
 79, 84–7, 90, 96, 101, 107,
 114–21, 141, 145
 as opposition leader 62, 163

resignation 53
retirement 15, 16, 19, 26, 37, 45, 52–3,
    146, 302
'winter of discontent' 101
women, votes for 147

Woolton, Lord 142
Wright, Peter 280

York, Duke of 204, 236, 240
Young, David, Lord 57, 59, 241

Lightning Source UK Ltd.
Milton Keynes UK
UKOW032123190912

199288UK00001B/2/A